The

FARCE

of the

FART

AND OTHER

RIBALDRIES

THE MIDDLE AGES SERIES

Ruth Mazo Karras, SERIES EDITOR

Edward Peters, FOUNDING EDITOR

A complete list of books in the series

is available from the publisher.

The
FARCE
of the
FART
AND OTHER
RIBALDRIES

Twelve Medieval French Plays
in Modern English

Edited and translated by

JODY ENDERS

PENN

University of Pennsylvania Press

Philadelphia

Published by
University of Pennsylvania Press
Philadelphia, Pennsylvania 19104-4112
www.upenn.edu/pennpress

Printed in the United States of America on acid-free paper

10 9 8 7 6 5 4 3 2 1

A Cataloging-in-Publication record is available from the Library of Congress
ISBN 978-0-8122-4323-9

For my students

Contents

The PLAYS

On Abbreviations, Short Titles, Notes, and Bibliography

It is my working principle that no reader of this performance-friendly anthology need read French, which is why there are no face-to-face translations. That is also why I have not signaled each and every primary source in Middle French (some of which are relatively inaccessible). When possible, I provide instead a more readily accessible source in English. Moreover, my goal of user-friendliness is why you will not see, in my Bibliography, numerous books and articles for which I have enormous respect and that I have frequently cited elsewhere, as in the mammoth bibliographies of my own books.

For ease of reading, I avoid notes whenever possible in favor of parenthetical documentation that works in concert with the Bibliography. When there is no confusion as to which work is being referenced, more often than not I do not provide a note at all. Frequently mentioned works are cited by abbreviations.

Many of the principal editions and translations on which I draw share titles that are quite similar. To facilitate consultation, I refer to them as follows:

ATF   *Ancien Théâtre françois.* 10 vols. Edited by M. Viollet le Duc.

FFMA   *Farces françaises de la fin du moyen âge.* 4 vols. Translated into modern French by André Tissier.

FCMF   *Five Comedies of Medieval France.* Translated into English by Oscar Mandel.

MFP   *Medieval French Plays.* Translated into English by Richard Axton and John Stevens.

Recueil   *Recueil de farces françaises inédites du XVE siècle.* Edited by Gustave Cohen.

RF   *Recueil de Farces (1450–1550).* 13 vols. Edited by André Tissier.

SMFF	*Six Medieval French Farces.* Translated into English by Thierry Boucquey.
TFR	*Le Théâtre français avant la Renaissance.* Edited by Édouard Fournier.

These are the abbreviations used for other frequently cited primary and secondary sources:

AG	*Aspects of Genre in Late Medieval French Drama.* By Alan E. Knight.
CE	*Les Caractéristiques essentielles de la farce française.* By Barbara C. Bowen.
CP	*Les Clercs du Palais* (1856 and 1875 editions). By Adolphe Fabre.
DBD	*Death by Drama and Other Medieval Urban Legends.* By Jody Enders.
FAH	*Farce: A History from Aristophanes to Woody Allen.* By Albert Bermel.
LD	*The Life of the Drama.* By Eric Bentley.
LM	*Laughing Matters.* By Sara Beam.
MBA	*Murder by Accident.* By Jody Enders.
MES	*The Medieval European Stage, 500–1550.* Ed. William Tydeman.
MTOC	*The Medieval Theater of Cruelty.* By Jody Enders.
Répertoire	*Répertoire des farces françaises.* By Bernard Faivre.
ROMD	*Rhetoric and the Origins of Medieval Drama.* By Jody Enders.
SRD	*The Staging of Religious Drama in Europe in the Later Middle Ages.* Edited by Peter Meredith and John E. Tailby.
TDF	"Towards a Definition of Farce as Literary 'Genre.'" By Barbara Cannings [Bowen].
TB	*Theatre of the Basoche.* By Howard Graham Harvey.

Preface

It all began in the fall of 2007 when I could take it no longer. Was I really going to teach comparative medieval drama one more time without teaching the anonymous fifteenth-century *Farce of the Fart*? Was I *really*?

My undergraduates at the University of California, Santa Barbara, were mostly theater majors and English majors. At best, they had perhaps read *Everyman* and the *Second Shepherds' Play*. They might even have heard vague rumblings about everybody's beloved Shakespeare having drawn heavily on medieval traditions of farce (as M. L. Radoff had noticed as early as 1933). Sure, there were plenty of English plays available in a variety of anthologies: unfortunately, David Bevington's marvelous *Medieval Drama* was out of print, but there was now Greg Walker's *Medieval Drama: An Anthology*, a hefty tome of over six hundred pages. And yet, the rest of the medieval dramatic picture—that vast and vastly enjoyable repertoire of French farce—was virtually unknown in the English language. Although scores of French plays had first been edited in the nineteenth and twentieth centuries by some of the greats of French theater history—Gustave Cohen, Eugénie Droz, Édouard Fournier, Emmanuel Philipot, M. Viollet le Duc, and, later, André Tissier, Bernard Faivre, and Jelle Koopmans—those painstakingly preserved farces had yet to reach the larger audiences that they so richly deserved because, for one thing, the vast majority had never been translated. What about all the English speakers out there? We weren't going to leave all the fun to the French, were we?

I think not. So let's start with a dozen in English.

To be fair, there have been some pioneering translations of medieval French farce—of about a dozen from the hundreds extant—most notably by Barnard and Rose Hewitt, Oscar Mandel, and Alan E. Knight. These are listed in the Bibliography, and I'll be alluding to them briefly in About This Translation. But, for the moment, what about my pedagogical dilemma about *The Farce of the Fart*? I wondered: What if I just translated it myself?

What do you know! The students *liked it*. So much so that, as their final project, four of them acted it out—Jeremy Cowan, Jessica Fleitman, Joey Axiaq, and Travis Wong—bringing the dialogue and the laughter to life. The next thing I knew, a graduate student, Andrew Henkes, was proposing to stage the play at our yearly Medieval Studies Conference. On 3 May 2008, the superb cast of Dakotah Brown, Michael Ruesga, Courtney Ryan, and Annika Speer acquitted themselves so well that students, colleagues, and friends inquired: What would we be doing next year? It was *The Farce of Master Mimin* (published here as *Birdbrain*), also directed by Henkes and featuring Jason Bornstein, Melani Carroll, Beth Faitro, Andrew Fromer, Jordan Holmes, and Sigmond Varga. One thing led to another, and then there were twelve. To my knowledge not a single one of the plays here assembled has ever been translated into English.

Why these plays? Why now? Humor is an important mechanism that perks us up, all the while teaching us to beware of those who would use it to keep us down. Mostly, we can laugh, we can learn something, we can do both. If nothing else, the farces demand that we take humor seriously: seriously enough to read them, act them out, watch them, and restore them to the larger conversation about the arts from which they have often been wrongfully marginalized (if not downright excluded) thanks to centuries of antitheatrical polemic. Predating the standard comic structures that we have come to know and love in Shakespeare, the commedia dell'arte, Molière, and beyond, the medieval French farce offers up a literal song and dance about what unites and divides us. From politics and religion, to learning and litigiousness, to marriage and social class, to theology and sexuality, each play satirizes social life through that most present of literary media, the theater. These plays are *funny,* and they have withstood the test of time, mostly by providing lots of laughter when things are tough. When it comes to human foibles, the farce is transcendent: the more things change, the more they remain the same.

Walter Kerr might well have summed it up best in 1967 when he endeavored to reelevate the farce to its heights—not *depths*—of days of yore. Disputing the commonplace of the so-called lowly farce, he extolled its considerable virtues by comparing it instead to the noblest of tragedies:

> Its purpose, of course, is to render [tragedy's] such high aspiration absurd; but it acquires a height of its own in the process of stretching to mock. Farce is the largest comic form we know, potentially the most di-

mensional; it offers us the greatest spaces to be filled in. If a playwright, or a period in history, fails to fill in the spaces and chooses instead simply to reproduce the cartooned outlines in a mechanical way, that is not the form's fault. It has matched the thrust of tragedy as best it could and left us the directions for making lunacy out of nobility; what we do with the legacy will depend upon our own capacities. (*Tragedy and Comedy*, 312)

Do something with the legacy we must. In fact, I keep telling my graduate students that there are umpteen dissertations just waiting to happen if only someone would turn seriously to these comedies. Perhaps they'll listen now, if not to me then to Mikhail Bakhtin, who cautioned, in *Rabelais and His World*, that "to ignore or to underestimate the laughing people of the Middle Ages . . . distorts the picture of European culture's historic development" (6). So let's bring that picture back into the focus, shall we?

I've fashioned the present collection with students, theater practitioners, theater aficionados, and general readers in mind. To them, I say now: If you think that medieval literature is esoteric, inaccessible, and endlessly enmeshed in scholastic debates about how many angels can fit on the head of a pin, this is not your mother's Middle Ages. From the outset, I must state a number of issues baldly—four, to be exact.

First, a curious thing: As many of my fellow pedagogues can attest, something odd seems to happen when you teach a farce. Reading one is fine. So is seeing one. Everybody cracks up. But just try to have an intellectual discussion about one, and you suck the humor right out of the thing. The silence is deafening. Once the guffaws are over, the students have nothing more to say. Is it that the laughter is so cathartic that literary analysis just plain ruins it? Maybe, maybe not. Or maybe Eric Bentley got it right when he asked: "Why do we laugh at jokes? The point of a joke can be explained, but the explanation is not funny" (*LD,* 229). I hope not, because I've done my best to make some of my explanations funny, walking a fine line between scholarly interpretation and pedantry. Farces are *meant to be fun;* so I've had some fun with them. This includes writing with a chattier, colloquial tone such as the one I'm using right now, which I temper a bit only in the Introduction—and only a bit.

Second, it is impossible to understand a medieval play independently of performance, my guiding principle throughout this volume. Without performance, medieval culture makes no sense. Epics and romances were declaimed by jongleurs in public squares; poetry competitions were waged and won before enthusiastic crowds; students and faculty filled the streets surrounding the Sorbonne for oral exams in theology (the quodlibet); crazed dancers processed through towns in the sexualized antics of the Feast of Fools. André Tissier is explicit: "The farce is originally written for performance, not for reading" (*RF*, 1: 55).[1] And, difficult though it might be to reconstruct the full scope of medieval playing, I have drawn on every resource I could find to help make that happen. But please be forewarned that casting a farce will prove more challenging than you might think. Although one needn't necessarily second Susan Morrison by invoking "fecopoetics" as the ultimate medieval habit of thought—*yuck!*—the sights, sounds, and smells of the body are everywhere (*Excrement in the Middle Ages*, chap. 10). When the stage directions of #5, *Blind Man's Buff*, call for the serving girl Thomasina to pee in a cup in one scene and for her employer to "shit himself all over" in another, it makes Rabelais look like child's play.

Third, there are aspects of this repertoire that are distinctly unfunny and worthy of our serious exploration. The recurring theme of domestic violence is one of them, in which many a playwright goes so far as to make the preposterous suggestion that *women* were the ones who regularly brutalized their husbands. If these plays are any indication, medieval men were always trying to put women in their place and with a plethora of misogynistic literature to back them up. To evoke a signature essay by the historian Natalie Zemon Davis, that place was not exactly "on top" ("Women on Top"). The female characters, however, are having none of it; and in at least a few instances, one might even say that they emerge victorious, Pyrrhic though their victories might be.

Finally, my twelve favorite farces, all anonymous, are not exactly politically correct, hence my humble offering of an Actors' Prologue that any company may recite prior to performance, the better to prepare its audiences. Allow me to speak plainly. I am not one of those historians who think that offensive language and content must be stricken from the record. Quite to the contrary, I firmly believe that we do a disservice to history by electing to ignore past scenarios that we now dislike and that we understand even less. I can only hope that the reader will adopt Bentley's sensible philosophy that "in farce, as in drama, one is permitted the outrage but spared the consequence" (*LD*, 222). Otherwise, I can best characterize my approach like so: If feminists can specialize in pornography, then I think I can translate farces. My wish is that this collection will provide a lot of laughs along with a heavy dose of serious reflection—all with a spoonful of sugar to help the good and bad medicine go down. No saccharin, folks. Have the courage of your convictions and read on! But not without one last caveat and one first parody. If these plays were movies, the following rating would probably apply:

WARNING: PG-13

Some material may be inappropriate for children under 13.
May contain moderate language, minimal strong language, some explicit nudity, intense violence, gore, or mild drug content.

Introduction

B awdy, scandalous, lewd, profane, obscene. Influential, dangerous, boisterous, subversive, even heretical.

Modern audiences are all too familiar with the arsenal of adjectives that
normally apply, even if they have never encountered a farce in their lives. It's
all part and parcel of the centuries of derision and mistrust to which theater
itself has been subjected by a veritable chorus of philosophers on the politics
and poetics of the human condition. From Plato to Marivaux to Adam Smith
to George Bernard Shaw, the farce has suffered an unusually bad rap. Shaw
famously excoriated it in these terms: "we find people who would not join in
the laughter of a crowd of peasants at the village idiot, or tolerate the public
flogging or pillorying of a criminal, booking seats to shout with laughter at a
farcical comedy, which is, at bottom, the same thing—namely, the deliberate
indulgence of that horrible, derisive joy in humiliation and suffering which is
the beastliest element in human nature" (*Our Theatres in the Nineties,* 2: 118).[1]

It was the sort of cruel nonsense up with which he would not put. And the
fact that apparent detractors like the great Jean Bouchet (1476–ca. 1559) had
shared that view (possibly with an irony that has escaped us) hasn't helped
matters very much. A lawyer and a longtime watcher, reporter, and producer
of theater, Bouchet had this to say in the 1530s about the "lewd, wicked,
and degenerate" comedies featuring "despicable adulteries" and "assaults on
women": "We call them in the vulgar tongue *farces* and often criticise the
actors of them, and it is right that those who earn their livelihood by such
means should be noted rogues. *Scholars should not be tempted by such knowledge*" (*MES,* E84, 332; my emphasis).[2]

I couldn't disagree more, and these dozen plays will show you why. There
is indeed a great deal that we might be tempted to learn—and enjoy—from
the bawdiest of dramas. If farces are all those terrible things above, they are
also witty, wise, linguistically ingenious, physical, and just plain fun.

Like it or not (and most audiences *like it*), at some point, any fan of Shakespeare, Molière, Ionesco, or Neil Simon, any premodern, modern, or postmodern theater student, any theater historian, theatergoer, or theater practitioner must address the European Middle Ages in general and the farce in particular, if only to explain how such a vital art form emerged, developed, and prospered in the West. During an almost unparalleled heyday from the mid-fifteenth to the mid-sixteenth centuries, the farce was as much a fifteenth-century genre as a Renaissance performance practice, troubling the standard historical periodization and emerging as one of the most popular literary media of all time. It was also one of the first to profit en masse from the advent of the printing press. Throughout what can only be deemed a "long Middle Ages" whose theatrical life extended well into the glorious Renaissance—some would say encroached upon it—the farce was a real crowd-pleaser.

What was it, then, that audiences flocked to public squares to see? And what exactly was the problem once the Middle Ages were over?

It seems that the farce answered, with hilarious stories like those that I'm about to preview, the most controversial questions of the day about law, politics, religion, economics, social stratification, and the battle of the sexes. *That's what.* Relegated though such stories have been to the role of poor stepchild of their more illustrious dramatic relations like the Passion play or morality play, the medieval farce has it all:

What happens when a woman pollutes the air of her home with the stench of her farts? She drags her husband's ass to court to get to the bottom of it, as it were (*Farce of the Fart*). What's the verdict when a married couple does battle over who's the boss at home? The wife's in charge, of course, especially when she can produce an edict establishing women's rights, even if its imaginary author was truly thinking "No way!" (*Edict of Noée*). What if you're one of those "gals" who suspects that your husband is cheating on you? Get your BFF Colette to dress up like a priest so she can wheedle an authentic confession out of your not-so-better half; but better watch out lest you learn more than you bargain for (*Confession Lessons*). How about if you want an education and you're dumb as dirt? Just *try* to get into the college of your choice: you'll only make a spectacle of yourself (*Student Who Failed*). If two overworked servants are waiting on a nasty old blind man, is it ever okay for them to take the law into their own hands? Sure it is! Take the curmudgeon out into the woods for a little fun and games and bludgeon his sorry ass (*Blind Man's Buff*). Is your dumb-ass husband getting you down? Do you need some doctoring? Get your neighbor to "stick it in" and say it's an enema (*Playing Doctor*).

Intermission.

How does a girl get rich on her husband's dime? *Courtly, shmourtly*. After taking money from three different suitors, she can always direct a little masquerade in their (dis)honor, the better to rebuff all three at once (*At Cross Purposes*). What about when everything is just plain "full of shit?" Concoct a farce that serves as a theatrical thesaurus, a distinctly unscholarly companion to your lowly subject (*Shit for Brains*). Are you sick of the lechery of your parish priest? No worries! Devise a drama that will show his true colors and provide his come-uppance (*Monk-ey Business*). Is your wife fooling around on you? Try catching her in the act; but, when you cast the scene of her entrapment, better make sure that everyone is only acting (*Getting Off on the Wrong Foot*). What about that dolt of a husband who's always locking you up inside the house? Typecast your priest as the Devil so that, next time your hubby shouts, "The Devil take you!" the priest can step right up in a Devil suit. *Could it be . . . Satan*? (*Cooch E. Whippet*). And, finally, what do you do when schooling turns a young man into such a jargon-spouting, Latin-speaking fool that he forgets how to speak his native French? Get him back on the farm for some homespun homeschooling (*Birdbrain*).

That's what.

While it would be customary to start out with a working definition of what farce *is,* I prefer to end where others might begin. (Any farcical resemblance to my doing things "ass-backwards" is purely coincidental.) It is only at the close of this Introduction that you will see a tentative sketch of the farce as literary genre; and that is because *performance* is paramount to all the usual, prefatory categories or heuristics. Performance (as exemplified here by space, mime, gesture, and costume) makes it difficult to treat independently such crucial access points as genre, history, authors, actors, and audience. Performance inflects all the questions that I propose to ask and answer in a version of the journalistic canon of *Who? What? Where? When? Why?*[3] As we shall see, *who* the performers of farce were had a lot to do with what came to define the genre over time. To put it another way, my questions are these:

Where does farce come from? (I am tempted to respond, paraphrasing Dr. Seuss: "I can't say. But I bet it has come a long, long way.") *Why did it develop in medieval France the way it did?*

Who wrote the farces? Who acted in them? Who produced them? Who watched them? Who recorded their impressions about farcical texts or performances?

In the world of farce, as in the *Recueil Cohen* (a remarkable collection of plays from which ten of ours are drawn), the men involved in writing, producing, and performing farces were members of a boys' club of sorts, an influential French organization of law clerks and legal apprentices known as the Basoche.[4] It is impossible to access the history, status, and *stature* of the genre, impossible to reply to *What is a farce?* without an understanding of the Basoche in the larger medieval dramatic picture.

History, Development, and the Actors of the Basoche

According to the standard narratives, the proverbial Dark Ages were dark indeed, hosting little art worthy of admiration. Spanning some ten centuries from the fall of Rome to the discovery of the New World, the entire era was typically relegated to that depressing middle ground between the apogee of classical antiquity and the oh-so-enlightened Renaissance, whence the very meaning of the term "Middle Ages" (*medium aevum*). Stuck in the middle. Certain critical allowances have been made for the fourteenth-century miracle play (in which the Virgin Mary comes to the rescue of a large variety of sinners), for the morality play, and for the monumental mystery plays of the fifteenth century (which were performed well into the sixteenth century). But otherwise, it doesn't seem to have mattered much that a bustling theatrical life was everywhere, drawing crowds to the *Play of Adam* as early as the twelfth century and ultimately, in 1515, filling an amphitheater for the *Acts of the Apostles* at Bourges with twenty-five to thirty thousand spectators.[5] Nor has it mattered much that, when the printing press first came on the scene, it was plays that were printed nonstop. Postmedieval readers have found it practical to dismiss the medieval dramatic art anyway, such that the commonplaces and stereotypes persisted. Even so respectful a reader as Albert Bermel devotes a mere eight of sixty-nine pages to the Middle Ages in his admittedly rushed historical contextualization of the farce or, as he calls it, "A Hurried Tour from Greece to the Twentieth Century" (*FAH*, chap. 5). He wasn't kidding: less than one page per century—and I am exaggerating only slightly—really *does* qualify as hurried.

It lies well beyond the scope of this anthology to detail, rehearse, and explain the intellectual investment in keeping the Dark Ages dark. For our present purposes, suffice it to confine ourselves to the story of the origins of medieval drama, which goes like this:

During those dim and inartistic centuries, bards and silly jugglers traipsed about their fledgling communities until, all of a sudden, liturgical drama sprang not-yet-fully formed from its mother Church. No antecedents to speak of, ex nihilo, totally unique, and hallelujah![6]

Not so fast.

Thanks to the paradigm-shifting work of E. K. Chambers, Karl Young, Grace Frank, and O. B. Hardison, any student of medieval art forms is cognizant of the sensible critical dogma that, at such key moments of the liturgical calendar as Easter and Christmas, religious services were becoming increasingly theatrical, for purposes, we think, of communication. It's true that, in France, a decision had been made by the Council of Tours in 813 that actual sermons would no longer be given in a Latin impenetrable by parishioners but, rather, in the "rustic Romance tongue." That *rustica romana lingua* was the emerging language that was to evolve into modern French (Price, *French Language,* 6); but adaptive measures were still needed for the Latin rituals of the liturgy itself. Within the expressive spaces of the Church, what better way to clarify the liturgy's message than to enhance its ecclesiastical delivery by means of additional music, costume, gesture, and mime? That is just what came to pass. The musical, vestimentary, and gestural interpolations into the liturgy are known as "troping"; and troping has long been cited, in any serious study, as the so-called origin of medieval drama.

The canonical example is the *quem quaeritis* trope (also called the *Visitatio sepulchri* or "visit to the sepulcher"), which is now taken to be a kind of playlet. In that trope, the three Marys (friends of Mary, mother of Jesus) seek the body of Christ in what proves to be an empty tomb because Christ has risen. So beautiful and breathtaking is the *quem quaeritis* trope that Eric Auerbach situated it within "one—and always . . . the same—context: of *one great drama* whose beginning is God's creation of the world, whose climax is Christ's Incarnation and Passion, and whose expected conclusion will be Christ's second coming and the Last Judgment" (*Mimesis*, 158; my emphasis). Also, the scholarly attention paid to that trope has gone a long way toward rectifying a modern tendency to indict the Church as the necessarily sworn enemy of all things theatrical.[7]

The problem arises, however, in positing that the Church was the *only* origin of medieval drama. Nor can we accept at face value the theory that D. W. Robertson proposed in the introduction to his *Preface to Chaucer* (1962), revolutionary at the time. Simply put, Robertson argued, from the writings of Saint Augustine, that all of medieval literature could be understood as a manifestation of charity (*caritas*) versus lust (*concupiscientia*), an exemplary way of modeling either positive or negative behaviors to be imitated or eschewed. But no single-origin theory fits all; and to insist on a single origin is to fail to account for the richness of medieval dramatic life. To illustrate my point, I present two curious scenarios:

First, I recollect my own experience from decades ago as a spectator of a reconstructed liturgical drama at the International Congress for Medieval Studies at Kalamazoo, Michigan (to which thousands of avid, mostly young medievalists make a yearly pilgrimage in the month of May). An eager student of medieval drama, I was seated behind a pillar, from which vantage point I saw . . . not a blasted thing. I could not help but conjecture that, if liturgical troping was the origin of medieval drama, then anybody with a lousy seat had missed it entirely. (This is akin to what I've long believed with regard to the dictum attributed to Gregory the Great about art being "the book of the illiterate." During my many visits to medieval churches, it occurred to me that, between the bird droppings, the dim lighting, and the overall height and inaccessibility of such a sculptural "book," the "illiterate" would have had an extremely hard time "reading" anything at all.)

Second, for as beloved an explanation of medieval drama's origins that troping has come to be, there are arenas in which it just doesn't make sense. Supposedly, after the *quem quaeritis* trope gave birth to "liturgical drama," that newly baptized art form crept slowly, gradually, and regularly from inside the church . . . toward the church doors . . . to the top of the stairs . . . on down the steps . . . into the public squares . . . where, eventually . . . What? The resurrected Christ was sharing a playing space with an unfaithful wife receiving an enema designated The Expunger (#6, *Playing Doctor*)? A single derivation for the two seems implausible, although, believe it or not, it's not quite as far-fetched as it sounds. Consider this salvo launched against a tortured saint in the grim hagiographic *Play of Saint Denis:* "Get a load o' Lord Shitter-in-school over there. . . ! I'll clean out his turdy asshole, all right!"[8] Or remember, with Jessica Milner Davis, that the Kyrie or Sanctus of the Mass itself "were often called *farsae* or *farsurae*" (*Farce*, 7).[9] If anything, we ought to infer not a single-origin theory but a nexus of reciprocal influences that moves us momentously beyond any *this* versus *that*, the Church versus popular culture, the serious versus the comic.

For example, in her unique and anything-but-foolish *Fools' Plays*, Heather Arden paints a nuanced portrait of the *sottie* (sometimes spelled *sotie*), a close companion of the farce. There, she takes the time to rehearse and, ultimately, to question the many theories of the origins of farce, *sottie,* and morality play. On one hand, Arden was skeptical of the "individual genius theory" that Joseph Bédier had elaborated for a glorious medieval epic like the *Song of Roland;* on the other hand, she found insufficient evidence to support the hypothesis that the *sotties* "developed from the dramatic tradition of Latin drama" (15). She was more receptive to the idea that farce, *sottie*, and morality play shared a parentage with the jongleurs who were singing and reciting epics and romances in public squares (with some acrobatics thrown in for good measure). Although readily acknowledging the impact of the liturgy and of bona fide religious drama on the French comic theater, Arden simultaneously acknowledged that extraliturgical comedy played a role of its own in the evolution of so-called liturgical dramas (15–18). Specifically, she signaled the supremacy of the raucous, carnivalesque festival of the Feast of Fools (*la fête des Fous*), a world turned upside down that attracted the attention of none other than Mikhail Bakhtin in *Rabelais and His World* (introd.).

Did the Christian liturgy influence the history and development of medieval drama? Absolutely. Did it influence the farce? Of course it did, if only in the sense that any play, any comedy, any satire requires an understanding of its object of imitation (even though our medieval writers likely had little or no access to Aristotle's time-honored discussion of the same in *Poetics* 1448b). But it is time to bury once and for all the long-held critical view that all things noteworthily artistic from those Dark Ages perforce stemmed from religion. The Church was by no means the sole origin or, for that matter, the sole enemy of the medieval theater. We cannot move forward without paying due attention to the peerlessness of mime, costume, and gesture (all three inseparable from our treatment below of "Performance and Performance Records" but in need of analysis here as well).

Just because few dramas of any orthodox sort survive prior to the fourteenth-century heyday of the miracle play, that does not mean that there was no medieval drama per se. Centuries before the cinema was but a glimmer in the eye of onlookers of daguerreotypes, the medieval theater was a highly visual medium, hosting numerous practitioners of mime, dance, and slapstick, all of them proficient in the art of gesture. Naturally, those mimes hit a roadblock or two, especially since priests and bishops were not their biggest fans.[10] But, throughout classical antiquity and the Middle Ages, mime evoked far more than the annoyance associated with histrionic begging for small change in tourist spots worldwide. Instead, it was a universal language, the communicative function of which was as crucial as that of any trope.

As early as the second century B.C., the acclaimed satirist Lucian of Samosata had praised pantomime as a philosophical art to be practiced by one who was "retentive of memory, gifted, intelligent, keenly inventive, and above all successful in doing the right thing at the right time" ("The Dance," sec. 74). And the first-century rhetor and educational theorist Quintilian just as pointedly categorized gesture as *body language:*

> [T]he hands may almost be said to speak. Do we not use them to demand, promise, summon, dismiss, threaten, supplicate, express aversion or fear, question or deny? Do we not employ them to indicate joy, sorrow, hesitation, confession, penitence, measure, quantity, number and time? Have they not power to excite and prohibit, to express approval, wonder or shame? Do they not take the place of adverbs and pronouns when we point at places and things? In fact, though the peoples and nations of the earth speak a multitude of tongues, *they share in common the universal language of the hands.* (*Institutio oratoria* 11.3.86–87; my emphasis)[11]

Even though the medieval farce did not exactly keep its hands to itself, its actors did all the things above; gesture is not limited to giving someone the finger. It was a *good* thing, a system of communication, a literal *sign language* unquestionably deserving of respect and without which farce texts, translations, or performances are incomplete. We needn't have waited for Marcel Marceau's virtuosity, Barry Unsworth's exquisite *Morality Play,* or FOX Broadcasting's physiognomic detective drama *Lie to Me* to comprehend that.

And yet, here is what Allardyce Nicoll had to say in 1949 in *World Drama:* "If there is any dramatic continuity between the world of the Greek and Roman temples and the world dominated by the fantastic imagination of the Gothic cathedral we must look for it in the *pitiful and despised gesturings of the mimes*" (99; my emphasis). How times have changed! So much so that actors and directors who are reading this collection with a view toward enactment do far better to turn to Jelle Koopmans, André Tissier, or Jessica Milner

Davis. Koopmans fancies that the plays of the marvelous *Recueil Cohen* are "less literary" and "all the more visual" (introd.); and Tissier finds that, in farce, "the text seems only a support; and what one could easily read inside of a half an hour might well justify a performance of one hour"—not because of any notable scenic complexity but because of how much room is left for pantomime (*RF*, 1: 43).[12] And their views are consistent with Davis's clarification that, "paradoxically, the crudest of all comic forms is a demanding, even a challenging style for dramatist and actor alike," all of it raising serious issues for anyone brave enough to cast a farce: "From the correct reception of custard pies to the precise machinery of a complex display of fireworks . . . it is the physical skills of the actor, and the corresponding visual imagination of the dramatist, which are at a premium. Verbal and literary artifice is simply overwhelmed by physical action in farce" (*Farce*, 17).[13]

I submit that the farce has been done a great disservice by a kind of prejudice against physical comedy, which is not unlike the prejudices faced by contemporary scholars who study the musical theater. (By the way, the French are not similarly prejudiced against physical comedy and slapstick. Witness all those bemused Americans who can't figure out why Jerry Lewis is *still* so popular over there.) Nicoll was right, but for the wrong reasons. Mime is precisely where we must look for dramatic continuity, and not because it's pitiful. Nor is the Church the only place to look for it.

In medieval France, it so happens that another strand of theatrical activity, another pervasive, spectacular ritual was equally influential (and perhaps many others besides, as yet undiscovered). It was the law, as exemplified by that most cathartic of denouements, trial and punishment (*ROMD*, 1–12): the law as practiced by those famous legal apprentices and theatrical fools, the Basochiens.

One of the most striking features of medieval French farce is its preponderance of legalistic scenes, whether these unfold in an official courtroom or in a domestic space in which husbands and wives negotiate and renegotiate their marital contracts. In contrast to its cousins across the English Channel, the French corpus is maniacally—and manically—juridical: full of noisy bodies and bodies of law. (Note that, to this day, the French expression *chercher des noises*—literally to *seek noise*—means "to instigate legal proceedings"). Lawyers are everywhere. They are onstage and behind the scenes, litigating their proverbial asses off, such that one senses a literal incarnation of another popular expression: "that trial is a *farce*!"

Why is that?

Theater historians have barely scratched the surface of the meaning and import of this noticeable difference between French and English drama of the Middle Ages. But one important lead is the prominence of royal court culture in England, as compared to the Basoche in France or to the learned and equally civic-minded "rhetoricians" or *Rederijkers* from the Low Countries.[14] My point is that the law is more than a recurring theme: it is a genuine dramatic structure that owes its prevalence to the theatrical leadership of the Basochiens. In one of the earliest scholarly assessments of the Basoche (1856), Adolphe Fabre honorifically dubbed that organization the "vulgar cradle in which comedy begins to utter its first whimpers."[15] That was no mere poetic turn of phrase. Nor, in my opinion, is it mere coincidence that, in her astute volume in the Critical Idiom series, Davis devotes more time to the medieval French farce than to almost anything else in her first chapter on genre (*Farce*, 6–14).

In 1941, Howard Graham Harvey authored the finest introduction in any language to the *Theatre of the Basoche*. That society was founded in 1303 and flourished in France between 1450 and 1550, at one time, boasting as many as ten thousand members apprenticing their future legal trade (*TB*, 17n). As they trained to practice in Parliament, the Basochiens played their civic roles as interns of sorts under the watchful eye of prosecutors and notaries; and, from what we know, they were chatty fellows. Theory has it that their very name derived from the Greek *basochein*, denoting loquacity but also histrionics, theatricality, and playfulness (*ROMD*, 130–31). The barristers-to-be learned their profession by adjudicating minor court cases that are roughly analogous to our contemporary small claims; and, frivolous though such proceedings have appeared, they are certainly no more so than the countless civil actions that flood the American legal system on a daily basis. (Sometimes, it feels like an *hourly* basis.) These were the tort cases of such minor personages as tailors, bakers, linen suppliers, barkeeps, and deadbeat students. Add cobblers to the mix—the lowest of the low on what emerges as a veritable hierarchy of footwear specialists[16]—and we have the dramatis personae of any farce (below, § "Question of Genre"). That realization, it seems, was not lost on the Basochiens.

When the Basochiens sallied forth to play at litigation, they drew on all the thespian talent that they could muster. Forerunners they were of today's most effective litigators along with their televised descendants, as seen in umpteen courtroom dramas from *Perry Mason* to the *People's Court* to *Judge Judy* to truTV (formerly Court TV network). The Basochiens came together officially twice a week, on Wednesday and Saturday afternoons, with one of those sessions apparently reserved for fictional cases (*causes fictives* or *causes grasses*), a tradition as old as the mock encomium of Greco-Roman antiquity and as new as the moot courts that spring up in law schools nationwide (to say nothing of rowdy, tension-releasing, end-of-the-year revues). Inside the Palais de Justice, the novice lawyers performed their playful pieces for one another with all the trappings of real court cases. Their play trials were fully loaded, so to speak, with bailiffs, court recorders, verdicts, and sentences.

In addition to those legal and theatrical antics, there is evidence of bona fide theatrical collaborations too. A subgroup called the Enfants-sans-Souci—literally, children without worries (*dudes?*)—branched off to devote themselves to the theater; and their repertoire comprised mostly farces, *sotties*, and morality plays (below, § "Question of Genre"). Indeed, Lynette Muir notes that "there was no real distinction made between a *basochien,* a *sot* [fool] and a farcer" (*MES,* E91, 336n). Meanwhile, by the mid-fourteenth century, other Basochiens had initiated a preliminary partnership with the Confrérie de la Passion, the company best known for the massive civic undertaking of staging Passion plays. In that respect, the study of the Basoche belongs to all three of our introductory categories of history, performance, and genre. It assists us immeasurably with our queries *Who wrote farces?* and *Who acted in them?* In both cases, the answer is the Basochiens (even if not exclusively).

As Aristotle had reported long ago, the finest author-orators of his day habitually acted in their own tragedies (*Rhetoric,* 1403b). That appears to have been the case as well for the Basochiens in their own comedies, with Sara Beam asserting that "most farces were written by the men who performed them, usually a bourgeois who enjoyed a certain level of education" (*LM,* 24).[17] If the Basochiens had an order of the day, it was theater and theatricality. The lads were not only good actors; they were good mimes, fluent in that universal language of gesture. In 1424, for instance, when a group of Basochiens performed the *Mystery of the Old Testament* for the Duke of Bedford, they did so without uttering a single word: "and this was done without speaking or movement, *as if they were images raised against a wall.*"[18] Arden might have dubbed it a "dumb show" (*Fools' Plays,* 1–4), and Tissier speaks of "gestural fantasy" (*RF,* 1: 43); but that performance of 1424 was positively protocinematic. In pursuit of their histrionic pleasures, the Basochiens even had special costumes, most notably their marvelous furry hats, to which they were particularly attached (*ROMD,* 136–41) and which would have rendered them identifiable on sight. To be sure, their "costumes" were as recognizable as anything worn by the farce's standard cast of characters: the lawyers, the judges, the priests, the teachers, the chimney sweeps, the cobblers (of whom she shall meet no fewer than five), and the *fous, badins,* or *sots* (that last group wearing floppy-eared bonnets that would do a Monty Python Ministry of Silly Hats proud).[19] Onstage or off-, costume constituted another sign system, another mode of nonverbal communication as powerful as gesture.

As interpreted by medievalists from Johan Huizinga to Jane Burns to Susan Crane, costume signified wealth (or lack thereof), social standing, and a host of other imponderables.[20] Costume was identity in the Middle Ages, and its symbolism or semiotics was by no means limited to heraldry and coats of arms. It was part of character and character development, about which Bouchet, himself associated with the Basoche (*TB,* 13n), spoke emphatically when offering, in the 1530s, some versified advice about putting on a Passion play: "[C]ostume must befit each player well. / It's not a pretty sight when you can't tell / The difference between learned men, you see, / And Pilate, lawyers, or a Pharisee, / Or Herod for that matter. . . ." (cited in *DBD,* 25). That precept held true all over medieval literature, as when a manipulative young wife opens the anonymous *Fifteen Joys of Marriage* by tricking her husband into buying her a new dress (8–15). (The typical medieval woman would have owned only one or two.) Or think about the *schmatta* that Chrétien's Énide is wearing when hero Erec first meets her and spirits her away from her humble upbringing (*Erec and Enide,* 6). Think about the joyous excesses of role-playing during carnival as we follow such guides as E. K. Chambers, Emmanuel Le Roy Ladurie (*Carnival in Romans*), or Mikhail Bakhtin in his stunning tour of the *fête des Fous.*[21] Above all, think about the twelve farces to come. In #3, *Confession Lessons,* good neighbor Colette figures out that her daughter has been deflowered when her girlfriend's lecherous husband describes the dresses that the girl normally wears. In #5, *Blind Man's Buff,* an entire scene is devoted to what the chambermaid, Thomasina, is wearing and how it looks on her. Indeed, the French farcical repertoire is exceptional for the frequency with which costumed actors don yet *additional* costumes as they impersonate yet *other characters* while staging little dramas of their own during a given play.[22]

All things considered, we already start to taste, in the activities of the Basochiens, the bread and butter of theater: privileged spaces, costume, gesture, imitation, impersonation, audience, and, perhaps even more important than costume, conflict (*ROMD,* chap. 2). But this was not just any conflict: it was and *is* the ultimate conflict about how people come together to form a civilized society. It is the conflict that is repeatedly incarnated and theatricalized by medieval drama as a whole. It is a conflict that may finally shed some light on that other notorious leitmotif: the prevalence of a violence that is as much a part of the farce's historiography as it is of its generic features, of its performances, and of the politics of its reception. The violence of the medieval French theatrical corpus comes into focus only when we resituate it within the relentlessly and, I dare say, *naturally* adversarial context of the law itself. The law illuminates much of what we know about farce, including how we come to know anything about medieval dramatic performance at all.

Performance and Performance Records

Before we move to a definition of farce that eventually encompasses the silent screen (with its mostly silent audiences watching things that have already happened), let us not forget that theater is always real, even when it delivers a fantasy. It is always *happening,* always of the moment, always present as it unfolds before spectators in real space and real time. Let us cling to that moment of being and becoming, even though it may be lost forever. Then again, maybe not quite forever.

I've said it before and I'll say it again: there is no understanding medieval farce without performance. And yet, notwithstanding Tissier's categorical affirmation that "the farce is originally written for performance, not for reading" (*RF*, 1: 55), that has not been so easy to see. Why not?

As present and influential as theater once was in the Middle Ages (as in classical antiquity), that is how absent it seems to be from contemporary debates about the effects of media on culture. There are many reasons for that: the soaring cost of tickets (which has tended to make theater the reserve of a cultural elite), the need to leave behind the television or the computer to get out and see a play (or, for the young, simply to go out and *play*), the relatively small audiences as compared to those of the more accessible and "universal" media like the Internet. Whatever the reason, theater has lost much of its collective rhetorical impact at the same time that print, cinematic, and electronic cultures have proved more meaningful. Be that as it may, if Marshall McLuhan's clarion call of the 1960s helped us to see that "the medium is the message," then the medieval theater was one of the most popular and widely available *media* of its era. Theater is not film, of course. It is not television. It is not live Internet streaming. And it is plain to see that medieval spectators gathering on public squares could never have imagined the exciting modes of artful and artless communication that reach audiences of the new millennium. But is just as plain to see that, with its clear and present messaging, theater is, in many ways, the place where our current debates about art begin.

Happily, a handful of specialists of medieval romance know full well that, if much was novel in the Middle Ages, not much was *novelistic.* (Most teachers of medieval literature need to admonish their undergraduates again and again that *roman* in Old or Middle French denoted "romance," not "novel.") Linda Marie Zaerr has been performing romance since the 1980s (http://www.boisestate.edu/english/ma/Linda_Marie_Zaerr.html); and, in a series of innovative programs with a website to match, Evelyn Birge Vitz has made New York University a receptive home to medieval performance practice (https://files.nyu.edu/ebv1/public/). We all play roles every day—some with greater histrionics than others. So we scarcely need a celebrated behavioral psychologist like Jean Piaget to stress for us that, to this day, "theater" serves as a persistent metaphor for many aspects of social life. Consider this sampling of popular expressions: "that trial is a *farce!*" (mentioned above) and "courtroom drama" (law); "military theater" and "staging arena" (battlefield; firefighting, construction); "piece of political theater" (elections; Congress [Please do not shout, "You lie!"]); "surgical theater" (classroom of sorts); and, Ladies and Gentlemen, I give you the "drama queen" (everywhere?).

From amid a host of daily activities that I have elsewhere called "protodramatic" (*ROMD*, 3–18), medieval theater was sprouting up all over the place. It was all part of what the eminent historian Jacques Le Goff characterized as a widespread predilection of that culture to "play itself out" (*Medieval Civilization,* 360–61); and that tendency is preserved by a large variety of medieval terms. *Ludus, ordo, jeu,* and *mystère* (*mystery* play comes from *ministerium,* the Latin term for daily activities): all refer to the "spectacles," "rituals," "play," "playing," and "performance" that informed a veritable "theater of everyday life."[23] Those terms applied to trials, punishments, parades, processions, sports, pageantry, mock battle, dance, song, allegory, dialogue, and even that public educational rite of passage known as the oral examination.[24] Although such spectacles have, of late, become integral to the academic discipline of "performance studies," it is imperative to realize that, as early as the seventh century, the great encyclopedist Isidore of Seville had already grouped them together.[25]

Therefore, in light of all those cultural performances, where does theater end and "real life" begin? With so many sites and venues from which to choose, did anybody whom we can trust—and in documentation that has actually survived—write down what it was like to attend a production of a medieval play? And what about our farces? What was it like to see one of those in the fifteenth or sixteenth centuries?

Tissier recalls that we have relatively rich records for French religious drama, as in Petit de Julleville's *Les Mystères* (2: chaps. 14, 15); and, for anglophone readers, there is Peter Meredith and John Tailby's helpful selection of translated stage directions in *The Staging of Religious Drama in Europe in the Later Middle Ages*. But the record is considerably more scarce for the comic theater, with Muir stating that the "performances of these genres are generally less well documented and rarely figure among civic financial records" (*MES*, 329). Pierre Sadron announced in 1950 that he was working on a book that would complete the performance picture for comedy; but it never saw the light of day (*RF*, 1: 45). Nevertheless, important records of comic performance in France have come down to us, especially in the hefty compendium entitled *The Medieval European Stage, 500–1550* (for which William Tydeman served as the general editor, with Muir taking charge of medieval France [277–349]). In that volume, a dedicated editorial team tackled any testimony that they could find about any medieval theatrical performance of any ilk: staging, costuming, payments, contracts, stage directions, audience reports, "reviews," legislation against the theater, and so on.[26] It amounts to more than six hundred primary documents translated or retranslated into English from some dozen languages—Greek, Latin, Old and Middle English, Welsh, Old and Middle French, Old Provençal, Old High German, Italian, Dutch, Old Flemish, and Spanish—and spanning some thousand years of interplay among theater, mime, music, law, ritual, religion, politics, folklore, and the beaux arts.[27] Their labors make it much less daunting to take on the questions that are on the floor.

Where were French farces performed? Anywhere and everywhere. Despite Muir's cautionary words about the paucity of historical evidence (*MES*, 329), the occasional record surfaces in the form of receipts, leading her to conclude that farceurs often performed at weddings. The actors of farce were "virtually professional and were paid in the same way as the musicians." Even Charles VI and his queen, Isabeau, are said to have enjoyed a farce or two: at least, there is evidence of payments made on their behalf to three troupes in 1388, 1409, and 1415 (*MES*, E78, 329–30). In contrast to the Passion plays, however, which were normally performed within some kind of enclosed space in which special scaffolding was erected, many farces were performed in open spaces: a raised platform at the marketplace, in the streets, at the fairgrounds, in a school or a room of a château (*TB*, 23–26; *RF*, 1: 49). In addition, while entrance fees were routinely charged for Passion plays, almost anyone could attend the less restricted farce.

When were farces performed? In *Tragedy and Comedy,* Walter Kerr reminds us that, from Greek tragedy to painful Passion plays, the farce was a form of quick comic relief that traditionally accompanied a longer tragedy (chap. 2). By analogy to the delectable comestible that we find inside a turkey, this type of play was literally *stuffed* into so-called serious dramas; in modern French, the word for *stuffing* is still *la farce*.[28] Or, in the franker language of Albert Bermel, a farce might be presented as an *interlude,* a "dinner theater that would be either sandwiched in between less frivolous material or served up between courses of a meal while spectator-diners groaned, belched, or otherwise responded to the dishes" (*FAH*, 76). The earliest known French farce, the *Boy and the Blind Man,* was thus stuffed into the Passion play from Semur, the better to resonate, it seems, with that other famous blind character, Longinus (*MES*, 330). Although not all "serious dramas" stuffed in a farce for good measure (*RF*, 1: 46–48), one can see why any alimentarily inspired stuffing might have been particularly welcome at the beginning of Lent, which was prime time for performing farces (*LM*, 30).

In some cases, we can learn a great deal from a single document. For example, thanks to a surviving report about a performance in Dijon (1447), we know: (1) that a farce was inserted into the *Mystery of Saint Eloi;* (2) that the company held rehearsals;[29] (3) that the actors were not especially literate; and (4) that there was a different cast for the mystery play than for the farce (*MES*, E80, 332). More generally, we know too that, when farces were performed in the company of other plays, they tended to serve as the grand finale in productions that contained an opening *sottie* (fools' play) and a morality play. But a farce needn't have been stuffing at all: it could readily be performed independently.[30]

Who was the audience? If the authors, actors, and author-actors of farce were, for the most part, Basochiens, then Basochiens were likely in the audience as well. But farcical performance was much more than an in-joke for the nobility and the bourgeoisie. In attendance were "regular folk too, all there to laugh" (*RF*, 1: 54); and the adjectives in force to describe that "popular crowd" are kinder and gentler than those that have typically applied to the attendees of mystery plays (who have long been denounced as cruel, naive, insensitive, jaded, you name it [*MTOC*, 20–24]). For Tissier, the habitué of farce was someone who loved to snicker, sneer, and smirk at all subjects, even the most intimate ones. That spectator also loved a good pun, a veiled obscenity, a satire, and any kind of slapstick (*RF*, 1: 54). At the same time, even the most astute assessments of those snickering spectators have damagingly impeded our ability to define the genre, detracting attention away from gifted medieval satirists only to spotlight a kind of lowbrow spectator. Such propensities have fostered a certain elitist association of the farce with the lower classes, as if only the most rustic of folk were capable of a good guffaw.[31] We are far better served by Alan Knight's scrupulous demonstration that farces were in no way "limited to a single stratum of medieval society. They were played for and appreciated by all social levels, including the royal courts" (*AG*, 48).

Finally, the larger question that concerns us in any initiation to this repertoire is why we have records in the first place. If history records the extraordinary, that is also true of the medieval stage. Chroniclers usually pass over uncommented the humdrum daily events that form the fabric of our lives and, sometimes—with my apologies to theater practitioners—seeing a play is merely part of the humdrum. Even though a theater piece is always an "event" of sorts, the performance might simply have been "uneventful" enough that nobody memorialized his or her opinion about it in a personal letter or a memoir. More commonly, we come to know that a play was performed for one reason only. It is the same reason that the *Saint Eloi* of 1447 in Dijon came to light: because something illegal, immoral, or at least exceptional happened in its wake.

How do we know that a play was performed? Something *stops* it, as when, in 1510 in Avenières, an epidemic of the flu-like *coqueluche* so decimated the cast of the nonfarcical *Mystery of Saint Blaise* that almost three quarters of the villains had recourse to the medieval equivalent of calling in sick (*DBD*, 134). How do we know that spectators turned up from everywhere to take in a play that was in town? Because, when a mystery play was rained out in Seurre in 1496, *"those who had come from the towns round about* decided to go away when they saw the weather so changed" (*MES*, E81, 331; my emphasis). And how do we know that a farce was a special treat? Because those who weathered that storm in Seurre were rewarded by the mayor with the *Farce of the Miller*. How do we know that medieval theater audiences were not exactly peaceful and quiet at the theater? (Apparently, they were blissfully unaware that, one day, Stanley Cavell would ruminate that the "first task of the dramatist is to gather us and then to silence and immobilize us" [*Must We Mean What We Say?* 326].) For one thing, it is not uncommon for mystery plays to begin with a prologue that ever so politely implores the audience to shut up. For another thing, the Town Council of Beauvais issued an edict in 1452 that strictly forbade physical intervention by onlookers, notably at a play's initial moments. Specifically, attendees were not to "do anything that is intended to or will have the effect of stopping the players from taking to the platforms and scaffolding" (cited in *DBD*, 58). It is logical to presume that, if spectators were chastened for interrupting, then they *were* interrupting. It is also logical to think that, despite Michel Foucault's theory in *Discipline and Punish* (which is justly à la mode), it doesn't entirely make sense that civil authorities would *create* the very behaviors against which they were inveighing or that they would legislate behavior that had not yet occurred.

Other happenings that rendered a medieval play "eventful" are far more sinister. In 1395, we know that a Passion play was performed in Chelles near Paris because of a legal proceeding initiated against a gang of toughs who raped a woman. The erudite Antoine Thomas discovered the document because he was sifting through the archives looking for any and all extant references to theatrical life, and he clearly perked up when he learned that the group of felons had spent the night on the *theatrical scaffolding* erected for the next day's play.[32] Indeed, the history of the French theater emerges from the shadows of crime and punishment. Our earliest records include that case from Chelles plus two mortal stage accidents from 1380 and 1384, in which two men were accidentally killed by the cannon fire of special effects gone awry.[33] Such knowledge must preface what we *do* know about the fifteenth- and sixteenth-century performance of French farce, whose infamous violence finally gains some much-needed perspective.

The farce, for Eric Bentley, is "notorious for its love of violent images" (*LD*, 219); and the violent images and realities of the medieval farce are too disturbing, too distracting, and too ubiquitous to be designated an undercurrent. Barbara Bowen (née Cannings) names violence an essential plot mechanism, judging that "in a farce something happens, if it is *only a beating*, and a point is made, however simple and obvious" (TDF, 558–59; my emphasis). Although I've occasionally been reproached, in my own oeuvre, for what appears to be an obsession with violence, I would counter that it is not my own obsession but that of the medieval playwrights. There is no such thing as "only a beating." Violence demands moral reflection and so too does the farce. The problem is that there has been a lot more scholarship on why some violence is inspirationally good and noble (such as René Girard's *Violence and the Sacred*) than on why other violence is risibly bad and ignoble. One can certainly disagree with the commonplace argument about the Passion plays' deployment of violence for the greater good. I can, I do, and I have (*MTOC,* 4–24). But what about violence in the farce?

All in all, the gory, turn-of-the-twentieth-century French "theater of horror" of the Grand Guignol has nothing on the farce and owes much to the medieval spirit.[34] Contemporary theater companies may well find clever ways to denounce, reverse, or cross-cast all the violence; but it is impossible to avoid it. If Gustave Cohen and, later, John Gatton took as a kind of medieval mantra the famous stage direction from the French Old Testament cycle that, in mystery plays, "there must be blood," one might almost say that, in farce, *there must be beatings.* No fewer than half of the plays presented in this anthology open or close with a bang, calling for sticks or staffs to inflict such beatings (or threaten as much): #3, *Confession Lessons;* #5, *Blind Man's Buff;* #6, *Playing Doctor;* #8, *Shit for Brains* (threat); #9, *Monk-ey Business;* and #10, *Getting Off on the Wrong Foot.* And, while I cannot do justice to this vast topic, I wish to assure the reader that, having pondered at length the interrelations of rhetoric, torture, pedagogy, spectacle, and musicality in the scourging and Crucifixion scenes of Passion plays, I can say with unhappy confidence that we encounter all those features in the flagellations of farce. Excruciatingly "playful" games of abuse abound (such as blind man's bluff), as do allusions to specific techniques of torture, all beating one and the same ideological drum about the pleasures of pain (or is that the pains of pleasure?). On one hand, the medieval French farce stages the pedagogical ramifications of corporal punishment, literally "teaching a lesson" to its wayward protagonists. On the other hand, its violence is quite the "song and dance," musically reflective of the singsong, rhythmic, metronomic "beats" that pound all those shitting, farting, and boisterous bodies.[35] Husbands beat their wives, and wives their husbands; masters torment their servants and vice versa; priests extort their female parishioners for sex; and, inside and outside the bounds of holy matrimony, all those parties engage in nonconsensual sex that we would likely define today as "rape." If I may, none of it is terribly funny. It suffices to read the harrowing legal case of Marguerite Vallée, as painstakingly reproduced by Natalie Zemon Davis. Mme Vallée was a victim who murdered her abusive husband in 1536 after enduring regular domestic violence (*Fiction in the Archives,* chap. 3).

According to Bermel, one of the hallmarks of farce is a brutality that is seemingly without consequence:

In farce, characters seldom get badly injured, almost never die. Although a character doesn't merely clash with other characters but also collides with the scenery and props, he stays more or less intact. Blood flows like wine in a heavy drama or melodrama. In farce the victim, who is apparently bloodless, looks dazed after a collision, then shakes his head, picks himself up, and goes off to meet the next collision. Farce shows us human bodies that are indestructible, sponges for punishment. (*FAH*, 23)

'Tis a far cry indeed from the buffeted, bleeding, and crucified Christ who "dies-but-not really," only to be resurrected (*DBD*, 55–57) and whose death-that-is-not-one is of the utmost consequence. Rather, it is all too close for comfort to the unmatched legacy of the philosopher who tainted our theatrical consciousness for millennia: Plato. Bentley embarks upon his signature chapter on farce with a long citation from the *Republic* that warned of off-color theatrical violence coloring offstage cruelty (*LD*, 219). Plato had complained bitterly that

> if in comic representations, or for that matter in private talk, you take intense pleasure in buffooneries that you would blush to practise yourself, and do not detest them as base, you are doing the same thing as in the case of the pathetic. . . . In regard to the emotions of sex and anger, and all the appetites and pains and pleasures of the soul which we say accompany all our actions, the effect of poetic imitation is the same. For it waters and fosters these feelings when what we ought to do is to dry them up. (*Republic*, 606c–d)

In essence, Plato's is a fear about what theater can *do.* In the sense outlined by the ordinary-language philosopher J. L. Austin, his was a fear that theater can do real things, that theater can be "performative."[36]

Austin is rightly revered for having revolutionized our understanding of how language is used. By no means limited to reflecting or describing reality, language can actually *create reality* under such fixed, ritualized circumstances as marriages, promises, threats, and bets. Thus, when the poker player says "I bet" while anteing up, he or she is betting and has bet. When the bride and groom say "I do," they are not speaking *about* marriage but are genuinely *marrying;* they are committing the performative act of getting married, after which, technically, they will *be* married (assuming that all the other requisite conditions have been properly fulfilled: they dutifully obtained a marriage license, their divorces are final, no one is a bigamist, etc.). Writes Austin in *How to Do Things with Words:* "the issuing of the utterance is the performing of an action—it is not normally thought of as just saying something" (6–7). On the stage of the medieval French farce, there was plenty of physical assault to go around and we need not—we *ought not*—think of it as "just saying something." In fact, myriad records survive about actors and spectators who barely survived their performances ... or who did not survive.[37]

Regardless of Bermel's belief that the farce's "family traits" of unreality, brutality, and objectivity create a culture in which "the unreality is objective ... [and] the brutality is unreal" (*FAH,* 22), physical violence, as enacted by real bodies in real space in real time, never leaves reality far behind. Whether it be a mystery play or a farce, medieval drama *did things;* and, notwithstanding many medieval and postmedieval perceptions and misperceptions about the scenic action of drama, everybody knew it. Therefore, I prefer to reframe our final question of what a farce *is* by asking instead something eminently pragmatic, especially in an anthology of plays destined, I hope, for performance: *What does farce do?*

The Question of Genre

Generally and generically speaking: *What is a farce? What are its subjects and plotlines? Who are its characters? What does it do?*

The trouble begins the minute that one attempts to distinguish farce from its partners, the *sottie* and the morality play. Both Beam and Tissier make such distinctions, the former noting that *farce* is "an umbrella term for all French comic theater of the fifteenth and early sixteenth centuries" (*LM,* 27); and, the latter, that "nothing would be further from the truth than to believe that these different genres are separate, independent" (*RF,* 1: 32). Still, Jessica Milner Davis regards the contrary as just as viable: "in France during the late Middle Ages, farce actually achieved ... structural independence and was both named and recognized as a distinct dramatic type" (*Farce,* 6–7). Enter Koopmans to advocate that all fifty-three of the plays of the *Recueil Cohen* require "nothing less than a new historicization of the farce" as literary genre. They are "sometimes passing strange," he avers, "sometimes surprisingly modern—correspond[ing] to no image of the genre provided by the standard histories of literature or theater."[38] Whom shall we believe? If medieval French playwrights and theater troupes referred to their creations as *farces, sotties,* and *moralités,* then it stands to reason that they meant something by it, right?

Defining farce is a tough call. It's almost as tough as defining satire, which is invoked repeatedly in the secondary literatures but which, with the notable exception of Martha Bayless's *Parody in the Middle Ages,* is shockingly neglected in the study of medieval comedy. As late as 1693, the Poet Laureate Nahum Tate admitted defensively: "I have not yet seen any definition of Farce, and dare not be the first that ventures to define it. I know not by what Fate it happens (in common Notion) to be the most contemptible sort of Drama."[39]

One understands his anxiety.

It proves useful nevertheless to review some of the enshrined definitions, incomplete though they may be, along with a number of areas of scholarly agreement.

When Randle Cotgrave compiled his famous *Dictionarie of the French and English Tongues* in 1611, he defined the farce in terms of performance. It was "a [foolish] and dissolute Play, Comedie, or Enterlude" akin to dancing a jig: "also, the Iyg at the end of the Enterlude, wherein some pretie knauerie is enacted" (cited by Davis, *Farce,* 16). Much later, Bentley summed things up nicely when equating farce to "joking turned theatrical" (*LD,* 234);[40] Tissier determined it to be a "very supple genre, which ranges from the simple parade to the makings of a comedy of manners" (*RF,* 1: 37); and, in virtually twenty-five words or less, Muir offered a remarkably apt sociocultural vision of the farce as performance. She insisted on segregating from the mystery plays the entire medieval theatrical pack of *sotties,* morality plays, and farces. The triumvirate of farce, *sottie,* and morality play, she contended, boasts markedly different settings, themes, characters, outlooks, and "community appeal":

> These fictional plays, though not civic, were essentially urban in their outlook and subject matter: the farce portrayed scenes and characters from contemporary society, the morality presented personified abstractions or allegories, and the *sottie* . . . was a peculiarly French type of satirical play performed by actors wearing the headgear of fools (*sots*), the traditional long-eared cap of the jester. (*MES,* 329; her emphasis)

(If you ask me, the easiest way to tell them apart is like so: think of the *sottie* as literal "foolishness," almost surreal, preabsurdist fools foolishly fooling around, sometimes engaged in "actions" that barely qualify as such and most certainly not as Aristotelian "imitations of actions" [*Poetics,* 1449b]. And for the morality play, think of *Everyman,* of a debate that comes to life among personified virtues, vices, and other character traits. And, if that sounds unfamiliar or inaccessible, then remember that, in the early 1990s, the nascent FOX network tried one out on television called *Herman's Head.* Back then, it could run for three seasons but it was not exactly a hit.)

Last but not least, one appraisal from a distinctly nonmedieval medium is refreshingly apropos regarding something that is frequently lost in the medieval critical shuffle. With an emphasis on performance (albeit privileging written rather than improvisational forms), Wikipedia gets it absolutely right that farce needn't be limited to so-called dramatic literature at all:

> A farce is a comedy [written for the stage or film] which aims to entertain the audience by means of unlikely, extravagant, and improbable situations, disguise and mistaken identity, verbal humour of varying degrees of sophistication, which may include sexual innuendo and word play, and a fast-paced plot. . . . Farce is also characterized by physical humour, the use of deliberate absurdity or/of nonsense, and broadly stylized performances.[41]

Naturally, one can debate some of the finer points; but Wikipedia also gets it right about the farce's telltale "frantic pace," "crazy costumes" (a qualifier that was subsequently deleted), tolerance of transgressive behavior, and status as a "highly flexible dramatic mode that often occurs in combination with other forms, including romantic comedy." Not bad at all, especially considering that the great Samuel Taylor Coleridge wryly but sketchily pronounced that "the definition of a farce is, an improbability or even impossibility granted in the outset; see what odd and laughable events will fairly follow from it" (*Coleridge's Literary Criticism,* 201). It's even tempting to speculate that Coleridge meant both the farce *and* its impossible definition!

Our key question of *what farce does* is elucidated somewhat by the scholarly consensus surrounding four of its principal components: length, settings, characters, and plotlines. Barbara Bowen's handy résumé helpfully brings them together, moving us beyond such thematic statements as Beam's that farces are "earthy" plays, "at their core, depictions of good and evil underpinned by basic Christian values" (*LM,* 27–28). Instead, Bowen opines:

Their characters, always few in number, are everyday people anchored in daily life, with names and nicknames, with homes of their own and professions and jobs which they are seen doing. Their scenes are the home, the farm, the open road, the market place. Their subjects are the accidents of humdrum existence—conjugal infidelity, debtors and creditors, petty thieves and swindlers, family quarrels. Their dialogue resumes and intensifies the elements of everyday conversation; its lyrical heights and abusive depths, its asides, tirades, incoherences, songs, tears and laughter. (TDF, 558)

With all that in mind and, and, all the while acknowledging that an enumeration is not, in and of itself, a definition, here are some of the canonical answers to those four canonical questions:

First: *How long is the typical farce?* Scholars generally stipulate, as does Bowen, that "several striking exceptions aside," the majority of the extant farces are short, funny "little scenes of everyday life" (*CE,* 4). Along with many other colleagues, Tissier seconds that motion, specifying that farce texts average 350–450 lines of verse (*RF,* 1: 35). (Length, by the way, is one of the things that makes the beloved *Farce of Master Pierre Pathelin* so exceptional.)

Second: *What is the setting?* Scholars also agree about where the farcical plotlines unfold, even if they disagree about what it all means. For Tissier, these are "situations in the frame of family life, married life, or of a profession" (*RF,* 1: 37); and for Bowen, farces are "simply 'slices of life' dramatically and comically distorted but still very close to reality" (TDF, 558). But Alan Knight is emphatic about refuting the notion "that the farce is a realistic genre": not unlike the universe of Hieronymus Bosch, it is a highly stylized, "abstracted, fictional, farce world that could never exist in reality" (*AG,* 49). (More on this below.)

Third and more complex: *Who are the characters?* From the least to the most controversial viewpoints, Tissier relates that the standard farce casts two to six *personnages,* usually three or four (*RF,* 1: 35); and Bernard Faivre divides those characters into two basic categories (although heaven only knows how he told them apart): men versus women and tricksters versus dupes (the preponderance of which dupes are men).[42] We shall encounter five cobblers (in #2, #6, #9, #10, #11), who are joined (in no particular order) by the scheming servant, the cuckolded or henpecked husband, the shrewish wife, the "dumb-blonde" daughter, the country bumpkin, the clever mom, the snooty professor, the "doctor" or apothecary, the woman who never shuts up, the lusty monk or priest, the adulterer (male or female), the dishonest merchant, the shyster lawyer, the overeager neighbor, the trickster tricked, and even the trickster who knows that he's about to get tricked but proceeds anyway. To that list, Bowen would add silly children and boastful soldiers (*CE,* 4), while Tissier would supplement it with tradesmen of all kinds, all-around jokers, and "the little people, modest folks, artisans and bourgeois: a shepherdess, a fishwife, a tripe merchant; valets; a schoolboy, a teacher; a doctor, a priest, a book vendor, a chimney sweep, a kettle maker, a stocking maker, a water carrier, a tailor or seamstress, a cloth merchant" (*RF,* 1: 36). In other words, who they *are* is inextricably linked to *what they do.*

The characters of farce are "types," warrants Tissier, who are frequently unnamed for the very reason that they *are* types; and he finds them "neither frankly sympathetic nor frankly antipathetic; they are morally and intellectually mediocre" (*RF,* 1: 31). I submit, however, that that phenomenon of "typing" and stereotyping aligns them, on one hand, with the exemplary characters of the morality play (whether the example be positive or negative), and, on the other hand, contributes to the historical disparagement of farce. The modernist take of Joan Dean is instructive in that respect. In "Joe Orton and the Redefinition of Farce," Dean suspects that "the belief that such plays are populated by caricatures rather than fully drawn, well-developed characters capable of growth and change" has encouraged a misleading but "prevailing assumption . . . that the farceur is not so much unwilling as unable to create three-dimensional characters" (482). It turns out, moreover, that that assumption has a great deal to do with farce's notorious violence (above, § "Performance and Performance Records"). Dean espies a misperception according to which "the gross physical action and slapstick violence of farce seem better suited to simple, readily identifiable characters than to complex or sophisticated ones" (482), all of it leading to the association of farce with the bloodlust of a lowbrow audience. Regardless of whether one accepts or rejects Dean's charge that the farce has been dismissed on socioeconomic grounds by intellectual elitists, none of it has nurtured a very high artistic opinion of the farce or of its characters. Those characters shall emerge nonetheless, on the pages that follow, as the three-dimensional creations of medieval authors who suffered from no authorial impoverishment whatsoever. Not at all. They were insightful humorists about the human condition. (And, yes, outside the ivory tower, one is allowed to speak of a universal "human condition.")

Fourth and finally: *What are those characters up to?* Usually no good. Etymologically, the word *farce* means (among other things) "trick," with trick upon trick structuring the vast majority of farcical plotlines. Drawing on that etymology to conflate plot and character, Knight specifies that "farce characters act in order to deceive, and often their actions are really reactions to other characters who have deceived them or are in the process of doing so. Their goal is virtually always to gain at another's expense some selfish, personal advantage such as status, power, goods, money, or sex" (*AG*, 51). It's true: that tricky structure is no conflict à la Greek tragedy, but conflict there is. No matter who plays and who gets played, the dramatis personae make love and war over sex, religion, education, domestic power, and the excesses of a legal system gone awry. In contrast, though, to all those Aeschylean deaths and demises, farce conflicts "tend not to be resolved, but only momentarily neutralized for the sake of bringing the play to a close" (*AG*, 51). If anything, a farce suggests an oxymoronic open-ended closing (as in everybody's favorite *Pathelin* or in our #10, *Getting Off on the Wrong Foot*): when all the fighting is over, it has only just begun.[43]

What actually happens in a farce? As I cursorily unveiled their plots above, our dozen plays adjudicate such conflicts as the legal liability of farting (#1), the domestic rights and duties of the sexes (#2), the presence of trickery at confession (#3, #9), the access of country bumpkins to an education (#4, #12), the social mobility (or lack thereof) of the "serving class" (#5), the penalties (if any) to be imposed upon a large variety of adulterers (#3, #6, #7, #10, #11) or upon libidinous priests (#9, #11), and, last but not least, the need to "clean up one's shit" (#8). Those twelve plotlines bring us, at long last, to that pesky question that I posed at the outset: If that is what happens, then *to what end? What does farce itself do?*

Tissier is quite right that, in art, "usage makes the norm" (*RF,* 1: 32); and he just as rightly emphasizes that farce and satire belong to one and the same generic universe. Channeling the wisdom of the classical Horatian dictum of art as both sweet and useful (*dulce et utile*), he nevertheless makes a problematic assertion. By dint of its unique mimetic mission to "perk up the crowd and awaken their laughter" (*RF,* 1: 32), the farce "seeks *only to solicit laughter*" (*RF,* 1: 38). Quoth Tissier: as a mere "comical divertissement, the farce proposes *neither to edify nor to instruct,* even when it is satirical (and however satirical it might be): it *is uniquely destined to make people laugh* by taking its subjects from daily life, even when its subject is our misery and ridicule" (*RF,* 1: 31–32; my emphases). For her own part, Davis is inspired by this pithy definition from the *Oxford English Dictionary:* "a dramatic work (usually short) which has for its sole object to excite laughter" (*Farce,* 1). She asserts that farce is "broad, physical, visual comedy, whose effects are pre-eminently theatrical and *intended solely to entertain*" (*Farce*, 1; my emphasis). My rebuttal is one that I have proffered elsewhere: for one thing, a play has never "intended" anything in its nonexistent life. Only *people* have intentions (*MBA*, 93–94). For another thing, there is no such divorce between didacticism and entertainment, no such arbitrary distinction between "didactic theater" and "diverting, satirical theater" (*RF,* 1: 28). The difficulty with Tissier's categorization is his simultaneous affirmation that satire—one of the most instructive literary forms of all time—is more relevant to the *sottie* (where it "predominates") than to the farce (*RF,* 1: 37). Is it reasonable that satire would be central to the *sottie* but a mere divertissement in the farce?

I think not.

Having laughed out loud at this repertoire for many years, I, for one, am still negotiating my way through the meaning of the farce's rampant legal injustice, domestic violence, and sexism (to name but a few eminently serious, didactic matters). One needn't be a medievalist geek to find these plays literally thought-provoking. And I have a hunch that, even in the midst of their own laughter, medieval spectators were thinking too: especially the battered women and legally unrepresented and underrepresented servants. Therefore, we do well to heed Knight's counterclaim about the "commonly held, but misleading, [notion] . . . that farces were played in the Middle Ages for the sole purpose of making people laugh" (*AG*, 48). Tissier himself concedes as much: "even the comic genre as a whole has no clear separation from the serious genre, laughter serving only as a dominant note of the mimetic theater, the serious serving only as the dominant note of the didactic theater" (*RF,* 1: 32). In that spirit, he wondered whether the "commingling" medieval comic genres might be disentangled by "the methods employed to address the public," with allegory emerging as the primary mode of communication for the morality play, "bizarre excesses of language" for the *sottie,* and "caricatures of daily life" for the farce (*RF,* 1: 37). Tissier further intuited more profitably that, if all three genres shared an overall satirical function, then perhaps one could invoke *degrees* of satire, an insight that lends credence to Beam's instinct that farce is less "satirical" and less "judgmental" than its theatrical partners of *sottie* and morality play (*LM,* 24).[44] So, since the binary between teaching and entertainment will simply not do, we might try something else. Happily, there is a cultural institution that interprets and promulgates those very modes of judgment, judgmentalism, and communication. It was as paramount to Greco-Roman government and medieval thought as it is today to contemporary media studies or social theory. It is called *rhetoric*.

The rhetorical tradition explored, rationalized, and codified all imaginable aspects of social life, its own three official genres focusing on praise and blame, politics, and the law. Briefly, the "epideictic" or demonstrative genre was "occasional" or of the moment, a presentist oratory that encompassed both the funereal eulogy and the bitter invective. The deliberative or political genre comprised the exhortatory or dissuasive orations of bodies politic working toward a shared future. And forensic or legal rhetoric classified and categorized juridical, fact-finding investigations into the past, the better to prosecute or defend alleged malefactors.[45] Most important, forensic rhetoric was not only the contextual frame in which most early rhetorics were articulated: it was the bread and butter of our farcically inclined Basochiens, who cast the widest of political and legal nets in their various performances, whatever the occasion.

In a flawed but ambitious book called *Satire and the Transformation of Genre* (1987), Leon Guilhamet argued suggestively that satire was not a literary *genre* at all but, rather, a *mode* that was decipherable only in the context of those three classical rhetorical genres of forensic, legal, and epideictic.[46] With Dryden, Pope, and Swift as his case studies (works dated 1681–1742), Guilhamet's tantalizing thesis—still underexplored—was that "all satires are imitations of rhetorical structures," despite their "fundamentally different actions and temporal schemes" (13). Shedding new light on the ethical open-endedness of farce, he hypothesized that "the basic difference between the satiric and the comic is that the satiric reinterprets the ridiculous in an ethical light" (8) whereas, implicitly, the farce would do so more gently, more merrily, or not at all:

> The satiric employs comic techniques of ridicule, but discovers harm and even evil in the ridiculous. *The ridiculous that is proper to satire cannot be reconciled to the good at the conclusion of a comic plot.* Rather the evil or perversity is isolated in expectation of some moral correction. The correction comes from the satire itself, as the evildoer is, to use a Renaissance phrase, "stripped and whipped." (8; my emphasis)

In light of the large amounts of dramatic stripping and whipping, literal and metaphorical, that we are about to see, one can only wonder: How valuable is it to separate the corrective satirical *good* from the farcically *good laugh*?

It is nothing if not dispositive that the celebrated lawyer, Basochien, and aficionado of the theater, Jean Bouchet (cited above), described thusly the theatrical duties of the "King of the Basoche": "to declare by grave tragedy, rude satire and feigned comedy, the good of the good and the evil of the wicked" (*MES*, E86, 333). Even more extraordinary was his explicit identification of the political, advisory, and monitory role of satire. In Bouchet's estimation, the *sottie* was not necessarily "a bad thing" just because it "sometimes attacks individuals and causes scandal." Far from it. In France, a play like the *sottie* was a powerful rhetorical tool by means of which players might advise their monarch more honestly and less opportunistically than a privy counselor:

> It is called a *sotie,* because *sots* re-enact on stages in polished language the great follies of high and low society. And this is allowed by kings and princes so that they shall know the disarray of their councils, which no one dares to tell them unless they are warned of it by Satire. The king, Louis XII, wanted them to perform them [*sotties*] in Paris and said that by these plays he learnt of many faults which were hidden from him by over-cautious advisors. (*MES*, E87, 334; Muir's emphasis)

By dint of that mission, the Basochiens were social, political, and theatrical satirists who were subject to all the perils thereof. Indeed, as Aristotle had long ago explained it, politics was second nature to actors, just as theatrical exhibitionism was—and is—second nature to politicians (*Rhetoric,* 1403b). At least, when constituents are looking. Given that the farce was one of the *sottie*'s comrades in arms, given that it was oftentimes written and performed by the self-same Basochial author-actors, it is unlikely that that satirical mission simply faded away during a farce. Quite to the contrary, there is every reason to suspect that the farce might have gotten in on the overtly political act. Certainly, all manner of medieval communities harbored suspicions to that effect, which led in turn to more theatrical and extratheatrical stripping and whipping.

With giggles and guffaws galore, the influential Basochiens negotiated quite the legal minefield as they spoke truth to power, their plainspokenness not always going over so well with the royal and ecclesiastical powers that be. Outside the plays proper (or farcically *improper*), actors frequently came forward to recite proclamations and prefaces—called "Banns" in medieval England—as well as epilogues in which they begged the indulgence of spectators. Among their most pressing requests: actors should not be held liable for potentially dangerous utterances not spoken *in their own voices,* as it were. For instance, during the Passion play from Angers of 1456, the play's expositor petitioned on behalf of his fellow thespians for a kind of freedom of speech, urging spectatorial judiciousness lest the company's onstage words trigger offstage accusations of heresy: "I protest publicly on behalf of all players in this mystery play, jointly and severally, that, in the event that anything against the faith should be said or done by anyone, it shall be deemed null and void. For we do not intend [*entendre*] to say or do anything against the faith."[47] Theirs were legally protected utterances, he postulated, all part of a theological tradition of safe haven for translators, interpreters, and exegetes of the Bible, as exemplified by Saint Jerome's own translation of the good book. Not coincidentally, all twelve of our farces conclude with a versified plea to the audience, with #1, #2, #8, and #10 praying in particular that their ribaldries be taken in stride. One thing is clear: the threat was real. Theater might have real juridical consequences.

Reconsider now the patently legalistic setting in which so many medieval performances come to be discovered in the first place and in which so many medieval dramas begin and end. It is a commonplace of satire that, "if evildoers cannot be brought before a real bar of justice, they can be tried in the court of satire where they have little chance of escape" (Guilhamet, *Satire,* 67). If, for Bouchet, foolish jokes were monitory, then, all over fifteenth- and sixteenth-century France, the monitory needed monitoring. With increased scrutiny and censorship, municipalities demanded the preapproval of dramatic materials—farcical stuffing included. For example, in Dijon in 1447, a group of hasty actors found themselves on the wrong end of the law because of misplaced allusions during a farce that they had illicitly inserted into the *Mystery of Saint Eloi* (above, § "Performance and Performance Records"). It seems that one member of the troupe had so enjoyed seeing a farce at Beaune that he had raised the possibility "of inserting a farce in the play of St Eloy." Alas, "[proceedings were started against] the players of this farce who *without permission from the authorities performed this scene*" (my emphasis). Although the outcome of those proceedings has been lost, we do know that even those actors who had not actually *performed* in the farce were investigated. The embroiled fan of the Beaune farce did his best to defend himself, hazarding that, "during the rehearsals no one had noticed in the words used anything derogatory or touching anyone's honour especially not of our lord the King or the Dauphin [. . .] and for his part if he had known or been told by anyone that it was wrong to play this farce [. . .] he would not have joined the group [. . .] but he was no clerk and could only read a little" (*MES*, E80, 331; Muir's ellipses). (Note that, today, the French still have a motto that "no one is permitted to be ignorant of the law" or *nul n'est censé ignorer la loi*.)

Almost a century later in Savoy, a theatrical censor was clearly quite busy making emendations to the "book" that he had been furnished for an impending performance of the *Mystery of Saint Sebastian* slated for 1547. He was loath to issue a blanket authorization to the troupe insofar as he had yet to peruse "some remarks by the fool [*stultum*] which are not included and the same will not be allowed unless they have been seen first. Provided other corrections or cuts are made as marked it is permitted to perform what has been seen in this book" (*MES*, E82, 332). Did the show go on? Unknown. But, back in Paris, under the reign of Francis I, three *farseurs* were imprisoned for having gone too far when they took on royal authority: Jacques *le Basochien*, Jehan Seroc, and Jehan de Pontalais. They were "taken before the king [Francis I] at Amboise in chains [. . .] for having played farces in Paris concerning the nobility: among other things [suggesting that] Mere Sotte [Mother Fool] ruled the court and was taxing, robbing, and pillaging everyone. The King and the Queen-Regent were very angry about this" (*MES*, E91, 336; my emphasis; Muir's ellipsis). The unholy trio escaped to Blois, we are told, and were pardoned shortly thereafter. (By the way, this was hardly the first time that Pontalais had gotten into hot water. According to a famous apocryphal tale, he noisily interrupted a priest *during a sermon*—going so far as to box his ears—so that he could advertise a performance by the Enfants-sans-Souci [*DBD*, 108–10].)

It is in the undeniably political context of such ruckus and commotion that we come full circle to that challenging definition of farce, a painfully delightful (and delightfully painful) art form that did, does, and will keep on keeping on doing what it does. Dancing in theatrical counterpoint to the tune of the human condition, the farce is the fun-house mirror image of tragedy, soliciting a laughter that may well serve the same cathartic function as tragedy's tears. We laugh until we hurt; we hurt until we laugh. To paraphrase Blotto of #9, *Monk-ey Business,* laughter and tears have always gone together in happiness and sadness alike: we're "laughin' one minute, cryin' the next: both at the same time when [the farce has its way with us] . . . if you know what I mean" (Scene 2). Enthusiasts of the stage can keep on citing Bentley or Henri Bergson. They can even add to the mix latter-day specialists of the biological basis of behavior, the better to theorize laughter. But the bottom line is that, when we are reading, writing, or attending a farce, the somatic release of laughter, tears, and tearful laughter comes naturally, instinctually, involuntarily . . . unless, of course, we're playacting or faking it (which is one of the repeated worries of our dozen plays). We laugh and cry at the law, at politics, and at all those other occasions that surround us. No matter if the cues be didactically *utile* or icing-on-the-cake *dulce.* We laugh when we are happy, and we cry when we are sad; but we also cry when we are happy and laugh when we are sad. Sometimes we cry at things that are silly and sentimental (like all those Hallmark Cards commercials). Sometimes we laugh at things that are not funny at all, say, the wounded and the dead in Iraq and Afghanistan—but only as mediated by the likes of Jon Stewart. We laugh at the humor of Andrew Dice Clay or at a resonant turn of phrase during the eulogy at a funeral. We laugh at the domestic violence of medieval French farce.

Theater is a hot medium; and the farce pushes plenty of hot buttons. Let's hope that it always will.

About This Translation

Once upon a time, in a universe not so far, far away . . .
It was perfectly acceptable to pontificate publicly about assholes, farts, piss, shit, and sodomy, so long as no one took the name of the Lord in vain: "Golly gee whillikers, husband, why did you fuck me up the ass?"

Such is the universe of the medieval French farce; so prepare to enter a world of jokes, gags, slapstick, and, above all, puns and double entendres that are frequently apparent in the characters' very names—when they *have* names—and evidenced by the titles that I have bestowed upon these largely untitled works. (I hate puns myself and habitually groan at them, but perhaps medieval audiences did too. Just imagine the sound of a gong propelling me offstage each time I make one.) In preparing these anything-but-literal translations, I have respected, to the best of my ability, the exacting philological and historical standards of medieval scholarship, but my priorities are accessibility, course adoption, and performance-friendly dialogue. Although I have endeavored to preserve carefully the literal sense of each and every speech of each and every character whom you are about to meet, I prefer to call these pieces "adapted translations." Why?

It's not merely because my beloved medievalist colleagues are notorious quibblers about the precise meaning of any given word. I am too. But even the best edition is a translation of sorts. Asks the archivist who is deciphering many sorts of medieval handwriting: What *is* this word? What does it mean? Did the scribe forget something here? What happened to the rhyme scheme? Is this is a mistake? The archivist then answers those questions, taking the first step in an interpretive process that future readers normally come to know only as a printed text that is definitive in name only. Recall as well that the textual editing of drama is rendered still more complex by both the oral nature of medieval literary traditions and by the ephemeral nature of theatrical performance. Much of what we know and love about theater is of the moment, often lost to history: the gesture that makes the speech, the actor's physiognomy, the inflection, the intonations, the singing voices, and the farce's freewheeling humor, always contextual. Faced with that translational lost and found, I have sought to preserve the farce's precious essence by transmuting an entire fifteenth- or sixteenth-century French universe into a recognizable American one. (That's right, say I, to my theorist friends: I believe in essences.) I hope that you will find the latter universe a rough but surprisingly timeless and timely equivalent.

In working with each play, I have asked myself repeatedly: What are the cultural touchstones? Which contemporary settings, sites, and spaces best capture the medieval communities at hand? How does one address the imperceptibles of Romance-language dialogue that oscillates seemingly haphazardly between addressing someone with the formal *vous* as opposed to the informal *tu*? What about the dexterity with which medieval dramatists mixed linguistic registers, creating a genre that is as teeming with the learned allusions of an intellectual elite as with the most vulgar street language? What about prose versus verse translation? What about all the songs or musical numbers that were clearly interspersed into the plays at key moments? And, forgive me for saying so, but what about the magic? These plays are sheer delight, and delight is transcultural, transhistorical, but also relentlessly site-specific.

For the most part, my response to those larger questions has been: American sitcoms, stand-up comedy, *Saturday Night Live,* political gaffes, widespread litigiousness, the excesses of university life, twentieth- and twenty-first-century slang, and whatever music rises and falls on the pop charts, especially country music. To put the problem in terms of American popular culture, think of the twelve farces to come as *Judge Judy* meets *Saturday Night Live* meets *Sister Act;* or, alternatively, *Guys and Dolls* meets *Father Knows Best* meets *The Simpsons.* (As far as I know, there was no medieval equivalent of *Survivor,* but give it time; I'm sure that argument is just around the corner.) So, by all means, think Molière but don't stop there. Think Monty Python. Think the Marx Brothers. Think George Carlin. Think *The Three Stooges.* I realize, of course, that all such touchstones are subject to the same ravages of time as the plays that I present here. I also recognize that my "contemporary" cultural moments belie my own arrested development and that my translations too will mutate into work that is anything but "up to date." However, it is my hope that, if the dialogue rings true, then the full sociocultural depth of its zaniness will endure when future readers, directors, and actors substitute their own selections in response to my dramaturgical allusions to vaguely analogous songs, sitcoms, news stories, and even cusswords.

The bottom line? In a way, it's a question of trust. As one who has spent the past thirty years or so living in the world of medieval drama, I feel justified in assuring you that I "get it." The farces are masterpieces of visual, linguistic, and even gallows humor. I'm sure that, were my subjects alive today, they might wince at my occasional misunderstanding of some obvious gag that has disappeared forever. But, if there is humor in the Middle French, it has found its way into this translation, even if that involves my taking a few liberties. Those liberties might take the form of an extra line, an extra term, an extra mimed scene, an extra nonspeaking character, an extra possible musical number, or an extra name (especially for the many unnamed female characters). "What's in a name?" I've asked myself; and I've answered, with the seventh-century encyclopedist Isidore of Seville, *everything.* His masterwork, the *Etymologies,* may not sound particularly catchy, but in many ways it was the key to medieval thought (and it is finally available in an accessible English translation by Priscilla Throop). As Howard Bloch has shown in *Etymologies and Genealogies,* if you understood a name, you have the gist, the essence of a person, place, or thing.

In the "Production Notes" to the individual plays, I strive to answer the principal questions that readers, directors, actors, and dramaturges are likely to ask. To help guide their choices, I provide a snapshot of each play in the prefatory Brief Plot Summaries. That information is subsequently embellished in the sections devoted to "Plot" in the "Production Notes" for each play. At all times, I refer to the plays and their characters by the titles and proper names that I have given them. On occasion, I also venture alternative titles or subtitles; it was too much fun not to. (Medieval plays were often untitled but were likely known to spectators by their story lines: a bit like all those episodes of *Friends* called "The One with … "). After a few words about context, I introduce each play with a brief discussion of the following categories: "Plot"; "Characters and Character Development"; "Language"; "Sets and Staging"; and "Costumes and Props List." Please do realize, though, that it is sometimes impossible to disentangle such canonical categories, especially when an entire play is based on an overarching pun or play on words (#2, #4, and #11), or when the *way* that a given character speaks French (or refuses to in #12) is integral to character development. In sum, I have done my best to tease out any information likely to enhance the understanding, appreciation, and production of these plays, separately or together. I even make the suggestion, here and there, that several farces might be *staged together.* Together they will stand with respect to challenges that are noteworthy for them all.

Needless to say, all translations from the French are my own unless otherwise indicated in the Bibliography. Compared to Middle French, modern French was a walk in the park.

And one final note about the French of the fifteenth century: There is no orthography, no absolute standard for the spelling of Middle French. Middle French was still evolving at the time when our plays were memorialized in writing. In practice, this means that the twenty-first editorial insistence on rigorous consistency is impossible. For example, we may find one character, as in #6, *Playing Doctor*, being called *Frigallette* on one page and *Frigalette* on the next. One edition of our #11 preserves its title character as *Martin de Cambray* while another names him *Martin de Cambrai*. Elsewhere, one cast of characters lists *personnages*, another *parsonages*; a nonaccented word in Middle French now bears an accent in modern French. I will not be indicating each such instance by *sic*: the farces are sick enough, thank you. Please simply recall that the many variant spellings that you shall encounter are not "wrong." They are merely evolving.

Editions and Printed Sources

First things first. *How many farces are there?* About two hundred medieval French farces have survived, starting with *The Boy and the Blind Man* of circa 1280, but with most dating from the fourteenth and fifteenth centuries (*RF,* 1: 15) or, for Barbara Bowen, from 1460 to 1530 (*CE,* 4). In terms of medieval survivals, this is an impressive number that, depending on how we add things up, accounts for almost half of the plays from the medieval comic theater (*RF,* 1: 31) and for almost one-third of *all* the extant medieval French dramatic texts. On one hand, we find the figure of "more than 300 texts" (*MES,* 329) if we consider together the genres of farce, morality play, and *sottie* or fools' play (above, Introduction). On the other hand, Bernard Faivre describes, categorizes, and summarizes the plots of 176 farces in his delightfully witty *Répertoire* (which I highly recommend if you read French). Either way, the entire extant medieval French theatrical corpus, be it comic, serious, or both, comprises some 550 theatrical works (whole and fragmentary), among which the farces join some 180 mystery plays (most cataloged by Graham Runnalls in *Études sur les mystères* and *Les Mystères français imprimés*), 80 morality plays, and 60 *sotties*. When we take stock of those numbers, the paucity of French farces in English translation is all the more striking.

What medieval French farces are available in English? Not many. But, as I mentioned in the Preface, it is well worth reading those that *are* available, even if they are not so easy to access. Barnard and Rose Hewitt's splendid 1938 *In the Suds* (*The Farce of the Washtub*) and Mandel's 1970 *Five Comedies of Medieval France* (*FCMF*) have long been out of print, whereas Knight's spot-on translation of the *Farce of Master Pierre Pathelin* is tucked away as an Appendix to a scholarly monograph: *Semiotics of Deceit* by Donald Maddox (173–99). In 1971, Richard Axton and John Stevens published some excellent translations in *Medieval French Plays* (*MFP*), of which only two are farces: *The Boy and the Blind Man* and *The Play of the Bower* (*Le Jeu de la Feuil-lée*). In 1972, Neville Denny included *The Pie and the Tart* in *Medieval In-terludes*. And in 1999, Thierry Boucquey offered *Six Medieval French Farces* (*SMFF*). By my count, that makes eleven farces in English out of hundreds: *The Bonnet* (Boucquey), *The Bower* (Axton and Stevens), *The Boy and the Blind Man* (Axton and Stevens), *Calbain* (Boucquey), *The Chicken Pie and the Chocolate Cake* (Mandel; or Denny's *The Pie and the Tart*), *The Chim-ney Sweep* (Boucquey), *The Gentleman and Naudet* (Boucquey), *The Kettle Maker* (Boucquey), the *Farce of Master Pierre Pathelin* (Knight; Mandel, the latter calling it *Peter Quill's Shenanigans*), *The Miller* (Boucquey), and *The Washtub* (Hewitt and Hewitt; Mandel). Unbelievably enough, the book that you are reading essentially doubles that number. Even if my count is off by the time you read these words, Stephen Wright maintains an exceptionally useful website, "Medieval Drama in English Translation," that lists any and all medieval plays translated into English from some dozen languages, from Latin to French to Croatian.[1] Practically speaking, that means that a few of the most delicious farces will not be included in the present collection—for my money, those would be *The Washtub* and the *Pathelin*—but the need to *re*translate them seemed far less urgent.

Otherwise, there are already available a large number of invaluable re-sources, not only for the rarefied circles who read the Middle French of the fourteenth and fifteenth centuries but also for those who speak or read mod-ern French. In preparing these translations, I have consulted every Middle French and modern French edition that I could find and, in my "Production Notes" to each play, I indicate where to find the source (or sources) for each base text. To those curious about my process: it was only after finalizing my own translations that I consulted those annotated editions—which was pos-sible for eight of our plays—reserving for absolute last André Tissier's terrific four-volume *Farces françaises de la fin du Moyen Âge* (*FFMA*), in which he assembled modern French translations of all sixty-five of the farces that he edited in his own masterful, thirteen-volume *Recueil de Farces (1450–1550)*. However, six of the plays presented here have never been translated into modern French nor, to my knowledge, into any modern language: #2, *Edict of Noée;* #3, *Confession Lessons;* #4, *Student Who Failed;* #5, *Blind Man's Buff;* #6, *Playing Doctor;* and #10, *Getting Off on the Wrong Foot.*

What are the original manuscripts or printed sources for French farce? Starting with the original-language documents of the farcical repertoire, four collections dominate the scene. All four were printed in the sixteenth century, and all reproduce playtexts thought to predate their publication: the *Recueil Trepperel* (thirty-five plays, of which five are farces, and all discovered in 1928), the *Recueil du British Museum* (sixty-four plays, forty-seven of them farces, discovered in 1840), the *Recueil La Vallière* (seventy-four plays, forty-eight of them farces, and sold by its owner, the Duke of La Vallière, in 1780), and last but certainly not least, the *Recueil Cohen* (the name I use; also known as the *Recueil de Florence*). Over the span of some twenty-three thousand verses, the *Recueil Cohen* contains fifty-three plays, all called "farces," all appearing in print (as in the other three collections) considerably after their dates of composition, between 1540 and 1550.[2] The *Recueil Cohen* was also discovered in 1928 in Florence—whence its alias, the *Recueil de Florence*—only to be lost again. Thus, it came to bear the name of the illustrious medievalist editor who had reportedly been the last to lay eyes on it: the Belgian-born Sorbonne Professor Gustave Cohen. Until very recently, the only trace of the original *Recueil Cohen* had been the edition prepared by Cohen, and that is my principal source: the *Recueil de farces françaises inédites du XVe siècle* (hereafter *Recueil*), published in 1949 for the Medieval Academy of America. (More on its particulars momentarily.)

Ten of our plays are from the splendid *Recueil Cohen;* the remaining two farces—the opening *Farce of the Fart* and closing *Birdbrain*—are both so delectable that I turned to another collection to be able to include them: the *Recueil du British Museum*. In addition to the facsimile edition of the *Recueil du British Museum* prepared by Halina Lewicka, I've elected to follow the editions of those who first attracted us to these plays. These are my base texts: for the *Farce of the Fart,* I follow Viollet le Duc in *Ancien Théâtre françois* (hereafter *ATF*); for *Birdbrain,* I follow Édouard Fournier's *Théâtre français avant la Renaissance* (hereafter *TFR*). In amplifying my readings, I have also sought guidance—when it was available—from Tissier's *Recueil de Farces,* which is the case for six of the plays (in order of appearance herein): *Farce of* the Fart, At Cross Purposes, Shit for Brains, Monk-ey Business, Cooch E. Whippet, and Birdbrain. Tissier's comparative analysis of the extant printed and manuscript sources of sixty-five farces is a tour de force of erudition some fifteen years in the making, every page of which is teeming with insights into philology and historical context as well as an exquisite attention to scenography, acting, directing, and staging. Particularly impressive, moreover, is Tissier's work on the plays from the *Recueil Cohen* in the absence of the original manuscript. With only Cohen's edited volume in hand, Tissier used his best judgment to expand and enhance Cohen's readings, which were thin on the ground in terms of annotations and explanations.

For the record, I have arranged the texts of the present repertoire in such a way as to prove pleasing to American audiences. If that fails, then let's just say that I've arranged them in a way that was more pleasing to *me*. I thought it might be fun if, toward the beginning of this anthology, we were to see— in flagrant defiance of all those stereotypes of the Middle Ages—a tale of women's rights (#2, *Edict of Noée*) and if, toward the end, *women* were to have at least the *semblance* of the last word (#12, *Birdbrain*). (The ten plays from the *Recueil Cohen* appeared in this sequence in that collection: *Confession Lessons, At Cross Purposes, Student Who Failed, Shit for Brains, Edict of Noée, Getting Off on the Wrong Foot, Playing Doctor, Monk-ey Business, Cooch E. Whippet, Blind Man's Buff.*)

Otherwise, I would say: caveat emptor. This is not a full scholarly edition and, by some measures, it is not a scholarly edition at all in the sense that, working primarily with Cohen's edition of the *Recueil Cohen*, I rely on published materials rather than on manuscripts. There is a very good reason for that.

As I specified above, everybody thought that the *Recueil Cohen* had vanished without a trace when—lo and behold!—enter Jelle Koopmans, who, in an academic cloak-and-dagger tale, managed to pick up the trail and arrange to see it. It behooves us to pause briefly to recall that stories like this are not so rare in the history of the serendipitous discovery of medieval works. For instance, one fine day at the Herzog August Bibliothek in Wolfenbüttel, Germany, Alan Knight found himself inquiring about a curious box, only to discover seventy-two plays from Lille that had completed eluded scholarly notice. (The multivolume publication of those plays is still under way for Droz as the *Mystères de la Procession de Lille*). The *Mystère des Trois Doms,* the subject of a famous performance of 1509, was romantically recovered in December 1881 in an attic (*DBD*, 131). The *Recueil du British Museum* was itself discovered in 1840 in a German attic. And, that's right: Koopmans found the *Recueil Cohen,* rebaptizing it in honor of its original Florentine discovery location. His hefty reedition (in press at the time of this writing) is entitled *Les Farces du Recueil de Florence.* It seems that the intrepid Professor Koopmans put out feelers everywhere imaginable until, on another fine day, he received a tip from an American librarian who suspected that the *Recueil Cohen* had recently been sold at auction. By contacting the auction house, Koopmans was able to communicate with the anonymous owner, who generously arranged for him to study the precious document at an undisclosed, neutral location. To this day, its whereabouts remain unknown to all but the lucky and very private owner, rendering the usual process of consultation nearly impossible. But here is what we now know about the *Recueil Cohen* thanks to Koopmans:

The first significant detail is that the *Recueil Cohen* is not a "manuscript" at all, despite Cohen's own implication that it *is* a manuscript. Tissier had already surmised as much from his reading of Cohen's edition, intuiting that the actual primary source and, in this case, primary *sources,* was what we call a *recueil factice:* that is, a group of texts that, while being *presented together,* don't necessarily go together and needn't even have been *conceived* together. The *Recueil Cohen* was "hastily compiled by an amateur," says Tissier (*RF,* 1: 17), a phrase that he repeats virtually each time he reedits one of its plays. More important, once Koopmans located the original, he was able to confirm that, yes, the *Recueil Cohen* is indeed a "collection of separate printed editions (that were designed to function apart). . . . These separate farces had their own histories (browning caused by sunlight, water stains, etc. prove it) before being bound together."[3] Some, he observes, even have different typographical conventions (introd., § "Description du Recueil").

Extraordinary by any measure, the *Recueil Cohen* contains approximately one quarter of all the known French medieval farces, most of them one-of-a-kind. Even when there are versions of the same play in the *Recueil du British Museum,* opines Koopmans, the playtexts of the *Recueil Cohen* are "older and better." They were "published" in Paris by some of the greats in the history of printing, the result of a "collaboration of actors and playwrights, amongst whom we find Roger de Collerye, François Girault, Jean de l'Espine, and Pierre Gringore." That collaboration was not to last. Koopmans goes on to explain that, in 1517, the group apparently broke up their collaboration as well as their repertoire, which they sold "to the Trepperel workshop, who printed it all (the *Recueil Trepperel* and the *Recueil Cohen*) within a matter of days." A first group of plays, reports Koopmans, were printed by the great Jean Trepperel himself, a later group "by Jean Janot and the widow Trepperel toward 1517." Some of the plays are older, "from Gringore's student days in Caen"; some are newer; others are partial texts only.

From the standpoint of theater history, of the greatest interest is that we may be dealing here with performance copies, actual *scripts*. Cohen thought so, noting that this particular "manuscript" was destined for actors (*Recueil*, xi); and Koopmans's analysis would seem to bear him out, were it not for his ultimate puzzlement about the following matter. The pages look so clean and tight that Koopmans wonders "whether it was consulted frequently in the 16th century or, to put it quite simply, whether it was consulted at all" (introd., § "Description du Recueil"). Any actor—or, for that matter, any musician—knows that a working script commonly becomes a marked-up mess; thus, a few contextual details about medieval "reading matter" may prove welcome at this juncture.

In the Middle Ages, "reading" meant "reading aloud," a process that might take place at considerable remove from the actual reading matter. On display in churches, for instance, were all those huge, unwieldy, ceremonial Bibles that are essentially too heavy to lift, to say nothing of read and study. In contrast, there were the tiny matchbook-sized "booklets" with their equally tiny lettering, unwieldy in the opposite way and designed not so much for reading as for prompting the memory. Elsewhere, there were the compilations and concatenations of many different texts into a single scroll, a single manuscript book, or a *recueil factice*. And, as it appears to be the case for the *Recueil Cohen*, there were the inelegant, portable copies that might readily have been used by actors or directors.[4] From what Koopmans tells me, "inelegant" is the right word: the *Recueil Cohen* is not in good shape, with some spots virtually indecipherable.

At this point, readers might well be wondering: If the *Recueil Cohen* is so far from perfect, then why give it a starring role in this anthology?

For one thing, there is something both comforting and energizing about returning to the recuperative work of Cohen himself (as to Viollet le Duc and Fournier for #1, *Farce of the Fart* and #12, *Birdbrain*). As one of the founders of the field of medieval studies, Cohen not only brought these plays to our attention in the first place; throughout his career, he also brought medieval French theater back to the life of the stage. In the 1930s, Cohen directed a troupe of actors called the *Théophiliens,* among them the renowned medievalist Paul Zumthor.[5]

For another thing, if the *Recueil Cohen* was a collection destined for actors (*Recueil*, xi), then this book is too; and I'm reproducing its texts, warts and all. Here are two small examples of what I mean. On the matter of those warts, I would like to report—without dwelling on the host of errors introduced when texts were copied—that actors have been known to commit to memory—and *deliver*—mistakes in a script. (I myself witnessed this in the first production of my *Farce of the Fart*, in which a silly typo emerged in production as part of a speech!) Second, among the features of the plays of the *Recueil Cohen* that have annoyed editors and prompted accusations of authorial incompetence is a tendency to repeat, at the beginning of one line, the word or two that just ended the previous line (more on this below, § "Repetition and Repetitiveness"). Sometimes, this is a print convention, enabling publishers to match up pages in the proper sequence. But imagine, now, that the texts were for *actors*. I'm no actress but I believe that this is what we call a *cue*!

Additionally, there was something stupendous about working with the edition of such an elusive group of plays . . . at least until Koopmans arrived on the scene as a deus ex machina. What could be more worthy of resurrecting and sharing than a document on the verge of extinction? Here is how Cohen characterized his own effort:

> From among all the worldly goods that I have lost to Fortune's wheel—the books, the notes, the manuscripts of forty years of scholarly life—fortunately, I was able to rescue a most precious document: a copy of a hefty collection of farces that are, for the most part, unknown, and which enhances and completes, in a most remarkable way, our understanding of the comic theater of the fifteenth century. (*Recueil*, xi)

I for one am very glad for Koopmans's remarkable find because, until that moment, I had come to doubt the very existence of the *Recueil Cohen*! Allow me to confess that, as the author of a book called *Death by Drama and Other Medieval Urban Legends* (which was all about the various untrue tales that had sprung up around the medieval theater), I was seriously beginning to suspect that there *was* no *Recueil Cohen* at all, that there never *had* been, and that the whole thing was an urban legend! Consider, in that respect, Tissier's oft-repeated, highly equivocal language about the *Recueil Cohen:* "a collection of theatrical works cobbled together (*recueil factice*) . . . which is known today only through the copy that Gustave Cohen either made himself or *had made* before the Second World War" (*RF,* 11: 117; my emphasis). Consider that, for his own part, Koopmans suspected that Cohen might not have actually seen the *Recueil* that bears his name with his own eyes. Wouldn't it be a riot, I thought—or a *farce*?—if it turned out that a crafty Cohen, as the ultimate trickster, had pulled the wool over everyone's eyes and had *written the plays himself*? (One of my colleagues, Richard Wittman, jokingly accused me of the same during the talkback after the Santa Barbara production of the *Farce of the Fart:* "I think you *wrote* that play!")

Furthermore, there has always been something playful, if not downright bizarre, about even some of the scholarly descriptions of French farce. In 1849, for instance, there appeared a volume entitled *Description et analyse d'un livre unique qui se trouve au Musée britannique* (*Description and Analysis of a Unique Book Located at the British Museum*), which presented a relatively detailed inventory of the contents of the *Recueil du British Museum* (again, the collection from which I take our opening and closing plays). I fear that the "analysis" part of that tome is not much use nowadays, with the exception of its priceless commentaries on the *Farce of the Fart* (#1) and *Birdbrain* (#12), a few of which I reproduce in the "Production Notes" to those two plays. But what about the author of those commentaries?

In an anonymous article published in *Notes and Queries* (25 January 1851), the *Description et analyse* is attributed to a certain "Breton Gentleman," one Tridace-Nafé-Théobrome, an appellation that resembles no French onomastic construction: "we strongly suspect that no such gentleman is to be found; and that we are really indebted for this highly curious and interesting book to a gentleman who has already laid the world of letters under great obligations, M. Del[e]pierre, the accomplished Secretary of Legation of the Belgian Embassy" (77). For myself, I am convinced that, just as Françoys Rabelais penned his raucous tales under the anagram of Alcofrybas Nasier, this "Tridace-Nafé-Théobrome" represents some kind of wordplay. All I can tell you at this time is that the words *tridace* and *théobrome* exist, both specialized chemical terms: *tridace* is related to lettuce, *théobrome* to chocolate (not eaten together, we hope). So, is Tridace-Nafé-Théobrome an anagram? I suspect so, but I've asked every francophone punster of my acquaintance, and we've just not yet been clever enough to figure it out! Perhaps it's a ridiculously complex spoonerism or what the French call a *contrepèterie*. We all know that a spoonerism in English interchanges parts of two different words in a phrase: "You missed my history lecture" becomes "You hissed my mystery lecture." But the French have a real talent for amplifying these, doubling and tripling them to form *double-* or *triple-contrepèteries*. (In English, a classic one is attributed to the Reverend Spooner himself, when he was alleg-edly proposing a toast to Queen Victoria. Instead of saying "Let us raise our glasses and toast the dear Queen," he apocryphally intoned, "Let us glase our asses and toast the queer dean.") So please let me know if you figure anything out for Mr. Tridace-Nafé-Théobrome.[6]

One last thing. As far as picking my favorites is concerned, it seems that I am in very good company. Tissier chose his favorites as well for his *Recueil de Farces,* drawing on all four extant manuscript collections. Likewise, Fournier had this to say when justifying his selections from the *Recueil du British Mu-seum,* the *Recueil La Vallière,* and several independent manuscripts: "I have picked over these collections to find what suited us best—skimmed the cream off their surface, as it were, for the plays that might best suit our readers—without, of course, offending their sense of propriety, which was the most challenging and delicate aspect of making our choice" (*TFR,* iii). As you shall see, dear Reader, I was little concerned with that issue of propriety and deli-cacy; but, for me, these dozen plays are definitely the crème de la crème.

Critical Apparatus

In addition to my working principle that no reader of this anthology need read French, I have sought to produce a user-friendly book that students would appreciate and that actors might stand a chance of *holding* while re-hearsing or performing. It seemed important not to overwhelm my scripts with the hefty critical apparatus that medievalists ordinarily expect to find . . . and that I myself ordinarily provide. True, over the years, my own students (who are not required to memorize their lines) have devised some ingenious remedies for avoiding entirely the need to hold their scripts. For example, during their classroom production of the medieval Dutch farce *Lippin,* Por-tia diPasquale, Dominique Moomaw, and Wilson Trang fashioned a series of handheld masks depicting a variety of appropriate facial expressions, on the inside of which they had transcribed their speeches.[7] The better to facilitate reading and performance by actors who may or may not be prepared to do quite so much transcription, I have kept the scripts free of distracting foot-notes, reserving interpretive, critical, historical, or philological comments for the endnotes. My rule of thumb is this: If I can reference a single English-lan-guage source that will clarify the matter, then that is what I do. The exception is Tissier's *Recueil de Farces.* His careful annotations in French are too crucial not to cite; besides, his scenographic charts are in the universal languages of mathematics and drawings, always well worth consulting.

In that sense, although my endnotes are scholarly, they are by no means complete. In these prefatory materials as well as in the Introduction, I have woven every reference that I could into the critical narrative; if all that is needed is an author's name or the title of a work, just look for those in the Bibliography. In the plays themselves, the critical apparatus is, of necessity, rather more dense, so I give fair warning. When Tissier or others have published editions of a given play, my notes get a good bit longer because I occasionally disagree with a reading or two. Otherwise, I intervene to annotate a playtext in order to clarify a conspicuously complex phrase in the Middle French, to tease out a pun or a double entendre, to highlight a proverb or a popular saying, to emphasize the difficulty of finding *le mot juste* (which I'm still finding months and even years later!), or to refer the reader to similar moments in other plays in this collection and beyond. In keeping with the spirit of the farces, I've even taken a stab, every now and then, at making the endnotes funny. I also beg your indulgence up front for citing a lot of my own work. It's not that there's a dearth of terrific scholarship out there (start with the excellent articles reprinted by John Coldewey in the four-volume *Medieval Drama*); but this collection is very much a part of my lifelong spin on how best to approach medieval theater history.

Last but not least, be forewarned that I'll be using this phrase a great deal: *Metacommentary alert!* Critics use that term when pointing to a kind of literary self-consciousness, a moment when the artifice of a play calls attention to . . . well . . . *the artifice of the play.* Time and time again, we shall see a sort of play within a play, a performance within a performance, or a scene of costuming, disguise, duping, impersonation, or role-playing, many of which make full and eminently noteworthy use of such resonant verbs as *contrefaire* ("to counterfeit") or *faindre* ("to fake"). Rest assured that I have tried to keep it in bounds for the generalist, the student reader, or the theater practitioner. All metacommentary and no play makes medievalists very dull.

Stage Directions

Many of the plays contain only minimal stage directions and scenic indications; for the most part, these are absent. To increase readerly enjoyment and to venture some guidance for future productions, I have made multiple suggestions for scene breaks, locations, sets, costumes, props, and stage directions. (Tissier and Koopmans do so as well; but I do not always agree with their advice, so I've provided my own.) All stage directions of the base edition that I follow are *italicized,* whether they be mine, Cohen's, Viollet le Duc's, or Fournier's. My own interpolations, additions, and emendations to any such scenic indications appear in brackets: for instance, [Scene 1] / [*At the home of Cooch and Wilhelmina*]. On occasion, a recommendation about pronunciation or a variant possibility for stage action appears in the notes.

We shall also have occasion to consider a variety of special effects (such as the smoke machine in #2, *Edict of Noée*) along with what I can only think to call "olfactory effects," especially in the "shittier" offerings, which call for farting, defecating, and the overwhelming stench of a filthy house or chicken coop (#1, *Farce of the Fart;* #5, *Blind Man's Buff;* #8, *Shit for Brains;* and #12, *Birdbrain*). There is a history of this sort of thing on the medieval stage, as for the roasted body of Saint Barnabas, which called for a "fake body full of bones and entrails."[8] As Trixie says in #12 (Scene 1), the nose knows.

Prose, Verse, and Music

Just as English-speaking readers and theatergoers have grown accustomed to Shakespeare's ten-syllable iambic pentameter, French-speaking audiences have done likewise, essentially from the seventeenth century onward, for the feel of the twelve-syllable *alexandrin.* But what about the farce's standard octosyllables? The primary versification pattern of all twelve scripts is rhymed, octosyllabic couplets (A-A, B-B, C-C, etc.). Periodically—if rarely—I give a flavor of the rapid-fire dialogue that occupies a single octosyllabic verse through formatting, that is, through extra indentations or line breaks. Occasionally, however, a play's overall metric scheme is interrupted, as when a character breaks into song or recites poetry (mostly, in five-syllable verses). Nevertheless, mine is a prose translation. Why?

Reaching across cultures and histories is complex enough—thank you very much—without further estranging these wonderful texts with English doggerel. This is not an indictment of all those true poets out there; it is simply to say that I am not one of them and, with the possible exception of Shakespeare, the American ear has no habit comparable to the medieval French attunement to verse drama. So I have translated French octosyllabic verse into English prose, except for certain musical or poetic set pieces in

---

the originals. When a character launches into a different rhyme scheme—mostly in the closing verses of adieu—I tend to provide a verse translation (for which I apologize in advance!). Sometimes, it is clear that the character is *singing* and, if that is the case, I make various suggestions regarding post-medieval songs, rhymes, or ditties that might conceivably bear a resemblance to the Middle French or that manifest a similar spirit. (All of those drama-turgical observations—which are guidelines, not citations—are consistent with the parameters laid out below in the Appendix: Scholarly References to Copyrighted Materials.) Sometimes, to give a better sense of the original, I reproduce the rhymed, Middle French set piece in an endnote. And speaking of singing . . .

Although I've subtitled as a "musical comedy" only #12, *Birdbrain*, many of these scripts might qualify as "musicals" or, certainly, they might be *performed* as musicals (with any and all requisite permissions having been cleared, of course, for performance). Among the first to draw our attention to the medieval musical theater was Howard Mayer Brown in his signature *Music in the French Secular Theater, 1400–1550*. Music plays a premier role in the farces and in medieval life in general, where, as Ritva Jonsson and Leo Treitler have demonstrated, there was no terminological distinction between speaking and singing (*dicere* and *cantare, dire* and *chanter*) ("Medieval Music and Language," 1). Not surprisingly, many farces open or close with popular refrains, not all of which have been lost to history. Indeed, in a learned book review of Cohen's *Recueil*, the musicologist Jacques Chailley identified at least thirteen medieval songs for which the music or lyrics have survived (Chailley, 66–68). Usually in the endnotes, I share a number of time-sensitive thoughts as to possible English-language, musical analogues that seem to capture the medieval song in question. However, the better to extend the life of these translations, it seemed wise not to be too specific about precise musical selections, not to "script them" officially, as it were. Therefore, I have adopted the practice of including, in any related endnotes (as for the poetic set pieces), both the original Middle French and a more-or-less literal trans-lation of its words. I do so in order to assist actors, directors, and readers in identifying music and lyrics that have the right feel for *them*, that are more consonant with what will become their own "contemporary" equivalents (such as rap, hip-hop, electronic music, and the like).[9] Of course, there is also the option, which I confess to preferring, of composing original music.

Another confession. The farces host a plethora of over-the-top verses de-voted to the pain and suffering—*oh, the pain! oh, the suffering!*—of love. To all you die-hard aficionados of medieval romance, sorry: I must admit that courtly love has never been my cup of tea. For me, it evokes all those trials and tribulations, all the cheatin' and mistreatin' of country music, which I consider to be the closest American equivalent. So don't be startled to see things "get country." If you're a hopeless romantic, this is probably not the collection for you anyway.

Repetition and Repetitiveness

Inextricably linked with music, musicality, and performance is another feature, that of *repetition* and even a seemingly annoying *repetitiveness*. Though related to both the musicality just discussed and to the linguistic matters of the subsequent section (§ "Language and Style"), this subject is more aptly introduced between those two categories because of its resemblance to refrains.

In any medieval text, it is almost impossible to know whether an author (or authors) *meant to be* as repetitive as they are. Did the scribe lose his place and mistakenly copy a line again? Is one of the lines an actor's cue? All this by way of saying that, when the original repeats something—and repeats it again . . . and again—so do I. The same holds true when a character uses a given phrase in Scene 1 and comes back to it, say, in Scene 3: I seek to preserve the echo.

There are a number of explanations for this phenomenon, some scholarly, some commonsensical, some both. The specialist of the French Middle Ages is familiar with the versification convention known as the *rondeau triolet,* a fixed metrical and sometimes *musical* figure that made frequent appearances in both poetry and drama. And please do note that, although modern readers usually prefer to speak of "poetry," "drama," "dramatic poetry," and literary "genres," I gravitate more toward the literary *media* of a large-scale medieval performance culture (above, "Introduction"). In such media, the *rondeau* normally signaled moments of elevated tension, turning points in the action, the arrivals and departures of characters, or changes of scene (which could also prompt bona fide musical interludes).[10] One of the most common forms of the *rondeau triolet* is based on an eight-verse sequence built around two rhymes like so (with the uppercase letters indicating repeated lines): *ABaAabAB.*

So much for technicalities. On a less lofty plane, recall also that repetition is the bread and butter of oral traditions, especially when plays were performed in noisy public squares. If you missed something the first time around because you were yakking to your neighbor or trying to get your kid to quit running around, then it could be helpful to hear the line again. I suspect that medieval dramatists, directors, and performers knew that. Compare the practice, for instance, to that of the fast-dying genre known as the American soap opera, in which a character's first name seems to get used in each and every sentence. What are you talking about *Erica*? Surely, *Erica*, you didn't think that you could enter an in-patient drug rehab, *Erica*? Are you pregnant again, *Erica*? This permits any viewer who tunes in at that very moment for the very first time to be introduced to a lead character, *Erica*. And it works in drama too.

Language and Style

Let's talk grammar, shall we?

Any high-school or college student will tell you that it is not so straightforward to learn French. There are the verb tables, the conjugations, the nasty subjunctive, and a grammar so complex that French-language instruction is the site where many speakers of English take their first in-depth look at their native language. Even in the twenty-first century, it is difficult to overestimate the esteem in which the French hold their spoken and written tongue. France is, after all, the home of the Académie Française, an entire governing body devoted to the careful, intellectual supervision of the rules, standards, practices, and evolution of French. Language is power, language is class, language is upward mobility.

Not unexpectedly, the inability to speak French correctly has been the butt of innumerable jokes since time immemorial. Grammar, syntax, slang, dialect, regionalisms: it's all fodder for humor and mockery, not to mention what any tourist has learned to his or her mortification: *accent*. Were it possible to reproduce for you, dear Reader, some of the withering punch lines of contemporary French jokes that target the pronunciation peccadilloes of the neighboring Swiss and Belgians or the once-colonized Algerians or Togolese, I would gladly do so. But even a collection of farces has to draw the line somewhere at certain kinds of insult. Suffice it to say that many a French rib-tickler is based on racist, classist, ethnocentric "mispronunciations" of standard French. I have conveyed some of those undertones with American slang, dialects, regionalisms, and accents (mostly Southern, y'all, and "New Yawk," the latter including myself in the mockery group so, at least, I've shared in the ridicule).[11] As part of the farcical picture, I've also had a lot of fun with anachronisms, a feature that I borrow from the Passion plays, which habitually allude to the Christlike dimensions of Old Testament stories that unfolded long before Christ was ever born. Medieval intellectuals called it "exegesis," a scholarly way of reading the Old Testament as a symbolic prefiguration of the New Testament; we call it anachronism, and it's not limited to gladiators wearing Reeboks.[12]

Our twelve scripts reflect all the tendencies above, which results in a real linguistic hodgepodge that is true to the originals and that scholars call "macaronic." One of the hallmarks of farce is its blatant oscillation between good and bad grammar, formal and informal modes of address, or French and "foreign-language materials" like Latin. This potpourri, moreover, is not necessarily attributable to scribal deficits. I enumerate below several of the principal challenges that we face, but allow me to summarize the situation with an example:

A husband and a wife are cursing each other out. No terminology and no expletive is off limits as "shit," "fuck," "assholes," "dicks," and "cunts" abound. And yet . . . it's all so very *polite:* flawless grammar, the linguistic decorum of the "courteous" *vous,* even an imperfect subjunctive thrown in here and there for good measure. *"Would you be so kind, good sir, as to go fuck yourself?"* That is the feel of the language of farce; and I mention it now in anticipation of what you are bound to ask: *Would these characters really talk that way?*

The answer is *Yes.* They do it all the time. They might even begin a scene, a speech, a *sentence* speaking one way and end up speaking another way. They might swear like a stevedore in one breath, only to preen grammatically in the next with the imperfect subjunctive, a verbal mode so pretentious that most French people would hardly dream of *writing* it, no less *speaking* it . . . assuming that they know how to. (By the way, it's easy to see why the imperfect subjunctive dropped out of the language. Take the verb *savoir. Fallait-il que je le susse?* means "Was it necessary that I *'knew'* that?"—although we would say *know* in English or find a way around it. But, in French, *"fallait-il que je le susse?" sounds* like, "Was it necessary that I *suck* it. . . ?") Enough said. It's all part of the fun, notably in the following arenas.

Formality versus Informality

Worldwide, Americans are known—some might say "notorious"—for the ease with which they address strangers or near strangers by their first names. What feels right to Americans may well feel plain wrong in Great Britain and in such languages as French, Spanish, German, Italian, or Russian . . . to name but a few. The better to convey what would otherwise be much too subtle in English, I have exaggerated some of my characters' linguistic tics. Sometimes, a seemingly curious "Screw you, *sir* [or '*madam*']!" will do the trick; sometimes an obscenity; more often than not, both at the same time: "Woe is me, alas and alack! Thou art full o' shit!"

Another source of comedy is a character's deliberate and histrionic (and often unsuccessful) change of linguistic register. To this day, when the French speak formally in official settings—the courtroom, the body politic, an illustrious academic conference—they deploy a number of honorific set phrases that make American English look like nursery school. Some of us call it the *grand style national,* a highfalutin effort to capture the urbane, erudite language of the cultural elite. Likewise, when a variety of husbands, wives, and would-be students shoot for flowery romantic banter or leave their domestic environments for the courtroom or the classroom, they too brandish (or mutilate) the vocabularies of courtly love, law, or academia.

"Foreign-Language" Materials

Consistent with the above, the dramatis personae of farce trot out the odd term or phrase in a "foreign language." That language is usually Latin, and it's usually dramatically *wrong*. In the context of #12, *Birdbrain,* I discuss at greater length the daunting task of translating a peculiar brand of humor that is based on grammatical errors—*real howlers*—in the Latin language. The problem is that most Americans do not understand Latin, and even the classicist isn't used to speaking or hearing that famously "dead language." Thus, what is hysterically funny in Middle French would likely fall flat in translation: whence my use of absurdities that *sound like* Latin, even pig latin. Elsewhere, I tend to preserve the sense of "foreignness" by having a given character use and mispronounce *French* words.

Cursing and Expletives

Who could have fathomed the veritable encyclopedia of ways to swear in Middle French? The American term "potty mouth" doesn't begin to cover it. There are so many expletives in this repertoire that I needed to consult multiple specialized dictionaries just to keep them coming. Middle French seems to have an individualized curse for each and every saint and each and every disease to boot. One must also admire the irony of shrieking "A pox on your house!" to one's own cohabitant, that is, to one's husband or wife *in* the same house! (The title character does so in #11, *Cooch E. Whippet.*) A pox on *my* house? Some of the French editions, especially Tissier's, make detailed and learned propositions as to why a particular character might swear by a particular saint when invoking a particular condition; but, for the most part, such "saintly" expressions are lost in translation, leading me to find other ways. Imagine the Whop! Bam! Pow! and Kerplunk! of a *Batman* comic book; or imagine the stand-up comedy of Kathy Griffin, who jokes that her devout mother has the foulest mouth of all when calling upon Jesus Christ, the Virgin Mary, Mary Magdalene, or just about any apostle. Most of all, imagine that, as expletive piles upon expletive, it seems just as important to pretend that these are *not*, in fact, expletives at all and that the characters are *not* taking the name of the Lord in vain: "God's Blood!" becomes "'Sblood!"; "God damn it!" becomes "Darn!" In those cases, I commonly add or subtract something, my expletives of choice being "Jesus H. Christ!" and "Christ in a bucket!"

One more expression requires explanation inasmuch as it recurs throughout: wishing upon someone the *fièvre quartaine.* Technically, this is a fever that returns after three days (*RF,* 10: 61n), and the term is also associated with the paroxysms of malarial fever. However, in the farces, this imprecation is used in as many tonal and syntactic contexts as the trendy "fucking," as in— begging your pardon, dear Reader—"are you *fucking* kidding me?" Throughout this volume, I offer a plethora of vernacular and vulgar equivalents for the all-purpose *fièvre quartaine:* everything from "on the rag" to "screw you!"

Masculine and Feminine

French is a gendered language. Nouns are masculine or feminine for reasons that mostly strike language students as frustratingly arbitrary . . . unless, of course, they're also trained as historical linguists. Such training would enable them to go back to a given Latin etymon to learn, for example, that the feminine "rose" (*la rose*) evolves linguistically from the Latin feminine *rosa,* or that the masculine "wall" (*le mur*) evolves linguistically from the Latin masculine *murus.* (So much the better, but I'm sorry to report that it's easiest to work that out for Latin nouns of the first and second declension.) Beyond that, most specialists of Old and Middle French are happy to remind you that the gender of nouns is largely conventional: linguistic gender is attached to the word, regardless of the sex of the speaker. *La sentinelle* is always a *femi-*

nine noun, even though the person standing guard is likely a man. *Le profes-seur* is always a *masculine* noun, no matter how many women are employed doing that work. (Come to think of it, contemporary women faculty seem to have had quite enough of that, thank you, creating *la professeure*.) And, check this out: to this very day *some* nouns in French are both masculine *and* femi-nine: the exquisitely delicious *délice* (delight) is masculine in the singular but *feminine* in the plural, as in *les grandes délices*. No comment.

Why am I telling you all this? Because there are a fair number of gendered linguistic moments—not coincidentally, I think, in plays that are *about* gen-der—that are bound to strike the modern reader as odd and that warrant explanation. Two examples will suffice here.

In #8, *Shit for Brains,* wife Harpee lets loose with a slew of *feminine* ad-jectives as she insults husband Harpo. Why? Because she's talking about his *head* (la *tête*). For his own part, husband Harpo then lets fly an equally impressive list of insulting *masculine* adjectives as he insults his wife. Why? Because he's talking about her *ass* (le *cul*). Thus, medieval audiences saw and heard a woman (or a man *dressed as one*) being repeatedly insulted in the masculine, and a man being repeatedly insulted in the feminine. Elsewhere, in #12, *Birdbrain,* the Professor proclaims the superiority of women, refer-ring to them with the masculine pronoun *ilz.* Is all that mere convention?

In many respects, sure it is. Readers of Middle French know full well that the masculine pronoun *ilz/il* was frequently employed interchangeably with the feminine plural pronouns. Christiane Marchello-Nizia says so in her magisterial study of Middle French, noting that "if the usage of *il* in the femi-nine singular is extremely rare, on the contrary, *il/ilz* appears fairly frequently in the feminine plural; in certain texts, moreover, that form is the only one to be utilized in that manner" (*Langue française,* 224). What is more, in versi-fied literary forms like our farces, that interchangeability of the masculine *ilz* and the feminine *elles* had the added advantage of offering writers the possibility of the one-syllable *ilz* as a better metric fit than the two-syllable *elles.*[13] In octosyllabic verse, the two-syllable *elles*—when accompanied by a two-syllable verb—immediately occupies the entire first half of the eight-syllable verse (regardless of whether we come down on the side of the erudite debaters who maintain that there is no metrical break at the end of the fourth verse . . . and that, even if there *were,* we may *not* call it a caesura, as we do for the *alexandrin*). And yet . . .

Whatever the versification needs of a given piece and whatever the lin-guistic conventions of a language like Middle French (whose grammar was still in flux), I would urge nonetheless that we be mindful of William Kibler's observation in his *Introduction to Old French*. When it comes to subject pronouns in Old French, he reminds us that "masculine and feminine forms are distinguished *only* in the third persons singular and plural" (75; my emphasis). In other words, at the very site where a linguistic distinction was in fact possible, we find no distinction between *il* and *elle* (or *ilz* and *elles*), no matter how *conventional* the absence of a distinction might be. I cannot help but wonder whether there was more at stake during an actual theatrical performance that takes on the very subject of the linguistic performance of gender. Consider this:

Weren't there other ways to do it? After all, Harpee of *Shit for Brains* could just as easily have targeted her verbal wrath at her husband's masculine *ass,* and he to her feminine *head*. Instead, it's the opposite. And what about the Professor in *Birdbrain*, who says of the female protagonists that, "they've really got it down pat! When it comes to talking, women rule the roost." (*Mais pour parler* ilz *ont le bruyt*.)[14] Couldn't the phrase have been turned another way? Certainly, and without doing any damage to the rhyme scheme. All that was needed was to drop the opening *mais* to obtain an eight-syllable verse: *Pour parler* elles *ont le bruyt*. Therefore, I submit that we heed the wisdom of Luce Irigaray, who is famous for having investigated and exposed (in *This Sex Which Is Not One*) the deep-seated sexism that resides in the linguistic conventions of gendered language. I invite readers, actors, and directors to consider what the performance of convention, linguistic or other, really means and, beyond that, what it might mean *onstage* when the men playing men point to the female characters—in all likelihood, *also played by men*— and say *ilz*. Theater stages conventions; but staging something can *make* a convention as readily as it might *break* one.

Other issues, from monetary currencies to the notoriously ambiguous verb *baiser* (to kiss or to have sex?) are addressed in the "Production Notes" and critical apparatus of each play. And what a production it shall be!

Brief Plot Summaries

Note: More detailed information appears in the "Production Notes" to each play.

1. *The Farce of the Fart* [*Farce nouvelle et fort joyeuse du Pect*]

    For four actors: Hubert; Jehannette, his Wife; the Judge; the Lawyer.

    When Jehannette "pollutes" her clean house by farting, she and Hubert appear before the Judge. The man of laws deftly and logically ascertains that, since Hubert sodomized his wife on their wedding night, then, ergo, Hubert married *all of her,* including her asshole. Hubert must thus share and share alike in all that it produces, including farts.

2. *The Edict of Noée,* or, *Shut Up! It's the Farce of the Rights of Women* [*Farce des Drois de la Porte Bodès*]

    For three actors: the Cobbler; the Wife; the Judge.

    Who should get up and close the door when the house is drafty? The husband or the wife? This momentous question requires forensic adjudication. At the very moment when the Cobbler is about to triumph in a court of law, his Wife produces, before the Judge, a curious edict that gives *her*—and all women—mastery and dominion over the household. And *that* is the titular Edict of Noée (i.e., *no way!*).

3. *Confession Lessons,* or, *The Farce of the Lusty Husband Who Makes His Confession to a Woman, His Neighbor, Who Is Disguised as a Priest* [*Farce de celuy qui se confesse à sa voisine*]

    For three actors: the Husband; the Wife; Colette, the Neighbor.

    An unfaithful husband makes a true confession to a false priest, that is, to his neighbor, Colette, who is disguised as one. Colette has donned that getup in order to help her girlfriend discover with whom the Husband has been cheating. Alas, the joke is on Colette! Her friend's husband confesses that he has indeed been cheating, but with Colette's own daughter, whom he has deflowered. The two women give him a beating as his "penance."

4. *The Farce of the Student Who Failed His Priest Exam because He Didn't Know Who Was Buried in Grant's Tomb* [*Farce du Clerc qui fut refusé à estre prestre*]

For three actors: Master Peter, the Teacher; John-Boy Priestley (Jenin Clerc), the "Student"; the Examiner.

A country bumpkin wants to become a priest but he is unable to answer the most basic question—in this case, the medieval French equivalent of Groucho Marx's famous softball that nonetheless stumped countless contestants: "Who's buried in Grant's Tomb?" No dice. Similarly stumped, John-Boy ends up with nothing.

5. *Blind Man's Buff*, or, *The Farce of "The Chokester"* [*Farce du Goguelu*]

For three actors: John-John Horny, the Blind Man (Jenin Cornet); Thomasina, his Chambermaid (Thomasse); and Goguelu, the Valet, the "Chokester."

John-John Horny's Chambermaid (Thomasina) and her pal, the Valet (Goguelu), scheme to get back at their cranky, blind master because John-John has first beaten the not-so-innocent Thomasina. (She peed into a glass and offered it to him as wine.) The roles of master and servant are reversed as Goguelu and Thomasina beat up the Blind Man; but it all ends with a song—in fact, with a bona fide musical number.

6. *Playing Doctor*, or, *Taking the Plunge* (*The Farce of the Woman Whose Neighbor Gives Her an Enema*) [*Farce d'une Femme à qui son Voisin baille ung clistoire*]

For three actors: Dummy Downer (Trubert Chagrinas); Frigid Bridget, his Wife (Frigallette); and Doc Double-Talk, his Neighbor (Doublet).

Doc Double-Talk (who is more snake-oil salesman than doctor) has the perfect cure for Frigid Bridget, the wife of the jealous Dummy Downer. His ruse? Bridget feigns illness so that the "Doctor" can get her to his "office." There, they make a plan to meet secretly for some real "doctoring." But Dummy overhears them and, when Bridget returns home, he beats her, and Double-Talk too, when the Doc tries to come to her aid.

7. *At Cross Purposes,* or, *The Farce of the Three Lovers of the Cross* [*Farce de trois Amoureux de la Croix*]

For four actors: Martin, the Bumpkin (Martin); Walter, the Welshman (Gaultier); William, the Geek (Guillaume); and the Lady [Beatrice] (La Dame).

A coquettish (married) woman outsmarts her suitors (Martin, Walter, and William) all at once, but not before accepting money from all three. She instructs each man to come in costume, under cover of darkness, to their secret rendezvous spot: the big cross at the cemetery. As directed by the Lady, who is quite the metteur en scène, Martin dresses up as a priest, Walter as a dead man, and William as a devil, such that each lover gives the others a terrible fright. Eventually, all three gents realize that they have been outwitted.

8. *Shit for Brains,* or, *The Party Pooper-Scooper* [*Farce de Tarabin-Tarabas*]

For three actors: Harpee, the Wife (Tarabin); Harpo, the Husband (Tarabas); Payne N. Butts, the Meddler (Tribouille Mesnage).

This is probably the filthiest farce ever written (about filth): a play that is literally "full of shit" and of people who have shit for brains. The plot—if it can be said to have one other than cleaning up piles of you-know-what—centers around grotesque puns on the head and the ass, as well as the *shit* (literal and metaphorical) that proliferates from both.

9. *Monk-ey Business,* or, *A Marvelous New Farce for Four Actors, to Wit, the Cobbler, the Monk, the Wife, and the Gatekeeper* [*Le Savetier, le Moyne, la Femme, et le Portier*]

For four actors: "Blotto," the Cobbler; Dottie, his Wife (unnamed in the text); Brother Peter, the Monk, also known as Pete or "Bro Holdup" (Serre-Porte); and the Gatekeeper.

The henpecked Cobbler, Blotto, falsely sings wife Dottie's praises to the horny Monk, Brother Peter. Blotto does so in order to play a trick not only on Pete, his old school chum, but also on Dottie (which involves her boxing the ears of the Monk-in-Blotto's-clothing). When Brother Peter makes a rendezvous with Dottie for a private confession session— she thwacked a *monk,* after all—it is Blotto, the Cobbler, who keeps the date, showing up in his *wife's* clothing. The lewd Monk then attempts to extort "her" confession in exchange for sex, but instead he receives a good thrashing from the Cobbler.

10. *Getting Off on the Wrong Foot, or, Who's Minding the Whore? for Three Actors, to Wit, the Lover Minding the Store, the Cobbler, and His Wife* [*Farce de Celuy qui garde les Patins*]

For three actors: Bootie the Shoemaker, [Jack's Wife's] Lover (unnamed in the text); Jack, the Cobbler; and Desirée, Jack's Wife (unnamed in the text).

Desirée, the Cobbler's wife, and Bootie (her Lover) come up with the perfect ruse so that they can have sex essentially right under the nose of her dopey husband, Jack. Bootie is to leave Jack minding Bootie's shoe store so that lover boy Bootie may head over to mind *Jack's* store. That labor of love is to include servicing Jack's wife, Desirée. Although slow on the uptake, Jack figures things out eventually and tans their hides.

11. *Cooch E. Whippet, or, The Farce of Martin of Cambray* [*Farce de Martin de Cambray*]

For three actors: Martin Eric Whippet, the Cobbler, better known as Cooch (Martin de Cambray); Wilhelmina, his Wife (Guillemette); and Father John, their Parish Priest (Le Curé).

Cuckold now and evermore, Cooch the Cobbler likes to lock up his wife inside the house while he is out hawking his wares. Annoyed by those impediments, Wilhelmina devises a ruse with her lover (their Priest, Father John) such that, the next time Cooch curses her out with "The Devil take you!," Father John will appear in a Devil costume and do just that: *take her*. He does, they do, and Cooch can but accept his lot as a henpecked husband or, in the more raucous language of the farce— sorry, folks!—as one who is "coochie-whipped" (Cooch E. Whippet).

12. *Birdbrain: A Musical Comedy? or, School Is for the Birds* [*Farce joyeuse de Maistre Mimin*]

For six actors: The Illustrious Professor (Le Maistre d'escolle); Master Mimin (Estudiant); Rollo, Mimin's Father (Raulet); Trixie, Mimin's Mother (Lubine); Wolfy Chewy, Mimin's future father-in-law (Raoul Machue); [and featuring] Dolly, the Fiancée of Master Mimin (Et La Bru Maistre Mimin; unnamed in the text).

Master Mimin, whose folks have sent him off to a tutor to make something of himself, is so besotted with his Latin learning that he has forgotten how to speak French. His parents are extremely concerned that he will no longer be able to communicate with his Fiancée; so both families—Mimin's and Dolly's—head off to the Professor's place to collect him. With the women taking the lead, Mimin is placed in a chicken coop. Caged therein, Mimin is like a talking bird, retrained by the others in his native French.

The PLAYS

Actors' Prologue

Medieval theater troupes often opened and closed their dramas (comic or serious) with a plea for understanding. There, the actors begged the indulgence of their audience, hoping that they would not be held liable for offensive utterances not spoken in their own voices. They were acting, after all, not engaging in treason, lèse-majesté, libel, heresy, or the like. In our own age, the aforementioned trespasses no longer pose the same momentous threat; but they do indeed risk offending on the grounds of political correctness. Whence this humble offering, designed to soften the blows:

ANNOUNCEMENT FROM THE COMPANY

> 'Twas many years ago, in ages dark,
> Misogynistic lit was all the rage.
> With every bite much worse than any bark
> Men wanted to put women in a cage.
>
> Today, we often find we wish to curse
> Their violence and abuse: 'twas very real.
> What's more, these guys suggested the reverse:
> That, thanks to women, *they* had the raw deal.
>
> And thus we humbly pray you, lest you flee,
> That, should you find upon our words you choke,
> We tender to you all proposals three:
> For one: Good God! Why can't you take a joke?
>
> Or, two: Do you think every man's an ass?
> All ignorant of gender, race, and class?

Recall that, if we don't look, we don't see
To what extent he is our enemy.
We can't imagine any worse a fate
Than that, one day, we might assimilate,
And tacitly condone—God, what a mess!—
The politics of those who do oppress.

And, last, to speak of race and class and genders,
If you don't like it, just blame Jody Enders.[1]

1.

The Farce of the Fart

Farce nouvelle et fort joyeuse du Pect

CAST OF CHARACTERS

HUBERT
JEHANNETTE, his Wife
THE JUDGE
THE LAWYER
[THE JUDGE'S CLERK]

Original production: *The Farce of the Fart* was first produced at the University of California, Santa Barbara, on 3 May 2008, directed by Andrew Henkes.

CAST

Dakotah Brown as the Lawyer
Michael Ruesga as Hubert
Courtney Ryan as Jehannette
Annika Speer as the Judge

PRODUCTION NOTES

The *Farce nouvelle et fort joyeuse du Pect, à quatre personnages*, #7 in the *Recueil du British Museum*, appears in Viollet le Duc, *Ancien Théâtre françois*, 1: 94–110; and as #48 in Tissier, *RF*, 10: 21–63.[1] This anonymous play, whose author was "doubtless a Basochien" (*RF*, 10: 32), was also translated into modern French by Tissier as *Le Pet* (#48 in *FFMA*, 4: 13–26). Although the playtext was first published between 1532 and 1547, Tissier sets its approximate date of composition at 1476 (*FFMA*, 4: 15). It is 300 octosyllabic verses in the Tissier edition. (Viollet le Duc does not provide verse numbers.) Finally, the most miraculous thing of all: we have a record of an actual performance of the play in Lyon in 1476, and before a king, no less! It was presented for René d'Anjou during his dicey territorial negotiations with Louis XI (*RF*, 10: 30–31); elsewhere, there is evidence of René having employed thrice, from 1447 to 1449, a variety of actors for his entertainment, we presume (*MES*, E79, 330).[2] Alternate title: *Home Is Where the Fart Is*.

Plot

On the subject of our play, a certain "Breton gentleman," the mysterious Monsieur Tridace-Nafé-Théobrome, had this to say: "The subject, dirty and insipid, warrants no analysis. We provide only a few verses from the judge's decision, which ought to be sufficient for anyone."[3] If anything, that assessment demonstrates how the tolerance (and intolerance) of obscenity has evolved. For myself, I say that a few verses are not nearly sufficient. I am delighted to provide, in its entirety, a play that is funny enough to open this whole collection.

If contemporary American audiences have *The People's Court* and *Judge Judy*, their medieval forebears had the *Farce of the Fart*, devoted to such weighty legal matters as "He who smelt it dealt it." Abuse of the legal system was as much a medieval concern as a modern one and the subject of much satire. So, when Jehannette sullies her home by farting, and is accused of so doing by her husband, she employs a strategy as beloved in sports as it is despised in politics: the best defense is a good offense. If her husband continues to insult her with his allegations—they're *true*, but never you mind about that!—then she'll haul his ass before a judge. *That* will get to the bottom of it, all right. Hubert can but call her bluff and, lo and behold! There just happens to be an attorney on the scene listening in, only too happy to profit from their dispute. He makes his presence known and promises to represent the interests of both parties (although he sure sells Jehannette down the river at the first possible opportunity). When the preposterous case comes to court, Jehannette complains of cruel and unusual punishment: her husband was rushing her to set the dinner table, you see, and, when she squatted down to move a pile of dirty linen, something *escaped her*. Hubert counters with his right to the peaceful, olfactory enjoyment of his own home.

With deft logic, the Judge takes a more *hole*-istic approach to his verdict. He ascertains that (1) since farts issue from the asshole and, (2) since husband and wife are united as one in perpetuity, then, ergo, in conclusion, what issues from the asshole of one is the bodily possession—or liability—of the other. To that *end,* Jehannette offers a most unusual piece of evidence: she testifies that, on their wedding night, Hubert first "took her there," sodomizing her—accidentally, he interjects—because he couldn't tell which end was up. Thus, on their first night together as husband and wife, Hubert married *all of her,* including her asshole. (By the way, sodomy was not considered okay, even if it seems that medieval ecclesiastics doth protest too much in their obsessively detailed discussions of the practice.)[4] The Judge rules that Hubert must share and share alike in all that is produced by the disputed asshole, including but perhaps not limited to farts. In the end, Hubert has no cause of action and his entire point is moot, if not mute.

Who really laid the fart? At the beginning of the play, both Hubert and Jehannette proclaim their innocence; but Jehannette eventually admits responsibility when speaking to "her" attorney in total confidence . . . except, of course, for those pesky theatrical spectators. In production, it would not be over-the-top to suggest that *Hubert* is the guilty party or, at least, that both Hubert *and* Jehannette are guilty of letting loose in (rectal) concert. Otherwise, as the Judge says at the end of the play, "prick up your noses," ye dramaturges! A scholarly work exists that will help you to answer almost any question that you might have about the history and philosophy of our play's illustrious subject: Valerie Allen's *On Farting: Language and Laughter in the Middle Ages.*

Characters and Character Development

Hubert's spouse appears throughout the playtext as "The Wife"; but I have scripted her by her name, which appears in the first line of the play: Jehannette. Scarcely a submissive spouse, she continuously goes tit for tat with Hubert. A healthy dose of overacting would not be out of place. She also understands the dangers and drawbacks of a corrupt legal system. This is a very smart character who—with or without eavesdropping on a juridical sidebar—sees the legal verdict coming from a mile away and who, to her husband's detriment, is able to produce the piece of evidence that closes the case (if not the body part in question).

In many ways, Hubert is a more hapless version of the traditional student participant in a Platonic dialogue with Socrates. He's a bit of a blowhard at home but, once in the courtroom, he is no match for either the Judge or his own wife. Under questioning, he simply doesn't perceive the impending logic of the inevitable conclusion. After conceding point after point, Hubert is ultimately forced to accept the Judge's unshakable determination that he must accept full liability for an asshole not his own.

We also meet here our first unethical (and unnamed) attorney. He is a kind of medieval equivalent of an ambulance chaser, trolling around town, listening in on the townspeople in the hopes of finding future litigants. In this case, he's a fart chaser. He is part of the boys' club of jurisprudence, pleased to be in cahoots with the Judge, if possible.

At Tissier's suggestion, a nonspeaking character—the Judge's clerk—might also be added to the production's final courtroom scene (*FFMA*, 4: 22; 305). And at the suggestion of copyeditor extraordinaire Michael Gnat, if so, that actor might struggle to keep his composure, fight against wrinkling or holding his nose, or even gag at some of what is said during the trial.

Language

The challenge of this particular play is to create a universe in which a couple wouldn't dare to take the name of the Lord in vain but, at the same time, has no trouble yelling, screaming, and *litigating* about anal sex. In the first scene, Hubert and Jehannette use both the formal *vous* and the informal *tu* when hurling insult upon insult at each other. To indicate these shifting levels of courtesy (if one can call it that), I have occasionally added such terms as "madam" for *vous* and the oh-so-appropriate "toots" for *tu*.

The text hosts other puns and wordplay as well, to which I call attention in the endnotes, especially regarding the pairing of *pet* (fart) and *paix* (peace, peace and quiet, legal resolution, or silence [as in "shut up!"]). Even if the late medieval pronunciation was not precisely identical, that pairing is certainly resonant. Readers might also be interested to know that this is one of the only plays in our collection to use, as we use it today, the curse word *merde* ("shit!"). I think you can see why.

Sets and Staging

In Scene 1, there must be an enormous pile of sheets (or laundry of some sort) blocking access to Hubert and Jehannette's kitchen or dining table and possibly *on the table*. (They are trying to prepare for their dinner, normally the noonday meal.) Among the more intriguing questions for the staging and the *sound effects* of the infamous fart are these: If the laundry is on the table, then how low does Jehannette really need to *squat* to clear it? It's the table where they eat, for heaven's sake, not the pig trough (which we shall encounter in #8, *Shit for Brains*)! The company must also decide whether some sort of sound should emanate from Hubert as well: a fart, a seam splitting, a lace popping, or what have you, which Jehannette claims is the source of the offending boom. There is also the matter of those "olfactory effects": how much to leave to the imaginative nostril is entirely up to you.

The Lawyer appears from out of nowhere; so it could be quite funny to have him roaming around different houses on the set, listening in for domestic disputes that might lead to a legal cause of action. Moreover, since the passage from "living room" to courtroom is almost imperceptible, the Judge too might appear from out of nowhere and litigate the matter in open air. After all, medieval judges traveled around from town to town as they exercised their profession, a fact well known to spectators of the impatient judge of the *Farce of Master Pierre Pathelin*.[5] It would also make sense for the trio to move to a nearby courtroom (however impromptu).[6]

Costumes and Props List

An enormous pile of laundry; various legal accoutrements, such as a judge's gavel. For costuming, remember that, prior to the days of zippers, medieval clothes laced up. Since Jehannette accuses Hubert of busting a seam or a lace (*esguillette*), he might be garbed in period costume; splitting his pants works just as well. Otherwise, the *esguillette* in question was a specific vestimentary item that attached stockings or hose to the "pourpoint" or quilted doublet (*RF*, 10: 36–37n). So have some fun, performers, with the medieval equivalent of a garter belt!

[Scene 1]

[*At the home of Hubert and Jehannette*]

[*The Lawyer may enter at any time during their argument and eavesdrop for awhile.*]

HUBERT *begins:*
   Jehannette!

JEHANNETTE
	Hubert!

HUBERT
		Ready or not, here I come! Isn't it dinner time yet?

JEHANNETTE
	Hold on.

HUBERT
		My blood is boiling! Jehannette!

JEHANNETTE
		Hubert!

HUBERT
		Ready or not, here I come! Isn't it dinner time yet?

JEHANNETTE
	So get over here! Help me get this pile out of the way so we can set the table.

[*Here Jehannette will squat down to move the laundry, precipitating the sonorous and olfactory crisis that dominates the play. That's right: it's time to simulate the sound of a fart! Hubert may also squat halfheartedly to do something else: he does not help his wife.*]

HUBERT
	Hark! What, on earth was *that*—pray tell—that I just heard ring out?

JEHANNETTE
	How should I know? Maybe you busted a seam or a lace or something[7] when you bent over.

HUBERT
	[*Taking a good whiff*][8] Jesus H. Christ! It was a fart! I don't know where it could have come from.

JEHANNETTE
You sure don't have to make *me* guess who did it.

HUBERT
You, madam.

JEHANNETTE
No way!

HUBERT
Yes, way! Jesus H. Christ, jumpin' Jehosaphat, and holy smokes![9] I know it was you!

JEHANNETTE
He who smelt it dealt it. And I'm not the one who smelt or dealt a thing.

HUBERT
No: I'm not saying it was *you*.

JEHANNETTE
Then who?

HUBERT
Your asshole. Let's just say it escaped you.

JEHANNETTE
May they hang by the neck from the gallows the one who farted or, for that matter, anyone who saw it or heard it or smelt it in any way, shape, or form![10]

HUBERT
Well, it would've come from behind; it's not like you woulda *seen* it, toots.[11]

JEHANNETTE
That's some kinda guy I married! I know how it goes. You don't have to draw me a map, you know.[12]

HUBERT

And yet, that is the usual route these things take. And, once it passed through, that's when I smelled it so sweetly.

JEHANNETTE

Gosh darn it! You lie, you big blowhard! And, if you're really gonna make an issue of it, then let me just say that I'm from a good family and a lot cleaner than you say.

HUBERT

And gosh darn it! I know full well that it was *you* who did it: the fart, that is.

JEHANNETTE

I categorically deny it!

HUBERT

Say what? She's denying her own asshole!

JEHANNETTE

You can say whatever you want, bub, but you'll pay for this dishonor! I'll have my day in court, gosh darn it! Don't think I'm so naive that I'm just going to put up with this and take it up the . . .

[*Enter the Lawyer "officially"*]

The LAWYER [*aside*]

What's this I hear? Some kind of debate between these folks? Hmmm . . . I wonder if there's any money to be made off their dispute. . . .

JEHANNETTE

May I die on the spot, or may the Devil take me[13] if, a single day o' your stinkin' life, you never did anything worse, I'm telling you.

HUBERT

And what if I have your ass cited? This fart shall be disputed in a court of law!

JEHANNETTE
    Oh yeah? Who's gonna prove it? You?

HUBERT
    I'll rely on the fact that you'll be under oath.

JEHANNETTE
    Okay, fine. So let's go to court so I can get what's coming to me. Just
    follow your nose!

HUBERT
    And by God, I can hardly wait to get you there. I'm gonna getcha!
    Wait'll you see. You're gonna be so ashamed!

JEHANNETTE
    Oh yeah? What of?

HUBERT
    Well . . . when I say that you laid that huge fart, woman!

JEHANNETTE
    And I'll just say that *you're* the one who did it, pal!
    Furthermore, I shall raise my right hand and swear to it.

HUBERT
[*When delivering the next lines, the actors are wishing that a lawyer
were nearby; but they might simultaneously suggest that the actor who is
playing the Lawyer has missed his cue.*][14]
    Where is there a lawyer when you need one anyway? *He'd* be able to get
    to the bottom of all this!

JEHANNETTE
    I wish to God he were already here. [Where the hell is he already?]

The LAWYER [*aside*]
    [Yikes! My cue!] It's high time I show myself.
    Hear ye, hear ye! Anyone needing a lawyer, step right up, folks! Right
    this way! Here I am!

JEHANNETTE

There you are! I was just looking for you, sir. Things were starting to go down the tubes around here. I think you know what's goin' down.

HUBERT

Hey, sir, over here! Let me tell you my side.

JEHANNETTE [*wringing her hands*]

No, me first, please. Talk to *me*.

The LAWYER

Why, of course, you two, tell me all about it.[15] Who would like to begin?

HUBERT

I'm seeking legal action . . .

JEHANNETTE

And so am I, cross my heart and . . .

The LAWYER

What does your heart have to do with it?

JEHANNETTE

If you'd just listen to me, sir . . .

The LAWYER

But you're just spewing out nonsense . . .

HUBERT

. . . and my case goes like this . . .

The LAWYER

The two of you can't seem to get it together to tell me what happened. Take turns.[16]

HUBERT

What really happened, what my wife did was . . .

JEHANNETTE
Did not! You're a liar!

The LAWYER
Let him finish, and then I shall hear you. I'll be able to represent you both.

JEHANNETTE [*sarcastically*]
Yeah, yeah, that sounds just great.[17]

HUBERT
In our household, sir, there has been a difference of opinion, if you will, between the little woman and myself, for no other reason than just a little bit of ill wind that I smelled and which—whoa, Nelly!—greatly displeases me.

The LAWYER
All together now:

HUBERT and JEHANNETTE [*together*][18]
It was a fart.

HUBERT
'Tis true, sir. And, let's not mince words here: get a load o' this . . .

The LAWYER
Where did it come from?

JEHANNETTE
My husband did it.

The LAWYER
And what was that?

HUBERT
A fart, that's what!

The LAWYER
    Where did it come from?

JEHANNETTE
    My husband did it.

HUBERT
    It came from *her*.

JEHANNETTE
    Oh for Chrissakes, did not!

The LAWYER
    What's that you say?

HUBERT
    A fart, that's what!
    'Tis true, sir. And, let's not mince words here: get a load o' this . . .

The LAWYER
    You'll need lawyers, all right, to litigate the matter.
    [*To Jehannette*] Now you, madam, be good enough to get your ass over
    here so you can tell me all about it in private: the motive, means, and
    opportunity of how things came to pass.

JEHANNETTE
[*She might look around at the Audience.*]
    Oh, I dare not, sir, everyone will make fun of me.

The LAWYER
    Nobody will ever know a thing about it. I'll keep your secret forever.
[*He might break his word immediately by drawing in the Audience.*]
    So: how did it all go down? However did this come to pass?

JEHANNETTE
    All right, I'll tell you:
    I was picking up a great big bundle o' sheets,[19] and my husband was

---

rushing me so much that I bent down a little bit too low and, then—
God help me!—something escaped me!

The LAWYER

And was it indeed your husband who charged you with such a load,
advising you to proceed in that manner?

JEHANNETTE

Yes, of course.

The LAWYER

Then he is clearly at fault because this is cruel and unusual punishment.
Rest assured: as soon as cases like this come to court, the husbands are
always found guilty.

JEHANNETTE

If you take my case and win, I promise, I'll make it worth your while.
You can take that to the bank!

The LAWYER

Shut up, would you? And don't you worry about a thing. Just put a lid
on it for a minute. Not another peep!
[*To Hubert*] And now you, my good man, tell me the whole truth, as
you know it.

HUBERT

It's true, sir, that my wife really did lay one heckuva fart—*right next to me*!
And I was so sore afraid at the boom that my butt is still quaking! Right
next to me, I tell you! I, who ask for nothing more than a clean home, free
of all filth and waste! I request . . . *rectification* for the indignity that she
has perpetrated in my own home! And that's the long and the short of it

The LAWYER

You're right, of course. Even though this sort of case comes up all the
time, if she's the one that let 'er rip with the aforementioned ill wind,
and if it's established that she's your lawfully wedded wife, then you can
be pretty sure that things will go your way and that, in a word, she's the
one who will be found guilty. You'll see when it all plays out.

HUBERT

So maybe you can take this up with the Mayor on my behalf; I could throw in a little extra somethin' for you.

[*Hubert might actually give—and the Lawyer might accept—a payoff.*]

The LAWYER

Enough about that for now. Let's get down to business.

[*Here, the trio should be heading to the "courtroom."*]

JEHANNETTE

Hey! And, for God's sake, sir, make sure you say that *he's* the one who did it.

The LAWYER

[*To Jehannette*] For now, just stop talking out of your ass[20] and go stand over there.
[*To Hubert*] You too. You'll be able to hear the whole thing.

[Scene 2]

[*In the courtroom*]

[*The Lawyer appears before the Judge and addresses him.*]

The LAWYER

God give you good day, Your Honor.

The JUDGE

[*He might address his first line to the Audience as well.*] Welcome, welcome, one and all!
[*To Hubert and the Lawyer, ignoring Jehannette*] So . . . what's up gentlemen?[21] What do you say?

JEHANNETTE

[*Offering up a prayer, perhaps because the Judge greeted the men only*]

For pity's sake, Saint Nick, I beg you: Ho-ho-ho, quickity-quick! Come
to my rescue today!

The LAWYER

The Devil take you, woman, shut up!
[*To the Judge*] Your Honor, the case is as follows.
[*To Hubert*] And you, what is your name?

HUBERT

I am Hubert.

JEHANNETTE

And my name's "Jehannette Hubert," on accounta bein' married to him
and all, the one who's hauling me into court today because . . .

The LAWYER

[*To Jehannette*] Shit! For God's sake, woman, shut up!
[*To the Judge*] Here, Your Honor, is Hubert, who states as follows:
While peacefully engaging in the quiet enjoyment of his dwelling—he,
who desires only to be left in peace to unwind—he was most unduly
and unjustly . . .

JEHANNETTE

He was nosing around trying to pick something up that was just too
heavy!

HUBERT

Was not! That's not how it happened at all![22]

The LAWYER

[*To Jehannette*] Not another peep out of you!

The JUDGE

Speed it up a bit, will you, Mr. Prosecutor? Chop-chop!

The LAWYER

Yes, Your Honor, I'll make it snappy.[23] Hubert says that he heard a fart.

HUBERT
> If you please, sir . . .

The LAWYER
> Stop talking out of your ass, Hubert!

The JUDGE
> Go on, Mr. Prosecutor.

The LAWYER
> Hubert is thus lodging a formal complaint in this matter because, firstly, it snuck up on him so quickly that he was quaking in fear. Secondly, he maintains that the odor brought stench into his household. Therefore, he has served his wife with due legal notice that she has no right to eject any vile waste into the home of her husband.

The JUDGE
> And what says Jehannette about all this?

The LAWYER
> With regard to this delict, she says that, if things went down that way, then she lays the blame entirely upon her husband.

The JUDGE
> Is that so? Do tell.

The LAWYER
> Because, it was upon the orders of her husband that she was burdened thusly by the pile that [*gesturing toward Jehannette who has just asserted the opposite*] she picked up. Whence, the wind that kicked up was the result of cruel and unusual punishment.

HUBERT
> It was not!

The LAWYER
> Will you please shut up!

JEHANNETTE

Was too! This is all the Devil's doing, I tell you, this whole drama.

The JUDGE

[*To Jehannette and Hubert*] If the two of you would step back now and await your *scent*ence.
[*Sidebar. Jehannette might sneak over to eavesdrop.*][24]
Mr. Prosecutor, let's figure this out. What shall we do?

The LAWYER

Your Honor, it's only right that, in one's own home, one cannot abide that another party dump all over it.

The JUDGE

But, by the same token, a man is obliged to endure any and all odors and stench from his wife.

The LAWYER

Lordy, Your Honor, Hubert is the first to acknowledge that man and wife are two spirits, two persons, two essences in one, if you will. He understands that perfectly. But, if *she*'s the one who farted or what have you, then he refuses to have any part of it and he opposes it . . . most *stenchuously*.

The JUDGE

Inasmuch as husband and wife are indeed a sole and single essence, then Hubert must understand and recognize that he plays his part in all that she does. When he married her, he married *all of her.*

The LAWYER

But here is what he offers in his own defense. He says that there is no proof whatsoever that he ever married his wife's asshole. He further alleges that, if an asshole produces filth, then it's all perfectly clear: it follows that he is to assume no role or responsibility in that whatsoever.

[*End of sidebar*]

The JUDGE

You now, Hubert, approach. Raise your right hand and [*to Jehannette*] you too.

Did you or did you not take this woman—and *all of this woman*—as your lawfully wedded wife?

HUBERT

No sir, no! I swear on my own baptism that I did not. When I took her in marriage, I took only her body! Did I marry her asshole? Up hers!²⁵

The JUDGE

And what if she had had no *derrière* at all? Would you have taken her to wife?

HUBERT

I don't know.

JEHANNETTE

Your Honor, I have proof! How's this for a piece of evidence? As soon as he married me, it was on that very first day, on our wedding night!—and you can rip me to pieces if I'm lying—that, to make a long story short, my asshole was the first place he took me.

HUBERT [*to Jehannette*]

That's because it was pitch black. The night, I mean! I couldn't tell which end was up! Believe you me, if it had been daylight, I would've turned you right side up before I ever took you *there.*

The JUDGE

That's enough. Now, step back! Go stand over there.
[*The Judge delivers the verdict.*]
Inasmuch as you hold title to the asshole that laid the fart, then it follows that you were the one who laid it. That is clear and compelling proof. What's good for the goose is good for the gander.²⁶
[*To Hubert*] And, therefore, I rule that you must acknowledge having done it. That is my verdict.

HUBERT
    I object!

The JUDGE
    Husband and wife are one entity together, are they not? Do you understand, Hubert?

HUBERT
    Yes . . .

The JUDGE
    And of the blessings that God has bestowed upon you, isn't it true that each of you should receive your fair share?

HUBERT
    Yes, that's true . . .

The JUDGE
    If a man is reduced to begging, his wife comes to his aid, does she not?

HUBERT
    Yes, sir.

JEHANNETTE
    And all those other times too!

The JUDGE
    And if you've got something—anything—she needs and she wants some?

HUBERT
    Then she gets some, whatever she needs and whenever she needs it. I hand it over.

The JUDGE
    And if she farted or what have you, or if, from her asshole, there should happen to escape a little bit of wind, then you, as her husband: Would

you really have this court believe that you are *not* to have your fair share of it, whether it be in public or in private? That you are *not* to suck it up? So suck it up! If the asshole of one emits something—regardless of whether you can touch it with your fingers or your toes—if it enters into the nose or the mouth of the other, then, upon my word, you must accept it with patience, take it all in stride.

The LAWYER

Hubert, my friend, in this fart case before us, you're going to have to admit that—albeit with no malice aforethought—you yourself are the guilty party.[27]

HUBERT

Well, by God, I never . . .

The LAWYER

And, by God, you have no choice!
Even if we imagine for a moment that you *didn't* do it . . .

HUBERT

But I *didn't* do it!
I swear to God that it came from the asshole of my wife because it never came from mine. And that's the truth, the *hole* truth, and nothing but the truth!

JEHANNETTE

Holy cow! The hell you say . . .

HUBERT

And you're just on the rag.[28]

The JUDGE

So, do you now duly acknowledge that all this hot air in question is, in fact, the fart about which you're litigating? *And* that you did it, *and* that you will now confess in what *manner* you did it?

HUBERT

Okay, fine! But by means of *her* asshole! I don't know what kinda show you're runnin' around here.

The JUDGE

I now so direct:
To all married couples who henceforth, shall have occasion to fart: Suck it up, folks! Drink up! Share and share alike in the duly apportioned stench. If one turns downwind, the other shall simply say, "Excuse *you*!"
So let it be written; so let it be done. That is my *scent*ence!²⁹

JEHANNETTE

God bless you, Your Honor, it's a glorious ruling, upon my soul!

HUBERT

You mean glorious for *you,* my wife: God only knows how this will help *me*.

The JUDGE

What's that you say?

HUBERT

If you please, Your Honor, I was just saying that you've ruled justly and in total accordance with the law. Home is where the fart is.

The JUDGE

Hear ye, hear ye!
Prick up your noses and your assholes, one and all, to all these *scent*iments and take it all in! Suck it up! You too, my lords, who are present here today, take it all in stride! And may this ruling be to your taste.

The END

2.

The Edict of Noée, or,

Shut Up! It's the Farce of the Rights of Women

Farce des Drois de la Porte Bodès

CAST OF CHARACTERS

> The COBBLER
> The WIFE
> The JUDGE
> [The Judge's Clerk]
> [Noé(e), The Great Jurist, in flashback]
> [Some extra nonspeaking female Trial-Watchers]

PRODUCTION NOTES

The *Farce nouvelle très bonne des Drois de la Porte Bodès et de fermer l'huis, à trois personnages* appears as #20 in Cohen, *Recueil,* 159–64. The play is 388 octosyllabic verses. To my knowledge, it appears in the *Recueil Cohen* only; I know of no modern French translation. Alternate title: *Marriage at the Thrash-hold.*

Plot

In the *New Farce about the Rights of the "Gate of Bodès" and about Shutting the Door* (as the French title translates), it is virtually impossible to present our usual five categories.[1] Plot blends with punning language, which has ramifications for characterization, staging, and even props. In this, another farce about who rules the roost, the Cobbler and his Wife (both unnamed) cannot agree about which of the two must get up and close the door. (Apparently, neither can say "Honey, while you're up . . ." because neither one is up.) And yet, get up someone must because it's getting smoky and windy in there in more ways than one . . . if not quite for the same reasons expounded in #1, *Farce of the Fart*. With blustery legal language—try comparing these two blowhards with Hubert and Jehannette of our previous play—the couple continues to argue the point as things threaten to go up in smoke. Trapped by the bonds of holy deadlock, the Cobbler and his Wife eventually make a wager: the first one of the chatty pair to utter the next word will rise to the occasion and shut the door.

Enter, at that moment—*quelle coincidence!*—a traveling Judge (also as in #1) who is seeking directions to his next legal gig. Because the temporarily quiet Cobbler and his Wife are still operating under the terms of their wager, they answer the Judge in sign language,[2] which he is unable to interpret (and which is scarcely a testament to his legal prowess). But when the lecherous Judge makes amorous advances toward the Wife, she breaks her silence to rebuff both him and her noninterventionist husband. In other words, she loses the bet. She welshes anyway and refuses to close the door; so the Cobbler hauls her before a judge for a legal determination about the proper division of domestic duties. Again, *quelle coincidence!* The man presiding over their case is the very same Judge who has just had truck with the couple and harassed the Wife.[3] (All three characters might manifest their surprise at seeing one another again.)

With the significant recent exception of Lisa Perfetti's *Women and Laughter in Medieval Comic Literature* (chap. 5), it's a wonder that this play hasn't attracted more scholarly attention. At trial, it seems that the Cobbler is just about to triumph when, suddenly, his Wife introduces as evidence a curious edict that grants to *her*—and to all women—mastery and dominion over the household. Who should get up and close the door when the house is drafty? The husband, of course! So says the titular edict that guarantees the "Rights of the 'Gate of Bodès.'" But what in the world is it?

The "Edict of the Gate of Bodès" appears to be a complete fiction, named after its equally fictional author, an illustrious jurist who had the foolhardy and farceworthy idea of empowering women.[4] It's bad news then, for readers hoping to espy a kind of protofeminism in this play: women's rights are a *farce;* and the term *bodès* itself—Basoche-like in sensibility—is etymologically linked to all that is bawdy, bold, arrogant, talkative, spirited, and in good fun. Like the play that does honor and dishonor to a farcical feminism, the momentous edict of the "Lord of *Porte Bodès*" is one big joke, necessitating an English name for the penetrating legal mind that produced this mess of a precedent. I briefly considered "Sir N. Pecket" (*henpecked*) and "Sir Jess Kitten" (*jus' kiddin'*); but my copyeditor and punster par excellence, Michael

Gnat, ingeniously suggested that a more *Bodèscious* effect might be achieved by calling the absent jurist "Noah" and pronouncing his name *no way*). What he didn't suspect is that, in French, that idea works even better inasmuch as one does not *hear* the difference between the masculine and the feminine form of Noah. Both *Noé* and *Noée* are pronounced identically as *no way*. To the ear as well, the French version of Noah has the added advantage of preserving the mystery surrounding the sex of the titular barrister; to the eye, you can see that, rather than go for something like Noé(e), I've come down on the side of her womanhood. Furthermore, since it's *Noah*, after all, the name even dramatizes a terrific piece of proverbial wisdom that basically means "Let the chips fall where they may!" Literally, the French say: "After me comes the flood!" as in *Après moi le deluge*! The play's message? Hallelujah, ladies! There's an edict that grants and protects the rights of women. Oops! Sorry, *no way*!

By the way, the play's key plot device of shutting the door was not only the stuff of balladry (as in the medieval Scottish "Get Up and Bar the Door");[5] it was a big deal in the Middle Ages for none other than the Basochiens. The Parisian legal apprentices could hardly wait for the official Parliamentary sessions of the Grand'Chambre to be over so that they could get in and start pleading their own silly cases. It's just that they were *so* eager to get in that they started congregating well before the appointed hour of 5:00 P.M., causing problems for Parliament, which normally deliberated with the doors open.[6] That august body attempted to postpone the Basochial séances until 6:00 P.M., the better to keep the raucous fellows at bay, but it didn't work. The young apprentices appear to have caused such a ruckus banging their drums to announce their takeover that an official complaint was lodged on behalf of court officials who "can no longer hear one another, and are forced to leave their seats and go on home because they can no longer do anything."[7] Poor lads of the Basoche! Somebody tried to close the door in their faces! And that was no joke.

A final observation: to my way of thinking, there are so many similarities with the *Farce of the Fart* that it would be possible to stage the *Edict of Noée* as a kind of sequel, imagining that, here, Hubert and Jehannette of #1 are appearing anew in court for further rulings.

Characters and Character Development

Of the three unnamed characters, we are about to meet the first of our five cobblers, the lowest of the low in the hierarchy of specialists of the shoe.

(If Hubert of #1, *Farce of the Fart*, is also a cobbler, the text doesn't say.) As Christopher Pinet recalls of the ubiquitous, humble guildsman, a cobbler traveled from place to place, offering his services, which were confined to "repair[ing] the shoes of those citizens who could not afford to buy new ones."[8] This particular drunken, cobbling weakling of a spouse is a *heel*.

In the Wife's case, lacking a name might, for once, serve her in good stead. With all due apologies to Chaka Khan, she's every woman.[9] And she's none too happy with her lowly husband, especially when he drinks away their income. (Compare her with Dottie of #9, *Monk-ey Business*. Or imagine the Duchess of *Alice in Wonderland* speaking roughly to her husband rather than to her little boy.) Like Shakespeare's Kate in the *Taming of the Shrew*, she does not hesitate to manifest violence or the threat thereof, even when waging the quieter legal warfare of the closing scene. Both the Wife and her Cobbler husband are also talented mimes. Considering their relative, initial sloth in not wishing to get up and close the door, they might be on the portly side.

Lascivious to the bone, the Judge is another traveling jurist. He has little respect for women, but he does indeed respect legal precedent when he rules in favor of the so-called fairer sex in accordance with the titular Edict of Noée. His tone is considerably more highfalutin when engaging with the Cobbler and his Wife than when he talks to himself or to the Audience. (Compare him, in that respect, with the Examiner in #4, *Student Who Failed*.)

By analogy to Tissier's suggestion for #1, *Farce of the Fart*, a nonspeaking character—the Judge's clerk—might also be added to the production's final courtroom scene along with some female trial-watchers.

Language

Particularly complex for nonnative French speakers is the play's two-part title. The subtitle, *de fermer l'huis*, means "about shutting the door," which refers to the action—or, rather, the *inaction*—that spawns the plot. But the play's signature line connotes something else as well. Literally, *allez le fermer!* can be translated as "Go and shut it!" (*it* being *the door*); colloquially, however, it is an extremely rude way of telling someone to "shut up," "shut your face," or "zip it." Thus, each time the Cobbler tells his Wife to "*shut it!*," he is also telling her to "*shut up!*" To reinforce the pun in production, one might have the Cobbler stutter: "Shut-t-t-t-t-t [i]t-t-t-t-t up!"

Another pun, this one on legal terminology, is noteworthy. At one point, the Judge deems the Wife a *malle fame,* which is technically a "bad wife";

but *mala fama* is also legalese for a "bad reputation." Keep reading: it's the Cobbler who will prove unable to keep his reputation intact when the day is out. Additionally, this farce boasts usage of the term *haro!*—a Norman cry for legal intervention which, for the fifteenth-century legal reformer Thomas Basin, "stirs up all the dustups, mockery, disputes, and altercations . . . [and] instigates the birth of all litigation" (*Apologie*, 258–61).

As the couple leaves their living room for the courtroom, their physical progress is reflected by the Wife's linguistic progress. Her grammar, syntax, and vocabulary become increasingly elaborate, formal, and downright legalistic as the action proceeds and as her power takes hold; so her entire demeanor and bearing might reflect those enhancements. She even uses the imperfect subjunctive! (See above, About This Translation, § "Language and Style"). In contrast, both the Cobbler and the Judge experience linguistic *regress,* mirroring their loss of legal power.

Sets and Staging

Over two scenes, the action moves from the interior of the couple's smoky home, to the threshold of its [back] door, to outdoors (where the Judge is in transit on a nearby road), to the locus of the denouement, the courtroom. For added comedy, one might stage the couple's opening argument at the threshold, the contested site of the play: the Cobbler and his Wife can hardly get to trial if the door is closed. (Note that both seem all too willing to get up and brawl and to continue their brawl in the courtroom—just not to get up and shut the door. The actors have multiple opportunities to pass right through that door without shutting *it* or shutting *up.*) The courtroom itself may be a formal or informal setting; and some extra nonspeaking female characters might be present. Alternatively, the trial might play out, in a more impromptu manner, outside the couple's house, not too far from the very door in question. Do they leave the door open before heading to court? You decide. To what other behaviors does this farce open the door?

Scenically speaking, two important elements symbolize the transformations that are about to occur. First of all, the house is full of smoke, literal and metaphorical, as husband and wife "blow one another off," clouding the issue, as it were. The smoke that precipitates the play's legal crisis is of unknown origin, but we can imagine two possibilities, either one of which would necessitate closing the door. It might be coming from *inside:* perhaps the Wife is unable to light a fire properly, or she's a lousy cook who has left something burning on the stove; closing the door would prevent a backdraft. (We do not know for sure whether the Wife's accusation, in Scene 1, that the Cobbler opened the back door is correct, although the Cobbler affirms as much in Scene 2. It's possible that, in a sonorous echo of the *Farce of the Fart*, it's *another* back door that he'd like her to shut. Either way, the action seems funnier if the couple is staged at the back door; the front door should probably be closed. It doesn't make sense for them to dig in their heels about who must close *one* door but to find the situation totally unproblematic for the *other* door. Or maybe it does. It's a farce.) Or maybe the smoke is coming from *outside:* imagine the medieval equivalent of your neighbor who barbecues every night and whose smoke gets into *your* kitchen. (Neighbor, you know who you are!)

Second, the Wife is spinning or weaving in the first scene, holding a staff (*quenoulle*) that will be legally assigned to her by the Judge in the play's final ruling. That staff is the symbol of her changing powers, which include the right—nay! the duty!—to beat her husband with it if he fails to perform his newly assigned domestic tasks to her satisfaction.

In a way, one of the most important characters of the play is not actually *in* the play: "Noé" himself. Or is that "Noée" *herself*? A pantomimed flashback might bring him or *her* to the stage.

Costumes and Props List

At the home of the Cobbler and his Wife: a smoke machine or other representations of smoke; a staff suitable for spinning and beating; plus, for the Wife, a variety of materials for the spinning, sewing, or embroidery of so-called women's work. For the trial: various legal accoutrements and vestments for the Judge.

Scholarly References to Copyrighted Materials (in order of appearance)

"Respect." By Otis Redding. (BMI)
"Smoke Gets in Your Eyes." By Otto A. Harbach and Jerome Kern. (ASCAP)
"Proud Mary." By John Cameron Fogerty. (BMI)

[Scene 1]¹⁰

[At and near the Cobbler's home]

The COBBLER *begins,*
[On his way home, he talks to himself and possibly to the Audience as well.]

> May God bless my fellow cobblers—and everybody else while I'm at it! It's a good and honest living, but, for God's sake, let us make a buck, why don'tcha?¹¹
>
> Boy, oh boy, I'm dyin' o' thirst here; but if I even go and have one lousy beer, I'll never hear the end of it! It sure does make a racket in my tummy!¹² If only I could get some better luck a-brewin'. . . . Then cobblers would be rich.
>
> But, no. Not happenin'.
>
> So I better watch my step and head on home. I think I already hear that cow a-mooin' in the distance, and I'm not even halfway there! God only knows the scene she's gonna make this time the second she sees me comin'.
>
> So she'll go: "I bid you a crappy day, asshole!"
>
> And I'll go: "Right back atcha, bitch!"

[Rubbing his belly]

> Yes sirree, it'll be a cold day in hell before I let 'er hear what's goin' on down there. Let's face it: the minute she hears it, I might as well be dead and buried! Naggin', harpy bitch! A guy's gotta make a livin', don't he?
>
> Oh well. Best I just keep a low profile and grin and bear it.

[Noticing the smoky state of his home]

> Boy oh boy! That's an awful lotta smoke comin' out of our chimney!

[He enters his home and promptly sits down.]

> I can hardly breathe!¹³ Hey! What's with all the smoke?

The WIFE

> Hey yourself, you big ape! You're dressed for summer and it's freezin' in here because you opened the goddamn back door. The draft's comin' in all over the place.

The COBBLER

So go and shut it the hell up![14]

The WIFE

You listen to me, I've got plenty else to do. It's your own damn job.

The COBBLER

Go and shut it the hell up. Please.

The WIFE

The hell you say! You think you can just boss me around like that?
What do you think? I'm gonna wait on you hand and foot around
here? Better think again.

The COBBLER

Hell's bells, woman! Fine! Let the whole place burn down! I'm busy
over here!

The WIFE

And so am I, over *here*! I'm busy doing *my* job. I'm threading the staff
for my spinning;[15] and I care a whole helluva lot more about *that* than
about what *you're* doing.

The COBBLER

And she's keepin' it up! Get over yourself, girl! One of us has gotta get
up and go or, I promise you, there's gonna be trouble.[16] Have I made
myself perfectly clear?

The WIFE

You think you can scare me? I really don't give a shit! You got a helluva
nerve asking *me* to go and shut my back door! Some fine lord o' the
manor, you are! Go and hire yourself a maid or a valet for Chrissakes.
And you can go straight to hell while you're at it! Besides, I'm the kinda
woman who deserves a maid or a valet anyhow.

The COBBLER

If you don't shut it, I guarantee you, there's gonna be hell to pay.

The WIFE

Jesus H. Christ, you're a liar! What? Me? *I'm* supposed to shut the door? Cow that I am? You smoked me out, all right! I'd rather head off to the slaughter! I *shan't*![17]

The COBBLER

And holy smokes! I can barely see a thing in here! So you better get off your ass and shut the door if you know what's good for you. This is not going to end well.

The WIFE

Your eyes can pop right outta your head for all I care. I'm kinda likin' the idea of not risin' to this particular occasion. You can ask till you're blue in the face. It's not happening.

The COBBLER

You goddamn fat-ass! Get off your lazy butt!

The WIFE

Same to you.

The COBBLER

A man doesn't take orders from his wife! It just ain't fittin'!
[*Here, he may gesture toward the Audience.*]
As God is my witness: what would all these people say? So go on now and shut it the hell up!

The WIFE

God strike me dead if I even come close to shutting it. But, please: [*possibly bowing ironically*] after you! Go on and do it yourself![18]

The COBBLER

I can guarantee you that, if you keep this up, I have ways of making you hop to it. Now get up and shut the goddamn door!

The WIFE

I will not.

The COBBLER
　You will not, is it?

The WIFE
　Nope.

The COBBLER
　Then we'll soon see what kinda lady you are and who's runnin' this here
　show. Am I not a man of honor? Get off your ass right now and shut
　that door!

The WIFE
　No, you.

The COBBLER
　God Almighty, what a life a poor man has to lead. . . . I don't get no
　respect. And no pleasure from my own wife. Get off your ass right now
　and shut that door!

The WIFE
　You want it so bad, you can go and do it yourself.

The COBBLER
　Are you finished?

The WIFE
　You bet I am. That about covers it. I have nothing in particular to add
　at this juncture.

The COBBLER, *hitting her*
　Shut that door, God damn it! I've already told you a hundred times!

[*During the assaults to come, husband and wife might move progressively
toward their front door, which should probably be closed, the better to
avoid precipitating a second crisis. The beatings should be staged near the
door or at the threshold so that their dispute is audible but not visible
to the neighbors. By the time the beatings are over, the couple should be
outside and visible from the nearby road, having left through the back.*]

The WIFE

God damn it to hell! You're hitting *me*, you scumbag? I swear on a stack o' Bibles that, by the time I finish with you, you'll be up shit creek without a paddle![19]

Let's see how you like the feel of this staff on your sorry ass!

The COBBLER

[*He might run into the Audience with the Wife giving chase, but only if he makes the Audience complicit in concealing the truth about who is wielding the stick. Either way, the Cobbler can't have it* both *ways: yelling for the police is the opposite of such concealment.*][20]

Help! Police![21] My wife's trying to beat me up! Help! Murder! Please, somebody help me! Anybody!

The WIFE

[*Catching up and thrashing him repeatedly*]

You think *you're* gonna keep beating *me*?

The COBBLER

I give up, I give up! See? I'm beggin' for mercy.

But just you do this one little thing now, so neither one of us loses face. I'm askin' you nicely: Just let out one big, blood-curdlin' scream so, when the neighbors hear the racket, they'll think that *I'm* the one beating *you*. Get it? For better or for worse, you can keep on hitting me; I'll just stand here and take it.

The WIFE

I get it, I get it.

[*Overacting as she continues to hit him*] Help! Murder! Somebody, help! My husband is killing me! Hurry up! Help! He's gonna kill me! Owwwww! Help! The bully! Owwwww! The louse! Owwwwww! What are you tryin' to do, kill me? You lousy, stinkin' dog? Alas and alack! He has beaten me black and blue!

The COBBLER

Oh, blow it out your ear! God damn it to hell! What have I gone and gotten myself into? I knew in my heart o' hearts that nothin' good was gonna come outta this. I certainly got the point from all these welts you left all over me. Look at me! I'm black and blue all over.

The WIFE

All *that* for a lousy door that isn't closed? *This* is what you had to make such a big deal about? It would've been a better course of action by far if you'da just kept your big mouth shut. Yeah, that's right: you men are always sayin' that we women are yak-, yak-, yakkin' all the time, but you're the ones, are you ever! You're the ones who can't zip it![22]

The COBBLER

[*He massages his wounded shoulder. As they make their wager, the couple should be at the threshold heading outside.*]

I get it, I get it. You taught me a lesson and I'll never forget it. But, hey! How's about a compromise? The first one who opens their mouth— you or me—that's who's gonna go and shut the door. What do you think?

The WIFE

You got it, Mr. Johnson![23]

The COBBLER

And, in my humble opinion, you'll soon be shuttin' it up.

The WIFE

And that's your conclusion because. . . ?

The COBBLER

'Cause, in all my born days, I ain't never seen a woman who could hold her tongue or resist the temptation to yak her head off and make trouble. God Almighty! A woman's tongue is like the wheel of a wind-mill: big wheel keep on turnin'![24]

The WIFE

And that's got nothin' to do with the case at hand or with our wager. Plus, you're the one who pitched it and named the terms! You talk twice as much as I do anyhow.

The COBBLER

All right, then, if you'd be so kind, let's begin then, shall we? I'm asking you nicely. And the first one of us guys[25] who speaks is gonna have to get up pronto and shut that door without another word about it.

The WIFE

That's fine with me.

The COBBLER

Me too.
So: we're both gonna shut up then . . . starting . . . now. [*He speaks.*] Don't you say another word now.

The WIFE

You're on. I hope you die trying!

[*In a veritable dumb show, the two continue to "converse" by means of gesture.*]

[Scene 2]

[*On the road outside the Cobbler's House*]

[*Enter the Judge*]

The JUDGE [*alone*]

All righty, then! Time for my next gig over in [Santa Barbara]![26] Because that's the business I'm in.
Hmmmm. . . . I think I see a cobbler just ahead over there. Maybe I can get some directions from him. There's probably a shortcut between here and [Santa Barbara].
[*To the Cobbler*]
Excuse me, you over there, *pardon monsieur:* I say, my good man!
[*He watches the dumb show for a moment.*]
Are you going to answer me? What's the meaning of this?
Yo! Hey, over here! Are you deaf or somethin'? You, my good man!

Holy cow! Maybe he *is* deaf!²⁷ Or maybe he's havin' some kinda break-
down . . . Well God damn! The hell with him! I don't think he understands a single word of what I'm sayin'!

*The Cobbler responds with finger gestures [and might even "give the Judge
the finger" at some point].*²⁸

The JUDGE, *continues*
What a bunch of lunatics! What's he trying to say there with his
finger . . . fingers? What's that? Five? Six? I don't get it. Could we talk
turkey here?
Oh. . . I get it. . . . He really *is* mute. I've been barkin' up the wrong tree.
Good God! What a piece o' work.
[*Trying his luck with the Wife*] And what about you, my dear lady? Are
you mute like him? Or can you muster up a couple of words for me?
Come here. Come right on over here and we'll have ourselves a private
little audience. I can already tell that you're a woman of distinction,
discretion, and class. Not the kind of girl to abandon a guy in his hour
of need. So, [*starting to lead her away*] come on along with me then, if
you please. Follow me.

The WIFE [*irate, to the Cobbler*]
God damn you, you lousy bum! I hope they hang you by the neck till
you're dead! You're just gonna stand there like a sleazebag and let this
guy just take me off and have his way with me? And no thanks to you?
He better hadn't oughta try!
[*The Wife might gesture toward the Judge during the subsequent tirades as
the Judge endeavors to beat a hasty retreat, eventually managing to do so.*]
I swear to God, I can't stand to look at you! You just stand there like
some kinda lowlife instead o' liftin' one lousy finger to come and rescue
your own wife! I hope somebody cracks your skull wide open! Or
throws you into a well or somethin'!

The COBBLER
Nyah, nyah, nyah, nyah, nyah! I win! You lose! You're gonna go and
shut the door now. You talked first!

The WIFE

Oh yeah? I'm the one in charge of this goddamn, stinkin' rat hole and, Jesus H. Christ! I *will* be mistress of this house!

The COBBLER

I don't get it. We had a deal! You promised that whichever one of us talked first was gonna go and shut the door.

The WIFE

Go on and give it your best shot! Go on and try! You'll never win. You can't beat me.

The COBBLER

Hey, that's no fair, woman! You have to keep your word and do what you promised. Plus you have to obey what I say! It's only fair. You have to go and shut the door now.

The WIFE

I'm not doing it. No way, no how. Like I'd obey you and your nonsense!

The COBBLER

Oh for God's sake! You know very well that you can do it.
Come on, now, my dear, I'm asking you most politely. In the name of the Blessed Virgin, would you be kind enough to go and shut the back door? Pretty please? What'll it cost you? It's only right, and you know it.

The WIFE

And I say it's not happening. I will never obey you. But you *will* obey *me*! [*Presciently*] And you'll see that things are gonna get even worse for you around here!

The COBBLER

Then you leave me no choice but to bring you before the judge; because I'm well within my rights to state my claim that *you*'re the one who's legally bound to shut the door. *And* . . . that, from this day forward, *you*'re the one who's gonna shut it. . . . *And* I don't care how much I have to pay him!

The WIFE

You rotten louse! You can go hang yourself. By the time I'm through
with you, you won't have a dime to your name anyhow!

The COBBLER

I know my rights.

The WIFE

You're in for a nasty surprise, you'll see.

The COBBLER

Good Lord, woman! I'm gonna sue you. I know my rights: "Don't take
the law into your own hands! Take 'em to court!"

The WIFE

Jesus H. Christ! You're the one who's gonna wind up payin'. And then
I'll be the one makin' rulings over *you*. You hear?

The COBBLER

That'll be one hell of an attorney you'll hire to pull that one off.

The WIFE

You pathetic loser! Do you really think I'm scared of—whoa!—your
great physical strength? Do you really think I'd miss my chance to take
you down? And make mincemeat outta you? And break your lousy
neck?

The COBBLER

I'll wipe the floor with you! Come on, then, let's go! Get a move on!

The WIFE

I'll beat you to it! You think I'm scared?

[*Here she might race him to see who can get to court first.*]

[Scene 3]

[Before the Judge, the same man as in Scene 2, and the recognition of which prompts double takes from all three characters][29]

The COBBLER
[Arriving rather breathless before the Judge]
> God give you good day, Your Honor. I've hastened here before you today so that I might have recourse to the courts, if you please.

The JUDGE
> Go right ahead. Tell me all about it. I'm listening.

The COBBLER
> Your Honor, I'll tell you the whole story.
> What happened is that, all in good faith and with no malice afore-thought, I made me a wager with my wife—and that's the truth—that, whoever would be the first one to speak, her or me: that's the one who was gonna get up and shut the door with no further ado.

The JUDGE
> Is that true?

The WIFE
> I don't deny it.

The COBBLER
> So I'm requesting that you sentence her.

The JUDGE
> I can't just pronounce sentence like that! You think I just fell off the turnip truck, buddy?[30] I first have to conduct some discovery and some fact finding[31] before I make my ruling. Was that all you wanted to tell me about the case?

The COBBLER

All she ever does is curse me out! She's always saying: "Pain in the ass! Your ass is grass!"[32] She does it, like, more than a dozen times a day, Your Honor.

The JUDGE

Well that's not good. I'll have to take this under advisement.

The COBBLER

And then, when I tell her, "Go on and shut the door!" she says that there's no way she's doin' it. And then she's cursin' me out and cursin' me out . . . and heapin' all the ills of the earth upon me: damn me, screw me, hang me, I should die of a disfiguring disease . . . And all of that . . . well . . . it so happens, not unrelated to her earlier meeting with *you,* Your Honor. And, then, here's the kicker: she opens up her big fat yap and tells me that *she's* the one in charge.

The JUDGE

I get it. Not a match made in heaven.[33] I get the picture. And it seems appropriate that, before she leaves here today, she ought to be punished.
[*To the Wife, possibly vengefully given her earlier rejection of him*]
So . . . what about you? What have you got to say for yourself now, honey? It's only fair that I hear *your* side of the story.

The WIFE
[*With a marked change in linguistic register*][34]
Your Honor, if it please the Court:
It is indisputable that I was indeed the first one to speak; and that I gave my husband quite the dressing down, the better to demonstrate the flaws in his reasoning and the error of his ways. But I was well within my rights to speak, and I had every right to do so. For, at all times, it is the law of the land that men are subject to *our* judgment.

The JUDGE

Say what? What the hell kinda law are you citing there? You better get right to the point and produce your precedent so that I can make my ruling. Because, no matter how big a louse a man may be, he is most certainly not obliged to obey his wife and do her bidding . . . unless he feels like it.[35]

The WIFE

Your Honor, I am prepared to cite momentarily the precedent that pertains to the rights and privileges that we women possess: to wit, that it is we who are empowered to correct and to chastise our husbands when they misbehave, or when they act in a manner that displeases us. It is our duty to punish them to our heart's content, and to beat them—and to do whatever else is necessary—should something need to be done around the house. It's all perfectly well within our rights. It is man's duty, moreover, to do *everything* and, if he knows what's good for him, to do so without protest or contradiction. Quite to the contrary: he shall complete his tasks most cheerfully.
And there you have it. That's the statute in its entirety. Those are the rights accorded to all women.

The JUDGE

I, for one, would like to know where in the world it comes from, that statute you just cited.

The WIFE

It's all perfectly legal. It is to be found in a certain place in our town. I prefer not to disclose the exact location.

The JUDGE

Good God! It's only fitting that I be informed as to . . . Who's the chucklehead who gave all that freedom to women? Who gave away the farm?

The WIFE

'Tis a great and illustrious jurist by the name of Noée; and the edict establishes henceforth, and in perpetuity, according to long-standing precedent, that it is we who wield authority over the household.
[*She produces a document, perhaps a scroll.*]
See for yourself. It's all in here. Read it and weep!

The JUDGE

Looks at the document and then says:

This appears to be your lucky day.

I find, in the exhibit that you have produced, that, indeed, man is, in each and every way, to be subject to his wife.

It is he who is responsible for cleaning the pots and pans, making the beds, sweeping the house.

And it is he who is also responsible, at all times, for being the first to rise in the morning and the last to go to bed at night. It is he who must blow out the candles—and he must perform these duties cheerfully and without rebellion.

He must also wash the dishes. And there shall be no griping whatsoever about anything that his wife does, lest he be deemed in violation of his office.

He must also sift the flour; and he is completely and wholly responsible for doing all the sewing and all the laundry, again, without the slightest lapse in those duties.

He must go to the mill and to the oven; and, upon returning to his dwelling, if he is found to have been somehow lacking in any of these tasks, then, to spare the rod is to spoil the husband. Two or three whacks of the staff ought to do it.[36]

[The Wife might produce the staff she was using in Scene 1.]

I see little point in continuing the reading of the statute; but, certainly, I've never seen an edict so favorable to the feminine condition.

Thus, I have little choice but to throw this case out of court.

Henceforth, I shall enforce the laws of Noée in this jurisdiction. [That's Noée! Noée! No way!]

[To the Cobbler, possibly with a wink about the interpretation of "no way"]

So, check it out! You're gonna have to comply with the statute of *No-Way* in accordance with the law, like it says here.

And I order you, without further ado, that, upon returning to your dwelling, you shall immediately shut it . . . shut the door. That's my ruling; and you better comply or risk a hefty fine.

So let it be written. So let it be done.[37]

The COBBLER

In other words, there's no point in even filing an appeal. God, I can't believe I'm gettin' screwed like this. I don't see a way out.

The JUDGE

You'll have to put up with it, for better or for worse. And I wash my hands of anyone who won't toe the line.

The COBBLER

[*To the women in the Audience*][38]

My dear ladies, henceforth, I shall be obliged to shut it . . . and my wife shall be the mistress of the house. Because I'm a moron.

The WIFE

Piss me off again, and I'll throw you into a well.

The COBBLER

My dear ladies, henceforth, I shall be obliged to shut it. Because I'm a moron.

And now, in my remaining meager capacities, I bid you adieu, hoping that each and every one of you has had a real blast here today! One more time!

[*Here, the Wife can start dragging him offstage.*][39]

Say, girls, I'm a submissive spouse!

I'll shut that door, 'cause I'm a tool.

My wife's the mistress of this house!

The WIFE

Be quick about it, rotten louse,

Or else I'll beat your ass, you fool!

The COBBLER

Say, girls, I'm a submissive spouse!

I'll shut that door, 'cause I'm a tool.

But now I bid you, folks, be cool!

The fool says "bye!" I've gotta go!

We hope that you've enjoyed the show!

The END

3.

Confession Lessons, or,

The Farce of the Lusty Husband Who Makes His Confession to a Woman, His Neighbor, Who Is Disguised as a Priest

Farce de celuy qui se confesse à sa voisine

CAST OF CHARACTERS

The HUSBAND
The WIFE
COLETTE, the Neighbor
[Genie, Colette's Daughter]

PRODUCTION NOTES

The *Farce nouvelle de celuy qui se confesse à sa voisine qui est habillée en habit de prestre qui est le ribault marié, ou maugré jalousie* appears as #2 in Cohen, *Recueil*, 9–20. It is 616 verses, mostly octosyllabic. To my knowledge, it survives in the *Recueil Cohen* only; I know of no modern French translation. Alternative titles: *Dress Up, 'Fess Up, Mess Up;* or *Mea Gulpa!*

Plot

Despite Sara Beam's observation that "specifically religious themes are rare in the farce" (*LM*, 28), *Confession Lessons* handily displays the contrary, as does the lusty monk whom we shall encounter in #9, *Monk-ey Business,* or the suitor-in-monk's clothing satirized in #7, *At Cross Purposes.* This is a farce that has it all: disguises, tricksters tricked, metacommentaries galore about what it means to play a role (onstage or off-), plus lust, adultery, religion, and, to top it all off, the violation of the sanctity of the confessional. What is an unnamed Wife to do when she suspects her unnamed Husband of infidelity? Turn to her BFF Colette, of course, who hatches a seemingly brilliant plot to get the truth out of him. Colette will dress up like a priest so that she can solicit, inauthentically, an authentic confession. But the women better be careful what they wish for. It might come true. The Wife's warning to her Husband in Scene 1 is uncomfortably prophetic, and not in any theological way: ironically, things will not turn out as the girls have planned.

Initially, theirs appears to be the perfect ruse. With able direction from Colette, the rightly suspicious Wife pulls out all the stops to make her Husband believe that he is so deathly ill that he must make his confession immediately, at which point Colette (having donned a priest costume), will make a pastoral house call to receive that confession. (Like Martin of #7, *At Cross Purposes*, Colette just happens to have a priest outfit lying around the house and one can only wonder how: Did their parish priest have occasion to disrobe at the time of his last visit? Was there a private confession session like the one proposed in #9, *Monk-ey Business*?) The Husband is wary that things are not what they seem; but, since he is hungry for his supper, he capitulates to the pair's demands, hoping to get fed faster. Although he is in need of a serious refresher course on the how-tos of contrition, the Husband reluctantly makes his true confession to a false priest, unveiling to Colette one hell of a shocker. Spoiler alert! Not only are the Wife's suspicions about her Husband's cheating thoroughly founded, but the joke is on Colette too. The object of the philanderer's affections is none other than Colette's own daughter, Genie, whom he has deflowered. He met the girl on pilgrimage. (Where else were medieval people supposed to hook up? Ladies and gentlemen, I give you Chaucer's *Canterbury Tales*!) And it serves Colette right, the play seems to suggest, for penetrating the secrecy of the confessional . . . which penetration is exactly what the play itself is staging as it makes visible the sacrament of penance. Hmmmm . . .

All joking aside, medieval scholastics pondered extensively, and with the utmost gravitas, two perplexing theological questions posed by this farce. After the Fourth Lateran Council of 1215, when confession became obligatory, how is it that the Husband doesn't know how to do it? And, if one makes a true confession to a false priest, does it "count?" (The answer is *Yes*.)[1] The extent of the play's reflection on those weighty questions is limited to the physical violence of a folk vengeance that appears to have struck as odd no one at all. The Husband's "penance" is to stand there and take it as his Wife and Colette beat the crap out of him.

Characters and Character Development

Boasting yet another performance within a performance, *Confession Lessons* stages three deceivers. There is the Wife who *pretends* to love her cheating Husband and to panic over his allegedly imminent demise, the better to catch him in the act of confessing; there is her gal pal Colette, who *pretends* to be a priest to extract that confession; and last and definitely least, there is the cheating Husband who, although bedding another woman—a mere girl—appears little committed to any pretense at all, since he boldly begins the play by singing a love song about his girlfriend. Interestingly enough, this is the only play in the repertoire to stage the friendship between two women, hosting several scenes of the Wife and Colette chatting, scheming, and enjoying one another's company. (Across the Channel, one thinks of Mrs. Noah, who prefers to share a beer with her "gossips" rather than to prepare for God's retributive deluge. One wonders what Noée of our previous play would have to say about that.)[2] The Wife displays some of the typical harpy features, especially the glee with which she contradicts her lout of a Husband. She is also a more sexual character than some of her counterparts (but not more than not-so-Frigid Bridget of #6, *Playing Doctor*, or Desirée of #10, *Getting Off on the Wrong Foot*). She is annoyed, for instance, not so much that her Husband is cheating on her but that he is distributing elsewhere her fair share of marital favors.[3]

Colette is our go-to girl, ready to help out her BFF by any means that her theater-ready brain can think up; the confessional minidrama is her idea. Colette's own Husband is neither seen nor mentioned at all: only her daughter, Genie. Otherwise, Colette is another lusty maid who appears to have a steady stream of lovers coming and going—among them, judging from her quick costuming, a priest. One could almost stage her as a prostitute who, under other more serious circumstances, might have attracted the attention of Hrotswitha's Paphnutius. (Father Paphnutius, in the drama that bears his name, pays a visit to the "harlot" Thais in order to get her to renounce her life of prostitution. Naturally, he does so disguised as a john.)[4]

Surprise, surprise! The Husband is an idiot who is more concerned with his bodily needs for food and sex than with leading a good Christian life. (Perhaps this is why he gives in to his Wife's ridiculous request that he confess his sins: he's hoping for food, sex, or both. Recall too that all Paphnutius needed to do to convert Thais was to utter the Latin equivalent of "stop whoring around!") At the beginning of the play, the Husband has no trouble baiting his Wife, lording his romantic conquest over her.

Finally, since the Husband's backstory is expounded in some detail, it would be possible to stage a mimed flashback in Scene 5 in which Colette's nubile daughter, a nonspeaking Genie, cavorts with the Husband.

As usual, the characters are painted in broad strokes, so actors will play broad comedy, especially when the Wife and Colette are playacting or, more to the point, *over*acting in order to extract the Husband's confession. To give you an idea of how over-the-top they are: some marvelous possible parodies come to mind, such as the Master Thespian developed by John Lovitz for *Saturday Night Live* or Dana Carvey's Church Lady.

At the beginning of the play, the characters of Husband and Wife are developed musically, with each one singing refrains that give voice to their amorous states (or lack thereof). As usual, I have proffered my own analogies about possible musical selections (all subject to clearing the requisite permissions); but, as these translations age, performers will doubtless wish to substitute their own ideas as to whether music is necessary and, if so, which music.

Language

The linguistic highpoint of this play is its unabashed, macaronic, grammatically incorrect, and some might say sacrilegious and even blasphemous borrowing of the Latin language of the confessional. So much the better if readers are familiar with Eddie Izzard's routine about the Vicar of the Anglican Church, whose advice to would-be penitents is to efface sin from their memories by drinking Bloody Marys (*Dress to Kill*). But there are other interesting features as well. When we first meet this Husband and Wife, she is using the formal *vous* form with him, while he uses the informal *tu* form when addressing her. Shortly thereafter, those forms of address are reversed when the Husband begins to beat his Wife, after which the *tu* form seems to take hold, but not definitively. (My use of such terms as *madam* or *mister,* on one hand, and *buddy* or *girl,* on the other, reflects those changes in register.) Also, when the Wife and Colette are together, *tu* is the order of the day, as is some particularly vulgar language. That's right: vulgar even by the standards of farce.

More striking still, since the Husband and Wife are developed through snippets from songs of medieval courtly love, it makes for an unusual hodgepodge. As they malign and degrade one another, their musical choices are chock-full of lovely lyrical content enhanced by the respectful courtliness of *vous*. In fact, these two characters barely know how to speak to each other at all—except in Scene 3, when the Wife is playacting during the "confession."

Sets and Staging

The action takes place in two interior spaces: the small and extremely humble abode of the Husband and Wife; and the home of Colette (which might display a bit more elegance, especially if the company wishes to suggest that she is having an affair with the parish priest). For the final beating scene, since the ladies invoke the violence of "teaching someone a lesson" as well as specific torture techniques (like beating the soles of the Husband's feet), one might draw inspiration from the choreography and musicality of the scourging scenes of Passion plays (above, Introduction, § "Performance and Performance Records").[5] Music is so key to this particular play that it would also be possible to produce it as a musical comedy (assuming that all requisite permissions for any selected songs have been cleared for performance).

Costumes and Props List

Sticks, staffs, switches, or whips for the final scene. Colette will need a mirror or antique looking glass, a priest costume, and various other priestly props: a holy book, a stole, and so on.

Scholarly References to Copyrighted Materials (in order of appearance)

"Hot Blooded." By Louis A. (Andrew) Grammatico and Michael Leslie Jones. (ASCAP)

"Jealousy." By Freddie Mercury [Frederick Mercury, Freddie Bulsara, Farrokh Bulsara]. (BMI)

"The Vatican Rag." By Tom Lehrer. (ASCAP)

"I Will Follow Him" ["Chariot"]. By Paul Julien André Mauriat, Jacques Plante, and Franck Marius Louis Pourcel. (ASCAP)

"Goin' Co'tin'" ["Going Courting"]. By Gene de Paul and John H. Mercer. From *Seven Brides for Seven Brothers,* © Metro Goldwyn Mayer, 1954. (ASCAP)

"Get Ready." By William [Smokey] Robinson. (ASCAP)

"Suite: Judy Blue Eyes." By Stephen A. Stills. (BMI)

"Anything You Can Do." By Irving Berlin. From *Annie Get Your Gun,* © 1946. (ASCAP).

"Mon Homme." ["My Man"]. By Jacques Mardochée Charles, Albert Lucien Willemetz, and Maurice Yvain. (ASCAP)

"Saving All My Love." By Gerald Goffin and Michael Masser. (ASCAP)

"Let Me Entertain You." By Stephen Sondheim and Jule Styne. From *Gypsy,* © 1959. (ASCAP)

"Get Down Tonight." By Harry Wayne Casey and Rick Finch. (BMI)

"Night and Day." By Cole Porter. (ASCAP)

"Gimme Some Loving." By Spencer Davis, Muff Winwood, and Stephen Lawrence Winwood. (BMI)

[Scene 1][6]

[At the home of the Husband and the Wife]

The HUSBAND, *singing*[7]
> "In spite of jealousy,
> I'll stand by you,
> my lady, my love,
> for as long as I live."

The WIFE
> Good God Almighty, mister! I'm gonna make you look like one helluva dumb ass in a minute![8]

The HUSBAND
> For Chrissakes, woman! What're you snappin' at me for? There you go! Contradictin'[9] me again! At least you could let me get to the chorus!

The WIFE
> And I say God damn it! Yes sirree, before this day's out, I'm gonna make you good and sorry about that song . . . *and* that you ever sung it in your life!

The HUSBAND

Good God Almighty! Keep rushin' me like that, woman, and I'm gonna do an encore!

The WIFE

And Good God yourself! Just keep it up and, well . . . anything you can sing, I can sing better! You know very well that I can sing anything better than you![10]

We'll see who's doin' an encore! For as long you live, eh? We'll see how long you're gonna live!

The HUSBAND [singing again, with a special sneer for the last line]

"In spite of jealousy,
I'll stand by you,
my lady, my love,
for as long as I live . . ."

The WIFE

[Cutting him off again before he reaches the chorus and singing a few verses back at him from another popular medieval song][11]

"If you've got a girlfriend,
Gonna get me a boyfriend . . ."

The HUSBAND

One of these days, madam[12] . . . POW! Right in the kisser!

[He begins to hit her.]

What do you gotta come around here for and mess me up?

The WIFE

Help! Stop! Are you tryin' to kill me? Goddamn, lousy, stinkin' wife beater! You're gonna get what's comin' to you, you big jerk! You'll see! It's not gonna turn out like you planned!

Good God Almighty! I knew darn well that you'd gone and gotten yourself a little girlfriend, and believe you me . . .

The HUSBAND

And you're a liar, I say! So what if I croon a little tune and have a little fun? Why do you gotta go and take it so literal? No need to have a cow!

What? I'm not allowed to sing a little love song just because *you* get
jealous? Well, by God, I'll sing if I feel like it! And I'll dance too!
[*Here he might do a little number.*]
And we'll have a real good time, yes sir![13] That's what I say: We'll have a
real good time!
You can bitch about it all you want! See if I care!

The WIFE
I swear to God, you'll soon be singin' a different tune![14]

The HUSBAND
And she's off again, shittin' a brick! A guy's gotta right to sing a little
song, you know, and do a little dance if he feels like it.

[*He might perform yet another musical song and dance.*]

The WIFE
I swear to God, you'll soon be singin' a different tune!

The HUSBAND
You can do all the squawkin' and caterwaulin' you want! I'm *not* gonna
stop singin' when I'm in a good mood.

The WIFE
I swear to God, you'll soon be singin' a different tune!

The HUSBAND
Shut up, woman! You don't know what you're talkin' about. For each
one o' my numbers, I'm gonna do ten more. Who's gonna stop me?
You?

The WIFE
I swear to God, you'll soon be singin' a different tune!

The HUSBAND
If you're gonna keep that little refrain up much longer, I'm gonna get all
hot under the collar, and one of us is gonna be sorry!

The WIFE

I swear to God, you'll soon be singin' a different tune!
One more time! There! I said it again!

The HUSBAND

Oh for Heaven's sake! I'm gonna get me a stick and [*beating out a rhythm*] beat the crap outta you!

The WIFE [*sarcastically*]

Oooooohhhhh, help me Mother Mary, I'm soooooo scared!

The HUSBAND

A bit off-key there, aren'tcha?

The WIFE

It's your own goddamn song that's goin' flat! I hope to God I never hear that lousy melody ever again!

The HUSBAND

I've got some business to attend to now. You keep an eye on the house while I'm gone. [*Gesturing*] The *whole* house.[15]

The WIFE

Oh yeah? Well, I hope you and them laborin' arms and hands o' yours burn at the stake and get fried to a crisp!

The HUSBAND

What's that you're babblin' about now? That a new tune you're whistlin'?
Better knock off all your whinin' if you're wantin' me to give you some lovin' when I get back!

[*He leaves.*]

The WIFE

Yeah, yeah. I got *your* number, all right. I know *that* song by heart and I can hum a few bars anytime without fakin' it.
How many times have I been beaten?

I swear to God, by hook or by crook, I'll get to the bottom of this and find out who he's been seein' behind my back! He's got a piece on the side, no doubt about it!

So I'm gonna be on my way now. Gonna get me some good advice ASAP from my girlfriend, that gal pal o' mine, my girl Colette.

[Scene 2]

[At the house of Colette, who might possibly be dispatching her lover]

[Enter the Wife]

The WIFE

Girlfriend! Whaddup? You all alone in there? How's tricks, girl?

COLETTE

Just doin' some spinnin'. What's up, girl? What's goin' down?

The WIFE

Catch this:

That good ol' boy I married has gone and gotten himself a girlfriend.

COLETTE

No way!

The WIFE

Yes, way! God damn it!

You can gouge my eyes out if it ain't the God's honest truth!

COLETTE

How do you know?

The WIFE

Oh, please!

I can't hardly wait to tell you the whole story:

So today, all he's doin' is singin' that goddamn song! You know the one: "In spite of jealousy."[16]

COLETTE

No kiddin'! Okay, hon, but listen for a sec, would ya?
Just because he's all happy and singin' all over the place . . . You really think that means for sure that he's got himself a girlfriend? I mean, isn't there a possibility that he's doin' it outta love for *you*?

The WIFE

That's a good one! What do you take me for? You think I can't see what's right under my nose? I'd bet my life on it. There's not a doubt in my mind.
If he loved me even just one little bit, he wouldn't beat me all the time; and he woulda shown me some kinda sign o' the love in his heart.

COLETTE

Hey, you wanna know a great plan for figurin' out what's goin' on in that heart o' his?

The WIFE

What choice do I have? I'm fit to be tied!
[*Continuing, with a marked change in linguistic register*][17]
At least if we were to proceed in that manner, then I would gain the knowledge that I seek and attain some kind of peace of mind.
So how might we proceed with the acquisition of that knowledge, pray tell?

COLETTE

Okay, here goes. Where is he now?

The WIFE

He had somethin' to do in town . . . or in the fields. Whatever. Some sort o' business to attend to, he said.

COLETTE

When he comes home, you're not gonna make a peep and you're not gonna complain about a thing, you hear?

The WIFE

Why the hell not?

COLETTE

Because you're gonna have to convince him that he's really sick and that, if he's gonna save his soul, he has to make a full confession and be quick about it! [*Demonstrating how the ruse will go*] Because you can tell just by lookin' at him that he's barely gonna make it another two hours. But you're gonna have to do lots o' cryin' and flailin' and pretendin' like you're all torn up about it.[18]

The WIFE

Oh yeah? What for?

COLETTE

Mary, Mother of God! Because here's how we're gonna catch him: I'm gonna disguise myself like a priest. I happen to have the clothes for it right here![19]

The WIFE

And then what do we do?

COLETTE

I'm gonna tell him, in no uncertain terms, real explicit-like, that it's absolutely imperative that he make his confession. And, no matter what he says, I won't quit till he agrees to it. Because then . . . here's how it's gonna work:
You're gonna come right back over here and get me, get it? And may God strike me dead if we don't get to the bottom of this whole affair, and right soon, honey! We'll find out what he's got on his conscience, all right. And whether he's got himself a girlfriend or not.

The WIFE

Holy cow! That's a fantastic idea! But for Chrissakes! You make sure that you look and sound so much like a priest that he gives it up—his confession, that is—to your priestly mug!

COLETTE

It'll be the performance of a lifetime! Just what the doctor ordered![20]

The WIFE
    I'll go and play my part now too. I'm the interested party, you know!
    Ready or not, here we go!

COLETTE
    You go, girl!

[*The Wife leaves and returns home.*]

[Scene 3]

[*At the home of the Husband and Wife*]

The WIFE [*alone*]
    Whoa! There he is! Okay . . . Quick! Gotta get into character here!
    Here I go: cryin' and flailin' and pretendin' like I'm worried sick about
    'im.

Pause

[*Here the Wife might "rehearse" briefly in mime.*]

[*Enter the Husband*][21]

The HUSBAND
    Yo!

The WIFE
    Welcome home, my darling!

The HUSBAND
    So is dinner ready or what? Have you at least got supper on?

The WIFE
[*Making the sign of the cross, possibly incorrectly*]
    In nomine patri et filii et spiritu sancto and *Gesundheit!* Where have you
    been? What's happened to you, my lord? You look terrible!

The HUSBAND
> Where have I been?

The WIFE
> Yes, that's right.

The HUSBAND
> I'm not sure that's any concern of yours!
> And I don't think I'm gonna tell you!

The WIFE
[*Wringing her hands histrionically*]
> Mary, Mother of God! I must away this instant with great speed and
> fetch you the doctor forthwith!

The HUSBAND
> What are you talking about?

The WIFE
> Because the end is near, I fear. You're sick! You've got no color at all!
> Why, you're pale as a sheet. I've never seen anything like it!

The HUSBAND
> I'm sick?

The WIFE
> That is the case, yes.
> And you know very well that we must all be mindful of our eternal
> souls. In the name of our Holy Mother . . . I think it would be a damn
> fine idea for you to make a little bit of a confession.

The HUSBAND
> What do you mean a confession? What've I got to confess? I'm not in
> the mood for that! I'm in the mood for some grub!

The WIFE
> Some grub? In your condition? You'll be lucky if you ever eat again!

The HUSBAND
    I will?

The WIFE
    Seems pretty obvious to me! Your fate's written all over your face.
    Alas and alack! Woe is me! Whatever shall I do? Why, only yesterday
    you were all happily singing and serenading and frolicking . . . You were
    in such a good mood.
    And yet . . . How our fortunes can change in a single day! Alas and
    alack! Woe is me! Poor wretch that I am, I am not wrong to weep!

The HUSBAND
    I'm not in any pain or nothin'. What are you on about now? What do
    you gotta be harpin' on me all the time?

The WIFE
    Shall I rush off, then, straightaway, and fetch our parish priest? Perhaps
    one of the deacons if he's not available?[22]

The HUSBAND
    God's Blood! What the hell for, woman? I'm fine! I'm as healthy as you
    are!

The WIFE
    Oh, my word! You're breaking out into a sweat! You've got one foot in
    the grave already!

The HUSBAND
[*When the Husband reprises her words verbatim, he might actually
imitate her.*]
    Oh, my word! You're breaking out into a sweat!
    For God's sake! I'm sweating, you're sweating, we're all sweating. Tell
    me another one.

The WIFE
    You're at death's door, good husband!
    What's black and white and dead all over? You! You're as jet black as
    anything you'd be wearing at a funeral![23]

The HUSBAND

> I don't know about that; but I *do* know that you're *wearing* me out! Say,
> you know what I'd like *you* to put on?
> How's about the tablecloth so's I can have my dinner!

The WIFE

> Alas, Holy Mother, let me die with you, my most beloved husband!
> Alas, my love, why, you're just a shadow of your former self. Your heart's
> ready to give out right here on the spot!

The HUSBAND

> So I guess you got yourself *another* tune you're whistlin' now! If I'm
> dyin', I'm dyin' o' hunger and thirst around here![24] And, if I'm dead, it'll
> be dead drunk! Come to think of it, I'm good 'n' ready for a drink—
> and a good meal—but ain't no one givin' me nothin'! It's really gettin'
> on my nerves.

The WIFE

> Bless my soul, my sweet husband, you're delusional! You're losing it!
> And you really *could* lose it all . . . which is why you better get yourself
> all contrite and repentant and make your confession!

The HUSBAND

> God's Blood! I've got plenty of time! Can't it wait till Lent?

The WIFE

> Just take a look at yourself! I can see what's right in front of me, you
> know! You're in a lot of pain, aren't you, my darling?

The HUSBAND

> No way. No!

The WIFE

> Alas! It shows in that pale face of yours!
> Alas! If you were to pass to the other side without getting your affairs in
> order and confessing, God would never forgive you your trespasses, nor
> the mortal sins with which you've sullied yourself. So for that reason
> alone, do the right thing:

Be a good boy, now, and make your confession in good faith. Do it while you're still of sound mind and body! Come on. You better spill the beans!

The HUSBAND

Good God, woman! And speaking of beans, how's about some dinner? Why in God's name would I confess when I'm not sick and there's not a damn thing wrong with my body that can't be fixed in no time with a little bit o' food and drink? You're really startin' to piss me off with all this talk about confession!

The WIFE

In the name of the Passion of our Lord Jesus Christ, stop fighting me on this and get yourself into a state of grace! Lie down now; your bed's all made up.

The HUSBAND

Oh, for God's sake! I get it already! Like it or not, I'm gonna to have to say that I'm all sick and suffering even though there's not a thing wrong with me.

The WIFE

Not a thing? Nothing at all?

The HUSBAND

For the love o' Mike, no!
[*Checking himself out*] Everything's in the right place: all my parts are in working order.
[*He inspects his arms, legs, and virile member.*]²⁵
My arms, my legs, my baloney pony . . .

The WIFE
[*She might give those parts an "adjustment."*]
Are not! Talk about baloney! That's all that's comin' outta your mouth, all soft and mushy. It's pathetic!

The HUSBAND

You gotta be kidding! I talk twice as good as you, woman! Will you listen to this!

The WIFE

Alas, Grim Reaper, why would you trick me thus?[26] Why would you wrest from my arms he ... *him* ... who wouldst bring me comfort and solace and who's always been so good to me.

The HUSBAND

Oh for pity's sake! I'm perfectly fine. Better watch out the Grim Reaper don't come for *you* first, because I could care less.

The WIFE

I swear, when I look at your face, all contorted like that ... What've I got to lose by asking?
[*Perhaps to the Audience as well*] Nothin' to gain, nothin' to lose, right?[27]
Are you sure you won't make your confession?

The HUSBAND

And since I'm perfectly fine, why on earth would I go and confess?

The WIFE

Perfectly fine? *You?* Surely you jest! You think I'm just makin' this stuff up?

The HUSBAND

Oh, for God's sake, I'd be better off sick at this point!

The WIFE

He who puts off till tomorrow what he can confess today is a fool awaiting sudden death.

The HUSBAND

Well looky, looky here! Who taught *you* how to preach like that?

The WIFE

Could it be . . . Satan?

The HUSBAND

And now you're the Church Lady! Too bad you're not our parish
priest: then we could do without one.[28]

The WIFE

My preaching is none of your concern. You just pay close attention to
everything I just told you.

The HUSBAND

And she's keepin' it up! Since when did *you* get religion? But I guess
that's the only number you're gonna be doin' for me today. I get it, I get
it.
[*Pondering his possibilities*] And yet . . . people *do* say sometimes that a
man oughta listen to his wife; so that's what I'll do.
All right, already. Fine, I'll make my confession. Go on, my dear: go on
and get the priest.

[*The Wife leaves the house and heads over to Colette's place.*]

The WIFE [*aside*]

At least I got him to take the bait! I really gave it to him but good.
At this rate, he'll be six feet under in no time. And that first step is a
doozy.[29]

[Scene 4]

[*At the home of Colette, where she might be otherwise occupied with
additional lovers*]

The WIFE

Quick! Hop to it, girlfriend! Aren't you in your priest costume yet?

COLETTE

How's it goin', girl?

The WIFE

Better get a move on!

You gotta go and get his confession right now! I really had to give him hell before he'd agree to it. Anyway, when he saw I wasn't gonna give in for nothin', he finally believed me.

COLETTE

You get a head start and I'll catch up. Be with you in no time.
[*Colette dons her priestly attire and models it for her friend and for the Audience, taking her sweet time and creating a comical meaning for "in no time."*][30]

So . . . How do I look?

The WIFE

I swear! That outfit fits you like a glove!

But what's your name gonna be anyway? How am I supposed to address you? Father John-John?

COLETTE

Mary, Mother of God! No way!

The WIFE

So what name?

COLETTE

Father William: you know, the name of our priest.

The WIFE

Jeez . . . I've sure had enough trouble from him already, I swear!

COLETTE

Who? The priest? Holy shit!

The WIFE

No, no, from my ever-lovin' husband.

But, we're gonna have the last laugh if he thinks he can screw around with me.[31]

COLETTE
[*Looking at her reflection in a mirror*]
Sweet Jesus! Just look at me! I'm sure ugly as sin as a confessor!

The WIFE
Come on, come on already! Don't worry about it. But whatever you do, just try not to laugh!

COLETTE
Come to think of it . . . What are you supposed to say when you confess somebody?

The WIFE
Benedicite.

COLETTE
Sssshhhhhh! Never you mind!
Now that I've become a priest, I remember. I'm all dressed up and ready to go! Hey! Shouldn't I have a breviary or somethin'?

The WIFE
Nah. But make sure you keep your distance so my husband doesn't get too close a look at you.

COLETTE
It'll be a lot easier to trick him when I cover up his face.

The WIFE
Say what?

COLETTE
That's right. That's what they do so it's, like, more confidential 'n' all. Gives great cover.

The WIFE
I'm just beggin' you, girl, make sure you ask him lots o' questions. You know, conduct a full inquiry.

COLETTE

Will do. But go on ahead of me now, go on! Just leave it all up to me.

[*They leave Colette's house, perhaps after more "hurrying."*]

[Scene 5]

[*At the home of the Husband and the Wife*]

The HUSBAND [*home alone*]

Oh, for God's sake! That wife o' mine's sure takin' her sweet time gettin' the priest!

The WIFE [*coming in alone*]

Here I am, darling! Sorry it took so long. Are you all right?

The HUSBAND

So where's the priest, dear?

The WIFE

He'll be right here; he was right behind me.

The HUSBAND

Holy moly! What the hell am I supposed to do at confession anyway? I'm freakin' out here!

The WIFE

He'll be able to explain the whole thing to you and show you what you need to say.[32]

The HUSBAND

He will?

The WIFE

Sure.

COLETTE [*enters as a priest*]

>God be with you. How's the patient doing?

The WIFE

>Not very well; he's pretty sick. He barely slept a wink last night.

The HUSBAND

>Goddamn lying wife! I slept like a log!

COLETTE

>How are you feeling, my son? How's it goin'? *Como va vobis?* You must
>now show your contrition and ask God for mercy, otherwise . . .
>There goes your soul! Straight to hell in a handbasket!

The WIFE

>You betcha! A tisket, a tasket, to hell in a handbasket!

COLETTE

>And, bless my soul! All your trespasses shall be forgiven and you shall
>dwell with the angels—for sure, for sure—if you do your Christian
>duty and confess all of your sins.

The HUSBAND

>Gimme a break here, Father, would ya? If you could just lay off the
>preaching until after I've had my supper . . .

The WIFE

>You're taking an awful chance, you know, my darling husband, because
>Death can sneak up on you . . . just like that! Suppose, for instance, that
>one were to wish to do the right thing but that one were lacking the
>time to do so.
>That's how come you better step on it!

The HUSBAND

>But don't I get my dinner first? It'll help me remember things better.

COLETTE

>My dear fellow, my son: think upon the glory of the heavens!

The HUSBAND
  At least a little something to drink, then, to jog my memory.

COLETTE
  It's very bad when a man refuses to make his confession and tries to get
  out of it.

The HUSBAND
  Oh come on, I have to get started without dinner?

COLETTE
  Why, yes. That's the whole point.

The HUSBAND
  Good God! Just my luck! Talk about your bad timing! I can barely
  remember what I'm supposed to say. Just tell me what to do.

COLETTE
  Holy moly, my son! Don't you know anything about it?

The HUSBAND
  Not really; but I suppose you're gonna teach me.

COLETTE
  Okey-dokey, then! Up and "Adam!"
  First, you make the sign of the cross. [*Demonstrating, ideally incorrectly*]
  Make sure to get it right. Get both sides.

The HUSBAND
  With this hand?

COLETTE
  Oh for God's sake, no! The other one. I never saw such a cursèd
  man! You're off to a pretty bad start there, pal. Have they taught you
  nothing?
  And, now, my son: Repeat after me:
  Bless me, Father . . .

The HUSBAND
Bless me, Father...

COLETTE
... for I have sinned.

The HUSBAND
... for I have sinned.

COLETTE
Mea gulpa! Mea maxima gulpa. Mea maxim I gulpa!

The HUSBAND
Mea gulpa! Mea maxima gulpa. Mea maxim I gulpa![33]

COLETTE
It has been ... How many weeks? ... since your last confession.

The HUSBAND
It has been ... How many weeks? ... since your last confession.

COLETTE
No, you. How many weeks?

The HUSBAND
No, you. How many weeks?

COLETTE
No, you say it.

The HUSBAND
No, you say it.

COLETTE
What? I'm supposed to confess to you?

The HUSBAND
What? I'm supposed to confess to you?

COLETTE
Yes, you are.

The HUSBAND
Yes, you are.

COLETTE
Where were we again?

The HUSBAND
Where were we again?

COLETTE
Are you nuts or something?

The HUSBAND
Are you nuts or something?

COLETTE
That's not what I told you to say.

The HUSBAND
That's not what I told you to say.

COLETTE
You're crazy! Make your confession, like you're s'pposed to!

The HUSBAND
You're crazy! Make your confession, like you're s'pposed to!

COLETTE
Saints alive! Are you refusing?

The HUSBAND
Saints alive! Are you refusing?

COLETTE
God in Heaven!

The HUSBAND
    God in Heaven!

COLETTE
    Jesus Christ! What a moron!

The HUSBAND
    Jesus Christ! What a moron!

COLETTE
    Say it: I confess my sins to God . . .

The HUSBAND
    Say it: I confess my sins to God . . .

COLETTE
    No, "to God!"
    Wait! Maybe if I say it in French! [*Possibly with supporting gestures such as waving the arms*] I confess—*Je me confesse*—*À DIEU. À DIEU.* [34]

The HUSBAND
    ADIEU to you too! Bye-bye, now Father William!
    You, wife, give 'im a little somethin' to drink before he splits.

COLETTE
    Hey, not so fast! I'm not goin' anywhere! Just because I said *À DIEU* doesn't mean I said "bye-bye!" Don't you speak French, for God's sake?

The HUSBAND
    Well golly, I was pretty sure you said "adieu!" Haven't you done enough preaching for one day?

COLETTE
    But you haven't made your confession yet. We're just getting started.
    So, let's try again. Now: repeat after me . . .

The HUSBAND
    I swear to God! All on account of her goddamn jealousy!

The WIFE [*to Colette*]

Hear that, hon? That's what he's always sayin'. Same old song, day in, day out.

COLETTE [*to the Husband*]

Got yourself a little piece on the side, do you? Better 'fess up now!

The HUSBAND

Well, yeah, if you must know . . . [*Looking around*] I mean, no. No way. Where's my wife? I think I see her over there. Get her ass outta here.

COLETTE

[*To the Wife*] Would you excuse us for just a moment, my dear? It's not appropriate for you to be listening in. [*The Wife may take some distance here.*]

[*To the Husband*] Okay, let's go: we can speak softly. Now, tell me what's in your heart. Tell me all about it. Have you broken your marriage vows?

The HUSBAND

It's true: I *have* gotten myself a girlfriend. I've been seein' the sweetest, the most adorable, the foxiest girl in this whole town.

COLETTE

You don't say.

The HUSBAND

Why, only two days ago, we were havin' us a grand ol' time. She must've kissed me 'bout a hundred times. She was all over me!

COLETTE

Can you tell me what kind of dresses she wears around town?[35] Go on. Now that the whole affair is out in the open, get it all off your chest. C'mon. Spill!

The HUSBAND

When there's a festival, she wears a green dress, with lotsa colors.

COLETTE

And what about holidays?

The HUSBAND

An exotic white one with fur trim.[36]

COLETTE [*increasingly alarmed*]

And what about to court? Or when the King is in town?[37]

The HUSBAND

Same as on Sundays: a greatcoat with a beautiful red belt, and, believe you me, a beautiful little jet-black hat in the finest silk.[38]

COLETTE [*looking panicked*]

And what did you say her name was?

The HUSBAND

Genie.

COLETTE

Genie?

The HUSBAND

That's right.

COLETTE

And do you know who her father is?

The HUSBAND

Duh.

COLETTE

And who's her mother?

The HUSBAND

Oh for Chrissakes! It's our neighbor! I got me acquainted with the chick on pilgrimage.

COLETTE

And yet . . . she seems like a very proper young lady. Everyone thinks she's a virgin.[39]

The HUSBAND

What can I tell you? I'm doin' her. Menfolk already done rode that pony. And that's the way it is.

COLETTE

If you would be good enough to wait here for a few moments. I shall return straightaway.
[*She heads for the Wife.*]
Oh my God! God damn him, girl! You'll never guess how that lyin', schemin', two-timin' prick has shamed me and brought dishonor to my household! How can you be married to such a lousy, cheatin' S.O.B.?

The WIFE

So, how did it go?

COLETTE

Not very well, for God's sake! That bastard has deflowered my daughter!

The WIFE

Your daughter? You've gotta be kidding!

COLETTE

I heard it with my own ears: his whole confession. He told me the whole thing: motive, means, and opportunity about how he got her into the sack. And I never suspected a thing. I don't believe this!

The WIFE

Damn it! I knew it, girl! I just had a feeling it was true!

COLETTE

You bet your ass, sweetie! You're not exactly his one and only, you know. And now he's gone and wrecked my daughter's reputation too. I'm losin' it here, hon.

The WIFE

You're losin' it? *I'm* the injured party! You gotta admit that I'm much worse off than you.

COLETTE

How do you figure?

The WIFE

I'm gonna tell you:
You know how he, like, owes me my fair share o' marital action? You know: day and night, night and day? You know how he's supposed to gimme some lovin'? Well, I barely got *half* o' what he owed me! He gave the rest to your daughter![40]

COLETTE

Jesus H. Christ, it's not like I appreciate his donation. I'm fit to be tied!

The WIFE [*preparing to lunge at him*]

I'll beat you to it! You mark my words: he's never gonna forget this for as long as he lives!

COLETTE

Not so fast. That's why I was thinkin' that we might find a better way to punish his ass like he's never been punished before.
And I just thought o' somethin' else: I'm goin' right back in there this minute and I'm gonna explain to him that he has to do penance if he wants to be pardoned for the mortal sin he just confessed to.

The WIFE

So what's it gonna be?

COLETTE

He's gonna strip naked and get down on his knees and beg you for mercy. And the two of us are each gonna have a big stick in our hands—or, at least, a couple o' really prickly branches. And then, from his head to the soles of his feet,[41] we're gonna beat the crap outta him!

The WIFE

That's the best idea I ever heard! You go, girl!

COLETTE

Damn straight! So go on and get the whips! I'll be right here.

The WIFE

You don't have to ask me twice! We'll have 'em in no time.

COLETTE
[*Returning to the Husband*]

My son, when one makes a confession to unburden one's conscience, one must patiently accept the assigned penance.

The HUSBAND

Holy moly! What the hell do you mean, *penance*? I'd really rather not, thank you very much.

COLETTE

Truth be told, you certainly deserve a really awful one. And yet, you could care less. You seem quite unconcerned by the grave error that you have committed in breaking your marriage vows.

The HUSBAND

Oh yeah? Who says so? Where's the proof? I don't even see it in the script![42]

COLETTE[43]

How the hell should I know? But, in order to receive God's forgiveness and escape the vile inferno reserved for you and all your kind, you must complete, most willingly, the task that I am about to assign you. You'll do it, won't you?

The HUSBAND

I don't know. It depends. If it's something I can do without too much trouble and if it'll get you off my back, I'll do it.

COLETTE

    Okay, so listen up:

    You gotta strip naked and ask your wife—right over there—for mercy.

    And, then, God will have mercy on your soul.

[*The Wife returns and approaches with her switches.*]

The HUSBAND

    To which I'd respond that I'd be quite pleased to decline. No, thanks.

COLETTE

    That's how it's gotta be if you want to get you your mercy and

    forgiveness.

The WIFE [*aside*]

    He'll get his, all right! We'll whup 'im from head to toe! He'll never

    know what hit him!

The HUSBAND

    What's all this?

COLETTE

    Never you mind. Nobody's talking to you.

    Now, step forward, my son. Because this is how you show your humil-

    ity when asking God's forgiveness. This is really the best way to go.

The HUSBAND

    As long as you don't trick me. I'm doing this in good faith, you know.[44]

COLETTE

    [*To the Husband*] Why, I'd *never* do a thing like that. Come on, then,

    come on over here.

    [*To the Wife*][45] Whatever happens, let's keep our voices down.

    Let's get 'im!

The WIFE
[*Beating her husband*]
   That'll teach you to screw around on me!
   You took a solemn vow, mister, to always be faithful to me!

COLETTE
[*Beating the Husband*]
   And take this too! There! That one's for shaming my daughter!

The HUSBAND
   Your *daughter*? Who the hell are you anyway?

COLETTE [*beating him*]
   In the name of the blessed Virgin, you'll know bloody well soon
   enough by the time I'm through with you!

The HUSBAND
   Jesus H. Christ! You're my neighbor, Colette! I recognize your voice!

COLETTE [*beating him*]
   Take that! And that!

The HUSBAND
   I give up already! I give up!

The WIFE
   You go, girl! Get 'im!

COLETTE [*beating him*]
   Take that! And that!

The HUSBAND
   I give up already, Colette!

The WIFE
   You go, girl! Get 'im!

COLETTE [*beating him*]
 I'm givin' it all I got!

The HUSBAND
 Yeah, I can tell. I get it, I get it.

COLETTE [*beating him*]
 You *get* it? You're gonna get it but good so you'll never forget it!

The HUSBAND
 I'm all black and blue.

COLETTE
 Serves you right for huntin' high and low and sowin' your wild oats all
 over the place and findin' my daughter and doin' your filthy business
 with her like a pig. That'll teach you!

The WIFE
 At least it wasn't all for nothin'. He got what was comin' to him. We
 whupped his ass but good!

[*Musical or choreographed interlude*][46]

The HUSBAND
 Oh unhappy man
 Thought I had a plan
 Now the joke's on me!

COLETTE
 Mind your Q's and P's!
 Mind your words and deeds!
 Got you in the end!

The WIFE
 Watch yourself, my friend!
 You cannot pretend.
 Tricksters, they get tricked.

COLETTE

    I ain't never seen—
    Ever—such a prick!
    Ain't heard news so crass.

The HUSBAND

    I know what you mean!
    Now my wounds I lick.
    Quel pain in the ass!

The WIFE[47]

    Maybe now you'll think twice next time you feel like singin' "In Spite of Jealousy." So . . . you were doin' your little girlfriend! Feel like doin' her again, do you?

COLETTE

    C'mon girl, for pity's sake: could we maybe drop that particular subject?

The WIFE [*to the Husband*]

    Next time you wanna sing your ass off,
    "standing by" your little tart
    remember that I played my part!
    Just stick it where those things belong!

COLETTE

    It's time to sing another song
    Forget about it! Zip it, please!

The HUSBAND

    The Devil take that bloody priest! That fake confessor can go straight to hell! First he goes and excommunicates me,[48] and then he beats the hell outta me with whips . . . without so much as fair warning. And I *still* don't catch on! Damn it! And I had a feeling! I could tell I was gonna get had in the end.

[*To the Audience*][49]

Alas, folks, see? I'm just a sap!
I fell into their goddamn trap!
And, in the end, look what I wrought!

So watch out openin' your trap!
Don't matter where! It's all for naught
If you're so dumb that you get caught!

Be smarter than I was, *oyéz!*
Good lords, that is my final thought.
We hope that you've enjoyed our play.

The END

4.

The Farce of the Student Who Failed His Priest Exam because He Didn't Know Who Was Buried in Grant's Tomb

Farce du Clerc qui fut refusé à estre prestre

CAST OF CHARACTERS

> MASTER PETER, the Teacher
> JOHN-BOY PRIESTLEY, the "Student" (Jenin Clerc)
> The EXAMINER
> [Blackie Grant]

PRODUCTION NOTES

The *Farce nouvelle du Clerc qui fut refusé à estre prestre pour ce qu'il ne sçavoit dire qui estoit le père des Quatre Filz Haymon, à quatre personnages* appears as #11 in Cohen, *Recueil*, 83–86. It is one of several extant medieval French plays devoted to the foolish country boy who thinks he is capable of learning. To my knowledge, this particular version, of 278 octosyllabic verses, survives in the *Recueil Cohen* only; I know of no modern French translation.[1]

Plot

To any reader who retains an unpleasant memory of an oral exam at college, I invite you to imagine the lot of the fourteenth-century student at the Sorbonne. All classes were canceled so that each and every student and professor could turn out to watch him take his master's degree in theology. That's right, *him:* no coeds yet in those days. In the crowded, noisy rue du Fouarre, he underwent the spectacular, pedagogical initiation ritual known as the quod-libet, during which anybody was permitted to ask him any question about any subject whatsoever, which is what the Latin *quodlibet* means.[2] Imagine now the plot of this play in any era: What happens if you want an education and you're dumb as dirt? Just *try* to get into the college of your choice: you'll only make a spectacle of yourself.

As is the case for #2, *Edict of Noée*, and #11, *Cooch E. Whippet*, it is ever so difficult to separate our customary categories. Plot, characters, language, sets, and staging are all organic to the play's principal, overarching joke. Here is the setup: John-Boy, a country bumpkin who is in service to Master Peter, wishes to become a priest and, unlike Master Mimin of #12, *Birdbrain*, he refuses to marry. Alas, our hick protagonist doesn't stand a chance. Predictably, he fails his entry exam (if one can call it that) because he is unable to answer the simplest question. (Apparently there are *other* questions but, in a bit that is eerily anticipatory of the knightly quiz in *Monty Python and the Holy Grail*, John-Boy cannot get past the very first question.) That question amounts to the medieval equivalent of what Groucho Marx famously asked on *You Bet Your Life* when lobbing this softball that always seemed to stump nonetheless: "Who is buried in Grant's Tomb?" Just as Groucho's contestants were often too flustered to supply the correct answer, poor John-Boy is similarly baffled. Literally, his killer question in Middle French concerns the protagonists of a celebrated epic poem (or chanson de geste): "Who is the father of the Four Aymon Boys [*les Quatre filz Haymon*]." And the answer, even if you don't know the story, is just as obvious: *Aymon*. Duh.

Still, you can't blame the poor simpleton for tripping up. *Les Quatre fils Aymon* (spelled thus in modern French) is a notoriously convoluted tale from the late twelfth century that relates, in excruciating detail, the long-standing feud between the Aymons and Charlemagne himself. Then again, one hardly needs to be a genius to divine that the father of the *Aymon* boys is *Aymon*! Needless to say, the not-so-upwardly mobile lad winds up worse off than when he started because his delusions of social grandeur also prompted him to quit his servant job. At least all the students watching the play—clearly its intended audience—would have had a good laugh at his expense![3] In a modern production, their laughter should not be too difficult to solicit in that the explication of the big joke plays out a bit like the beloved "Who's on first?" bit of Abbot and Costello. Detailed endnotes in the proper place will take readers through the joke.

Characters and Character Development

We know very little about Master Peter except for the fact that he employs John-Boy, that he loves to eat, and that he has connections to academia; he may be an academic himself. In the playtext, he is *Maistre*, which might be understood as something between "teacher" and "boss" (and in other contexts, such as that of #8, *Shit for Brains*, "lawyer").

As for John-Boy, it is he who knows very little. He is a dolt, a hillbilly, a moron, a would-be *parvenu* who is unable to *parvenir*: think of Jim Nabors as Gomer Pyle or, for that matter, any member of the cast of *Hee Haw* (if readers can remember as far back as those TV shows). He is Gracie Allen to George Burns, Dick Martin to Dan Rowan, Tommy Smothers to Dickie Smothers. I'm certain that there are many contemporary analogues with which I am too decrepit to be familiar.

The unnamed Examiner appears to be a professor of theology; at several points, both Master Peter and John-Boy refer to him as a priest—an expert in canon law perhaps?—although the lad is not the most reliable of sources. Maybe Master Peter is no expert either. The Examiner should be an intimidating figure: John-Boy's Darth Vader. Alternatively, one might imagine John Houseman's frosty contract-law professor from the 1973 film *The Paper Chase*. Clearly, however, the Examiner's professorial persona is merely a role that he plays; his asides are more colloquial, presumably addressed to an in-crowd audience of Basochiens. Think of the great and powerful Wizard of Oz, whose formidable elocution (from behind the curtain) gives way to unpretentious statements when he is *in front of* the curtain as Professor Marvel.

Finally, it is helpful to the demonstration of the joke to stage a nonspeaking character in the role of Blackie Grant, the town blacksmith.

Language

To serve the comedy, I have exaggerated John-Boy's dialect and speech patterns somewhat. His French isn't actually quite as bad as the English that I have him speaking; but this is a farce: everybody exaggerates, so why not the translator? Also, he shall utter a number of French phrases and he should mispronounce them all: *bon appétit, chardonnay, adieu,* and so on. John-Boy uses *vous*, of course, when addressing both Master Peter and the Examiner; but both those characters use *tu* when speaking to John-Boy, exactly as one would to a child, a servant, or an underling of any kind.

Sets and Staging

An especially amusing choice for performance on a college campus, this farce has as many as three sets: the home of Master Peter, the local college or university, and the road between the two, which should look as much like a medieval village as possible. Scene 3 plays better if the audience can see a blacksmith's shop and the town cemetery. For the "examining room" (*en court*), one might create any setting where an examination (potentially open to the public) might take place. In John-Boy's case, it helps the comedy that he doesn't even seem to know the difference between a medical exam room and a university examination room.[4] During the inquiry about "Grant's Tomb," the Examiner might make every effort to involve the audience in mocking John-Boy's ignorance.

Costumes and Props List

At the home of Master Peter, there should be substantial evidence of his gourmet tastes and gourmandise, plus paper for a letter with sealing wax. For the scenes with the Examiner: some academic regalia and furniture to suggest a schoolroom. I also suggest that John-Boy have an extra piece of clothing, such as his finest hat—perhaps a Fool's hat (see Introduction, § "History, Development")—which should look quite silly: he will want to look his best (and fail to) when he presents himself to the Examiner.

Scholarly References to Copyrighted Materials

"(What a) Wonderful World." By Lou Adler, Herb Alpert, and Sam Cooke. (BMI)

[Scene 1][5]

[At the home of Master Peter]

MASTER PETER *begins:*
    Hey! John-Boy!

JOHN-BOY

    Whatcha need, Master Peter?

MASTER PETER

    Set the table! Where's my chair? I need a footstool! And a cushion. Hop to it!

JOHN-BOY

    There you go! It's all right here. *Bon appétit!*[6]

MASTER PETER

    Go on then! Get the pitcher and go get the wine.

JOHN-BOY

    Comin' right up. They was sellin' some right nice *Chardonnay.*[7] Should I git ya a pitcher o' that?

MASTER PETER

    Where's my baguette? Bring it here, with some of that nice chicken paté and a little Roquefort.

JOHN-BOY

    You don't got nothin' to be howlin' about, fer sure.[8]

MASTER PETER

    I'm just going to come right out and say it, boy: I want to see you marry well. That shall be the reward for all your trouble.

JOHN-BOY

    Don't that just crack your yaller![9] A wife ain't no sure thing, if I can tell ya straight up. I was thinkin' that you was maybe gonna make me into somethin' that don't involve livin' with no woman.

MASTER PETER

    What's that now, John-Boy?

JOHN-BOY

Like one of them smart priest fellas. I'd kinda like to earn me a livin'
like that. Ya know?

MASTER PETER

[*Possibly to the Audience as well*] How do you suppose that such an
uncultured lout is ever going to make it into the priesthood?
But, I'll tell you what: if you're a very good boy, I'll write a letter for
you, requesting that you be examined. And, if it turns out that anyone
needs to knock back a few when it's all over, then the drinks are on
me![10]

[*Master Peter drafts a memo, places it in an envelope, seals it, and gives it
to John-Boy.*]

JOHN-BOY

So maybe could ya write a little somethin' on that there envelope? Otherwise, how am I a's'pposed to know wh*ooo*m to speak t*ooo*m?

MASTER PETER
[*Taking in the boy's ongoing stupidity*]

It's for the priest who's giving the exam. Go on, then, boy, Godspeed.

JOHN-BOY

Amen. I bids you *adieu*. I'm a-headin' off to that examinin' room[11] right
now!

MASTER PETER
[*Mocking the boy à la* Beverly Hillbillies]

As soon as you're done, y'all come on back now, ya hear?
[*Aside*]

He's had no schooling and, all of a sudden, *that*'s what wants to become
a priest!

[*John-Boy dons his best hat and apparel and makes his way toward the
Examiner. He may dawdle along the way, providing opportunities for
physical comedy.*]

[Scene 2]

[*At the Examiner's*]

JOHN-BOY

> Well golly! Times a-wastin'! It done took me too long to git here if I'm
> a-wantin' to git this over with today!

[*Searching for the letter*]

> What did I do with that there letter from the boss man that I'm
> a's'pposed to bring to the exam? Dagnabbit! I musta forgot it at the
> house! I gotta go on back now and git it!

[*Finding the letter*]

> Well I'll be! Nope. Don't hafta! Here it is! I done found it! It was in my
> left hand, it was!
>
> Well golly! There's some kinda priest-lookin' fella over there. I'm just
> gonna go right on up to 'im and say somethin' like: [*rehearsing so loudly
> that the Examiner hears him and responds*] "Yo! My Lord, who's this
> here letter addressed to anyhow? Can I git you to take a gander and
> give 'er a read?"

The EXAMINER [*taking the letter*]

> This letter is addressed to me. I'm going to open it right now; and then
> I'm going to read it:
> "To the Noble and Honorable Examiner:
> "To Whom it May Concern:
> "Most Esteemed Friend,
> "I am most pleased to recommend to your good graces, sir, the suppli-
> cant who stands before you; and, I pray you: should you deem his intel-
> lect to be of sufficient quality, he wishes to enter into the priesthood.
> "Leaving him in your hands, and begging you to receive my most hum-
> ble expressions of gratitude and prayers on your behalf, in the name of
> Saint Peter, I am your most faithful servant."
> And blah, blah, blah, blah. . . .
> From what I can gather, boy, you want to be a priest, then, do you?

JOHN-BOY

> Why yes sirree Bob! That's why I done come to this here examinin'
> room.

The EXAMINER

    Shall we get right down to it, then, boy? What do you know? Have you engaged in the requisite course of study?

JOHN-BOY

    You betcha! Honest to God! I'm a right good scholar, I am. I'm singin' all the time round the house: *Sanctus doodle-ee-doo* and *Kyrie Lesson.* I was always a real good student.

The EXAMINER

    Where are you from anyway, kid? Massanutten?[12]

JOHN-BOY

    Whoooeee! Massa-hootin'! How'd ya know? All my kinfolk's still there, but I ain't there no more!
    But if I could *pree-vail* upon ya, if ya please, sir, if y'all would be kind enough to take me to that there place where they's holdin' that exam today . . .

The EXAMINER

    I am endeavoring to ascertain whether you are sufficiently knowledgeable, sonny, about the matters on which I shall examine you. And if you give the correct answers, then I shall allow you to proceed to the next stage.

JOHN-BOY

    Wait'll ya git a load o' me, sir!

The EXAMINER

    I shall begin by asking you whether or not you know, from olden days, the name of the man who is buried in Grant's Tomb. Please tell me his name now.

JOHN-BOY

    Golly Moses! Ain't got no idea!

The EXAMINER

You don't know the name of that man? The man who is buried in Grant's Tomb?

JOHN-BOY

I gotta think about it. I can't just guess some kinda name I ain't never heard of!

The EXAMINER

Then you shall not become a priest. Go on back home now to your master and tell him that you possess insufficient knowledge for the priesthood.[13]
[*Aside*] This moron must be drunk or something if he thinks he can become a priest. These guys are a dime a dozen: all dressed up [*giving John-Boy the once-over*] and no place to go.[14]

JOHN-BOY

Boy, oh boy. Folks say ya cain't go home again. It's worser now than when I done left!

[Scene 3]

[*Back at Master Peter's house*]

MASTER PETER

[*Aside*] I think I see my little priest out there on his way home. Let me go catch up with him.
[*The remainder of the scene takes place outside. The two might stroll peripatetically as they converse.*]
Welcome back, Father! How did it all go?
[*Aside or to the Audience*] He's such a hillbilly, I just can't help myself!
[*To John-Boy*] So ... When are you going to be singing your first mass to your family and to mine?

JOHN-BOY

Golly gee whillikers! I dunno. I'm back just the same as when I done left.

MASTER PETER

That's what all the successful ones say.

JOHN-BOY

Golly gee whillikers! I dunno.

MASTER PETER

I don't understand what you're getting at. What happened? Surely it cannot be that you failed to pass the exam.

JOHN-BOY

Somethin' done happened, all right! He done asked me the meanest most hardest question I ever done heard in my life! I just didn't get it. He might as well've been talkin' Hebrew![15]

MASTER PETER

Did he ask what material God used to fashion the wings of Saint Michael? Or with which blue He colored the firmament?

JOHN-BOY

What he done asked me was much harder than that.

MASTER PETER

Oh . . . I see. . . . Then he must have asked you what happened to the scrolls that the Angel Gabriel was holding during the Annunciation to the Virgin Mary.

JOHN-BOY

Nope, that ain't it, and that's the God's honest truth. But you don't gotta keep on askin': I'm fixin' to tell ya, if ya like.

MASTER PETER

Go ahead, then. Proceed.

JOHN-BOY

I think he was just tryin' to trip me up! Thass what I think! He done asked me somethin' right particular: "From olden days, what is the name of the man who is buried in Grant's Tomb?"
Boy oh boy! You gotta be a real genius to git that one![16]

MASTER PETER

I can give you an example that will teach it to you in no time at all.

JOHN-BOY

How's about you go on and tell me, then.

MASTER PETER

[*As the two continue to walk, Master Peter points out the various sites and persons of his lesson, beginning with the town blacksmith.*]
You know that fellow right over there, don't you? Blackie Grant?[17] The blacksmith?[18]

JOHN-BOY

I sure do. Sure I knows him.

MASTER PETER

And doesn't his family have a tomb in their name over at the cemetery?[19]

JOHN-BOY

Who? Blackie? Oooooooh! I git it! The *Grants!* Sure they do. I seen it myself. I know 'em all. He got four boys. We's buddies.

MASTER PETER

So, come on then. If someone were to ask you the name of the father of Blackie Grant's kids—the same name that appears on the *Grants'* tomb—what would you say, dumb ass? Who's buried in the Grants' tomb?

JOHN-BOY

Oh . . . I git it now! It's Blackie the blacksmith's granddaddy, all right! I knowed him way back when, and I know all them grandkids too. . . .

[He might make a sexual gesture about the seed that sired the whole family.]

I don't think I'm gonna need no more o' them letters from ya now. Folks is just wastin' their time with you. So I'm gonna git, on accounta I got lotsa learnin' to do and I ain't fixin' to wait on ya hand and foot no more.

MASTER PETER

Well if that doesn't take the cake! Go on and do your worst, you idiot. Follow your nose.[20]

JOHN-BOY

You ain't gonna have me to kick around no more! I'm gonna be me a priest. You can count on it! And I'm gonna make a good livin' just like other folks is doin'. I don't hafta be no servant no more!

MASTER PETER

That's enough out of you! Get out of here! Don't let me catch you around here again.

[Scene 4]

[Catching back up with the Examiner]

JOHN-BOY

Lordy, lordy! I do believe that I see me that priest I done talked to just now. I'm a-goin' right over there and say howdy in the name o' God. That should butter 'im up. Got me a right good *sal-u-ta-tion*, I do: *[To the Examiner]* Yo! Monsignor! God give y'all good day! Here I am again. Lemme git right to the point: I done come back so's I can see if you'd gimme another chance at becomin' a priest.

The EXAMINER

What? You went and got your college degree since I last saw you?

JOHN-BOY

Nope, that ain't it, my lord. But I done figured out the answer to the question you done asked me.

The EXAMINER

And which one was that?

JOHN-BOY

You know. The one where you done asked me the name of the man who's buried in Grant's Tomb. I went out and I done learned it, mister!

The EXAMINER

That's right, sonny. You were unable to answer. I gave you quite the intellectual workout.

JOHN-BOY

Lordy! But I really knows it now! The name! I knows it good. 'Cause my boss done explain it to me. He told me so.

The EXAMINER

Is he dead at least?

JOHN-BOY

Nope! He's alive. He lives right on my street.

The EXAMINER

Who? Grant?

JOHN-BOY

Yup. Him too.

The EXAMINER

I believe you're mistaken, kid.

JOHN-BOY

And you're always tryin' to trick me! I knows him like the back o' my hand!

The EXAMINER
Nevertheless, I wish to ascertain whether or not you know who it is that is buried in Grant's Tomb. Tell me his name. Make it snappy.

JOHN-BOY
It's Blackie the blacksmith's granddaddy! The one who done made the church bells.

The EXAMINER
Blackie the blacksmith's. . . ?[21] How on earth could *he* be buried in Grant's Tomb? What did he do? Go off and become President of the United States—which don't exist yet, by the way? Go on. Tell me. In what universe is that possible?

JOHN-BOY
Yup! That's his granddaddy, all right! I don't right care what you say! And my four buddies ain't got no other granddaddy but him!

The EXAMINER
Your buddies are not related to . . .

JOHN-BOY
Are too! Are too! I swear to God!

The EXAMINER
Good God, son, take my advice. If you've got some money in your pocket, go and buy yourself a drink because priest material you're not. You're as dumb as a bag o' hammers.

JOHN-BOY
That's what *you* say! Quit makin' me wait and make me a priest right now!

The EXAMINER
If you've got some money in your pocket, go and buy yourself a drink because priest material you're not.

JOHN-BOY

Saints alive! They all done me wrong! I ain't got no collar and no parish and no congregation and I don't even got no job no more!

[*Changing his tone radically for a moment*]

Why, if I should merely have been capable of hazarding a guess,[22] then I dare say that I should be a priest at this very moment! What I mean is . . .

[*Back into character*]

If only I coulda just guessed who they done buried in Grant's Tomb, then I'd be me a priest right now!

[*To the Audience*]

But, as for y'all, all you students out there, take it from me:

If y'all wanna pass your exams,[23] then y'all better be able to name that fella who's buried in Grant's Tomb. Otherwise, you ain't never passin' no test.

And now, God bless y'all—all of y'all—and give y'all a good night.

The END

5.

Blind Man's Buff, or, The Farce of "The Chokester"

Farce du Goguelu

CAST OF CHARACTERS

JOHN-JOHN HORNY, the Blind Man (Jenin Cornet)
THOMASINA, his Chambermaid (Thomasse)
GOGUELU, the Valet, "The Chokester"
[A few nonspeaking extra Musicians]

PRODUCTION NOTES

The *Farce nouvelle à trois personnages* appears as #45 in Cohen, *Recueil*, 357–67. The play is 616 octosyllabic verses. To my knowledge, it appears in the *Recueil Cohen* only; I know of no modern French translation. Alternate title: *The Butt of the Joke*. (Cohen abbreviates this play as the *Farce* du *Goguelu*, which suggests that the character is indeed a type who is known by his nickname.)

Plot

If you're a starving theater company, what kind of production should you mount to please the crowd, make a buck, and vent some hostility all at the same time? How about a show in which you all appear onstage to pass the hat—or the cup—as the play itself asks *this* question: If you're a servant waiting on a curmudgeonly blind man (or an actor sucking up to a capricious patron), can you ever gain the upper hand? Sure you can, and be sure to use your hands! Take the surly old soul into the woods for a violent game of blind man's bluff and beat his sorry ass. Finally, if this is another game of "stripping and whipping" (Guilhamet, *Satire*, 8), you might even have him receive his punishment in the *buff*.

Thomasina the Chambermaid, with her boyfriend Goguelu the Valet, devise just such a ruse to get revenge on John-John Horny, who has earlier beaten Thomasina. In this instance, John-John happens to be rightly furious because Thomasina has peed into a cup and offered the potion to her master as wine. (Anybody else hear the proverbial wisdom of Judge Judy Sheindlin's dad from her book of the same title: "Don't pee on my leg and tell me it's raining"?) Ultimately, we shall see who calls whose bluff as the various offenses of this plot pile up: sexual harassment, misogyny, physical abuse, and derision of the handicapped,[1] all at the hands of the allegedly down-on-its-luck Company putting on *Blind Man's Buff*. Time and time again, there are moments when Goguelu and Thomasina seem to be going at it right under John-John's nose. Any number of risqué readings of their speeches is possible and I've even go so far as to suggest that the pair is having a quickie. Exceptionally, I've scripted the half dozen words representing the "climax" *in French* so that you can see and hear for yourself.

The two servants lure the cantankerous John-John into some horseplay, a pleasant little game that involves—what else?—bondage, beatings, and literally *sticking* it to the Blind Man as they spear his ass with a branch. Thomasina and Goguelu do not adhere strictly to the clearly stated rules of their game, changing the plan as they go along; but, obviously, John-John gets the worst of it. Their ruse calls further for a performance within a performance in which Goguelu pretends to be a policeman patrolling the woods. In that role, he accuses John-John of being a bandit lying in wait and imposes corporal punishment in the form of yet more beatings. Needless to say, Goguelu can pretend to be anything he wants right in front of a blind man.

Even with the roles of master and servants reversed, all's well that ends well. Everyone lives happily ever after as the Company comes together for the musical finale that they have been promising throughout. As Faivre concludes in another witty résumé, John-John does well to "close his eyes to a bad situation" (*Répertoire*, 198–200). Or, if I may, Thomasina and Goguelu have literally settled the score.

Characters and Character Development

In the original text, the characters are scripted as the Blind Man, the Chambermaid, and Goguelu (or, sometimes *Gauguelu, Gouguelu,* the *Valet,* the *Varlet* and so on); but I've scripted each by their proper names, all three of which appear in the text. In *Blind Man's Buff,* moreover, the Company itself is a bona fide, collective character in the play. From their opening song to their grand finale, John-John, Thomasina, and Goguelu are all three keenly aware that they are characters in a broad comedy *as well as* struggling actors who are begging for a handout, eager to perform a number or two in exchange for a financial contribution. All through the play, they transition seamlessly between those roles, especially when speaking, as *actors,* directly to the Audience.

What's in a name? The blind master is *Jenin Cornet,* which suggests the cuckold's horns (*cornes*): whence, John-John Horny. (I also thought of calling him Mr. Johnson because, in a word, he's a dick!) Gustave Cohen thought of him as a descendant of such holy blind men as Lazarus, who was miraculously cured in the Passion plays.[2] And John-John might also be channeling an illustrious predecessor who came to life in one of the earliest extant French farces: the thirteenth-century *Boy and the Blind Man,* which features (as does our script) begging, "whoring," trash-talking, and the now familiar but ever troubling physical abuse of farce in general.[3] Think of him too as a cross between the cartoon character Mr. Magoo and a variety of characters portrayed by Walter Brennan in westerns.[4] Since John-John mocks Goguelu's silly name at some length, he might potentially parody momentarily Rob Schneider's Richard Laymer from *Saturday Night Live.* (Of course, "Googue, the Googuemeister," couldn't possibly have been "makin' copies" in the Middle Ages). A final particularity of this character is that, for all his so-called handicaps, he is sure and strong enough to administer beatings so severe that the only way Goguelu and Thomasina can get him back is by tying him up. Toward the play's end, the actor playing John-John will also need to brave "shitting himself all over." He is literally "scared shitless" by his apparent run-in with the law.

Enter now one of the most beloved dramatic characters from ancient Greece onward (two of them, actually): the scheming servants, who found as hospitable a home on the medieval stage as they would later in Molière. In *Blind Man's Buff,* both are exceptionally talented thespians, especially Goguelu, and both have multiple opportunities throughout for pantomimes in which John-John is the butt of the joke.

Goguelu (pronounced \Go- gǝ- ′ loo\) suggests joy, satire, mockery, and, to my ear, his mug (*gueule,* as in the variant *Gauguelu*) and his throat (*gosier*); so I've dubbed him "The Chokester," but "Deep Throat" or "Hoarsey" would work well too. Key to this character is his skill as a master impersonator who plays so many roles that it is difficult to know who he really is. Indeed, as early as his first entrance, he is playing a role, cheering on John-John sarcastically as the latter beats Thomasina and pretending to mediate the dispute between master and chambermaid; later, he will play a policeman in the woods. Goguelu "does voices" as well, for which any number of possible parodies might enhance the comedy, such as two characters created by John Lovitz for *Saturday Night Live:* Tommy Flanagan, the pathological liar (*yeah, that's the ticket . . .*); and Master Thespian (he's *acting!*).

Thomasina (whose name appears only once in the text) is the wily chambermaid, responsible for a lot more physical comedy than some of her more civilized successors. *Note to actors and directors:* before you select this play, beware! The actress playing Thomasina will be harder to cast than you might think. She needs to pee in a cup and, later, to "take a shit" (or at least *say* that she has). Scatology aside, she reminds me of the sassy and more castable maid Florence Johnston, as created by Marla Gibbs for the long-running CBS television show *The Jeffersons* (1975–85). (I told you I was decrepit.) Thomasina's talents are not confined to acting: she is quite the director too, and the little drama of folk vengeance is *her* idea.

One ambiguity in the play concerns the extent to which Goguelu and Thomasina are already acquainted with each other. When she first calls upon him for help, for example, she says *mon amy* ("my friend"); but how far that "friendship" goes is anybody's guess. In production, one might conceivably choose to convey the dark side of a chambermaid's life. Such girls were frequently the targets of abuse and even rape not only from their masters but from their valet coworkers.[5] Farce or no farce, there is really nothing funny about a serving girl being forced, as she might be interpreted to be forced in this play, to choose between two abusers: John-John, with his physical threats and deeds, and Goguelu, with his sexual ones. In their closing number, both men want to be "back in the saddle" with Thomasina as they morph again into the two male actors who, with unbridled lust, seem to offer her up as a whore for sale.

Language

Not surprisingly, this play boasts numerous theatrically resonant verbs, especially *faindre* (to feign) and *contrefaire* (to counterfeit, act, pretend, engage in hypocrisy, and the like), along with some notably cruel moments when Thomasina asks the Blind Man to *look at* or to *see* something. Also, the beating scenes contain richly rhymed pairings of *batre* (to beat or pummel) with *esbatre* (to take [sexual] pleasure); and *lier* (to bind, tie up) with *liesse* (joy or pleasure). Sexual happiness is of a piece with physical pummeling, and the transitions between musical "beats" and physical "beatings" are just as seamless as those between actor and character. Such language, moreover, is the stock in trade of many a Passion play, where similar "fun and games" dominate the endless scourgings of Christ.[6] The beating scenes in *Blind Man's Buff* also take full advantage of the many meanings of the term *discipline,* which denotes intellectual discipline, teaching, learning, and the whip besides (from the Latin *disciplina*). The two servants really *discipline* John-John, teaching him a harsh lesson that he'll never forget (*MTOC*, 129–52).

Individual speech patterns include the following. As is customary, Thomasina uses the formal *vous* when addressing her master, whereas he uses the informal *tu* when addressing her. Goguelu and Thomasina mostly use *tu* when addressing each other, and Goguelu uses slightly better grammar when speaking with John-John than with Thomasina. When impersonating an officer, Goguelu uses *tu* to chastise John-John.

There are multiple exclamations in this play, many from the arena of food preparation; and swearing is particularly profuse, the most popular imprecation being *le corps bieu,* which refers to "God's body" but with the "proper" *bieu* substituted for the blasphemous *Dieu.* (What a relief! Glad they got that straight.) I have usually translated it as "Christ in a bucket!" And, yes: the characters really *do* say it that often. Also, the company will have ample opportunities throughout to underscore the frequently disgusting, scatological pairing of bodily waste and eating.

Sets and Staging

There are two sets: the home of John-John Horny and the woods, both the sites of extreme scatology and violence that may prove daunting to stage. A number of contemporary equivalents might help us to put the vulgar dimensions into perspective: urinalysis during doctor's visits; employee drug testing (for baseball players on steroids or others); Molière's doctors with their specimen bottles, the contents of which one such doc even goes so far as to drink (*The Flying Doctor,* sc. 4). The actress will squat down to pee into her master's cup (with the aid of special effects, we hope), which is, perhaps, the same cup that he uses for begging. Or perhaps it is the very same cup that has been passed around to the audience for contributions (of the monetary variety, we hope, *again*). But will Thomasina really "take a shit" in Scene 2 or just pretend to? Will John-John really "shit himself all over?" And, if so, since he does so toward the end of the play, will he sing the final number as it drips all over? Naturally, it would be possible to convey those moments from offstage, or to include a privy on the set near John-John's home or a nice big tree in the woods to provide some cover. The olfactory effects are a matter of choice.

Equally delicate—and far more difficult—is the matter of the two beating scenes. In Scene 1, Thomasina endures an unpalatable thrashing from John-John, as does John-John from the servants in Scene 2. In keeping with the model of the scourging scenes of the Passion plays, I suggest that these scenes of battery be choreographed in such a way as to exploit rhythm (using a metronome?), music, bandleading (wielding a conductor's *baton*?), dancing game, battle play, and even cheerleading.[7] However, there is no escaping the fact that a brutalized servant takes revenge on a brutalized handicapped person, so directorial vision is key. There is a very real way in which one could actually stage *Blind Man's Buff* as a tragicomedy or a tragedy pure and simple.

Costumes and Props List

A staff, a cane, or both for John-John; a cup or two plus a barrel (or keg) of wine; a variety of sticks, branches, broomsticks, and ropes for the final beating scene. For Thomasina, some "high-fashion" clothes and accessories, including a hat, a veil, a petticoat, a fancy dress, and so on. A number of musical instruments, preferably a lyre, should be onstage at all times (or, if you prefer, a guitar or a ukulele). Goguelu will tune and play this string instrument for the closing musical number, and Thomasina might play a tambourine or, perhaps more appropriate to the play's subject, a triangle.

Scholarly References to Copyrighted Materials (in order of appearance)

"If Ever I Would Leave You." By Alan Jay Lerner and Frederick Loewe. From *Camelot,* © 1960. (ASCAP)
"Going Up the Country." By Alan C. Wilson. (BMI)
"Nowhere to Run." By Lamont Herbert Dozier, Brian Holland, and Eddie Holland Jr. (BMI)
"You Can Leave Your Hat On." By Randall S. Newman. (ASCAP)
"Let the Good Times Roll." By Shirley M. Goodman and Leonard Lee. (ASCAP)
"Back in the Saddle Again." By Gene Autry and Ray Whitley. (ASCAP)

[*Before anyone speaks, the actors bring some musical instruments to the stage, which they begin to tune before launching into their prayer of sorts.*]

The COMPANY
Everyone sings in unison, singing the song that follows to the tune of "When Will the Good Times Return?" etc.[8]
> Ladies and Gentlemen,
> The Lord bless you and keep you.
> Give us this day our daily bucks
> And help us out.
> Give us this day our bread and wine
> And bless us with some good times
> Because we sure need 'em
> To fill our purses ... and,
> Ladies and Gentlemen ...

[*As the Company passes the hat, John-John, the Blind Man, with backup from the cast, might break into song, provided that all requisite permissions have been cleared prior to performance.*]

[Scene 1]

[*At John-John's house*]

JOHN-JOHN
[*To both the Audience and the absent Thomasina*]
> Help! Help! My lords, I swear to God, we're practically dying of hunger over here. And we've come from very far away. Why, we've barely been able to make a living lately.[9]

Groping around
> Where did my chambermaid go? Did she maybe run away? The nerve o' that girl!
> Has anybody seen her? Hello out there! Anybody? What *is* this? *Gaslight*? You wanna make me nuts? Won't anybody talk to me?
> Come on, answer me!

Okay, fine! The hell with all o' you!¹⁰

[Pause]

All right, I'll give it one last big old shout:

Somebody have a heart, would ya?

Hitting someone ["accidentally"] with his stick

Is she around here somewhere? Speak up!

Fine! All o' you can burn in hell!

Where has she got off to? That trash-talkin', soup-slurpin' little slut?

Out gallivantin' and partyin' right and left, all over the place!

Enter Thomasina

THOMASINA

Whatcha need now, Johnny-boy? What gives with all the hollerin'?

You're just givin' it all you got today, aren'tcha, with all that gobblin'?

Don'tcha know, sir, I could letcha shit yourself silly if I felt like it!

JOHN-JOHN

Is that you?

THOMASINA

Yes.

JOHN-JOHN

I swear!

I thought maybe you were lost or somethin'.

THOMASINA

Get lost yourself! Anyhow, better late than never. I always come back
to the house, don't I?

JOHN-JOHN

Come on over here now. I can never stay mad at you for very long.

[Lecherously] Can you fill 'er up? Can you fill my cup?

Get yourself over here! Come closer!

THOMASINA
You got it! I've got some nice fresh wine for you right here. Good, strong, spicy bouquet. Here, give it a try!

She pretends to pee [in the cup or glass].[11]

JOHN-JOHN
Are you pissin' into that thing? I hear that disgusting drip, drip, drip![12]

THOMASINA
That's just the drip, drip, drippin' you hear from the cask into the cup.
[*Handing him the delectable libation*]
Here, come on. Oh, for God's sake, take a little sip and you'll see what it tastes like!

JOHN-JOHN, *trying to drink*
Well . . . at least, if you could just raise the glass up just a little bit . . . please. Then I'd be able to take a drink.
Taking a sip [and spitting it out]
UGH! Damn you, you dirty slut and your filthy juice! You just pissed in there! Are you trying to poison me, you lousy little bitch?
He beats her.
Bleaaaahhhhh! It's still warm! You just oozed it outta your dirty hole! Aaaaarrrrggggghhhh! Christ in a bucket! I'm dying!
[*The beating continues.*]

THOMASINA
Help! Murder!
You're way off about this! It's on accounta it comes right outta the barrel that it's all hot like that. It's been in there for almost a week!

JOHN-JOHN
I'll give you six lashes! And then some! You lousy, dirty, stinkin', piece o' lyin' trash! That's what you are! Every last inch o' you!
Beating her
Take that! And that!

THOMASINA

Help me! Murder! You're killing me!
Please, I'm sorry. Enough now.

JOHN-JOHN

[*Continuing to beat her*]

You think you can fool me? You contemptible little whore? Bitch! Slut!
It'll be a cold day in hell before you ever break free of these hands! Boy,
are you gonna rue the day!

THOMASINA

Owwwwww! I think you broke my shoulder! Mary, Mother of God,
help! I'm gonna die!

[*Enter Goguelu, cheering him on*]

GOGUELU, *the Valet*

That's it! There you go, now! Five or six in a row! That's the way to
do it! No mercy! Get her in the arms! In the legs! She's a lousy bitch!
[*Cheerleading*] Hit 'er again harder, harder, harder!
Hey, if you'll let me get in on the game, I could go off and hang her
for you! Come on: she done you wrong! Hey, I could even play the
executioner!
You hear what I'm sayin' to you?

JOHN-JOHN

I do, I do.

THOMASINA

Help! Goguelu! Come over here and help me! I'm begging you.
If you see to my poor little body *now*, then you can see to it plenty
later! I'll make it worth your while, I promise. Honest. Helping me is
like helping yourself. And you can help yourself to whatever you like.

GOGUELU

[*To Thomasina*] Well, seein' as you put it that way... You got it! I'll
handle this with a firm... hand, God willing!

[*To John-John*] What are you gonna do to her now, you blind old bat? Cut her throat?

JOHN-JOHN

I'd never harm a hair on her head, I swear to God! So long as I live!

GOGUELU

Poor, miserable wretch that she is . . . All she ever does is wait on you hand and foot, and *this* is the thanks she gets: you beat her. Jesus H. Christ! If I have anything to say about it, she's never gonna wait on you again and she'll be *my* chambermaid from here on in, whether you like it or not!

THOMASINA

Cross my heart, you got that right! That's how it's gonna be: I give you my word.

JOHN-JOHN

[*To Goguelu, Thomasina, or both*] Please, please, enough with all the arguin' now, okay?

GOGUELU

Arguing? This is nothing!

JOHN-JOHN

Come now, my good man, let's just make this whole thing go away. Here, look: I'm imploring you most humbly. For all your trouble, I'll give you this gold crown. [*Taking out his purse*] Here you go.

GOGUELU

Most welcome, that, for sure.
All right, then, not to worry, I'll do it. I'll be your go-between. I'll go over there right now and have a private little chat with her.[13]

JOHN-JOHN

Don't be gone too long now or, I swear to God . . . if ever she would leave me . . . I think she'd die of hunger . . .[14]

[*To Goguelu*] And nuts to you,[15] by Jove! You keep your paws off her you-know-what!

GOGUELU

I said don't worry about it. I won't touch it. I'm not worthy—not even to get anywhere near it! Whatever would people say? Besides, the only say-so that matters is yours. Scout's honor.

JOHN-JOHN

Proceed, then. Please. Go to it. Go and conclude our business.

GOGUELU

It'll be done before you know it, I assure you.
[*To Thomasina for John-John to hear, perhaps indulging in sexual groping that John-John can't see*] Hey, baby, listen up, my beauty! So . . . here's the deal. . . . Well . . . it's like . . . deep down, he really and truly loves you and he . . . uh . . . most sincerely repents—yeah, that's the ticket—for ever hitting you. If you go away, he's gonna die. . . . So, ummmm, you really need to . . . yeah . . . take this into consideration. . . . If you could be just the teensiest bit less pissed off. I'm beggin' you.
[*Sotto voce to Thomasina*] Just play along with me here, babe, if you know what's good for you! You're gonna be mine—all mine—soon enough and we're gonna hop right into bed and go at it like nobody's business. And all on *his* tab! *That's* what I call gettin' down to business. And *givin' him* the business!

THOMASINA

[*Sotto voce to Goguelu*] I'll do it outta love for *you*—not outta love for him—but under one condition: If I'm stayin', then you're stayin' too.

GOGUELU

[*Sotto voce to Thomasina, with some grabbing*] It's a deal! Go on now. Go on and tell 'im that it's tit for tat: that you won't be stickin' around here unless I stay too.
[*To John-John*] Nuts! This is some job you gave me. I'm givin' it my all here.

JOHN-JOHN

Uh-huh, sure, I'll just bet you are. You're workin' for *yourself* over there, boy, and undoin' everything I've done. Workin' *her* over and workin' *me* over! What's takin' so long? What are you up to anyway?

GOGUELU

Jumpin' Jehosaphat! Are you kidding me? You're jealous? Honest, I don't even *want* to do what you're thinking.

JOHN-JOHN

Uh-huh. Sure you don't. . . . Like it would be hard for you to find plenty to do . . . here and there. But, believe you me, if I wanted you to knock her up so I'd have another mouth to feed around here . . . well . . . then I'm serving you with legal notice right here, right now: we all know who's the father! The father *and* the mother!

GOGUELU

Then you won't have a chambermaid for much longer.

JOHN-JOHN

And Jesus H. Christ! See if I care.

THOMASINA

I'd rather be burned at the stake like a pig![16] And here comes the green-eyed monster![17] Him and his rotten ugly mug can go straight to hell! I'm not pullin' any punches here: If I stay on with you, then you're hiring *him* too. Period. And *he's* gonna be staying on too, right here with me!

JOHN-JOHN

I can see that I've got no choice. Jeez Louise, you've got me over a barrel here.[18] Serves me right, I guess. You just wrap me around your little finger.
Oh well. I guess, in the good old days, I would've had me a chambermaid *and* a valet. What have I got to lose? I just can't win.[19]

THOMASINA

Good. So that's how it's gonna be! He's gonna be your servant—I win!—and I'll stay on too, as the maid. Besides, he's a good man, a real straight arrow.

JOHN-JOHN

Oh, for God's sake, fine already! I'll take him! Let's just not talk about it anymore.
[*To Goguelu*] Fine! Since my chambermaid says that, if you go, she goes too, then you'll stay, if you're willing. So tell me what you'll need for the next three years.

GOGUELU

It's gonna cost you, all right: three big ones, for starters. Plus living expenses.[20]

JOHN-JOHN

That's a living, all right. What else?

GOGUELU

Shirts and undershirts.

JOHN-JOHN

Okay, fine. What's your name anyway, sport?

GOGUELU

My name's Goguelu. They call me "The Chokester."

JOHN-JOHN

Goguelu?

GOGUELU

That's right.

JOHN-JOHN

Leapin' lizards![21]
What kind of a name is that?

All right then, what's your face, Goguelu, Gogue-*luau*, Go-Go, Gobbledey-Gook, Googue, The Googue-ster, The Googuemeister, are you a good singer?

GOGUELU

You bet I am! I don't know a cantor in Paris who's got a better voice than me. You can take that to the bank!

JOHN-JOHN

At least *that's* a good thing. [*Metacommentary alert!*] Because, in just a few minutes, we're gonna tune that lyre over there and do a right nice little number, all three of us.[22]

THOMASINA

[*In a very ladylike manner*] Why, that sounds like a perfectly marvelous plan to me. How absolutely delightful! But before we do anything else, I'll have to get all dressed up.
[*More likely, Thomasina performs various stages of* undress, *possibly as a striptease for Goguelu that, of course, John-John can't see. To John-John, it all sounds like she is modeling her outfit; but it seems that what Goguelu and Thomasina* really *have in mind is "servicing" each other with a quickie.*]
Well? How do I look? Go on, give me the whole once-over! Tell me if there's anything wrong. Is my slip showing?

GOGUELU

[*Inspecting his own lower regions too*]
Boy oh boy, you're ready to roll. Nothin' peekin' out, as far as I can tell.

JOHN-JOHN

Come on, Tommy-Girl! Step lively! Get over here! You can get yourself all dolled up later.

THOMASINA

Jesus H. Christ! When I'm good 'n' ready, you old creep. You'll wait till I'm all dressed up and ready to go!

JOHN-JOHN

Yeah, right. And who was it that got you all those latest fashions any-how? All that, so you could go around holding hands with Goguelu over there and so *I'd* be the one goin' beggin' from the likes o' him?

GOGUELU

And what of it? I'll serve you the best I can and her too, likewise.[23] But, I swear to God, there's lots more I gotta do for *her* than for you.

JOHN-JOHN

Mademoiselle over there can go to the Devil![24] Get over here and help me right now this minute!

THOMASINA

What makes you think you're more important than *me* and that he can't help *me* first?

JOHN-JOHN

Say what? Gosh drum it! You've gotta be kidding me! Whose valet is he anyway? He's at *my* service!

THOMASINA

He's at *my* service.

JOHN-JOHN

Jesus H. Christ! You lied to me! I'm the one that hired him!

THOMASINA

And what of it, my good sir? If you can say he's yours, then I can say he's mine.

JOHN-JOHN

You think so, do you?

THOMASINA

I do.

JOHN-JOHN

Good God Almighty! Get a load o' her, tryin' to make me think *she's* the lady of the house!

[*To Goguelu, possibly as the couple's interaction is heating up*] Get over here! Right now! On the double!

THOMASINA

He's not goin' anywhere!

JOHN-JOHN

Come over here right now, I say!

GOGUELU

I'm scared.

JOHN-JOHN

Who of?

GOGUELU

Of her! She'll beat me like an egg![25]

JOHN-JOHN

What the devil. . . ? If that's not the most ridiculous thing I ever heard! You're more afraid of her than me?

GOGUELU

Yes.

JOHN-JOHN

So you've had her, then.

GOGUELU

What I have is a she-devil! Look! I'm shakin' like a leaf here!

JOHN-JOHN

So let her be for a minute and come on over here.

THOMASINA

He's not going anywhere! Am I not the mistress of this house?

JOHN-JOHN

And am I not the master?

THOMASINA

I'm conceding the point; but, for the moment, no two ways about it: he's still gonna be helping me first.

JOHN-JOHN

What a pair I've got! This is some chambermaid and valet! Two peas in a pod, they are. Let 'em both go straight to hell before I lose my temper! [*To the Audience*] And now, before I get any help around here, I have to just cool my heels while the two of them finish horsin' around, if you know what I mean.

[*Goguelu and Thomasina are still attempting to finish their business. Thomasina might craftily adopt the language of modeling her hat for John-John's benefit. Meanwhile, for Goguelu, she might well be modeling only her hat. In other words, she can leave her hat on.*[26]]

THOMASINA

Goguelu, honey, tell me: how does my bonnet look?

GOGUELU

You look really good in it. It's as well made and tasteful a bonnet as I ever did see in this town.

THOMASINA

I sure can pick 'em. This one cost the boss a bundle! It's one in a million. Does it do anything for my face?

GOGUELU

Of course it does: it's *couture*![27] None o' them fancy ladies in town pull it off as good as you.

JOHN-JOHN

Yo! You, boy! What's takin' you so long? Aren't you finished by now?

GOGUELU

I'm just gettin' started. Just let me finish up over here. Gotta keep on keepin' on.

JOHN-JOHN

What the devil can she possibly need that's taking so long?

GOGUELU

Stuff. This and that.

JOHN-JOHN

Just leave her be now and get back over here!

THOMASINA

No, he's stayin' right where he is 'cause . . . that is my wish!

JOHN-JOHN

You can both drop dead!

[*The couple is likely more interested in* la petite mort *than in John-John's invocation of* malle mort]

GOGUELU

Same to you, buddy. Oh for God's sake! You can get along by yourself for once for two minutes.

THOMASINA

He's pathetic! He's just doin' it outta spite, you know. Get a load of all that grumblin'.

[*Continuing to imply the fit of her clothing to John-John while Goguelu receives another kind of physical demonstration*] Now: What do you think of this new veil? See how it wraps around my neck here, just like so?[28]

GOGUELU

    It's a real beaut, all right.

JOHN-JOHN

    Yo! Hey, Goguelu! [*Hau! hau! Gauguelu!*]

[*The "climax"*]

GOGUELU

    Yo! Oh! oh! oh! oh! oh! [*Hau! hau! hau!*]

JOHN-JOHN

    Are you done yet?

GOGUELU

    In a jiff.

JOHN-JOHN

    It's takin' you quite a while to dress up that little tramp.

THOMASINA

    You don't like it when I'm all dressed up and ready to blow, do you?[29]

JOHN-JOHN

    If I'm lyin', I'm dyin'.

[*Returning to duty, the couple gets dressed again, if necessary, and plans the next scene.*]

GOGUELU

    Can you please knock it off already and figure out somethin' else to do? Nuts to you, Mr. Magoo! You're all fired up over nothin'![30]

JOHN-JOHN

    And I know whereof I speak! Ergo why shouldn't I speak? I'd have to be outta my ever-lovin' mind to take orders from a crazy woman!

THOMASINA

[*Aside*] I swear to God! Ain't no schoolmaster ever done learn a student so good as I'm fixin' to learn you when I beat the crap outta you! An eye for an eye! I'd stake my life on it! That's some hazin' you're gonna get![31]

[*Off to the side, she and Goguelu speak softly, formalizing their plot for revenge.*] Only now . . . I got me an idea for a little game we're gonna make 'im play with me.

GOGUELU

Just name it. Tell me the name of the game.

THOMASINA

It's called Shit-Kebabs.[32]

GOGUELU

Jesus H. Christ and good golly, Miss Molly! That's a great idea! Sounds like a ball!

THOMASINA [*demonstrating*]

So here's how we're gonna stick it to 'im: him and me, we're gonna be all tied up by the hands and feet, see? Like this . . . and then each of us—him and me—we're gonna have a skewer in our hands: that's the first thing. And then—you listenin'?—you're gonna tie us up good, only my rope's gonna come undone. Not his, get it?
And then, Good God Almighty, we'll spear his ass good. And we're gonna whup 'im till his lousy goose is cooked!

GOGUELU

That's some kick-ass gag! What a riot! Except we better take 'im into the woods. Don't want no one blowin' it for us.

THOMASINA

Good idea!

GOGUELU

[*To John-John*] Come on, let's get going!

JOHN-JOHN
    Where to?

THOMASINA
    Goin' up the country.
    Ain't nothin' doin' 'round here.

JOHN-JOHN
    You said it. Okay, let's go.

GOGUELU
    Off we go!

JOHN-JOHN
    I'll be hangin' onto you for dear life. So let's be off: we'll have us a real
    good time out there. It's always so nice in the country, with the nightin-
    gales singin' and all.

Pause

[*The Company moves to the next location with some appropriate mime.
On the way, Goguelu and Thomasina begin to collect some of the
implements that they will use to torment John-John, all with a possible
musical interlude.*][33]

[Scene 2]

[*In the woods*]

THOMASINA [*to John-John*]
    You just wait here in the shade for a sec. I gotta go take a leak.

GOGUELU, *softly*
[*Taking aside Thomasina, who might then uncomfortably gesture toward
the Audience watching*]
    It's not like he can see you, you know.

Okay, so I'm gonna go and make the switches like we planned, and you can hang around here with him while I'm gone. Here are the brooms.[34]

JOHN-JOHN [*to Thomasina*]

Please don't make it a long stop, though, will you? Do you hear me, my dear? I can't get along without you.

THOMASINA

I'll be right back, honest. 'Cept now, nature calls.

JOHN-JOHN

Delighted to hear it. But don't be long now, you hear?
[*Goguelu and Thomasina continue to plot their revenge off to one side.*]

THOMASINA

So, Goguelu, here's what I need: You're gonna go and make some big ol' sticks with a nice fat paddle and you're gonna beat his ass as hard as you possibly can. And I'm gonna scream too—just as loud—like you was hittin' me too. You gotta do it that way, or else he's gonna say I'm in on it.[35]

GOGUELU

Well, looky, looky what we got for Mr. Magoo over there! And nuts to him! May I catch a disfiguring disease and marry a moron if I don't dance to your tune!
But [*gasps*] . . . I could no more whack you than I could whack myself. . . . [*begins to search for sticks elsewhere on stage*]

THOMASINA [*returning to John-John*]

So, that wasn't so long, was it? Eh? Whaddaya think o' that, sir?

JOHN-JOHN

Not that long . . . which is one heckuva shock, by the way, because you're always up to somethin'.

THOMASINA

Well, if you must know, that's what happens when you have to take a shit.

JOHN-JOHN

Let's just hope that you covered up your thingy again, you dirty girl![36]

[*Depending on how seriously Thomasina has taken her alibi, she might now take a good whiff of her "output," alluding to an odor that still lingers in the air.*]

THOMASINA

Mmmmm. This whole place smells of spices.[37]
Okay! Let's all play a little game now. Hit it![38]

JOHN-JOHN

Goguelu, where *are* you?

THOMASINA

I just saw him headin' off thataway into the woods. It's hot as hell out here, and he's off to have himself a grand ol' time.

JOHN-JOHN [*lasciviously*]

Good for him! So . . . what's this game we're gonna be playin' while he's off gallivantin' in the woods? Tell me.

THOMASINA

Heavens to Betsy, I'll make one up that you never heard of before.

JOHN-JOHN

And what game will it be? Tell me all about it, my dear.

THOMASINA

It's called Shit-Kebabs.

JOHN-JOHN

If you please, then, let's give that game a whirl. Because, bless my soul, I don't know how you play it.

THOMASINA

Oh no?

JOHN-JOHN

No.

THOMASINA

Well now, holy moly! Then I'm just gonna have to teach it to you! Okay, first, I tie you up. And then, I tie myself up. [39]

JOHN-JOHN

Well, okay . . . er . . . that sounds good, I guess . . . and I'm certainly willing to play along . . . and stay in the game. . . . But remember, I've always been good to you. No tricks now, you hear?

THOMASINA

Mary, Mother of God! Of course not! I'd only do unto others like I'm wantin' them to do unto me!

[*She starts to tie him up at the feet and may or may not get to the hands. As the action unfolds, she might make some grand gestures such that he will feel her allegedly tying herself up as well.*]

JOHN-JOHN

Ow! Ow! In the name of all that's holy! You're tyin' me up too tight! Loosen it up a little bit here, will you? Or go off and play with yourself . . . [*correcting himself*] that's *by* yourself. This is the Devil's work!

THOMASINA
[*Thwacking him accidentally on purpose*]

Oops! Will you look at that! I kicked you in the groin. I guess I just wasn't payin' no mind.

JOHN-JOHN [*doubling over in pain*]

May you burn in St. Elmo's fire! You didn't have to get me all hunched over! I'm wrapped as tight as a nun's ass! [40]

THOMASINA

[*Aside*] It's time to pay the piper! If I'm lyin', I'm dyin'.

JOHN-JOHN

This is some fine mess you've gotten me into!
Please, God, let me get out of here safe and sound!

[*Thomasina rejoins Goguelu, who is returning to the site of the game bearing sticks.*]

THOMASINA

Whatcha think, Goguelu? He's tied up right, eh? And *habeas corpus* to you too.[41]

GOGUELU

Hail Mary! We're gonna laugh so hard we'll piss our pants. I couldn't've tied him up better myself. He's not goin' anywhere! *Sacrebleu!* He's really gonna get what's comin' to him now with these here switches! He's gonna bleed all over the place if it's up to me!

THOMASINA

Go ahead, do your worst. Tan his hide—and no faking!

GOGUELU

I'll give it my all! And I'm playin' it straight! I'd never break my word to you.[42]

[*Goguelu might stand erotically behind her to demonstrate how he will help her beat John-John. Afterward, he will move to another vantage point, despite his promise of tanning John-John's hide. At some point, if Thomasina is doing a good job, he might even take a seat in the Audience to watch her work.*]

JOHN-JOHN [*either alone or* thinking *that he is alone*]

I don't think I'll last much longer in this place.
Hello? Where are you?

THOMASINA

Look, *see?* I'm right here! Did you think you'd lost me?

JOHN-JOHN

God in heaven, you bet your ass! Aren't we supposed to be playing a game? Where have you been anyway?

THOMASINA

Lookin' for wood to make our skewers.

JOHN-JOHN [*lecherously*]

Nice, bulging, fat ones, eh?

THOMASINA

Big 'n' fat as a rolling pin.[43]
[*Giving him one stick while smacking him with another*] Here. Take this one![44]

JOHN-JOHN

Hey, hey, hey! Let's get this party started,[45] by God! And no fair gettin' a head start!
Okay, get your ass ready because I'm all hot to start pokin'!

GOGUELU, *from afar*

Just wait till I get my hands on you. . . . I swear . . . if I don't beat the crap outta you during this little game of Shit-Kebabs, I might as well go take vows and join a monastery.[46] This game's gonna cost you . . . plenty.

JOHN-JOHN

Are you ready to roll?

THOMASINA

What are you talkin' about? I don't play first. You're the one that's supposed to start, you big pussy!

[*John-John begins the beating game with great exertion and likely misses the target.*]

JOHN-JOHN

Okay, then, take that!

THOMASINA

Come on, you can do better than that!
Okay, good luck. Now, start again.

JOHN-JOHN

I think we better stop.

THOMASINA

We just got started.

JOHN-JOHN

I'm tired already.

THOMASINA

Nyah, nyah, nyah, nyah, nyah! You lose, I win!
[*Thomasina pretends to see a policeman, who is really Goguelu pretending to be one.*]
Oh my God! What's that I see over there? It's a cop! How am I gonna get outta here? He looks like a mean one too, sir.

[*She might stage her fake fear in a possible musical interlude.*][47]

JOHN-JOHN

Get over here and untie me so I can get outta here too!

THOMASINA

Oooooh. There's gonna be trouble. He's got his arms full o' switches. Oh my God! Praise the Lord and all the saints: I've gotten myself untied![48]

JOHN-JOHN

I pray you, then, my dear: Would you be good enough to come over here and untie me please?

THOMASINA

What? I can't stop now! I'll get beaten silly! Gotta make like a tree and leave!

JOHN-JOHN

Oh unlucky man! Alas! Nobody knows the trouble I've seen. I better
start sayin' my prayers.

Yo! Goguelu!

THOMASINA

Goguelu's already gettin' away! And me too, right behind him as fast as
I can!

[*For her own part, Thomasina now heads to a better vantage point from
which to observe the action, possibly taking the seat that Goguelu has
vacated in the Audience.*]

JOHN-JOHN

Our Father who art in heaven, I'm a dead man, for sure.

GOGUELU

*Here he feigns a different voice to sound like the officer as he beats the crap
out of the Blind Man, saying:*[49]

Come out, come out wherever you are! I'm gonna tan your lousy hide!
Now you're *really* gonna get it! Fifty-three lashes on your butt, you
punk! A real ass-kickin'!

JOHN-JOHN

Alas, officer, I surrender. I wasn't doing anything wrong.

GOGUELU

Come out, come out wherever you are! I'm gonna tan your lousy hide!

JOHN-JOHN

Help! Help! Somebody! Help!

GOGUELU

No use yellin' and screamin'! There's nobody gonna hear you in these
here woods.

[*Goguelu delivers the alibi speech for himself and Thomasina.*][50]

Boy, oh boy . . . if I could get my hands on that chick, I'd beat *her* ass good too! Two hundred lashes for *her*! And her boyfriend too! The one I saw runnin' away with 'er just now!

JOHN-JOHN

Alas! Woe is me, officer, you're scaring me! I didn't do anything, I swear. Honest.

GOGUELU

Aha! And I'm just gettin' started! Now: let the games begin!
[*As if cuing a band*][51]
And-a-one, and-a-two, and a-one-two-three,
And-a-three, and-a-four,
And five, and six, and seven, and eight.
Come on, baby, let the good times roll![52]
Nine, ten, eleven, twelve, thirteen,
Feelin' good now? Think you're gonna come into the woods like that and rob folks blind?
Okay, one more time:
Two, four, six, eight!
Who is it we really hate?
Two, four, six eight!
Whack again now, don't be late!
Hit 'im again harder, harder, harder!
That'll teach you to lie in wait!

JOHN-JOHN
[*At some point, John-John loses control of his bowels.*]
Alas, woe is me!

GOGUELU

I've got a few more good ones in me yet! I'm just gettin' warmed up over here!

JOHN-JOHN

Woe is me! Officer, please, I've had enough now!

GOGUELU

You highway robbers—you and your lousy kind! People can't even go out walkin' in the woods no more!

JOHN-JOHN

Woe is me, officer, please, I've had enough now! I'll never come back again.

GOGUELU

You better see that you don't because if I ever catch you 'round here again, you're gonna be strung up by the . . . neck! And now, I bid you farewell.

JOHN-JOHN

That goddamn Goguelu!

GOGUELU [*still as the "officer" as Thomasina heads back from her vantage point to join them*]

What's that I just heard over there? You got somethin' else to say to me?

JOHN-JOHN

Why, no, officer, honest. I'd never!

GOGUELU

You just cursed me out, boy!

JOHN-JOHN

I'd never do a thing like that.

GOGUELU

Seems to me that, since you just got yours, your best course of action would be to shut up!

JOHN-JOHN

I'm not sayin' a thing.

GOGUELU [*aside to the Audience as Thomasina rejoins the party*]
Sacrebleu! Mr. Magoo over there is such a moron that he couldn't even tell it was me!

THOMASINA
We sure learned him good![53]

JOHN-JOHN
[*Still bound and, thus, unable to maneuver to attend to his bodily needs*]
Help me! Sweet Mary, Mother of God, I don't know what to do! I've scared myself shitless all over myself! It's drippin' out all over the place!

[*"Enter" Goguelu and Thomasina*]

THOMASINA
We'll have to take you down to the river, sir, you really reek!

JOHN-JOHN
A fine lady you are, leavin' me alone like that in my hour of need—you and that other son of a bitch, Goguelu. You can both go to the Devil!

GOGUELU
You can't really be surprised that we ran away. Holy cow! He woulda beat us to death! And that's no joke.

JOHN-JOHN
The Devil himself brought him right here to break *your* balls! But when the pair o' you saw me in mortal danger, you just ran off and left me there to get busted!

THOMASINA
Good Golly! If you keep on cursin' us out, if we hear one more word against us outta you, we've gotta mind to leave you stuck right here where you are!
You've gotta be kiddin'! *You're* threatening *us*? You think we even care about ya enough that we're gonna let ourselves get beaten within an inch of our lives for *you*? You best try singin' a different tune and start

fixin' to make it up to us. Else we ain't gonna hang around here no more.

And yet, Goguelu is [hanging around] tuning the lyre.

GOGUELU

A different tune, you say? So knock it off with all that fightin' already! As soon as the lyre's ready, how's about the three of us do a nice little number?

JOHN-JOHN

That's what I was calling you for to begin with, Goguelu! So, what's the story? Is everything ready or not?

GOGUELU

How should *I* know? Did you tune it before or not? If it's all fired up, then me too. Ready to roll!

JOHN-JOHN
[Possibly trying out his own "instrument"]

Everything seems fine to me, thank God! You now, house girl, enough horseplay! Come on over here and use your big fat blowhole for somethin' else! Try it out to the sound of the lyre when we do a new song. Hit it!

THOMASINA

It's all very well and good to say "hit it!"; but we're the ones that settled the score. Plus, you better tell us what song we're doin' first.

GOGUELU

Good point. Let's think about it for a second before we begin.

[Brief pause]

[The COMPANY] ALL TOGETHER

Listen up now, y'all. We've got something to say to all you folks out there:

[They sing their song to an original melody chosen by the production or they deliver the upcoming verses in rap. If Thomasina and Goguelu mime the events described in the song, the nonspeaking extra Musicians may now join them on stage with the appropriate instruments. Once again, they pass the hat for any spectator who failed to pony up the first time the Company asked for donations.[54]*]*

A cowboy and a gal, I say,
Were learnin' 'bout the birds and bees,
Back in the saddle, 'neath the trees.
A highfalutin girl—hooray!—
Was bouncin' up and down. You see?
And they were really makin' hay!

The filly's 'bout eighteen. *Touché*!
The cutest tits I've seen! *Oyez*!
If you're the kinda *chevalier*
who's fixin' on some choice horseplay,
then mount that saddle! Make 'er sway!
You'll have yourselves a fine ballet.
So step right up boys! Right this way!
Venez! Let's play! Step up and pay!

You wanna take 'er for a whirl?
Say, boys, this service ain't for free.
A pony ride with this here girl,
who's got herself a pedigree,
is gonna cost a little fee.
Put up or shut up! Have away!
It's virgin flesh, I guarantee!
Venez! Let's play! Step up and pay!

So pony up, boys! Make 'er bray!
This chick's a babe from head to toe.
Shout giddy-up! Hear 'er say "neigh!" [or "nay"]
Come pop your coins in, 'thar she blow!
As cowpokes reap, so shall they sow.

But just don't put that purse away.
Come dance the cowpokes' do-si-do!
Venez! Let's play! Step up and pay!

The END

6.

Playing Doctor, or, Taking the Plunge
[The Farce of the Woman Whose Neighbor Gives Her an Enema]

Farce d'une Femme à qui son Voisin baille ung clistoire

CAST OF CHARACTERS

DUMMY DOWNER (Trubert Chagrinas)
FRIGID BRIDGET, his Wife (Frigallette)
DOC DOUBLE-TALK, his Neighbor (Doublet)

PRODUCTION NOTES

The *Farce nouvelle trezbonne et fort joyeuse d'une Femme à qui son Voisin baille ung clistoire, à III parsonnages* appears as #28 in Cohen, *Recueil,* 219–26. The play is 388 octosyllabic verses and, to my knowledge, it survives only in the *Recueil Cohen;* I know of no modern French translation. Other possible titles or subtitles: *The Doctor Is In; The Medicine Man.*

Plot

It is a relatively simple matter to summarize this particular plot, as long as you are not scared by a profusion of scare quotes. Is your dumb-ass husband getting you down? Do you need some doctoring? Get your neighbor to "stick it in" and say it's an enema! Doc Double-Talk (who is more elixir-toutin' salesman/apothecary than "doctor") has the perfect remedy for Frigid Bridget, his current love interest and the wife of his neighbor, Dummy Downer. If only Doc could get her alone for a piece and out of the grasp of her jealous husband. Doc and Bridget soon agree on a scheme by which Bridget will feign illness so that Double-Talk can get her to his "office," where "the doctor is in," all right. The scheme works, at least at first. When Dummy fetches Doc for expert advice about Bridget's ersatz condition, Doc makes a house call and escorts the patient away with him, promising to cure what ails her with the best treatment he knows: he shall administer a super-duper whopper of an enema that he is more than happy to stick in. (As in #1, *Farce of the Fart*, the specter of anal sex is dredged up as one big joke.)

For all the frank sexuality, the most unusual aspect of the execution of their plan is that, once the illicit couple is "alone" for the actual doctoring—with the exception of all those theater spectators—it's pretty much all talk. Dirty talk, plus whatever goes along with it, but no sex. Doc and Bridget do not actually (re)consummate their relationship. They do not "take the plunge." (This may have something to do with our practitioner's seemingly customary practice of treating his patients out in the open air at the same spot where he hawks his pharmaceutical wares. Apparently, there's a thing or two that even a farce won't stage.) Instead, Doc and Bridget make a plan to meet up again shortly, and secretly, at another location, the better, of course, to protect Bridget's impeccable reputation. (What *is* this? The medieval equivalent of getting a motel?) But Dummy overhears the lusty pair, so when Bridget returns home, he beats her as well as Double-Talk, who tries to come to the rescue. And they all live (un)happily ever after.

Characters and Character Development

Prepare to make the acquaintance of the quintessential geezer of a hubby who can no longer "perform." He is a real dummy who is a bit depressed by his lot in life, and he has a surname to match: he goes by *Chagrinas* (from *chagrin*), meaning grief or sadness. So I have dubbed him Dummy Downer. His first name, Trubert, who is a character from a comic fabliau, comes into the language as a synonym for "nobody's fool"—in this case, *everybody's* fool.[1]

Dummy's wife has a revealing name too. She is Frigallette, an intriguing etymological admixture that is evocative of frigidity (*frigide*), erotic tastiness (*friandise*), cookery or frying (*frire*), and even the yummy *galette* (she's a real cookie, all right). Needless to say, she reserves some properties for her husband and others for her lover (or is that *lovers*?). Interestingly enough, the *frire* of frying also comes to be used in expressions devoted to "having nothing left to eat in the house" as Bridget goes out of the frying pan and into the fire. More grotesquely pertinent still: *frire* connotes "buttering or greasing things up." Dare I remind you, dear Reader, of the infamous scene from *Last Tango in Paris*?

Although the playtext refers to our third character as a doctor (*médecin*), Double-Talk's profession would be more closely aligned today with that of the pharmacist or, for Faivre, of the "sexologist" (*Répertoire*, 142). Two words help to convey the essence of his character to modern actors and audiences: snake oil. Plus this apothecary has another suggestive name: *Doublet* denotes a double-talker, a doubler (of prices?), an impostor, a simulator, a stand-in, and so on. Other possible names for this character: "Doctor Impostor" or "R. Satz" (*ersatz*).

Language

In addition to its medically inspired wordplay, this is the only play of our entire collection in which all characters use the courteous *vous* form throughout. That's right, all the suggestive dialogue is so terribly polite. That is even the case when Bridget and Dummy are parrying their insults back and forth. Nice to know that there are no hard feelings.

A number of Dummy's insults to Bridget play on the proverbial "women's work," such as *que fillés vostre quelongne*! Literally, this means "go do your spinning"; metaphorically, it's "mind your own business"; and contextually, it's *Go spin yourself!* which should be clear enough.

Elsewhere, some of the business at hand strikes at least this reader—*moi*—as ambiguous. Perhaps I've lived in the universe of farce for far too long but, throughout Scene 1, there is, shall we say, a running ambiguity as to the kind of "business" in which Dummy is engaged as he calls repeatedly for his wife. Yes, he's a cobbler, so it makes sense that he might be working with leather on a mount. But, when it comes to the phrase *il veult ouvrer à sa selle*, I see him "mounted" elsewhere, answering nature's call; and there is evidence in other farces in this very collection that such intestinal purges were not off limits. Consider that, to this day, *aller à la selle*—literally, to "go to the saddle" (with lovely echoes of our #5, *Blind Man's Buff*)—means "to move one's bowels" and that the *seel* in #8, *Shit for Brains* is the bucket in which the master of the house "takes a dump." So what does Bridget understand when Dummy asks for his *sellete,* his little stool? In my humble opinion, Bridget may suffer some confusion as to whether he is requesting his stool for setting up shop or his chamber pot so that he may "open up" for a very different *stool.* Lest the Reader fear that I have lost my mind, I hasten to emphasize that Pierre

Pathelin famously requests a "clarification of his shit" (sc. 5) and that *Playing Doctor* is, after all, a play about the curative and purgative power of an *enema!* The ultimate catharsis.

Sets and Staging

Playing Doctor calls for these sets: the house of Dummy and Bridget, the very nearby marketplace, and the house of Doc Double-Talk, with repeated movement between those sites. The farce offers multiple possibilities for pantomime, especially during Scene 3, in which Bridget and Doc hatch their plan: Dummy later complains that it takes about an hour. For the delicious Scene 5, in which dumb Dummy spies on his wife's not-so-secret assignation, Molière's *Tartuffe* comes to mind. Remember how Orgon seems to wait *forever* under that table as he listens for more and more . . . and still *more* evidence that Tartuffe is trying to seduce his wife, Elmire (act iv, scs. 5 and 6)? Same problem here. Dummy waits overly long for the evidence that should be smacking him right in the face.

Otherwise, there are two principal challenges posed by staging *Playing Doctor*. A first difficulty lies in ascertaining exactly where Dummy and Bridget are at various moments, beginning with the opening scene in which Dummy wants her in at least two places at once. The couple appears to be at home, with Dummy preparing to head to market to set up shop; Doc Double-Talk is close by, already hawking his pharmaceutical wares from a spot that is within earshot of their argument. Doc must then draw closer to eavesdrop on his neighbors. Part of the humor lies in Dummy's demands that Bridget attend to his needs simultaneously at the privy (if you believe me), at the market, and in their house (cooking, cleaning, spinning). For a good gag, one might stage the two outside their home, with Bridget setting off to market with Dummy, following him out the door, trailing along behind him, and even carrying all his stuff for him,[2] including some dishes for a meal or a *casse-croûte* where bread won't be the only thing broken (*casser*). Or Dummy could be making his ridiculous ruckus about Bridget accompanying him to a spot that is merely a few feet from the house (near Doc's spot). Or Bridget and Dummy might be staged *already* at the marketplace, but close enough to their home for Dummy to be ordering her to attend to her household tasks by rushing back and forth between the two locations. Given the cues in the dialogue, I have staged the couple traveling that very short distance between home and marketplace.

A second difficulty is the play's closing violence, in which Dummy beats Bridget repeatedly before turning on Doc Double-Talk. Such moments do not translate well across time, nor should they, if I may say. Indeed, it is unclear how the relentless mockery of the very real problem of domestic violence would have translated even in its own time. For the seventeen verses in question, in which several bona fide refrains occur, I suggest that the beatings be choreographed as a kind of violent ballet. As previously noted in the context of #5, *Blind Man's Buff,* scholarly work on the mystery plays has long established that the scourging of Christ was a veritable dancing game.[3] Since, in one of his closing lines, Dummy basically tells Doc to shove a stick up his ass (another enema?), Dummy could also wield that stick as a conductor's baton.[4] Physician heal thyself? The yucky question is: Does he do it? Shove the stick up Doc's ass, that is? And, afterward, does he use the same implement on Bridget? I know that sounds disgusting but, again, this *is* a play about an enema.

Costumes and Props List

In the home of Dummy and Bridget: a massive pile of tools of the cobbler's trade; a few sticks of furniture, among them a stool, a chamber pot or two, a set of dishes, some materials for both knitting and spinning, and a staff for the final scene. For Doc Double-Talk: a pharmacological bag of tricks that includes some bottles of alcohol of various sizes, among these brandy and perhaps cognac: we're looking for impressively high *proof,* as in alcoholic content.

Scholarly References to Copyrighted Materials (in order of appearance)

"All That You Dream." By Paul Barrere and William H. Payne. (ASCAP)

"Bad Case of Lovin' You" ["Doctor, Doctor"]. By John Moon Martin. (BMI)

"Smooth Operator." By Helen Folasade Adu, Paul Anthony Cook, Andrew Ralph Potterton, and Raymond William St. John. (ASCAP)

"Hard to Handle." By Alvertis Isbell, Allen Alvoid Jones Jr., and Otis Redding. (BMI)

"Hot Blooded." By Louis A. (Andrew) Grammatico and Michael Leslie Jones. (ASCAP)

"I'm Called Little Buttercup." By William Schwenck Gilbert, Cameron Nicholas Patrick, and Sir Arthur Seymour Sullivan. From *H.M.S. Pinafore* (1878). (BMI)

"Handy Man." By Otis Blackwell, Jimmy Jones, Charles Merenstein, and Un-art Music Corporation. (BMI)

"Come and Get It." By Paul James McCartney. (ASCAP)

"Adelaide's Lament." By Frank Loesser. From *Guys and Dolls*, © 1950. (ASCAP)

"Night and Day." By Cole Porter. (ASCAP)

"Let the Good Times Roll." By Shirley M. Goodman and Leonard Lee. (ASCAP)

"I Think We're Alone Now." By Ritchie Cordell. (BMI)

[The play might include an opening mime by Dummy, showing that life has got him "down."][5]

[Scene 1]

[At the marketplace near the home of Dummy and Bridget]

[Enter Doc Double-Talk, possibly to some opening music][6]

DOC DOUBLE-TALK, *a doctor, begins:*

[Hawking his wares]

Life-sustainin' elixirs o' life right over here that keep everything a' sproutin'![7] Juices that'll keep you goin'! Keep you safe from any malady on earth! I got it all right here!

Life-sustainin' elixirs o' life right over here that keep everything a' sproutin'! Step right up folks! Looky, looky here! Don't be shy! Hurry up now, while supplies last!

Life-sustainin' elixirs o' life right over here that keep everything a' sproutin'! Juices that'll keep you goin'!

[Settling on his spot very near the home of Dummy and Bridget]

This looks to me like a good spot right over here to set up shop and tout my wares. *[Setting up his table]* Table goes right here, like so; I'll stand right over here like so. Maybe see if I can get a nibble from some sucker walkin' by.

Step right up folks! Step right up! I got everything you need.

Is your hair fallin' out? You got kidney disease? I got your cure right here, fresh outta the woods.

You a guy who's madly in love? Got a little bit o' gentian violet gonna stop you dead in your tracks. Alls it takes is three days—guaranteed— and you'll go from lovesick sap to jealous fool in a flash! Fix up all that sentimental stuff in no time!

And I got me an ointment right here! A real special lot it is, got magic powers to boot! Gonna make any woman *always* tell her husband when she's makin' a cuckold outta him! And the exact time too: just like you had a fortune-teller right there inside your own home!

And right over here, take a gander at this here potion I got, made o' wine gonna make you look ten years younger!

Step right up folks! Seek and ye shall find! Have a good look! I'm at your service.

[Scene 2]

[*At—or near—the home of Dummy and Bridget*]

[*Dummy prepares to head to the nearby market—a matter of mere steps away—as Doc Double-Talk listens in.*][8]

DUMMY DOWNER
    Bridget! Are you there?

FRIGID BRIDGET
    Yeah, yeah, I'll be right with you, Dummy.

DUMMY DOWNER
    Are you coming already?

FRIGID BRIDGET
    Christ! I said I was coming!

DUMMY DOWNER
    Bridget! Are you there? Bring me over the . . .

FRIGID BRIDGET
    What?

DUMMY DOWNER
    I need my little stool: I've gotta go open up![9] Bridget! Are you there?

FRIGID BRIDGET
    Yeah, yeah. I'll be right with you, Dummy!

DOC DOUBLE-TALK [*aside*]
    What's this I hear?
    My neighbor over there talks a good game at the market but, I swear
    to God! Christ in a bucket! He sure does treat his wife badly.[10] I can't
    believe anyone coulda married her off to such a louse! Orderin' her
    around like that! Not givin' her any TLC. It's enough to make you shit
    a brick! Or lose your cookies! Or at least get a cough.[11]

DUMMY DOWNER
    Bridget, are you coming already?

FRIGID BRIDGET
    Here I am, Dummy, what do you need?

DUMMY DOWNER
    Didn't you hear me yelling for you?

FRIGID BRIDGET
    So? What was all the yelling about?

DUMMY DOWNER
    Put a lid on it, woman! I wish to have you here, by my side, as needed,
    whenever I'm doing my business![12] You can bring your knitting if you
    want, but there's work to do around here! If you want to make batter,
    you've gotta beat some eggs.[13]

[*Dummy finishes his first order of "business"; the couple prepares to head
to market.*]

FRIGID BRIDGET
[*Possibly wiping his ass or dealing with her husband's "output"
in another way*]
> Is this the wedded bliss you promised me, Dummy?
> You're always tellin' all my friends about how you're gonna do right
> by me. So far, I haven't noticed a thing. Same old, same old ... every
> morning when I wake up, and when I lay me down to sleep.

DOC DOUBLE-TALK
[*Aside or to the Audience*]
> Holy moly! You can say that again! And, speak of the devil ... I hear
> the poor little hussy right now. She's a newlywed, and that's the cause of
> all the trouble. *She* wants her little bottom attended to, *as needed;* and
> all that gets *him* off is business!
> He's hangin' by a thread over there, and he's this close to losin' it all.

DUMMY DOWNER
> Let me get right to the point, Bridget: there is no rest for the wicked.
> So, if you please, *do something*! Are you gonna do something or not?

FRIGID BRIDGET
> What am I supposed to do?

DUMMY DOWNER
> Think of something!

FRIGID BRIDGET
> Like what?

DUMMY DOWNER
> Like the housework. Go and do the dishes.

FRIGID BRIDGET
> They look fine to me.

DUMMY DOWNER
> Then go and clean your house!

FRIGID BRIDGET
It's not the season.

DUMMY DOWNER
Go on! Roll up your sleeves! Time to get those hands dirty.

[*Bridget inspects her unclean hands, especially if she assisted with a certain business.*]

FRIGID BRIDGET
Just calm down. What's the hurry?

DUMMY DOWNER
Go put the kettle on!

FRIGID BRIDGET
Don't worry about it. I'll get to it.

DUMMY DOWNER
Then hop to it and go make your bed!

FRIGID BRIDGET
You're some taskmaster, all right.

DUMMY DOWNER
I submit to you, madam, that you should already have been finished by now.

FRIGID BRIDGET
And I submit to you, Downer, that you turn your attention to other things.

DUMMY DOWNER
Like what?

FRIGID BRIDGET
Christ, such dicking around![14]

DUMMY DOWNER

Am I not doin' right by you?

FRIGID BRIDGET

I know exactly how you're doin' and *not* doin' by me; that's the whole trouble. And I have every right to complain.

DUMMY DOWNER

So just do unto me what I tell you, and things will be a lot more peaceful around here.

FRIGID BRIDGET

So how come you don't do unto *me* when nature calls same as you expect *me* to practically shit myself helping to do unto *you*? You can't just wipe the slate clean you know!

DOC DOUBLE-TALK [*aside*]

Well butter my butt and call me a biscuit! What a racket over there! If I could just get you alone—maybe borrow a little love nest from one of my cousins—then *I'd* help you out, all right, neighbor lady, and *really* do unto you. You can count on it.

DUMMY DOWNER
[*Having worked up an appetite, his business accomplished*]

Bridget, get dinner on the table right now this instant! I'm gettin' good and tired o' starvin' around here. And you better not make me ask you twice! Go get it!

[*Bridget heads home, cursing out Dummy and goes inside.*]

FRIGID BRIDGET [*aside*]

You're the one that's gonna get it, all right. Whoever put us two together so I could put up with all this crap . . . May his balls dry up like raisins![15] All that jack-off ever does is harp on me all week long. Talk about givin' me the business! He can't do a single thing for himself. But one of these days, he'll be sorry!

[Scene 3]

[At the home of Dummy and Bridget]

[Doc Double-Talk approaches the house and intercepts Bridget on her way home.][16]

DOC DOUBLE-TALK

God give you good day, neighbor dear. How's it goin'? Havin' a grand ol' time with Downer over there?

FRIGID BRIDGET

God willing, he'd be six feet under.[17]

DOC DOUBLE-TALK

Why heavens to Betsy! I'm so sorry to hear that! What's up? What ails you?

FRIGID BRIDGET

Anyone can see plain enough that Downer's gettin' me down.

DOC DOUBLE-TALK

Not to worry! He's just breakin' you in as a wife. Golly Moses, you'll just have to put it up with it!

FRIGID BRIDGET

Put up with it? I'd rather he die a bloody death!

DOC DOUBLE-TALK

Well, you do have a point there. Frankly, I overheard the whole argument and I still can't believe my ears! All that bellyachin'! And that whole list of grievances as long as the day is . . . well . . . long.[18] I don't know how you put up with it.

FRIGID BRIDGET

And do you think, good neighbor Double-Talk, that he ever wants to show me a good time? Not a chance. All I do, day in, day out, is work, work, work. Pain and suffering, suffering and pain.

DOC DOUBLE-TALK

If you're game for takin' my advice, then, believe you me, we can conduct a little business of our own on the side. I'll do unto you and you'll do unto me.

FRIGID BRIDGET

What a guy!

DOC DOUBLE-TALK

You got that right, girl! Listen: let Downer get everybody else down, and you just concentrate on makin' hay while the sun shines. Come on, baby, let the good times roll.[19]

FRIGID BRIDGET

Now you're talkin', I swear!

DOC DOUBLE-TALK

Frogs and snails and puppy dogs' tails, that's what little boys are made of.[20] If you want it, here it is, come and get it[21] while you're young.

FRIGID BRIDGET

I'll be goddamned if I'll do without![22]

DOC DOUBLE-TALK

If you'll just put yourself in my hands, then—I swear!—I'm yours for the taking: at your service, night and day, day in, day out.[23]

FRIGID BRIDGET

You sure do have a way of puttin' things. Nice o' you to lend a hand.

DOC DOUBLE-TALK

So you know what you're gonna do when you get back to your house? If he starts in on you again, you just flat out turn your back on him. Bottom line? You're gonna tell him that you're at death's door and that, if someone don't see to you right quick, then you're gonna drop dead. It's a . . . sudden-onset disease that strikes a poor young woman so hard that she falls over prostate—that's *prostrate*—and passes out! She faints . . . once an hour—why, twenty-two times a day![24] That is, unless somebody makes a "house call," if you catch my drift.

FRIGID BRIDGET

 My hubby's gonna be pretty embarrassed by all those details. But not as much as he's gonna be when we take . . . appropriate measures!

DOC DOUBLE-TALK

 I'm gonna tell him that it's a dangerous bug that's goin' around. And that he'd better step up to the plate and send you over to my place, where I can give you the treatment that you need—and need but good! And then, according to our dastardly plan, not only are we gonna make a damn pimp out of him, we're gonna get fringe benefits and have a grand ol' time while we're doin' it!

FRIGID BRIDGET

 Okay, I get it. Enough said. I see what you're up to. But pity the fool who breaks his promise to me. May he break out in hives!
 Later, neighbor, I'm off now.

DOC DOUBLE-TALK

 Later, neighbor, dear. But don't you forget me, now! [*He might make an obscene gesture.*] I'm all yours.

FRIGID BRIDGET

 So I see.

DOC DOUBLE-TALK

 We're gonna give it to him but good.

FRIGID BRIDGET

 You got that right!

DOC DOUBLE-TALK

 Straight up.

FRIGID BRIDGET

 I'll just bet it is.

DOC DOUBLE-TALK

I'll fuck the living daylights outta you. It'll be a world record![25] How's about a little kiss to tide me over?

FRIGID BRIDGET

You can bet your ass—or *my* ass—that he's not gettin' any sugar outta me.

DOC DOUBLE-TALK

Who's talkin' about sugar? He wants his dinner? I'm talkin' about cooking his goose![26] If you want, we can use this scheme o' mine to give him a taste of his own medicine.

FRIGID BRIDGET

Later, neighbor, I'm just gettin' warmed up here! I better step on it so I can get to work on his appetizer. Don't you worry 'bout a thing. Since I've put my mind to it, he's gonna get the business all right!

[*Bridget rehearses in mime the imaginary scene that she will soon describe to Dummy: i.e., that she passed out in the middle of the street.*]

[*Exit Doc Double-Talk but not too far: he remains close enough to eavesdrop.*]

[Scene 4]

[*At—and near—the marketplace near the home of Dummy and Bridget*]

[*After her mimed performance, Bridget sneaks over to stage her "return" home after the traumatic nonevent. She makes very sure that Dummy will see her as she struggles exaggeratedly on her way home.*]

DUMMY DOWNER
[*Aside, still at the marketplace*]

Hmmmm ... Come to think of it, Bridget's been gone for well over an hour and there's no sign of her. Oh, the happy man who's got a wife who never contradicts him!

["Reenter" Bridget in an apparent daze, struggling histrionically as she walks right by Dummy]

FRIGID BRIDGET

Here I am, Dummy! Sweet Jesus! I almost didn't make it!
I swear to God, I've been in quite a state. In fact, I woulda passed out flat on my face if it hadn'ta been for our good neighbor rushin' up to help me. All outta the kindness of his heart! I woulda been out cold right there in the middle of the street, splayed all over for all to see!

DUMMY DOWNER

I don't think people die from that sort of thing. It's more like: any excuse'll do to strut your stuff. It's just a play for attention.

FRIGID BRIDGET

You should talk. You and your sorry ass.

DUMMY DOWNER

Give me a break, will you? It'll pass.

FRIGID BRIDGET
[Pretending to gasp for air]

Help me, Holy Mother Mary, Mary Magdalene, and all the saints! It's happening again! I'm dying! I can't breathe! It's the sickness again!

DUMMY DOWNER

Is this for real?

FRIGID BRIDGET

For real? Alas, Dummy, it's plain and simple that you don't love me even just one little bit! If you can just stand there and watch me dying and not come to my aid in my hour of need and still gimme the business . . .
If you don't want to help me, then at least call me a doctor![27]

DUMMY DOWNER

I'll go give our neighbor a shout.

FRIGID BRIDGET
    Go do it before I drop dead!

[*Exit Dummy to find Doc Double-Talk, who should be unusually close by.*]

DUMMY DOWNER
    Alas, good neighbor, come quick! Help me or I'm a dead man!

DOC DOUBLE-TALK
    What's the trouble?

DUMMY DOWNER
    It's my wife. She's got it into her head that she's gonna die if someone
    doesn't come right away and help her out. She told me that the pain's so
    horrible and so sudden that she's at Death's door.
    In the name of God, I'm begging you, neighbor, please! Come and at-
    tend to her, would you?

DOC DOUBLE-TALK
    Why, certainly. I'm more than happy to come and help out. It's the least
    I can do.

DUMMY DOWNER
    Then, for God's sake, let's get a move on!

DOC DOUBLE-TALK
    We better hurry!

DUMMY DOWNER
        After you.

[*A pantomime might ensue in which they "hasten slowly."*[28] *Each man
attempts to let the other pass first—"After you, my dear Alphonse"—after
which Dummy and Doc Double-Talk reenter Dummy's home.*]

DOC DOUBLE-TALK
    So ... How now, my dear neighbor? How are we feeling today?

FRIGID BRIDGET
    Leave me alone.

DOC DOUBLE-TALK
    Benedicite! May our blessed Lord, Jesus Christ, be with you.
    Let me just feel her . . . pulse. She's very seriously ill.

DUMMY DOWNER
    What's she got?

DOC DOUBLE-TALK
    Her veins are poundin' all over the place!

DUMMY DOWNER
    What a world we live in! This is a catastrophe!

[*Bridget continues to display her dramatic symptoms as the two men converse and, sometimes, ignore her completely!*]

DOC DOUBLE-TALK
    This illness is stress-induced. It comes from getting angry.

DUMMY DOWNER
    Oh no! What are you telling me here, neighbor?

DOC DOUBLE-TALK
    It's a real killer, this illness. Well, in layman's terms . . . the nature of this
    dread disease is such that . . . an abundance of superfluids builds up in
    all her extremities, such that she faints and loses consciousness, almost
    like she was in a coma.
    Now: if she wants to alleviate her condition, she's gonna have to use a
    special compound for an entire year. She's gonna have to use some *Echinacea* compounded with—are you familiar with Gotu Kola powder?[29]

DUMMY DOWNER
    Oh my God, neighbor! Coca-Cola? What kind of disease is this
    anyway?

DOC DOUBLE-TALK

I swear upon the soul of my good professor who taught me everything
I know! In short, that's the reason she's dying. If you want to keep her
in good health, then she'd better come along with me right now 'cause I
got somethin' to give her. I'll administer a particular type of enema that
we call The Expunger.[30]

DUMMY DOWNER

Woe is me, good neighbor, I'm sure you mean well but, I swear on my
mother's life that I don't think she'll be able to take the plunge!

FRIGID BRIDGET

Alas, Mary, Mother of God! How long are you gonna leave me here like
this? My heart's gonna give out!

DUMMY DOWNER

Hang in there, Bridget, help's on the way. You're gonna have to get up
now, sweetheart, and then you're gonna take this medicine that our
good neighbor wants to give you.

FRIGID BRIDGET

So hurry up and get me outta here already or I'm gonna drop dead right
on the spot!

DOC DOUBLE-TALK

All right, then, by God, let's go! I'm hoping for a full recovery. Gonna
purge her of what ails her!
Farewell, neighbor, next time you see her, she'll be good as new.

DUMMY DOWNER

For pity's sake, neighbor, I pray you, do all you can for her.

DOC DOUBLE-TALK

I'll give it everything I've got. No more and no less than if she were my
own wife. Farewell!

DUMMY DOWNER
Farewell!

[*Double-Talk and Bridget leave Dummy's home. The two might perform a possible musical interlude to celebrate their exit.*][31]

[Scene 5]

[*Two interiors: Dummy's house and Doc's house with movement between the two*]

[*Bridget and Doc leave Dummy's house and make the "Doctor's appointment." The illicit couple then proceeds to Doc's place, both railing against Dummy as soon as Dummy is out of earshot. Part of the comedy involves a great to-do about leaving separately for a destination that is only a few steps away.*] [32]

DOC DOUBLE-TALK [*expressing his exasperation with Dummy*]
    Go on, pal, suck on it! Mary, Mother of God! What a schmuck!

FRIGID BRIDGET [*also railing against her absent Husband*]
    I swear, Downer, I can get what's comin' to me all by myself![33]
    [*To Doc*] Listen, it's better if we leave separately.

DOC DOUBLE-TALK
    Not to worry, Bridget, we'll figure out a disguise. And we're gonna
    make one joyful noise. It's party time![34]

[*Doc and Bridget go inside Doc's place.*]

FRIGID BRIDGET
    Cross my heart, sounds good to me, babe.

DOC DOUBLE-TALK
    My little honey bun.

FRIGID BRIDGET
    My Prince Charming.

DOC DOUBLE-TALK
My little darling, my cutie-pie.

FRIGID BRIDGET
My little golden boy.

DOC DOUBLE-TALK
My sweetheart. My little chickadee.

FRIGID BRIDGET
My little devil.

DOC DOUBLE-TALK
My love!

FRIGID BRIDGET
My little boy toy!

DOC DOUBLE-TALK
So, let's have us some fun! Let the games begin! Let the good times roll![35]

DUMMY DOWNER [*home alone*]
Talk about your cuckolded saps! Chump, chumpier, chumpiest! A pushover pussed . . . that's *pushed* over! And a real fool . . . foolishly fooled! What the heck was I thinkin' anyhow? I shoulda gotten my sorry ass over there with my wife in tow.[36]
If my neighbor's over there playin' hide the sausage,[37] then he's really got me by the balls.[38] Anyhow, if they're playin' doctor, then I'd better hop to it right now and go listen at the door. Suspicion, heal thyself! That's how this little game is played. Besides, it says so in the script! Then I'll know what they're up to.[39]

[*Dummy approaches the couple and may begin spying any time, through the keyhole, for instance, or through a window.*]

DOC DOUBLE-TALK
And now, I pray you, dear lady, let's get down to business.

FRIGID BRIDGET
    Please, after you.

DOC DOUBLE-TALK
    How are you feeling, my dear?

FRIGID BRIDGET
    How do you want me to feel, my dear? It's just that . . . when I think
    that my husband could come over here any minute and catch us in the
    act . . . I wouldn't be able to get out of it. I'd be a dishonored woman.

DOC DOUBLE-TALK
    Here's how you're gonna get out of it.
    As God is my witness, on Monday, when you head out of town on the
    main road by the hills, there's a little room at an inn along the way. In the
    name of Saint Martin, maker of miracles, no one will ever find you out
    there, so you won't have to worry about somebody or other seeing you.[40]

FRIGID BRIDGET
    Well I'll be! You got it. I'll take the high road.

DUMMY DOWNER [listening in]
    Will you listen to that, Dummy Downer! Jesus H. Christ! Is this what
    she's been servin' up all along?
    I'd rather die—die!—than not get my revenge before this day is
    through!

DOC DOUBLE-TALK
[Seeking to shake Bridget's hand]
    Put her there!

FRIGID BRIDGET
    You're on! But, hey! Your palms are all sweaty! You got it: Monday
    without fail.

DOC DOUBLE-TALK
    That's my plan: thought it up all by myself, I did. And, that way, we can
    really get down to business.

DUMMY DOWNER [*aside*]

Down to business, my ass! You're both gonna get the business, all right!
We'll see who gets played![41]

DOC DOUBLE-TALK

Don't you stand me up now.

FRIGID BRIDGET

Perish the thought! I'll be there, come hell or high water!

[*Bridget heads back home.*]

[Scene 6]

[*At the home of Dummy and Bridget*]

[*Enter Bridget*]

DUMMY DOWNER

Back already, are you, my fine lady? God damn it, now you're really
gonna get what's comin' to you!

FRIGID BRIDGET

That's some nice welcome! Are you ever gonna stop bitching?

DUMMY DOWNER[42]

So . . . how's that disease o' yours? Feeling better now? Treatment hit
the spot, did it? I've got the cure for what ails you! Time to take your
medicine!
[*Here, the violent "ballet" begins as Dummy begins to beat Bridget.*]
How now my dear? All better now?

FRIGID BRIDGET

I'm all fixed up![43] Why, glory be!

DUMMY DOWNER, *hitting her*
>I've got your cure here! One-two-three!
>And here it comes: watch out, ker-pow!

FRIGID BRIDGET
>Help! Murder! Ow! You're hurting me!

DUMMY DOWNER [*still hitting her*]
>I've got your cure here! One-two-three!

FRIGID BRIDGET
>Help! Murder!

DUMMY DOWNER
>I'll scream too! You see?
>How now, my dear, feel better now?

FRIGID BRIDGET
>I'm all fixed up! Why, glory be!

DUMMY DOWNER, *hitting her*
>I've got your cure here! One-two-three!
>And here it comes: watch out, ker-pow!

FRIGID BRIDGET
>You rotten louse! You're hurting me!

DUMMY DOWNER [*still hitting her*]
>I've got your cure here! One-two-three!

FRIGID BRIDGET
>Help! Murder!

DUMMY DOWNER, *hitting her*
>I'll scream too! You see?

FRIGID BRIDGET
>You're killing me! Stop! Quit it! Ow!

DUMMY DOWNER, *hitting her*
> I've got your cure here! One-two-three!
> And here it comes: watch out, ker-pow!

[*End of the ballet*]

DOC DOUBLE-TALK [*aside*]
> What's this? Isn't that Bridget I just heard over there, screaming her
> head off?

[*At the door of Dummy and Bridget, Doc addresses Dummy.*]
> What's up, neighbor? What's with all the roughhousin'?

DUMMY DOWNER
> And Christ Almighty! You'll get yours too since you're gettin' in my
> way!
[*Dummy hits Doc Double-Talk with a stick.*]
> You wanna stick it in? Here! Take *this* and bring it to your little love
> nest! Go on, say your prayers! You can use this stick as your votive
> candle!

DOC DOUBLE-TALK
> Pretty little thing let me light her candle but mama was too hot to
> handle.[44] I think I'll be on my way now, thank you!
> And now, I bid you adieu. Come to think of it, that's what I do best!
> Hit and run!
[*To the Audience*]

> For now, good folks, I've gotta run
> But I sure hope you had some fun
> Except for now, I'll tell you square
> I had to get me outta there!
> Please, no offense to all our jokes.
> Bye-bye to all and [*à la Porky Pig?*] that's all, folks!

The END

7.

At Cross Purposes, or,

The Farce of the Three Lovers of the Cross

Farce de trois Amoureux de la Croix

CAST OF CHARACTERS

MARTIN, the Bumpkin and "Priest" (Martin)
WALTER, the Welshman and "Dead Man" (Gaultier)
WILLIAM, the Geek and "Devil" (Guillaume)
The LADY [Beatrice] (La Dame)

PRODUCTION NOTES

The *Farce nouvelle de trois Amoureux de la Croix, à III personnages* appears as #8 in Cohen, *Recueil,* 57–66; and as #57 in Tissier, *RF,* 11: 115–81. To my knowledge, the complete play survives only in the *Recueil Cohen.*[1] It was also translated into modern French by Tissier as *Les Trois Amoureux de la croix* (#57 in *FFMA,* 4: 147–66). There is a sixteenth-century prose version of the story too which might well have been influenced by our play: Tale 13 in Nicolas de Troyes, *Le Grand Parangon des nouvelles nouvelles.*[2] The *Farce de trois Amoureux de la Croix,* in 574 octosyllabic verses (or 575 in Tissier), appears to be of Norman origin. Little is known about its date of composition, such that no one has ventured a precise date. Alternate title: *Graveyard Shifts.*

Plot

Martin the Bumpkin, Walter the Welshman, and William the Geek are, all three, pursuing one and the same married Lady, who may or may not be called Beatrice of Dantesque fame. Whatever she's called, the Lady could scarcely be less "ladylike" or less interested in the fellows' romantic efforts—although she does accept their money in anticipation, she promises, of better things to come. In truth, the coquette has devised a ruse by which to dispose handily of them all. Out of alleged concern for everyone's safety from her jealous husband, she assigns a different costume to each suitor. Martin (dressed as a priest), Walter (dressed as a ghostly dead man), and William (dressed as a devil) shall each come, under cover of darkness, to the secret rendezvous spot. She and each suitor are to hook up at the large, titular cross located at that oh-so-romantic site, the cemetery, for a series of "graveyard shifts."[3] Although the Lady has no intention of meeting any one of them, her choice of venue makes sense: Where else would a priest, a dead man, and a devil be likely to be marauding?

With ingenious metacommentary, *At Cross Purposes* stages costumed characters, the better to demonstrate how costuming itself can be used for trickery—all of which might lead audiences to wonder in turn whether someone means to trick *them*. Brace yourself: the action seems confusing on the page but, thanks to the three gents' costumes, it would not be confusing in performance.

In an unusually tongue-in-cheek plot summary, Tissier points out that the three besotted dolts are rather slow on the uptake, missing a number of important cues (*RF*, II: 122–30). The Lady has already tipped her hand by the mere fact that she does *not* find it necessary to disguise *herself* for the secret meetings. And yet, the gentlemen barely manifest surprise by their "director's" costuming choices! Despite her having timed the entrances of her "actors" at one-hour intervals, all three show up at around the same time—coming prematurely, as it were—and they are each frightened by the others (whose costumes are apparently quite convincing): Martin panics at the sight of a dead man and a devil; Walter, at the sight of a priest and a devil; and William, at the sight of a priest and a dead man. Since the Lady is not only one hell of an actress but an equally savvy playwright and director, it is no leap to assume that this is exactly how she wanted her little farce to play out. Ultimately, the three men unmask themselves, all realizing that they have been had. Whether or not they are clever enough to realize that they were all had *by one and the same woman* is anybody's guess. Not the sorts to hold a grudge, they do a little song and dance to conclude the theatrical proceedings.

Because of the great potential for readerly confusion during the denouement of Scene 7, I have expanded the stage directions considerably; I also indicate the speakers of that scene such that readers will see together both the character and his costumed alter ego: Martin-as-Priest, Walter-as-Dead-Man, and William-as-Devil. (Sometimes, Martin actually *does* attempt to play a priest but, otherwise, please note that Martin, Walter, and William are speaking *as them-*

selves and *not* as the characters that were assigned by the Lady.) Once extensive stage directions have been interpolated into the script, the scene actually makes a great deal of sense. Martin-as-Priest is afraid when he sees a zombie-like dead man at the cemetery and so he begins to pray. His prayerful posture then reinforces for Walter-as-Dead-Man that the individual whom Walter encounters at the cemetery (Martin in his cassock) really *is* a priest. Naturally, in Walter's eyes, a priest is a particularly poor third wheel for a romantic assignation. Now enter William, costumed as a devil, who observes what appears to be a storied conflict between a priest and a dead man. Of course, William also seeks to get rid of the priestly third wheel, only to become terrified of a "dead man" whose logical abode might well *be* a cemetery. As the three suitors chase one another, they are essentially going around in circles. So too are you, dear Reader, if you've managed to get through this explanation.

Characters and Character Development

Is the translator allowed to have a favorite character? If so, it's the Lady, hands down, who knows all about courtly love; she's just not buying any of it. In fact, she's literally cashing in on it. Although Faivre does indeed call her Beatrice (*Répertoire,* 41–43), that name appears only once, in Scene 7 on the lips of a flustered Martin; it may represent a poetic allusion only to the Dante character rather than to the sole female character's actual name. The Lady is probably the smartest female character of this entire collection, albeit a less than ethical one, and one of the only ones to win at her own game. My model for this scheming theater maven is Adelaide from *Guys and Dolls,* so I've written her with a New York accent or, more precisely, with a dialect from Queens.

The three suitors, all distinct character types, have three distinct speech patterns in the French, so I have undertaken to capture that spirit by writing each one with a different regional accent. Martin the Bumpkin, Walter the Welshman, and William the Geek might be further distinguished in production by the choice of an individual theme song for each man as he makes his entrance. Of course, any company performing these pieces is responsible for clearing all requisite permissions, but here are some possibilities that might capture the proper medieval mood. For Martin, one could consider "Hey, Marty" (from the 1955 film *Marty*), "Rescue Me," or "Walking the Floor Over You." For Walter, a Welshman, one might select a British Invasion tune like "Tired of Waiting for You," especially given Walter's allusion (in Scene 1) to the dangers of getting "tired out" before his big date (or "knackered," as they say across the pond). And for William, a good fit might be the sublimely geeky "I'm Telling You Now" or "In the Midnight Hour." (See below, Appendix: Scholarly References to Copyrighted Materials.)

Those distinctions between the three male characters are also reinforced during their respective *tête-à-têtes* with the Lady, where each suitor uses a different currency with which to buy her off. Remember that music and language are currencies in a love economy, but so too is cold, hard cash. For Martin, the sum is ten *ducats*, for Walter, ten *écus*, and for William, ten *royaux*.[4] Without getting into the complex chronological vagaries of currency conversion—as anyone planning a trip to Europe at the time of an unstable dollar knows full well—let's just say that these are all gold coins, all in the amount of ten, and that there are several ways to emphasize their different valuations. (More on things monetary momentarily, below, §§ "Sets and Staging"; "Costumes and Props List.") The point is that the Lady disdains their offerings, and seems to find Martin particularly cheap.

While I was tempted to imagine Ernest Borgnine's Marty for our own Martin and to give him a vintage Brooklyn dialect, Martin works better as a bumpkin. So, imagine a hillbilly à la Gomer Pyle (think of John-Boy in #4, *Student Who Failed*); he shall mispronounce any foreign words. Besides, one can still evoke the famous tagline from *Marty* in the eerily well-timed line of Scene 1 when Walter asks, "So whaddaya doin' tonight, Marty?" There is also something inherently comical about having the most rustic of our three characters speak, for the first and only time, Beatrice's Dantesque name.

Walter is the subject of a terrific pun about welshing during a later bit that conjures Abbott and Costello's famous "Who's on First?" (Again, compare to the bit in #4, *Student Who Failed*.) It will be explained in detail in the related endnotes; but suffice it to say that Walter's French name is Gautier. To insult a man by calling him *Gautier* is to accuse him of welshing on a bet, of being a welsher or, thus, a "Walter." Thus, in Scene 7, when Martin-as-Priest promises *to* Walter that he means Walter-as-Dead-Man no harm, Martin utters the following phrase that causes Walter considerable confusion: "And if I break my word," says Martin *to* Walter, "you can call me a welsher," i.e., *You can call me Walter!* Except Martin says that *to* Walter. One more time: Martin says *to* Walter that Walter can call him—i.e., *Martin*—Walter! Who's on first? It is in an effort to translate this routine that I have made this character a Welshman; the actor shall speak with a Welsh accent—or at least a British one.

William uses more flowery language than the others and, as you shall see, I've found that a parodic evocation of Martin Short's geeky character from

Saturday Night Live conveys the gist of this personage well. William seems a kind of Ed Grimley *avant la lettre*. (To actors: if you prefer a different inspiration, please do feel free to drop a few instances of "I must say!" with which I've peppered his speeches.)

Language

Literally, the "three lovers of the cross" are the "three lovers *at* the cross": that is, at the cross that is located at the rendezvous spot. However, in the hallmark punning of farce, an *amoureux de la croix* also denotes a certain kind of religious zealot: one who is capable of the famous Pauline folly of the Cross and even of crusading in the name of God. Not surprisingly, the Lady makes the most of their courtly zealotry; she cunningly double-crosses all three suitors, crossing them off her list in a single night.

In the macaronic language characteristic of this repertoire, all four characters occasionally make relatively failed forays into the highfalutin language of courtly love; eventually, they shift back to their vernaculars, usually midspeech and sometimes midsentence. The Lady's linguistic oscillations between frank, vernacular dialect and much more formal modes are especially dramatic, mostly when she talks to herself or to the audience. Also, as is the case in #12, *Birdbrain*, we find a fair number of highly idiosyncratic Latin phrases, most of these uttered prayerfully at the cemetery by the frightened suitors who are awaiting the Lady, the no-show. Naturally, at the sight of a priest, a ghostly dead man, and a devil, the three gents start saying their prayers—or, rather, pieces of those prayers, such as they know them—in "Latin." It seems that they haven't been to church in a while.

Sets and Staging

While there is some liberty in production as to how many sets are necessary, *At Cross Purposes* actually calls for quite a few scene changes.[5] Each lover visits the Lady at her home; each one goes to his own home to change clothes; and the denouement takes place near the big cross of the play's title, located just outside of town *at* or *near* the cemetery. Readers will note, by the way, that, in older French villages, one still sees today the large crosses that traditionally marked the town's entrance (although their magnitude is not comparable to that of the celebrated cruciform welcome to Rio atop Corcovado). Given the symbolics of costuming throughout the play and the frequent metacommentary, actors and directors might make the most of the three scenes of clothes changing as well as the unmasking(s) at the play's conclusion.

It is also possible to stage this play as a bona fide musical and to have the Lady perform an appropriate musical number after each of her three scenes with her suitors. In the endnotes, I share a few thoughts as to songs that seem to convey the medieval characters' *états d'âme* at those moments—all subject, once again, to clearing all requisite permissions.

Each suitor must be armed with his currency of choice; and, although that might appear to belong to our "Costumes and Props List," it is integral enough to the question of character that it warrants discussion here. The appropriate monetary units depend on whether these characters are portrayed as stingy or extravagant. One possibility is to have each suitor "up the ante" of the previous offering. Accounting for inflation and, the better to emphasize similarities as well as differences, I have opted for three versions of *fifty-something:* Martin the Bumpkin might speak of "a fifty" or "fifty bucks;" the Welsh/British character, Walter, proposes a sum in pounds sterling; and William tenders dollars but, since he is a geek, I suggest that he come with fifty one-dollar bills and count them out. If these offerings are to be visible to the audience, purses of coins are probably more effective than bank notes; but here, companies may use their imaginations.

Costumes and Props List

The three gents might wear codpieces: after all, the Lady has got them by the . . .

Otherwise, the most important props are those associated with Martin-as-Priest, Walter-as-Dead-Man, and William-as-Devil. Martin shall be dressed in priestly black, and—what a coincidence!—like Colette in #3, *Confession Lessons* (Scene 2), he just *happens* to have a priest outfit lying around at home! What is it doing there? Who knows! But one cannot help but chuckle along with Tissier at the idea that there were so many amorous priests roaming the countryside that, should a priest show up for a secret assignation, then no disguise was necessary (*RF,* 11: 129). Martin shall also tote a Bible or a book of prayers (or both).

For his dead man, Walter shall be a wandering spirit, possibly draped in an apparitional white sheet and wearing a mask (*visagière*).[6] (Think, dear Reader, about Eddie Izzard's bit from *Dress to Kill,* in which the Holy Ghost sports such a white sheet, as if that person of the Holy Trinity were a protagonist in an episode of *Scooby-Doo*.) Alternatively, imagine any number of zombies from any number of films: *Night of the Living Dead* comes to mind.

As for William, who might don devilish red, directors may not wish to undertake the fire-breathing menace that his devil seems prepared to simulate; but he can certainly wear a nonflammable mask or headgear (*testiere*) that is just as frightening.[7] He requires a chain, a favorite medieval accoutrement for the spooky hell-raiser, or, for contemporary audiences, perhaps a pitchfork.

The Lady may be as elegant or inelegant as desired; she might wear a different T-shirt in each scene with a would-be lover, starting with Martin: "Marty loves me and all I got is this lousy T-shirt."

Scholarly References to Copyrighted Materials (in order of appearance)

"Lover's Cross." By James J. Croce. (ASCAP)

"She's Not There." By Rod Argent. (BMI)

"Can't Buy Me Love." By John Winston Lennon and Paul James McCartney. (ASCAP)

"Madeleine." By Eric Blau, Jacques Romain G. Brel, Jean F. Corti, and Gérard Emile Jouannest. (BMI)

"I'm So Lonesome, I Could Cry." By Hank Williams. (BMI)

"Come Away Death." [Words by William Shakespeare.] By Danny Apolinar and Hal Hester. From *Your Own Thing*, 1968. (ASCAP)

"I Have a Song to Sing-O!" By William Schwenck Gilbert and Sir Arthur Seymour Sullivan. From *The Yeoman of the Guard* (1888). Revised version of Gilbert and Sullivan classic also attributed to Milton T. Okun, Noel Paul Stookey, Mary Allin Travers, and Peter Yarrow. (ASCAP)

"Hey, Marty!" By Paddy Chayefsky and Harry Warren. Theme song from *Marty*, © United Artists, 1955. (ASCAP)

"Poor, Poor, Pitiful Me." By Warren William Zevon. (BMI)

"Walking the Floor Over You." By Ernest Tubb. (BMI)

"Silver Threads and Golden Needles." By Dick Reynolds and Jack Rhodes. (BMI)

"Rescue Me." By Raynard Miner and Carl William Smith. (BMI)

"Hound Dog." By Jerry Leiber and Mike Stoller. (BMI)

"Tired of Waiting for You." By Raymond Douglas Davies. (BMI)

"Nowhere to Run." By Lamont Herbert Dozier, Brian Holland, and Eddie Holland Jr. (BMI)

"I'm Telling You Now." By Frederick Garrity and Mitch Murray. (ASCAP)

"In the Midnight Hour." By Stephen Lee Cropper and Wilson Pickett Jr. (BMI)

"Creep." By Colin Charles Greenwood, Jonathan Richard Guy Greenwood, Albert Louis Hammond, Michael Edward Hazlewood, Edward John O'Brien, Philip James Selway, Thomas Edward Yorke. (ASCAP)

"The Vatican Rag." By Tom Lehrer. (ASCAP)

"Quando, Quando, Quando." By Charles E. Boone, Elio Cesari, and Alberto Testa. (ASCAP)

"Upside Down" ["Round 'n' Round"]. By Sandra Jacqueline Denton, Bernard Edwards, Cheryl James, and Nile Gregory Rodgers. (ASCAP)

"Volare." By Francesco Migliacci and Domenico Modugno. (ASCAP)

"By the Light of the Silvery Moon." By Hawley W. Ades, Gus Edwards, and Edward Madden. (ASCAP)

"Rocky Raccoon." By John Winston Lennon and Paul James McCartney. (ASCAP)

"You Really Got Me." By Raymond Douglas Davies. (BMI)

"Hard to Handle." By Alvertis Isbell, Allen Alvoid Jones Jr., and Otis Redding. (BMI)

"Bye Bye Baby." By Bob Crewe and Robert Gaudio. (BMI)

[The play may open with a vignette demonstrating the rich connotations of being a lover of and at the cross.][8]

[Scene 1]

[In town]

MARTIN, *the first lover, begins by singing:*[9]
> I'd rather die than see another day.
> For that would be less pain!
> But, since I can't be cured another way,
> Then, let Death come for me without delay.
> My suffering's in vain.

[Martin seems to feel better after the performance.]

Well, golly! I best be fixin' to head off to that *ren-dez-vous* where I done promised to meet her. Whooooeeeee! My whole body's achin' for her! She's my one and only, she's my every-thang.

WALTER, *the second lover [with a Welsh accent]:*
Good heavens! I'd best run along, then. I've got a date to keep, I do, with my ladylove! What a stupid git I'd be to get knackered now!

WILLIAM, *the third one, begins:*
To whomsoever is fortunate enough as I to find himself in Love's grasp: may he live a joyful and happy life, I must say, free from all worries and cares.

WALTER
The bloke who swears allegiance to love: he loses fame and fortune, he does, lads. But everyone tosses him out in the end.

MARTIN
The hell you say! Ain't no way that's so!

WILLIAM
Way! Plus it certainly does behoove you to cease and desist immediately from spouting such nonsense, I must say!

MARTIN [*to William*]
Since we're back in the good ol' summertime, aren'tcha off to see them girly-girls o' yours? Come on, now, tell us all about it, boy! How's about some details! Is they good lookin'?[10] Can we see 'em from here? Point 'em out to us, would ya?

WILLIAM
With friends like you I hardly need enemies, I must say. Two's company, three's a crowd.

MARTIN
Whaddaya mean, boy?

WILLIAM

Don't you get it? You're cramping my style, I must say. And now, I bid
you gentlemen farewell! In a word: get lost!

WALTER

Very well, then. As you like it. Not another word about it. Must go
now. Somewhere I need to be, you see.
[*To Martin*] And you?
[*With a deliberately incongruous New York accent, Walter paraphrases
and parodies the famous line from the film* Marty.]
So whaddaya doin' tonight, Marty?

MARTIN

I'll catch ya later, ol' buddy. But, right now, I'm fixin' to be off myself.
Lordy, lordy, lordy! On accounta I'll be goddamned if I don't hook up
right quick with my little sweetie pie!

[Scene 2]

[*At the home of the Lady*]

The LADY

[*She might possibly open with her own musical number.*][11]
Boy oh boy oh boy! Them twists and turns on that path o' love! All
them fellas all lookin' for love in all the wrong places, all of 'em just out
for themselves! But you don't gotta put out for 'em, really. Lotsa times,
yuz can just get away wit' a buncha empty promises!

[*Enter Martin*]

MARTIN

Well, golly! Here I am already at her door!
[*Overacting Romeo*] There is my lady! There is my love! I been cryin'
like a polecat over her. I gotta go pay my respects.
[*He approaches the Lady.*]

My Lady, my honeychild, I ain't nothin' without you. [*Dropping to his knees*] See, baby? I'm on my knees here. I'm beggin' you, all soft and sweet and humble-like: if you'd just lemme set a spell.

Ain't nobody else like you. Why, you're . . . the fairest of 'em all. And, besides, everybody likes ya!

The LADY

Oh, it's you.

So, come on in, why don'tcha. Take a load off. What brings ya by?

MARTIN

Why, lemme tell you all about it, honeychild.

You gotta rescue me, yes ma'am: I just can't take no more o' this pain. Oh the pain! I been courtin' you a right long time now, I has, 'cause I ain't never loved no woman the way I love ya. So I'm beggin' you please, mercy me! Please don't break this heart o' mine. Gimme just a little bit o' cause to keep on hopin'! Pretty please now.

The LADY

Oh, that.

So lemme ask ya, mister: You really that in love wit' me, or what?

MARTIN

I'm hangin' my head, here, I done fell so hard! I'm all tied up in knots over you.

[*Martin might do a pantomime to demonstrate that he's "tied up in knots."*][12]

So come on, now, honey, and undo me. Come on now and rescue me! Take pity on me and set me free . . . else, I'm just gonna lay down and die.

The LADY

You boys in love! All o' yuz know all them same old tricks. You pretend like you're all sick or somethin'—all that tremblin' and stuff—but it's just an act.

MARTIN

You speak the truth, honeychild. There's some gold-diggin' boys out there. They's thinkin' that, with them bedroom eyes in your general direction, they can just get ladies to fall in love with 'em.
But, Praise Jesus! Ain't no silver threads and golden needles gonna mend this heart o' mine![13] Everything I got is yours!

The LADY

You sure do talk a good game. But I'm telling you: one o' them whatchamacallits—one o' them *swain* guys—who wants to do his lady proud . . . Well, he's gotta keep an eye on the time . . . and the weather . . . and the season . . . and the street where she lives. And he's gotta be . . . you know, discreet-like. Can't make such a big to-do about the whole thing.

MARTIN

What's that now, honey?

The LADY

My husband would end you if he was to find out I was havin' these private little talks wit' you. That's what!

MARTIN

Lord have mercy, girl! Here [*presents a greenback*]: Would a fifty do it?[14] You just hang on to that there, now, sugar, till I come on back. But I'm beggin' you: gimme a chance here, baby. Gimme a chance at love. I'm all yours. I swear by the hair on my chinny-chin-chin.[15]

The LADY

I think it would be, like, most rude of me to refuse your gift. Thanks a million, really. I'm just thrilled by your love, honest. A girl would hafta be pretty darn coldhearted if she was to refuse you. But I'm telling you: you mark my words. You can't come by the house no more!

MARTIN

Lordy, lordy! Why not, for heaven's sake?

The LADY

Why not?

Duh!

My husband's, like, the jealous kind. It's . . . *pathological*. There's no tellin' what he might do to you!

MARTIN

What in tarnation are you talkin' about? So where we gonna get together, then, baby doll?

The LADY

We gotta do it all secret-like. So here's what you're gonna do:

You're gonna go on home now, and you're gonna dress up like a priest, see? That's how it's gonna be and . . .

[*Here, as at other moments when referring to people watching—like the Audience—the Lady makes a momentous linguistic shift to better grammar.*]

. . . in that guise, if anyone were, perchance, to espy us, it would therefore be impossible to divine what is beneath the surface.

Get it?

MARTIN

I reckon that could work.

The LADY

And you're gonna make sure you bring a book wit' you—like a breviary or somethin'—you know, for your part and all—so you'll be all dressed up like how them priests is supposed to look, like I told ya.

And then, you're gonna head right off to that great big cross over there. See it? It's not far from where we're standin'. And that's the spot. That's where I'm gonna come meet up wit' you, for sure, at ten o'clock tonight. . . . Unless somethin' comes up.

MARTIN

Boy howdy! Yes ma'am! I'll be there!

But you better show up now, ya hear?

The LADY

Yeah, yeah. Certainly. I'll be there!

[*The Lady alone: Aside or to the Audience*]

[*À la* Beverly Hillbillies] Y'all come back now, ya hear!
As if! And fiddle-dee-dee! You can huff and you can puff all you want,
but you ain't blowin' *this* house down! Come to think of it, you can
blow it out your ear! I'm gonna make sure you're coolin' your heels but
good out there . . . sputterin' all over the place and nosin' around me
like ya do.[16] Oh for Chrissakes! He talks till he's blue in the . . . face.
And all I get outta him is this lousy gift! Talk about your bill o' goods!
Yeah. He can hang around in the moonlight till the cows come
home . . . Or at least till I can get the rest off 'im.

[*Optional: The Lady might perform a musical number about Suitor no. 1.*][17]

[Scene 3]

[*At Martin's home*]

MARTIN [*getting into costume*]

Yes sirree Bob! Gotta get me all dressed up now. Gotta slip me into this
here priest robe . . . tuck it in just like so. . . . There we go!
Now, I gotta make like a chicken and split! Lickety-split! Gotta get me
over to that there cross. Bless my soul and Godspeed! But it's gotta look
right:

[*He tries out in mime the more solemn gait and mien that he will adopt as
a priest.*][18]

Hangin' my head, trials and tribulations at the spot where Christ done
died for our sins. That don't sound too good, do it?
But I'm gonna be a happy ol' boy from here on in with my gal!

[*Martin may be offstage awhile; but he is the first to arrive at the cross.*]

[Scene 4]

[At the home of the Lady]

[Enter Walter before the Lady.]

WALTER

God give you good day, milady, and good health and well-being to you
as well.

What brings me here before you today, do you suppose?

The LADY

I really couldn't say . . . but I'm sure you're gonna tell me.

So . . . what can I do you for?

WALTER

Oh dear, dear, dear, dear, dear! Do allow me to explain it all to you,
then, won't you, madam?

I fear, you see, that you are the sole author and origin of my malady, and
only you might help me out a bit, eh?

What more can one say? It's the pain, you see, and the suffering that I
endure on your account. Bollocks! If you don't soften it up a bit and
give a bloke a hand, then I'll surely die of it. I'll be hanging on . . . yes,
that's what you call it over here in the New World . . . a "lover's cross"
for you.

The LADY

What did I ever do to you, sir, that you'd go off and die on accounta
me? You're way, way off there, seems to me, bringin' up that kinda topic
o' conversation wit' me. I'd be some kinda hard-hearted and proud lady
to let a fella die over *moi*!

WALTER

And yet, upon my word, I am dying . . . unless you were to grant me just
a wee bit of affection and take pity on me in this, my great distress.

And thus, I humbly beseech you to accept this small token of my affection which I now present to you, oh kind and virtuous lady. And, if you

would only be so kind, if you would grant me in return, your love that I so long for.

The LADY

Egad, milord, I can't possibly take your money, honest. Please don't mention it again.

WALTER

Please, in the name of God, do accept these fifty pounds, dear lady. If not, the price to pay is far too dear for the love that I carry for you in my bosom.

The LADY

Oh, well, seein' as you put it that way . . . Sure. [*She might put the money in* her *bosom, which will prove a challenge for the fifty bills yet to come from William.*] Knock yourself out. If you say it'll help you out a little bit with all that pain you're s'pposed to be in and all . . . well, okey-dokey, then. I'll take the cash.
But you know what you're gonna do for me now? You're gonna go on home right this minute, 'cause you're gonna dress up like a dead man.[19] And then, you're gonna be quick about it and make a beeline for that great big cross that's around here, get it? That's where I'm gonna meet-cha. That's the spot where I'm gonna come to you, for sure, come what may, at eleven o'clock tonight. . . . Unless somethin' comes up.

WALTER

Fuck me! That's a super plan! I'll bugger off at once to prepare! But you won't change your mind, eh?

The LADY

Why, heavens to Betsy! Of course I won't. Can't hardly wait. See if I don't beat you to it!

WALTER

Then I bid you adieu, luv. But do be sure that you keep that promise, eh?

The LADY
    Go with God, honey.
[*Exit Walter*]
[*The Lady alone; aside or to the Audience*]
    Yeah, that's right. Run, baby, run! Pesterin' me every night like ya do
    with all them pathetic requests that I, like, grant yuz my love and such.
    What was your name again, buddy? Walter? Well, after tonight, you're
    gonna go by a new name for sure: you're gonna be Walter-the-Wimp![20]
    We'll see who's gonna fall into Love's trap!

[*Optional: the Lady might perform a musical number about Suitor no. 2.*][21]

[*Enter William*]

WILLIAM
    May our Father, who art in heaven, extend to you his glorious grace and
    love.

The LADY
    Uh-huh. Likewise, I'm sure.
    Yeah. You too, sir, may our Father, who art in heaven, do . . . yeah . . .
    that stuff you just said.

WILLIAM
    Love has sent me winging toward you.

The LADY
    You don't say! Is that a fact? No kiddin'.

WILLIAM
    May our Father, who art in heaven, extend to you his glorious grace and
    love.
    Allow me, then, to proceed, without further ado, to the matter that
    brings me before you and to present my case: to wit, in my heart, I am
    indeed prey to such grievous suffering, I must say, that, to be perfectly
    clear about it—and to coin a phrase—I'm ready to give up the ghost if
    you don't come to succor me immediately.

The LADY

What kinda talk is that?

Yeah, yeah. I heard it all before. You love me. That's a good one!

WILLIAM

[*William brandishes a huge wad of dollar bills and proceeds to count out all fifty.*]

Here, please, accept these fifty dollars, at least to get you started. Consider it a small down payment, if you will. But I'm begging you most submissively, I must say, that you allow me to be your most humble servant and your oh-so-loyal friend.

The LADY

Okay, let's have it then, if that's how it's gotta be. Delighted, I'm sure. You know what you're gonna do now? You're gonna go put on a disguise and, then, you're gonna see one heckuva show!

WILLIAM

Whatever do you mean?

The LADY

You're gonna dress up like a devil. And you're gonna make it look real good.

WILLIAM

May the Lord condemn me to the fires of hell if I ever fail you! I'll do it! You can count on me, I must say!

The LADY

So, you're gonna go and you're gonna get, like, a huge chain. And then, you're gonna drag it around behind ya, get it? And then—no ifs, ands, or buts—you're gonna go and wait for me—you hear me?—over by that great big cross: that tall one over there. That's where we're gonna make our little party. . . .

But we're gonna wait till the midnight hour: you know, like when my love comes tumblin' down.[22]

WILLIAM

 I'll be there, believe you me, I must say! Come hell or high water!

The LADY

 Then ya better show up, 'cause I'm gonna be there too.

WILLIAM

 Ah, my lady, God only knows that I'll never fail you! I call upon all the
 saints as my witnesses!
 And you hurry it on up too now, don't be late!
 I'm off right now this very minute, hippety-hop! Must get my act
 together, I must say, for our secret rendezvous!

The LADY

 Off ya go, then. Hippety-hop and all. *Adyooo* to you too!
 [*Exit William*]
 [*The Lady alone; aside or to the Audience*]
 [*Optional: the Lady might perform a musical number about Suitor no. 3.*][23]
 And God only knows what fun's waitin' for you too. All three o' yuz are
 in for one helluva night. All o' yuz can count on it!

[*Exit the Lady*]

[Scene 5]

[*At Walter's home*]

WALTER

 Righty-ho! I do believe I'm all set to go!
 [*Looking in a mirror, checking his "dead man" costume*]
 Good heavens! I do look like death warmed up! I'll be off, then, to the
 cross, under cover of night. Righty-ho! Off I go!

[Scene 6]

[At William's home][24]

[William gets into his costume for his devilish look.]

[Scene 7]

[At the cemetery]

Martin, in his priest costume, is already at the cemetery.
Enter Walter-as-Dead-Man who sees Martin-as-Priest.]

WALTER-as-Dead-Man

Sacrebleu! What on earth is that? I say, there's another bloke out there at the cross already! Mary, Mother of God! I do believe it's a priest praying for the souls of the dead!
Bloody hell! That blasted priest will throw a spanner in the works, I say! Sod it! What is it they say? *[Pausing for the anachronism]* I'd send him off to Australia if I could![25] If my lady love comes to me now, then we're all done straightaway. Must get that bloody fool to piss off!

[Walter doesn't want anybody spoiling his rendezvous—least of all a priest—so he gives chase to the clerically costumed Martin, whom he naturally mistakes for a real priest.]

MARTIN-as-Priest
[Seeing that a zombie-like Walter-as-Dead-Man has appeared and is coming right at him]

Holy cow! I think I see me a dead man over there. Lordy, Lordy, have mercy! Deliver me from evil!

WALTER-as-Dead-Man *[continuing to give chase and praying]*

Heavenly Father, mightn't we just . . . hang that bloody priest over there?

MARTIN-as-Priest [*running away from Walter-as-Dead-Man*]

Dagnabbit! I'm a goner, fer sure! All my sins done caught up with me.[26] I'm gonna die! Right here tonight! Ain't no way out of it now.

[*Calling to Walter-as-Dead-Man*]

Shoo! Shoo! Git back in your tomb! Go on, git!

[*During the upcoming exchange, a terrified Martin falls to his knees to pray at some length, which is an appropriate position indeed for a priest. This appearance of priestly action also causes Walter-as-Dead-Man to stop short to observe Martin-as-Priest. In turn, Walter's hesitation might lead Martin to believe that the prayer is working; so during Martin's lines below, he may keep eyeing Walter-as-Dead-Man to see whether his prayer is still working. If Martin is also holding a cross as part of his clerical costume, he might even hold it up to ward off Walter-as-Dead-Man, as one would a vampire.*]

Dang! How does that prayer fer dead folks go again? *In pluribus unum, kyrie eleison,* and *caveat emptor!*[27]

Jumpin' Jehosaphat! If dumb was dirt, I'd cover 'bout half an acre! Comin' round here to mess around at the foot o' the Holy Cross, where God done suffered His grievous death for our sins. God's a-punishin' me, all right. The sun don't shine on the same dog's tail all the time. My number done come up.

WALTER-as-Dead-Man

Bloody hell! Bollocks! Good Lord! And bugger him! I'll scratch his eyes out, I will! Bloody priest![28]

[*Exasperated by the duration of the prayer of Martin-as-Priest*] What on earth is he doing over there? Offering a bit of a prayer to each one of the Twelve Apostles, for fuck's sake? I'd like to string him up by the . . . neck. He's pissing on my chips, he is!

And wouldn't we have a jolly old time—wouldn't it be lovely?—if my lady were to arrive now. I'm spitting tacks!

[*The fact that Walter-as-Dead-Man has stopped to observe the lengthy prayer of Martin-as-Priest makes it possible for the actors to continue their interaction in silence as William now makes his own entrance as a devil. William is occupied primping or preening, perhaps trying out a few diabolical tricks during the upcoming dialogue between Martin-as-Priest*] *and Walter-as-Dead-Man. At first, William doesn't even notice the other two nor do they notice him.]*

WILLIAM-as-Devil [*heading off to the cross*]
Ready or not, here I go, I must say! I'm off now incognito to the cross, because my sweet and gracious lady love doth command it, why, yes she doth! She was quite specific about it: crystal clear, I must say. And God only knows that I couldn't be happier than if someone had given me a pile of gold! I simply cannot wait until I hold her in my arms. She should be along any moment now.

[*Martin-as-Priest sees that his prayer hasn't worked. He starts to flee again as Walter-as-Dead-Man gives chase.*]

MARTIN-as-Priest [*fleeing Walter-as-Dead-Man*]
Mercy me! I'm as nervous as a long-tailed cat in a room full o' rockin' chairs. Death's a-gainin' on me!

WALTER-as-Dead-Man [*gaining on Martin-as-Priest*]
Sod off! You can go straight to hell!

MARTIN-as-Priest
Mercy me! I'm as scared as a sinner in a cyclone! I better git outta here!

WALTER-as-Dead-Man
[*Mocking the priest's Southern accent as he continues to give chase*]
Indeed: "Git outta here," lad, or I'll have your guts for garters!

MARTIN-as-Priest [*still on the run*]
Woe, woe is me! What's gonna become o' me? Death's a-gittin' closer 'n' closer! I'm so scared my hair's a-standin' on end! Ain't nothin' else could![29]

WILLIAM-as-Devil
[*William notices first Martin-as-Priest, whose presence annoys him, so he will head over to chase the priestly third wheel away.*]
What's this I see before me? Right over there where my lady is supposed to meet me?

The Devil take him and hang him by the neck! It's a priest, I must say. [*Now noticing Walter-as-Dead-Man, whose presence frightens him*] Golly Moses, my heart is racing! Oh my one true God! *Mon Dieu!* There's more! I do believe that I see something else out there as well! It appears to be some kind of a dead man. Help me, Heavenly Father!

[MARTIN-as-Priest][30]

> [*Guilt-stricken*] Ain't nothing less than what I done deserved. I'm gonna die fer sure, on accounta my sins I done committed....

WALTER-as-Dead-Man [*now seeing William-as-Devil*]

> Wait just a moment! What is *that*? It's a devil just over there, I say! He's coming straight toward me! He'll take me straight to hell, he will! Perhaps if I were to start praying....
> In the name of the Father, the Son, and the Holy Spirit:[31] Bless me Father, for I have sinned. Sweet Mother Mary, I pray you: come to my assistance!
> [*He proceeds to offer up his best guess at a prayer.*]
> *Asperges et collocavit;* Asparagus and Cauliflower,
> *Memento, Domine David;* in memory of King David . . .
> and Simon Magus. . . and Simon Cowell.
> *Agnus dei, Agnes Magnus. . .*
> Aggie-Maggies, Aggie Magic, Magic Johnson . . .[32]
> Save me, sweet Jesus, save me from that blasted devil!
> Get thee behind me Satan, minion of Lucifer! Cease and desist your deadly pursuit!

[*At a loss, a frightened Walter decides to seek help from the "priest," inspiring utter terror in Martin. Meanwhile, as Walter-as-Dead-Man approaches Martin-as-Priest, William-as-Devil thinks that Walter-as-Dead-Man is approaching* him.]

MARTIN-as-Priest [*still terrified of the "dead man"*]

> Well bless my soul and *gesundheit*! I'm just a poor miserable sinner, a wretch. I'm a-goin' to hell in a handbasket!
> [*Now noticing, in terror, William-as-Devil*] And what in tarnation is *that*?

Well I'll be hog-tied! That thar' devil's fixin' to break my neck. He's
a-headed thissa way to put an end to me!

WILLIAM-as-Devil [*terrified, in turn, by the approach of Walter-as-Dead-Man*]
I can barely contain myself, I must say! There's no way in and no way
out! Heavens to Murgatroyd! I'm shaking like a leaf from the sheer terror! Heavenly Father, my one true God, have mercy on my soul!
That dead man's trying to ask me for something. I'll give him something, all right . . . well . . . only if it be Thy will, of course. He must
be some kind of lost soul or something, wandering this earth with his
unfinished business so that he can make amends.
In the name of Saint Peter's Pearly Gates, perhaps a little prayer would
do the trick: a quick little piece of devotion to end his penance and
help out all those other folks that are dead and buried out here![33]
[*Falling to his knees*]
Our Father who art in heaven,
Forgive us our trespasses,
as we forgive those that trespass against us.
And lead us not . . .
How does it go again . . . ?
[*To Walter*] Will you get out of here, Dead Man! . . .
[*Praying again*]
but deliver us from evil.
Deliver us from evil . . . and . . .
[*Dropping momentarily his characteristic flowery language*]
Let me get right to the point:
Could you just plain deliver us, period?[34]
Amen!

[*William-as-Devil remains on his knees in prayer while Martin-as-Priest
prays too. Logically, William might well think that the "priest" is praying
for the "dead man" and that prayer is working. He rises when done.*]

MARTIN-as-Priest [*also falling to his knees*]
Salve Regina.[35]
Mater Mary, Mother of God,
blessed be the fruit of thy womb.

Beatrice, honeychild, to the Lord, I commend my spirit! I'm dyin' for the love of a lady. Ain't no one can help me now, and all this misbehavin' be woman's doin'! Help me, sweet Mother o' God!

Salve Regina and hiya, Mary, *mater misericordiae!* And you, *Diabolus*, tell me why! Tell me *quando, quando, quando?*[36] All this misbehavin's on accounta *you* too![37]

[*On his feet again*] Every inch o' my body's a-shakin' from head to toe! Things is pointin' every which way.[38] Right side up, upside down . . . Upside down, she done turn me . . . inside out, and round and round![39]

WALTER-as-Dead-Man

Had I more than five hundred pounds, I'd gladly give it all away just to be delivered safely back to my hearth and home.

[*Walter decides that, since William-as-Devil is pursuing* him, *then his own prayer isn't working. Thus, he will approach Martin-as-Priest for assistance.*]

Alas! Woe is me! I'd best go over there to that priest and ask him to hear my most humble confession. Can't have me dying, eh?, without getting into a state of grace.

You, there! Over there! I say, milord! Confession, please!

MARTIN-as-Priest [*swatting away Walter-as-Dead-Man*]

Lord have mercy! Git outta here! Go on now: git! Dang it! Ain't nothin' no one can do for you no more! You can burn in hell! Whatcha comin' round here for anyhow?

WALTER-as-Dead-Man

Alas, good sir, I'm a Christian: I'm not dead. No wandering spirit, I!

MARTIN-as-Priest

You're lyin'! I can tell just by lookin' atcha! You got one foot in the grave already!

WALTER-as-Dead-Man

It's Death that's chased me here.[40] Bollocks! And all because of that confounded woman!

[*Possibly to the Audience*] It's all rather confusing, I'll grant you.

MARTIN-as-Priest

You're lyin', I say! I can tell just by lookin' atcha! You got one foot in the grave already![41]

[*Perhaps addressing or indicating the Audience as well*]

A fella'd hafta be as dumb as a bag o' hammers—or some kinda monk or somethin'—if he was just to hang around here waitin' on you! [*Martin-as-Priest might also point to William-as-Devil, who is still on his knees in prayer. Otherwise: Metacommentary alert!*] This ain't the kinda thing folks just sit around watchin'!

WILLIAM-as-Devil [*still praying that he be saved from a dead man*]

Sweet Mary, Mother of God! Do I dare try that death chant to call him over to the other world? I don't know, I must say . . . although . . . for God's sake, all right, now that I mention it . . . I might as well just give it a try:

Miserere, miserere, dominus deus,

Scarribus all over your visagio,

I banish thee, presto change-o!

And let the angels cantare and volare[42]

Against the inimicos enemies domine Deo,

Gratias ad hoc for miraculis tuis!

Deo gratias parce que he banisheth all evil!

Now: get your ass out of here, why don't you? Get away from me! Get lost! Vamoose! Beat it!

WALTER-as-Dead-Man

Sweet Fanny Adams! If that devil gets his hands on me and spears me with that pitchfork,[43] I'm going straight to hell, I am! I'd best bugger off [*with an American accent*]—get the hell outta here. She'd have to be quite the love of my life, eh?, if I were to stay here another instant on her account! [Perhaps I'd do well to speak to that priest after all, eh?]

[*Walter runs toward Martin-as-Priest, having decided that his best bet is to make his confession.*]

WILLIAM-as-Devil

[*William has decided that prayer isn't working on a "dead man" but that he stands a good chance of scaring off a "priest." He stands up and gives chase to Martin-as-Priest.*]

At least I can get rid of that priest! If he thinks he's in any position to . . . Case closed! Enough of him already, I must say!

[*To Martin-as-Priest*] Boo! Ha! Ha! Boo! Ha! Ha! Brouhaha! Boo laka laka laka laka! Boo laka laka laka!

Watch out! I'm coming to get you! So wait up, preacher man, for you are going to die!

MARTIN-as-Priest

[*Martin is now fleeing both Walter-as-Dead-Man and William-as-Devil*]

[*First, to Walter-as-Dead-Man*]Dang it, boy! You gotta outrun me first! I'll be goddamned! You think you can catch up with me, y'old gravedigger?

WILLIAM-as-Devil [*to Martin-as-Priest*]

I'm going to get you!

MARTIN-as-Priest [*to William-as-Devil*]

Holy moly! If you come any closer, devil, I'm gonna knock your block off with this here breviary! Go on home now, ya hear? Git back! Go on, git! You're Satan! I'd know you anywhere!

WALTER-as-Dead-Man

[*Walter is still chasing Martin-as-Priest to make his confession as Martin is himself being chased by William-as-Devil. William is still thinking that he can scare off a priest.*]

Woe is me! Alas! You there! Slow down, Father, wait for me! Jeezy Creezy! Won't you hear my confession?

MARTIN-as-Priest

[*Still running from Walter-as-Dead-Man*]

You again! Quit it! Quit makin' trouble 'round here! You're a dead man! Skedaddle! Ya hear?

WALTER [*again, with the best Welsh accent the actor can muster*]
   I say, you might give me a bit of a chance here. Two minutes: that's all
   I ask. I'll just give you the good bits of all my sins! Because, I swear to
   you as a good Christian that I'm still alive! Death hasn't come for me
   yet! That's the truth, that is.

[*Walter might offer up a brief pantomime—unconvincing, at least at
first—in order to show that he is not dead. Have some fun choosing exactly
what he should do. At this point, William-as-Devil might be genuinely
winded so he might stop to rest, watching from a safe distance as Martin-
as-Priest converses with Walter-as-Dead-Man.*]

MARTIN-as-Priest
   Well, if that don't put pepper in the gumbo! You're lyin'! Christ
   Almighty! You're just wantin' me to believe you, is all. You done come
   here straight outta Purgatory. You can't fool me! I know exactly who
   you are! You're a wanderin' spirit, you are!

WALTER
   No, I'm not! I most certainly am not! I'm a regular bloke, just like you.

MARTIN-as-Priest [*still trying to ward off a dead man*]
   Git outta here! Go on, git! Or I'm gonna whup ya! You're just wantin'
   to see me come to no good! I command you: get thee, y'all, from this
   place! I command you . . . uh . . . in the name of all them wretched
   descendants of Adam . . . in the name o' twenty-thousand devils, all
   loaded up with silver and gold . . . and Hi ho, Silver! And by the light
   of the silvery moon . . . and Rocky Raccoon and Gideon's Bible and
   Daniel Boone and the whole platoon . . . and the late Tom, Dick, and
   Harry, and all them other goddamn spirits![44] Git on back now, straight
   to hell with all them other damned souls!
   In spiritu sancto, for Chrissakes!
   If you don't git the hell outta here, I'm really gonna bust a gut! Ya hear?

WALTER
   If you'd listen for just a moment, please! Bloody hell! I'm not dead!
   But I've got something on my conscience, I have. I'm remorseful, I am.
   Honestly. Won't you allow me tell you all about it, then, please?

MARTIN-as-Priest

The hell you say, boy! Git outta here! Go on, git! What are ya waitin'
for? Ya think someone's fixin' to say a Mass for you?

WALTER

Alas! Woe is me, Father, I'm hardly worthy of even a *morning* Mass!
But I do most solemnly swear to you, upon my faith, that I'm not dead
at all! Honestly.
Bless me Father, for I know what I do! I'm only here in fancy dress like
this at the request of a lady: so no one recognizes my gob!

MARTIN

So go on, then: take off your mask so's I can see if you're tellin' me the
truth.

WALTER

Only if you promise to keep this absolutely secret between us.

MARTIN

If you ever hear a single word about it, it ain't gonna come from me!
It'll be just between us two. Darn tootin', ol' buddy, that's a promise. I'll
be as quiet as a church mouse.
[*Playing a priest again for a moment*] That's right, my son, I shall handle
the matter with the utmost discretion.

WALTER

You promise, then, do you?

MARTIN

I done give you my word, as your brother in Christ. And if I break my
word, you can call me Walter-the-Welsher![45]

[*Perhaps shtick here along the lines of "Who's on First?"*]

WALTER

Go on, then: raise your right hand. Do you swear to keep your word?
On that book you've got there?

MARTIN

[*Perhaps confused about his right versus his left, he eventually raises his right hand and places it on the good book.*]

In the matter before I us, I swear to tell the truth, the whole truth and . . . uh . . . not a word about it to no one.

WALTER

Righty-ho, then, that'll do. [*He removes his mask.*]
So: have a good look at me, then. Am I a dead man? You've got quite the wrong idea about me. Go on, then: take a good look at my face.

MARTIN

Well I'll be a monkey's uncle! It's you! My good ol' buddy, Walter! Why, we was just hangin' out earlier today at the church by the monastery with Billy-Boy!

WALTER

Sacrebleu! When I think what could have happened! What, then? You went off to take vows since this morning, eh? I didn't recognize you at all!
Jeezy Creezy who died on the Cross! Tell me, then:
How on earth did you happen to come to this place and in this condition?

WILLIAM-as-Devil [*aside*]

What's this now? I swear to God, that dead man has come back to life! And that priest is in conversation with him!
I'd better get over there right now, I must say. In fact, I better get rid of this crazy mask so they won't be afraid of me!

[*William should have some difficulty getting rid of all the clothes and props that go with his costume. He is still wearing his mask as he approaches Martin and Walter.*]

WALTER

Bloody hell! What the devil . . . ? If that's not that devil again heading straight toward us . . .

WILLIAM [*removing his mask*]

Well, hello there, my brothers! What are you two up to?

MARTIN

What in tarnation . . . If it ain't good ol' Billy-Boy, who done become a devil!

WILLIAM

And that's a fine how-do-you-do, I must say! Good God! Who put you up to this? What in the world possessed you two? How come one of you is playing a priest and the other one's playing a dead man?

WALTER

I do believe that the three of us best spill the beans and confess . . . give up the ghost on our little secret.

MARTIN

You got that right. [*Perhaps gesturing toward the Audience*] But if folks was to find out, we's gonna look like a bunch o' hillbillies.

WILLIAM

So, let's all swear to it. Not a word ever to a single living soul, man or woman.

WALTER

I'll keep my end up. No worries at all.

MARTIN

Me too, boys. Quiet as the grave. Believe you me. I swear!

WILLIAM

And I'll keep quiet too, I must say, about our getting . . . well . . . screwed over like this.[46]

WALTER

Well, lads, if you must know, here's my story, then:
This is all because of some tart who's got me quite besotted. She's the one who arranged for this little performance.

MARTIN

    Same here.

WILLIAM

    And same here too. Seems to me that the three of us all got taken. All
    for one and one for all, I guess.

WALTER

    And same here as well.
    Righty-ho. So, all for one and one for all in a little musical number?
    What do you say, lads? Off we go, then!

*They sing [together a song whose melody has been lost to history and which
is rendered below in rap. If the Audience applauds, they might ask, "One
more time?" and do an encore. The Lady might appear elsewhere onstage,
perhaps dancing gleefully to the beat.]*[47]

WALTER

    At both ends we three burned our candle,
    And hoped that it would last the night.[48]

MARTIN

    But pretty little thing's too hot to handle.[49]

WALTER

    At both ends we three burned our candle.

WILLIAM

    She burned me good; God! what a scandal.
    Now let her burn! I wish she might!

MARTIN

    At both ends we three burned our candle,
    And hoped that it would last the night.

WALTER

    'Twas but a farce for her, our plight!
    And we were had. No telling why.

MARTIN

> She ripped us off! Left high and dry!
> But now, it's time to say good-bye.

WALTER[50]

> The time to leave is drawing nigh.
> How dare she play this little farce!
> She made me tumble on my arse!
> The price for fools is rather steep!

WILLIAM

> You boys who dig yourselves in deep,
> You watch out for a lady's traps.

MARTIN

> The lesson of this play was cheap,
> You boys who dig yourselves in deep,

WILLIAM

> Remember beauty's just skin deep
> And ladies treat us guys like saps.

WALTER [*joined by Martin and William, as they rap in unison*]

> You boys who dig yourselves in deep.
> You watch out for a lady's traps.
> She gives her word, but, oh the gaps!
> We walked right in like bloody fools.
> But, if you liked our show, please clap
> Bye-bye! We're just a bunch o' tools!

[*Closing music.*][51]

The END

8.

Shit for Brains, or,
The Party Pooper-Scooper
Farce de Tarabin-Tarabas

CAST OF CHARACTERS

HARPEE, the Wife (Tarabin)
HARPO, the Husband (Tarabas)
PAYNE N. BUTTS, the Meddler (Tribouille Mesnage)
[A few nonspeaking Children of all ages]

PRODUCTION NOTES

The *Farce nouvelle à III personnages fort joyeuse* appears as #13 in Cohen, *Recueil,* 95–101; and as #49 in Tissier, *RF,* 10: 63–116. The play is 325 octo-syllabic verses; and, to my knowledge, it survives only in the *Recueil Cohen.* Tissier also translated the play into modern French as *Tarabin, Tarabas, et Tribouille-Ménage* (#49 of *FFMA,* 4: 27–41). We know nothing of its date of composition, performance history, or provenance except for a scholarly suspicion that the text is from the Western part of France.[1] Alternative titles: *Up Shit Creek; Beyond the Pail.*

Plot

Perhaps the best way to begin this summary is by evoking the closing image of John Waters's *Pink Flamingos,* in which Divine, I'm sorry to say, actually *eats shit.* Rabelaisian in the extreme, *Shit for Brains* is a filthy farce about filth. Quite literally, it is full of shit from head to toe and of people who have shit for brains. Its characters are execrable and its plot—if it can be said to have one other than cleaning up piles of you-know-what—centers around grotesque puns on two principal body parts. Which two, do you think? The ass and the head, as well as all the shit (literal and metaphorical) that proliferates from both. In a way, the entire play amounts to little more than a theatrical thesaurus for all sorts of shit. It's a sustained rant that life is shit.

Tissier politely notes that "taboos on bodily functions had not yet been imposed" (*RF*, 10: 78), but that barely begins to cover it. *Shit for Brains* opens with a Husband and Wife in the midst of one of their countless arguments, this particular dispute revolving around a linguistic contest of sorts. The couple trots out every proverb, every idiom, every popular expression they can think of, so long as it contains the terms "head" or "ass" (much as I myself have done thus far—and will continue to do—with the term "shit"). Harpee, the Wife, lets 'er rip about her husband's head; Harpo, the Husband, runs his mouth about his wife's ass or—*excusez-moi*—about any of her holes that come to mind, especially her asshole. (The wifely anus is a subject already sufficiently probed in #1, *Farce of the Fart*). Enter our third character, the troublemaking Payne N. Butts who makes his presence known to the couple and offers to mediate their quarrel. That mediation amounts to hauling all their crap down to the river to clean it up, for which Payne prepares an excruciatingly detailed, legalistic, and contractual inventory of the contents of the household.

However, Payne (pain that he is) will not "clean up" remuneratively for his efforts. Far from it, it is he who shall pay for his intrusion. The denouement is not so much an "unknotting" as an "unloading" in which an impressive variety of receptacles consecrated to the collection of waste come apart, unwrap, leak, ooze, drip . . . you get the idea. Tissier even makes the ingenious suggestion that the coup de grâce shall be when a chamber pot breaks—while *full*, one surmises—on top of the meddlesome Payne's head (*RF*, 10: 98n)! That's what he gets for being a smart-ass. Eventually, enough is too much when Harpee and Harpo attempt to dispatch Payne to wash their "shit," sending him up shit creek without a paddle. Heads, the couple wins; tails, Payne loses and gets lost. By the end of the play, he doesn't know which end is up! And there you have it. That is the foul matter of this play.

Characters and Character Development

In this broadest of comedies, the characters' names are just as broad. In the French, the Wife is Tarabin and the Husband is Tarabas, both evocative of *taborie* (a "commotion" or "din") and, for Tissier, of *tarabat* (a "noise" or "racket").[2] I thought of calling the Wife Toots (for obvious reasons) and the husband Toot Sweet (*tout de suite*); but the best fit for a contemporary audience seemed to be Harpee (a shrew) and Harpo (with the all the zaniness of the Marx Brothers intended).

As for physical attributes: Harpee unceasingly insults her husband's head, at one point suggesting that it is the size of a small planet; Harpo targets his wife's ass. (Baby got back?) So I suggest that costuming be used to exaggerate these body parts in the extreme and to enhance the multiple occasions for physical comedy. Plus there is some evidence that Harpo is older—perhaps much older—than his lovely wife, as when he refers to the "couple o' good years left" in him.[3]

Since the couple finds our third character a pain in their respective butts, I've named him Payne N. Butts. In French, he is called *Tribouille Mesnage*, literally someone who "troubles the household" (*trouble-ménage*); and his name itself has caused quite a bit of scholarly trouble. First and foremost, it's ironic in that Payne causes no trouble at all; rather, he attempts to cause the *opposite* of trouble by mediating a domestic dispute. It is no coincidence, moreover, that the root of *Tribouille*'s name is *bouillir* (to boil), which is exactly what it would take to clean up the couple's rubbish. (This, by the way, is not among the antiseptic solutions proposed in the play, although Payne sure does bring things to a boil.) But here's the problem—and, I confess, dear Reader, that this appears to be a problem only for *me:* Who exactly *is* this character?

Everybody who's anybody thinks that there's not a doubt in the world that Tribouille Mesnage is none other than Harpo and Harpee's drunken fool of a valet. Certainly Tissier says so without hesitation (*RF*, 10: 69), as does Faivre (*Répertoire*, 411–12). Their apparently logical reading is based largely on his frequent use of the words *maistre* ("master") and *maistresse* ("mistress") when he is addressing both the Husband and the Wife.[4] It is also true that, when Payne makes his entrance, he asks the couple, as would any servant, what they need. Pretty straightforward, right?

Not entirely. And please do not think that I am full of you-know-what or that I have my head up my . . .

Going out on a limb here, I confess that, ever since I first read the play, I've heard Payne as another interloping, troublemaking attorney (*avocat*) who habitually *noses around* trying to rustle up business, eavesdropping at people's doors like those other nosy barristers of #1, *Farce of the Fart*, and #2, *Edict of Noée*. In fact, it took no time at all to dig up a *lawyer troubling the household* in

Champfleury's curious work from 1870 called *L'Avocat Trouble-Ménage*! So, as another Payne N. Butts, let me provide an itemized inventory of the issues:

Item: Tissier reads the play as a tale of social justice in which a wily, good-time-guy servant eventually has enough of his shitty employers and resigns (*RF,* 10: 76). At the same time, however, Tissier dismisses Faivre's reading of the name *Tribouille Mesnage,* noting that a valet is *not* "one who troubles the household." That would be contrary, protests Tissier, to what a valet normally does (*RF,* 10: 73). To which I say: Tissier is absolutely right! Either Payne is no trouble at all or he's *not a valet!* In a pinch, he's a valet that causes a heap of trouble, a male soubrette. (Would the politically correct version be a *soubret?*)

Item: The more standard reading of Payne as a valet fails to account adequately for a large number of linguistic anomalies. Payne often uses *tu,* for instance, when addressing Harpo and Harpee. Tissier floats the idea that Payne is simply inexperienced, but even Tissier has to admit to finding it "curious" that a valet would interact linguistically with his "mistress" in so disrespectful a manner, treating her as if she were a hick (*RF,* 10: 113n).

Item: While one of the most beloved character types of seventeenth-century comedy is the sassy soubrette of a serving girl who gets between master and mistress, it is also the case that Payne's language of mediation is highly juridical, especially when he prepares a legalistic accounting of the household items. How would a normally illiterate medieval valet know to ask Harpee to "put her complaint in writing" (v. 107)? Or even to *read* such a written accounting? How would he be able to draft *item* after *item,* formal legal articles memorializing the contents of the household (all under the contractual rubric of *Item,* as in my list here)? (He *wouldn't;* but a Basochien *would.* More on that in a second.) And, if Payne were indeed the valet, then wouldn't he know all too well the items inside the house that he is employed to maintain? (Then again, maybe the place is so heinous because he's not doing his job.)

Item: Much of Tissier's reading rides on Payne's alleged resignation in his final speech: *Plus ne seray vostre servant!* The literal meaning of that line is "I'll be your servant no longer"; but the problem—again, only for me, it seems—is the exceedingly ironic meaning of a host of such phrases. This type of statement was to become the popular and extremely insulting *je suis vostre serviteur,* an expression that literally means "I am your humble servant" but that connotes anything but respectful submission. Its idiomatic sense is more along the lines of "up yours!" "screw you!" "as if!" or, in keeping with the sensibilities of this play, "stick it up your ass!"[5]

There are other possibilities too, given the likelihood of Basochial author-ship. One could imagine that not only is Payne the quintessential *shyster* (shit-ter) of an attorney but that Harpo—who is called *maistre*—is *also an attor-ney*. After all, *maistre* is the polite appellation for both "master" *and* "esquire." Frankly, I suspect that the truth lies somewhere in between: the play, written by a lawyer, is written in the way that lawyers talk, which means that perhaps even a valet walks, talks, sounds, and "bullshits" like a lawyer. Maybe Payne *is* a valet who just happens to enjoy playing the role of adjudicator, especially if the actor *playing* Payne is an Enfant-sans-Souci: that is, a Basochien from a fool's play (above, Introduction, § "History, Development"). Or maybe, in a preab-surdist world, such a legal-minded fool—or foolish-minded lawyer—simply wanders into the couple's unholy mess of a house.

So let's split the difference, shall we? I'm writing Payne as a meddlesome attorney (who uses better grammar than would a valet); but each use of *mais-tre* or *maistresse* is open to interpretation. For each "my good man," "milord," "my good woman," or "madam," those who prefer the "valet" reading may substitute: "boss," "boss man," "sir," "boss lady," "ma'am," or the like.

Finally, since Harpee and Harpo clearly have children, a number of squalid, nonspeaking offspring could be staged roaming around the fetid en-vironment of this manifest shit-house. (Maybe they had so many children, they didn't know what to do.)

Language

Readers might be interested to know that, of the sixty-five farces edited by Tissier, this is among the most heavily annotated: too much "shit" to account for, I guess. One has to adore the irony that the most frankly vulgar farce has produced such a profusion of scholarly erudition, of learned running off at the mouth (which is not analogous, we hope, to Harpee and Harpo's verbal diarrhea).[6]

First, a brief remark on *tu* versus *vous*. Harpee and Harpo use *tu* between themselves, but they tend to refer to each other in the third person: that is, if you can call a *head* or an *ass* a *person*. (It's not as far-fetched as it sounds: there was a medieval-Renaissance genre called the *blason* devoted to the symbol-ism of body parts. Besides, we do it today each time we call someone an "ass," a "hothead," or worse.) Payne mixes registers throughout with Harpo, but he prefers *tu* when addressing Harpee. All this, however, is not what stands out linguistically in *Shit for Brains*.

In the veritable thesaurus of insults that opens the play, there are subtle features that might be emphasized in performance. Although there is nothing grammatically wrong with Harpee and Harpo's "bulleted lists," something feels "off" nonetheless about the slew of *feminine* adjectives that apply to a *husband* and the *masculine* ones that apply to a *wife*.[7] French is a gendered language, of course, so it is entirely normal from a linguistic point of view that Harpee's insults to her *husband* about *his* "head" (the feminine *la tête*) would pair that feminine noun with feminine adjectives. To give you the flavor, it looks like this: *Teste testue, teste verte, / Teste posée . . . / Teste lunaticque et fumeuse . . .* (vv. 8–12). Likewise, it is entirely normal that Harpo's insults to his *wife* about *her* "ass" or "asshole" (the masculine *le cul*) would pair that masculine noun with masculine adjectives. It's just that, in his own long list, it turns out that Harpo matches a masculine noun with a masculine adjective a single time only, when pontificating about her fat, round ass: *cul rond* (v. 29). For the duration of his speech, he finds synonyms for *cul* and deploys a variety of adjectives based on *cul* that apply to *himself*, such as *baculé* or *aculé* (vv. 26–27). It is my own interpretation that something is afoot here, even though the foot is not one of the body parts in question. That is to say that it would have been just as easy to insult a gendered *person* rather than a gendered *body part*, or to assign wife Harpee the fat head and husband Harpo the fat ass. (I guess, as witnessed by the *Farce of the Fart*, talking out of one's ass is the province, alas, of medieval women.) For actors hoping to emphasize gender-bending in production, my reading is that Harpee's opening tirade helps her to do what she does all through, as when calling a Harpo a "queen" or a "fairy": emasculate her husband.

Additionally, at key moments in the inventory scene, my farce-beriddled brain perceives scatological spins on at least three pieces of proverbial wisdom that seem to run through the narrative, as it were. Bear with me as I set these up:

The proverb *tant va la cruche à l'eau qu'enfin elle se casse* is a version of "never cry wolf"; but its literal meaning is "if you take the pitcher to the well too many times, it breaks." In *Shit for Brains,* it seems that a different receptacle—a chamber pot—has been used one too many times, such that it breaks on somebody's head!

Elsewhere, there is an allusion to another receptacle: the pot or jug of milk (*pot au lait*). The milk pot is a component of a well-known fable that would later captivate the great Jean de La Fontaine in the seventeenth century, in which a milkmaid is so busy fantasizing about everything that she will do with the money she earns at market that, distracted, she drops the jugs and spills all the milk. With apologies for the mixed metaphor, today we translate the moral of the story as "Don't count your chickens before they hatch." (The meaning of this particular moral is different from the similarly themed English-language expression "Don't cry over spilt milk.") What is noteworthy here is that when La Fontaine penned "The Milkmaid and the Milk Jug," he observed that "This sorry tale *a farce became* / In time, 'The Milk Jug' was its name."[8] It is unclear which chickens Payne hopes to hatch—his own financial reward, perhaps—but all he gets in the end is a pile of shit.

Finally, a seemingly innocent reference to the "pot for making cabbage stew" (*le pot aux choux gras*) might well have invoked yet another proverb: *faire ses choux gras*. Literally, the phrase refers to preparing one's cabbage with plenty of fat (*gras*); metaphorically, it means "to take advantage of a situation," "to cash in on something," "to screw with someone," or "to screw around." Our three characters are engaged in all those things. Moreover, *gras* (often spelled *cras*, from the Latin *crassum* or "thick") denoted not only "fat" or "lard" but "vulgar" as well, like the English "crass." Considering that the Basochiens performed silly mock trials called *causes grasses*, our crass play cashes in on that metaphor too.[9] *Shit for Brains* is the *coup de graisse*!

Sets and Staging

How lovely is their dwelling place. *Not.*

One set is all that's needed, and it's a doozy: the filthy home of Harpee and Harpo.[10] All three characters might be swatting away flies throughout the scene. Among the multiple opportunities for physical comedy, one of the more amusing bits is the "loading up" of Payne, who is tasked with carrying all the dreck to the river. Harpee and Harpo need to outfit him with numerous bundles and packages. They even engage in a comical debate about trying to find the right spots on Payne's overladen body on which to position their "shit." Not surprisingly, that debate—up or down? higher or lower?[11]—revolves around spots that are closer to either the head or the ass.

Costumes and Props List

Oh dear. Where to begin? Whatever the couple wears, it should be dirty; and Payne should be dressed as the joker he is, whether he be a valet or a lawyer. Since he's a fool, he might wear a jester's hat.

Otherwise, one can only imagine the putrefaction of Harpee and Harpo's home. That's okay: Payne is kind enough to imagine it *for us*. Before he takes legal charge of the articles being entrusted to him, Payne produces a detailed inventory that, conveniently, amounts to a props list, to which I add only sticks or staffs. Do I need to clarify that everything on this list is in pitiable condition? Dirty, filthy, greasy; fetid, sullied, squalid; and stained red, brown, or yellow? Brace yourselves for the list:

Various ass-wipes of assorted shapes and sizes or, perhaps, used toilet paper all over the house; dishtowels; underwear; an enormous pair of trousers (perhaps the fishing gear known as waders, for wading through you-know-what) with a conspicuous yellow-brown stain that I'm attributing to Harpee—you'll see why in a later endnote; handkerchiefs; shirts; pillows; cheesecloth; pots and frying pans; crockery; buckets; cups; glasses; plates; pitchers; spoons; sheets; aprons; wineglasses and wine paraphernalia; salt and pepper shakers; ladles; a trough (or more rudimentary pots from which animals feed); a soup strainer; a laundry tub (borrowed from the famous denouement of *The Washtub*?); a vinegar cask; bottles; baskets; a whole series of pots, pails, and "shit-pots and piss-pots"; some laundry soap (the brand Cheer would be fitting!); and, last but not least—you'll see where—a whoopee cushion (obviously, in good working order).

Scholarly References to Copyrighted Materials (in order of appearance)

"Goin' Out of My Head." By Teddy Randazzo and Bobby Weinstein. (BMI)
"Over My Head." By Christine McVie. (BMI)
"Baby Got Back." By Anthony L. Ray. (BMI)
"Gett Off." By Prince. (ASCAP)
"Proud Mary." By John Cameron Fogerty. (BMI)

———————

[The entire play takes place in the filthy home of Harpee and Harpo.]

[To preface the opening tirades, the production might consider a brief medley of songs dealing with the head and the ass, provided that all requisite permissions have been cleared.]

[*Harpee and Harpo might address their respective diatribes to the
Audience,*[12] *backing in from stage left and stage right until they bump into
one another's backsides.*]

HARPEE, *wife of Harpo, begins:*
> You wanna see a miserable wife? Just look what you done to me! A
> poor, harried wife! What a pain![13] Day in, day out. Wanna see hell on
> earth? This is it, bub! They sure fixed my wagon, all right, the day they
> hitched me to the likes o' you! And now you done made me sink so low
> that Lucifer himself couldn'ta done no worse by me.
> Goddamn hard-headed lout!
> Always bitin' my head off!
> Can't keep my head above water!
> And I'm sick o' bangin' my head against the wall!
> You done gone soft in the head, you moron!
> And I think I'm goin' outta my head over you![14]
> I'm tired o' runnin' around like a chicken with its head cut off!
> I'd put a price on your head if I could!
> Yeah, that's right: I'm over my head—and it don't feel nice![15]
> Every time you rear your ugly head, I wanna head straight for the hills!
> That's it! I hit the nail on the head!
> Heads are gonna roll!
> Heads, I win! Tails, you lose!
> Heavenly Father, any day now, will I be relieved?

HARPO
> Oh yeah? Wanna see a miserable husband? Just look what you done to
> me! A poor, harried husband? What a pain! Day in, day out. Wanna see
> hell on earth? Right here, baby! Bang! Bang! Bang! Enough to turn a
> man into a criminal, rottin' in jail for life in a lousy stinkin' hole where
> the sun don't shine. And all on accounta my wife's fat ass!
> Asshole!
> Goddamn pain-in-the-ass lard-ass!
> I'm ready to kick ass now, I am!
> You can bet your ass!
> Baby got back![16] but I'll get back at her, all right!
> I'll put her butt in a sling, God willing!
> Her and her goddamn dirty asshole, and that other hole too!

That stinkin', putrid asshole . . . all full o' shit!
That dirty, brown crevasse! That crack all caked up with crap!
The filthiest asshole of all the assholes in the world!
She makes me feel like shit!
She can stick it up her ass!
Her ass is grass!
Heads, you lose! Tails, I win!
Heavenly Father, how's about me? When will *I* be relieved?

HARPEE

Goddamn hothead!
You and your dumb ol' swelled head.
You oughta have your head examined. Ain't nothin' left in there.
All you ever do is bitch your head off!

HARPO

Bugger off, bitch!
Talk about takin' it up the ass!
You and your fetid, stinkin' hole, where all stench is born![17]
Pollutin' my sleep all the time! Three hundred times a night sometimes!

HARPEE

Yo! Shit-for-brains! You think you're gonna bring things to a head?
Oooooohhhhh, I'm quakin' in my boots!

HARPO

Yo! Shit-for-brains! Shut your smelly piehole and that other one too!
It's all red and brown down there![18] I never get any sleep on accounta
you.

HARPEE

You can go straight to hell with all your bitchin' and complainin'! Go
on! Better get a head start before I sputter all over you!

HARPO

Witch! Bitch! You're goddamn raving mad! Have you sniffed yourself
lately?

HARPEE

Quit breakin' my head!

HARPO

Quit breakin' my ass!

HARPEE

Just keep on oinkin' like a pig.

HARPO

Blow it out your ass!

HARPEE

Shit-head![19] Eat shit and die!

HARPO

Enough, you blowhard! Kiss my ass!

[*Enter Payne N. Butts*]

PAYNE N. BUTTS

Enough yourselves already! Settle down! What the devil's going on here? Are the pair o' you drunk or something?

HARPEE

Will I ever be delivered from this torment? You bet I will!

HARPO

Delivered? You're gonna get a special delivery in a minute! I got a couple o' good years left in me, you know.

PAYNE N. BUTTS

What in the world is wrong with you? What's with all the racket? You're making enough noise to raise the dead! That's some fine talk around here!
[*Indicating the Audience*] Keep the volume up like that and folks'll walk out![20]

HARPEE
    What a shit-head!

PAYNE N. BUTTS
    I beg your pardon?
    What is it you need, exactly?

HARPO
    What an asshole![21]

PAYNE N. BUTTS
    What the devil's the trouble anyway? I'll settle this! I'll just step right in and mediate your quarrel. Why don't each one of you tell me what's your beef?

HARPEE
    What a schmuck!

HARPO
    What a whore!

HARPEE
    Who are you callin' a whore?

HARPO
    You and your old caboose!

PAYNE N. BUTTS
    Come now, Harpee, tell me the origin of this commotion.

HARPEE
    Am I lucky gal or what?

HARPO
    Butter wouldn't melt in her mouth.

HARPEE
    One of these days, buddy, POW! Right in the kisser!

PAYNE N. BUTTS
    Harpee.

[*Harpo makes a move against Harpee: given the content, he might smack her behind.*]

HARPO
    Gotcha!

PAYNE N. BUTTS
    Listen to me, now, Harpo! If I could just have a word with you, my good man . . . What's wrong with you?
    Knock me over with a feather! I've never seen anything like this from husband and wife! Not in my life!
    Harpee? Harpo? What are you fighting about? What's the cause of this dispute? Tell me all about it, please.

HARPEE
    Goddamn hothead is always harpin' on me. He gets all hot under the collar over nothin'!

HARPO
    And that one never stops shittin' and fartin'! It's like somebody lit a fire underneath her! You could burn down the whole town with what she spews outta her asshole!

PAYNE N. BUTTS
    As I understand it, then, the contested matter emanates from the head and from the ass. So let me take charge from here on in. I'll restore peace and quiet—[*yelling, as if to say "shut up!"*] that's *peace and quiet!*—to your household!

HARPEE
    He's a lyin' scumbag. The whole problem's all in his head.

PAYNE N. BUTTS
    Now see here, Harpo, you really shouldn't be yelling at her all the time. It's just not right.

HARPO

Oh for God's sake! I'd hardly have to—would I?—if I weren't downwind all the time while she's lightin' 'em up right under my nose!

PAYNE N. BUTTS

Touché, Harpo. I'll grant you that. But come on now: kiss and make
up!

HARPO

I'm okay with that.

HARPEE

I'm not! If he says yes, I say no!

PAYNE N. BUTTS

Okay, Harpo, you first. Will you agree to binding arbitration and submit yourself to my judgment?

HARPO

It's okay with me.

PAYNE N. BUTTS [*to Harpee*]

And, in the matter before us, will you comply with my ruling?

HARPEE

If I hear one more word outta that dumbhead . . .

HARPO

If she could just plug that leakin' asshole o' hers for five minutes . . .

PAYNE N. BUTTS

And you, sir:[22]
If you would be good enough to shut your face for a moment, my good
man . . .

HARPEE

[*To Harpo*] You swellheaded fairy![23]

PAYNE N. BUTTS

And, for God's sake, girl . . . er . . . *madam,* my good woman: please put your complaint in writing.

HARPO

It's the asshole, I'm telling you.

HARPEE

And I'm telling you . . .

PAYNE N. BUTTS

Just wait a second, would ya? Let him finish.

HARPEE

And I'm telling you: he's outta his head.

HARPO

And I'm telling you that that asshole o' hers is bubblin' over as we speak.

PAYNE N. BUTTS

Are you an idiot, man?

And, you, woman, are you nuts? Let Harpo tell his side of the story, otherwise I won't be able to render a verdict. Go on. Go ahead!

HARPO

So, I . . .

HARPEE

So, I . . .

PAYNE N. BUTTS

You need to shut up now, toots.[24]

HARPEE

He's like one of the crowned heads o' Europe: a real queen![25]

PAYNE N. BUTTS

For God's sake, honey, let the man finish. And then, you shall have the opportunity to speak next.

[*To Harpo*] Go on. Continue.

HARPO

From that wind comin' outta her britches, there's one helluva stench.

HARPEE

But . . .

PAYNE N. BUTTS

Oh, all right already! Go on and speak first, otherwise we'll never hear the end of it. Go ahead.

HARPEE

It's his noggin.

HARPO

No, it's her farts.

PAYNE N. BUTTS

It's hard for me to tell *which* end is up . . . or down.

Order! Order! I'm instructing you to take turns in an orderly manner. Or wait: How's about this? Keep on fighting! See if I care! There you go! I *forbid* your reconciliation! Case closed!

Mark my words: if you can't stand the heat, get out of the kitchen! And your kitchen, by the way, is a real mess. This is the worst case I've ever seen.

HARPEE

Whenever he gets some idea into his head, you can see the cobwebs flyin' out! Yak, yak, yak! Always runnin' his mouth! You can hear the cranks and gears a-squeakin': big wheel keep on turnin'![26]

PAYNE N. BUTTS

If you please, now, Harpee, my good woman, a little bit of a change of heart would do you good. A little peaceful enjoyment of the home. It's good for the soul. Now calm down.

HARPO

Payne N. Butts is sweet on you—and [*perhaps gesturing toward her backside*] he's always on your side.

PAYNE N. BUTTS

So go on then, now, Harpo. Go on and give her a little kiss. And I'll have my fee as well, since I've reconciled you two. Or at least a tip. [*To Harpo*] You: don't you complain anymore about her asshole. [*To Harpee*] And you: no more complaining about his head. You know very well why Harpo's head is the size of a small planet and why *you're* always blowin' the big brown horn.[27]

The two of you are always bustin' out all over!

HARPEE

I'll quit harping on him.

HARPO

As long as she quits farting! That's the (w)hole problem.

PAYNE N. BUTTS

All right then, Harpee, Harpo: there must be agreement on this point. You, ma'am, you must realize that, sometimes, you simply have to fix the plumbing down there, clean out the pipes.

HARPO

Get everything spic and span!

HARPEE

[*Nodding in feigned agreement and eyeing one of the chamber pots suspiciously*]

Hmmmm . . . speakin' o' cleanin' things out . . . it could get *really* rancid around here if I was to break *one* of those pots . . .

[*Harpee cleverly lures Payne into position—you decide how—so that she can "accidentally" break a chamber pot on his head, the contents dripping down his ass.*][28]

[*Victorious*] You can lead an ass to water, and you *can* make it stink![29]

[*Harpo might join in and break a second pot on Payne's head.*]

HARPO

Make it *two*! You get two shots—that's two *pots*—period. Get it?

PAYNE N. BUTTS

Hey! No fair! You're busting my head *and* breaking my ass! Who would want a pile o' shit in a pot?

HARPEE

What of it?

PAYNE N. BUTTS

What of it? Good Lord! Harpo! Just for the sake of getting you two back together, here I am in the filthiest house I've seen in over a year. Truth be told, my dear father, Feyerbutt, and my blessed mother, Holly Baloo[30] slurped off their dishes like cats and dogs. But they licked everything clean, they did! And they barely had a penny to their names: just a few threads on their backs, from head to toe. Now, *this* place: it's a horse of a different color! It's beyond the pale. [*For the pun, he might kick a pail.*] It's a garbage dump!

HARPEE

So clean it up for me![31] If I can dish it out, you can take it! And it's not like *I'm* gonna do it! Snake those pipes, give it all a good scrub, wring stuff dry 'n' shit, get it all sparklin' clean!

PAYNE N. BUTTS

You keep an eye on the house, then; I'm gonna go and collect all your crap.

HARPO

Better wash all of it, Payne N. Butts! It really smells like shit in here.

PAYNE N. BUTTS

You're telling me!

HARPEE

Go on down to the river now, where the water runs all clear. Go on! I thought it was all decided. Haul ass! What the hell are ya waitin' for?

PAYNE N. BUTTS

Not much, in fact. Just get me the laundry soap, Cinderella.[32] Had I
known beforehand that this would do the trick, then I would most
certainly have done it already.

Harpee, Harpo: at this juncture, I require a writing table.

HARPEE

What for?

PAYNE N. BUTTS

I must take an inventory of the contents. All the household items being
entrusted to me. What you're dumpin' on me and so forth.

HARPO

What is that your business? We don't give a shit.

PAYNE N. BUTTS

I don't want you to feel taken.

HARPO

Don't worry about it, man.

PAYNE N. BUTTS

Whatever you say . . . but I repeat my earlier point: it's so that no one
can take issue with me later. You know: mess me up or take me down.[33]

HARPEE

Get outta here already.

PAYNE N. BUTTS

Whatever you say . . . but am I wrong here? What are we gonna do?
Insure the stuff by weight?[34] I mean if I should, unintentionally, leave
behind some of your crap . . . er . . . pots.

HARPO

So go ahead! Count it up!

PAYNE N. BUTTS

But I'm not wrong about this, right?

HARPEE

Just do it already! Step on it!
[*Payne proceeds to air their dirty laundry, as it were, by providing an inventory.*]

PAYNE N. BUTTS

Perhaps if I were to conduct a brief inventory . . .
First, we appear to have here . . . What the devil is this thing? It's all red and brown!
This is your asswipe, madam! Jesus H. Christ! It's ready to get up and walk away! Talk about bein' on the rag![35]

HARPEE

Yeah, well I hope you choke on it, God damn it!

PAYNE N. BUTTS

And what *is* it, pray tell?

HARPEE

That one belongs to the kids. Now off you go! Get goin' already! Hop to it! March!

PAYNE N. BUTTS
[*Proceeding with his inventory*]

They're all caked up with doo-doo! I beg your pardon . . . I thought that . . . Let's just proceed with the inventory:
Article 1: *Item:*[36] here, we have one dishtowel.
And I'm almost afraid to ask: What on earth is *this*? Seems to be Harpo's old britches and his best Sunday handkerchief.
Article 2: *Item:* some of Harpo's long-sleeved shirts and . . . some kind of pad . . . Whoopee! It's Harpee's cushion.[37]

[*Harpo might grab the whoopee cushion from Payne and use it to mock the noises that emanate so frequently from Harpee.*]

HARPEE

And I say you're lyin', you lousy schmuck!³⁸ Those are the guest towels!

PAYNE N. BUTTS

[*Displaying a particularly fetid item stained yellow—ideally, an
enormous pair of trousers or waders to accommodate Harpee's fat ass.*]³⁹

And this? Jesus H. Christ! They're enormous! This looks like a saffron
stain right here.

HARPEE

The hell you say! It's shit! Put your nose right in there and take a whiff!

PAYNE N. BUTTS

If this is shit, then somebody's got the runs! What've you people been
eating around here anyway?⁴⁰

Holy shit! How could it possibly be. . . ? This is gross! Harpo, this is
either saffron or shit. Might you shed some light on this . . . *matter*?

HARPO

[*In response to Payne's questions, Harpo does as Harpee has suggested:
rubs his nose in it to take a whiff.*]

By God, you're right!

PAYNE N. BUTTS

[*Continuing the inventory*]

And the Devil take me if I can figure out what *this* might be! Aha! It's
an absorbent pad. [*With a patently ridiculous suggestion that brings
Harpo's emasculation to a head*] It must belong to the *master* of the
house! Either that, or it's another small asswipe. [*To Harpee*] What do
you think, milady?

HARPEE

What are you, crazy? That ain't it: that's his very best apron!⁴¹

PAYNE N. BUTTS

Hold your fire! No need to piss yourself!⁴² I must merely have
forgotten.

[*Payne continues to sift through all the "shit," picking out individual items from the fetid piles and holding them up to the couple for inspection.*]

And, *Item:* What, pray tell, is this folded object here? It stinks to high heaven! Holy crap, man! Holy crap! It's enough to get you to make like diarrhea and run!

HARPO
   That's just cheesecloth.

PAYNE N. BUTTS
   [*Indicating a particularly dark spot*] And over there?

HARPEE
   Just a bit o' Montezuma's revenge.[43]

PAYNE N. BUTTS
   And this?

HARPO
   A Crock-Pot.[44]

PAYNE N. BUTTS
   And that?

HARPO
   That's our Sunday ass-best britches.[45]

PAYNE N. BUTTS
   And what about this?

HARPO
   That's just some more crockery.

PAYNE N. BUTTS
   And what's this here?

HARPO
   The throne—you know, the bucket.[46]

PAYNE N. BUTTS

And how about this? [*He begins to gag.*]

HARPO

The frying pan ... and into the fire! Will you get a move on, for God's sake! Quit lollygaggin'! And quit gaggin'!

PAYNE N. BUTTS

Well good golly Moses and in the name of Saint Francis of a-sissy![47] This constitutes rather a large number of tasks! How on earth can these items be refurbished?[48]

HARPO

How, shmow! That's a fine how-do-you-do-doo-doo-doodle-ee-do! And peace be with you too, bro! Why *couldn't* they be? You have your head up your ass or what?

PAYNE N. BUTTS

And what about all those pots over there? No one cryin' over spilt milk around here![49] And all those spoons, and all those goblets ... and all those plates ... and all those ... other plates. I'm supposed to wash all that too?

HARPEE

You betch'em, Chuck! All by yourself.

PAYNE N. BUTTS

I beg your pardon?

HARPO

What to you think? Get your ass down to business! Let's see a little elbow grease!

[*Payne might pause to look at the grease spots all over the house.*]

PAYNE N. BUTTS

Come now, my good man, if you'd just pay attention to the inventory. I seek merely to confirm that it's all here.

HARPO

    Enough already! Get the hell outta here!

PAYNE N. BUTTS

    Item: First of all, we have here . . . I must prepare the formal inventory.
    A place for everything and everything in its place:
    These sheets that I must wring out.
    And these teaspoons.
    And all these loose towels and rags.
    This spigot for the wine cask.
    Harpee's apron.[50]
    Harpo's small wipes.
    Item, and here, inside this basket . . . Wait a minute! What *is* this?
    These are scoopers! These are pooper-scoopers!
    And, *item,* here are four small handkerchiefs, the saltshaker, and
    other . . . er . . . vessels.
    [*He might hold up an exceptionally large serving bowl*] And here's the
    trough for the pigs.
    Item: and the soup strainer.
    Item: and the laundry tub and the vinegar cask, which, *item,* stinks to
    high heaven, by the way . . . and . . .
    Christ in a bucket! What the devil can *this* be?
    Aha! I'm afraid I know all too well! This is where Sir Harpo goes to
    take a dump! This is the shit-pot and the piss-pot! If you'd be good
    enough, kind sir, to get me a horse so I can carry all this dreck . . .

HARPEE

    Holy shit! I'll give you dreck in a minute! And a couple o' dog turds
    too, for good measure![51]
    You want a horse? Quit horsin' around or you'll be up shit creek with-
    out a saddle!

PAYNE N. BUTTS

    Wait: am I expected to pile up all this garbage and carry it on my
    person?

HARPEE

    No shit, Sherlock![52]

PAYNE N. BUTTS [*extending his arms*]

All right, then, hand it over: fill 'er up. I'll head down to the river. But if you could at least fetch me the wheelbarrow. I think everything might fit in there.

HARPO

Nope, no way. Forget it! Roll up your sleeves. Put your paws on all these pots and pitchers. Get your hands dirty.

PAYNE N. BUTTS

That's the least of my worries. But how are we going to fit all this laundry in?

HARPEE

On your head.

PAYNE N. BUTTS

I'll look like a schmuck.

HARPEE

Jesus H. Christ on the Cross! If you lose one single goddamn thing . . .

[*The couple begins to load him up.*]

PAYNE N. BUTTS

Whoa! Hey![53] Everything's falling down! There's too much stuff! My charge is simply too unwieldy . . .

HARPO

Stand up straight!

PAYNE N. BUTTS

Christ in a bucket! Everything's spilling out all over. Put it a little bit lower. Down! Down! Down, dooby-doo, down down![54]
[*Harpee and Harpo try to find the right spot on Payne's body for their "shit": Up or down? Closer to the head or to the ass? Harpo will also make some kind of comical, almost chiropractic "adjustment," perhaps "accidentally" kicking Payne in the groin.*]

HARPO

Here! Take this!

PAYNE N. BUTTS

Harpee! Give me a hand!

HARPO [*more "adjustments"*]

Right hand don't know what the left one's doin'!

PAYNE N. BUTTS

Gimme a break, Harpo!

HARPEE

Man o' man! Ya big fat wino![55] That's too high! [*More "adjustments"*]
Like this! This hits 'im just about right.

PAYNE N. BUTTS

Harpo! A hand!

HARPEE

Get a load o' him! He's tryin' to pull a fast one! [*To Payne*] I swear, ya'
big lout, if you drop one more thing I'm gonna smack you around!

HARPO, *hitting him*

Take that, you dirtbag! Take that, you lousy, stinkin' crook![56] Go on
now. Get the hell outta here! Make like horse shit and hit the trail!

PAYNE N. BUTTS

Mary, Mother of God! Forget it! Take care of your own shit! The Devil
take me if I stick around here one more minute and traipse around with
your spoons and your fruit baskets and your pots and your bottles and
your laundry soap!
[*Dumping the contents right back in the direction of Harpee and Harpo*]
Here! To market, to market with you two pigs![57]
I shan't be at your service any longer![58] In other words, up yours!
And that's all I have to say about that! The end. See you later. Much!
[*Harpee and Harpo are left speechless as Payne addresses the Audience.
As he speaks, the couple might begin reengaging in foul behavior of the*

company's choice. For example, Harpee might hit Harpo over the head
with the frying pan or chamber pot as he kicks her in the ass.]

Ladies and Gents, please do forgive us if our farce was a tad on the dirty
side. Don't mind the potty mouth! I hope you all took it the right way!
Farewell to all and to all a good night!
One more time in verse! How about it?

Forgive us this, are little farce
'Twas all about the head and arse!
Just take in stride our foul-mouthed jokes:
[*Given the content, à la Porky Pig?*] Bye-bye for now, 'cause that's all
folks![59]

The END

9.

Monk-ey Business, or,
A Marvelous New Farce for Four Actors,
to Wit, the Cobbler, the Monk, the Wife,
and the Gatekeeper

Le Savetier, le Moyne, la Femme, et le Portier

CAST OF CHARACTERS

"BLOTTO," the COBBLER
DOTTIE, his Wife
BROTHER PETER, the Monk, also known as Pete or "Bro Holdup"
(Serre-Porte)
The GATEKEEPER
[A few extras : Nuns, Priests, or Monks for the "cloister-bar scene"]

PRODUCTION NOTES

The *Farce nouvelle tresbonne et fort joyeuse à quattre personnages* appears as #33
in Cohen, *Recueil,* 259–68; and as #44, *Le Savetier, le moine, et la femme,* in
Tissier, *RF,* 9: 127–94. The play is 572 octosyllabic verses; to my knowledge,
it survives in the *Recueil Cohen* only. Tissier, who places its date of composition between 1480 and 1492 (*RF,* 9: 132–33), also translated it into modern
French (#44 in *FFMA,* 3: 153–74). Alternate title: *All Over Him.*

Plot

Monk-ey Business is zealously devoted to the importance of confession as a
gateway to Heaven. But, wait! It's a farce, so the Pearly Gates are barred by

all sorts of earthly creatures, all up to no good. One of those creatures guards the metaphorical gates: *Brother* Peter—not *Saint* Peter—a lusty man of the cloth; the other is a lowly, literal Gatekeeper, who serves several functions, including barkeep.

In *Monk-ey Business* we encounter another henpecked Cobbler, another everyman with a plan. After an impromptu meeting with his old school chum, Brother Pete, the two men head off to have a few drinks at the monastery (where else?). There, the Cobbler, "Blotto," falsely sings his Wife's praises, the better to play a trick on both the horny cleric and his shrewish Wife, Dottie (whom he impishly and tantalizingly describes to the Bro as marvelously loving and docile). Dottie is always all over him, claims the relative newlywed, Blotto, whenever she comes to fetch him. And she *is:* just not in the way that Blotto implies. Brother Pete takes the bait, aroused enough to want Dottie all over *him.* To facilitate the experience, the two men exchange clothes to set the scene for her arrival. The plan of their little masquerade—a practical joke and the first of *Monk-ey Business*—is that Dottie will be true to form and greet Brother Pete in her habitual way.

Needless to say, the Cobbler has omitted from his charming narrative the fact that Dottie is indeed "all over him," with great frequency and most unpleasantly, each time she drags him out of the bars where he spends most of his earnings during most of his days. Enter Dottie, who arrives at the tavern—sorry, that's *monastery*—in a foul mood, presumably having hunted high and low for her drunken churl of a husband. She immediately curses out the man who is wearing her husband's clothes, proceeding logically to box the ears of Brother Pete. Since Pete is now fit to be tied, the two men plot their dramatic revenge on Dottie, which calls for her to repent shamefacedly—to the priestly Pete himself—for having sinfully walloped him. (In the playtext, Pete is identified as "the Monk," but it is clear that he also functions as a kind of parish priest.) In point of fact, Brother Peter has other plans for her: without sharing his directorial vision with his coconspirator, Pete fully expects to go erotically off script. When Blotto tells Dottie that she has assaulted a priest, her perturbed reaction is what the men had predicted. Dottie endeavors to make amends: she's a good Christian, for heaven's sake (as Faivre emphasizes in another tongue-in-cheek plot summary [*Répertoire,* 395–97]). Dottie then accepts Pete's priestly invitation to a private, nocturnal confession session, where "Bro Holdup" will really "hold her up." It is a session that, as in #3, *Confession Lessons,* will not exactly go as planned by those who seek to misuse the sacrament of penance. She even tells her husband about it! (What *is* this? The *Princesse of Cleves*?).

Upon being informed of the rendezvous, our intrepid Cobbler, less dolt-ish than some of his fellow guildsmen, perceives instantly what the would-be private confessor is after . . . and it's not the *after*life. With directorial skill that rivals that of the Lady in #7, *At Cross Purposes,* Dottie turns the tables, devising an alternate mise-en-scène involving yet another costume change. It is her *husband* who will show up for the blessed event, in drag as Dot-tie. Blotto consents. At the spot for the sacred assignation—the Monk's cell—"she" meets the Gatekeeper, whose collusion Brother Peter has already enlisted and who wishes to partake in the offering that "Dottie" is there to make. "She" rebuffs the Gatekeeper's unintentionally homoerotic advances. Once "she" (Blotto) finds "herself" *en tête-à-tête* with Bro Holdup, the lewd Monk does in fact "hold her up," attempting to extort "her" confession in exchange for sex. He gets a beating instead from the Cobbler in women's clothing. So does the Gatekeeper, who demands his fair share of the booty as "she" attempts to leave. That'll teach 'em!

Characters and Character Development

With costume changes, role-playing, and trickery galore, no one here is who he or she seems to be, except perhaps for Dottie in the first scene, where she is *exactly* what she seems to be: a shrew, and the only one who is not in on the gag (at least, not at first). All four characters are practical jokers who make fine forays into directing their various performance pieces within this play.

I was tempted to call the Cobbler "Joe Six-Pack," but he already seems to have a nickname: *Fin Vertjus,* which might indeed be translated as "Blotto," or as "Perfect Lush" or "Helluva Drunk."[1] In Scene 1, we learn that he has recently married, that he's a lazy bum, and that Blotto is a fairly jolly drunk who might even be staged with a hangover. Initially, he seems a bit of a bump-kin, but he smartens up right quick. He's also a damn fine actor, soon to be a drag queen. By the way, he has big ears, which he covers up with an ill-fitting chapeau that is not just any hat. The subject of a medieval in-joke, this hat is, in all likelihood, the floppy, rabbit-eared fool's hat traditionally worn by the *badin* in fools' plays (*sotties*).[2] The closest American equivalent might well be the jester's cap and scepter, the latter of which could come in handy when Blotto beats the sleazy ecclesiastic and Pete's accomplice at the end. I suggest that Blotto sport a mustache or a beard (more below, § "Sets and Staging").

The randy Brother Peter might have a pot belly (like Friar Tuck), which is not so well camouflaged by ample vestments. He is a monk, a priest figure, an unprincipled extortionist, a liar, and a promiscuous cheat with a checkered past, although neither he nor Blotto will disclose the details of a certain notorious incident from their youth (Scene 1). Most important, his nickname, *Pierre serre-porte,* is the site of multiple puns. Literally, that's the doorstop, the "door stopper," the one who bars the gate, or, as Tissier advises, the one who holds the keys (*RF,* 9: 135), albeit *not* to the Kingdom of Heaven.[3] To give linguistic voice to all those vices, I have called him Bro Holdup to preserve the following: he wishes to be *holed up* with Dottie; he *holds her up* on her path to penance and salvation; and he has a criminal past that coincides with both those delicts, perhaps another sort of *holdup.* Moreover, since the play might begin with a sketch called *SERRE PORTE,* a mimed skit might convey all the "holdups" to come.

The Wife is unnamed in the play, but I have given her the name Dottie in order to make the most of a sort of knock-knock joke (Scene 2). She is quite sharp, as in quick on the uptake, but, for character development, I fear that that other sharpness of any fishwife will do. Does anyone recall the old *Star Trek* episode featuring Harcourt Fenton Mudd's shrewish wife, Stella (and her multiple android—I guess that's *feminoid*—clones)?[4] That's Dottie, harping on her husband for drinking again.

At the monastery where Brother Peter resides, the unnamed Gatekeeper (*portier*) guards the door, admits visitors, serves meals, pours wine, and, of course, entertains special requests, like smuggling women into cells. While "doorman," "innkeeper," and "barkeep" convey some of those duties, "gatekeeper" reminds us that the gates that really matter here are of the pearly variety.

Language

This is one of the most linguistically rich plays of the collection, boasting numerous puns and double entendres. One group of puns is related to theatrical representation: *farce, farcer, faire signifiance, contrefaire,* and so on. Another group concerns academia and student life, generally exemplified by the macaronic admixture of French with grammatically incorrect Latin phrases.[5] Blotto in particular mixes French and Latin midspeech and even midsentence (although, on rare occasions, he *does* get his Latin right). A similar situation obtains for his French, which is peppered with the improper—but occasionally proper—usage of that oh-so-pretentious imperfect subjunctive.

He tends to use *vous* with Brother Peter, as he attempts to outsmart him, all with the utmost courtesy. He and Dottie also use *vous* with one another.

Brother Peter's grammar is better than Blotto's, even as he alternates between formality and informality when conversing with his pal (it's *tu* for Dottie); and Dottie's grammar is better than her husband's. The actor playing the Monk might speak with a faux aristocratic accent. Furthermore, it is difficult to overestimate the blasphemy of all three characters but especially of Brother Pete, who frequently invokes his God while plotting sexual advances against Dottie.

Sets and Staging

When we first meet Blotto the Cobbler, he is leaving home, allegedly to set up shop to earn his daily bread; Tissier thinks that Blotto actually *works* for a time period that encompasses all of about three verses (*FFMA, 3:* 157). I think, however, that Blotto never quite makes it to work and simply walks right on by the usual spot where he hawks his wares. (If he is staged leaving home, what about a parody of Cary Grant and Katharine Hepburn at the opening of *The Philadelphia Story*?)

The play's setting is a *convent,* for which I provide the consistent option of *monastery* (more familiar to American audiences as the place where monks reside). Then again, there is something to be said for a convent with a proverbial fox in the henhouse. Considering the comportment of Bro Holdup, that setting could be played for laughs, in that the nuns would be in quite the pickle as the play makes light of the Monk's ongoing interest in a pickle tickle. Additionally, by analogy to the joke about the "nuns' bar" of the film *Sister Act*, imagine a "cloister bar" with nuns and/or fat tonsured fellows on their spindly barstools, nursing—or guzzling—their beers. But it would also be possible in production to accentuate the dark side of the isolated life of monasteries and convents: specifically, the painful realities of physical and sexual abuse. We needn't have waited for Denis Diderot's Enlightenment *The Nun*, the film *The Magdalene Sisters* (2002), or today's relentless disclosures about the criminal behavior of abusive priests to understand that there is really nothing funny about it. That goes, potentially, for the final beating scene too, which might be "choreographed" along the lines of #5, *Blind Man's Buff*, or #6, *Playing Doctor*.

Elsewhere, the text gives little guidance about the rapid scene changes. I have extrapolated to the best of my ability that the action unfolds in the great outdoors (possibly at some remove from both Blotto's home and his clearly delineated spot at the market), at the market (even if Blotto only walks right on by), at the gate of the monastery on the outskirts of town, inside its tavern-like refectory, inside Brother Peter's cell, possibly at the home of Blotto and Dottie, and at various spots between any of those locations.[6] Productions might thus make space onstage for all those sites simultaneously. Because at no time are we told that the Cobbler and his Wife are actually *inside* their house, it could be quite amusing to stage some of the clothes-changing scenes "out in the open." For example, Brother Peter and Blotto might execute the first switcheroo behind a pillar at the monastery; Blotto and Dottie might do so behind a tree if they are staged outside rather than inside their home. In light of Dottie's remark that Blotto has been gone for almost an hour, additional mimed scenes might be inserted at will.

Finally, the "humor" of the denouement might be amplified if our Cobbler is a mustachioed fellow who does not shave for his drag performance but, rather, who attempts (occasionally unsuccessfully) to conceal his facial hair with a veil, scarf, or shawl, such that his "costume" fails to camouflage what is most obvious: that he's a *man*.[7] How soon does Brother Pete catch on—if *ever*—that it's actually his "friend" Blotto who is taking him down? You choose. Choose also how much you'd like to make of what turns out to be numerous homoerotic interactions by Pete and the Gatekeeper toward Blotto. Or get a load of the exponential metacommentaries if, say, Blotto and Dottie are cross-cast, with Blotto, played by a woman . . . playing a man . . . who is "disguised" as a woman . . . and so on.[8] (I've always loved the movie *Victor/Victoria* myself.)

Costumes and Props List

Costume changes are profligate enough that Tissier invokes carnival and, at one point, even a cabaret, old chum (*FFMA*, 3: 156). Brother Peter requires some ecclesiastical vestments, a cope and a surplice to be exact: that is, a long robe and a white tunic worn as an overgarment. Both articles of clothing were well known to the medieval audiences of such fabliaux of mistaken identity as "Estula" (which features two thieves, lots of punning, and a priest who loses *all* his vestments while fleeing the scene of the alleged miracle of a talking dog).[9] For contemporary audiences, the instantly recognizable priestly collar and black robe (or cassock) should do the trick. Dottie needs a veil, a scarf, or a shawl, which she lends to her husband: something to cover his face during his final drag performance, for which he also requires a large stick or staff.

Scholarly References to Copyrighted Materials (in order of appearance)

"Behind Closed Doors." By Kenny O'Dell. (BMI)

"The Happy Wanderer." By Friedrich Wilhelm Moeller, Antonia Florence Ridge, and Florenz Siegesmund. (ASCAP)

"The Lusty Month of May." By Alan Jay Lerner and Frederick Loewe. From *Camelot,* © 1960. (ASCAP)

"Eight Days a Week." By John Winston Lennon and Paul James McCartney. (ASCAP)

"I'll Take You There." By Alvertis Isbell. (BMI)

"It's My Party." By John R. Gluck, Wally Gold, Seymour Gottlieb, and Herbert Wiener. (ASCAP)

"Think." By Aretha Franklin and Ted White. (BMI)

———————

[*Opening Mime:*] *HOL(E)D UP*[10]

[Scene 1]

[*Somewhere near Paris, in the great outdoors near a monastery or convent*]

[*Blotto, the Cobbler, might awake with a hangover, collect his tools, say good-bye to his wife, and ostensibly leave for work, singing a happy folk song.*][11]

BLOTTO
"The other day, I roamed across
A lovely field, for auld lang syne.
I didn't know what I had lost
Nor what it was I hoped to find."

I swear! Who gets up at this hour? This would go a whole helluva lot better with a little drink in me! Just a shot or two and I'd be singin' like a tweetie bird in no time!

[*Noticing the Audience*]

Come on over, folks.[12] Anyone wanna come along with me? Come on, now. Don't keep me waitin' like that![13] Come on along with me! It's springtime, you know, and a young fella's thoughts turn to . . . you know . . .

He sings [*another tune*][14]

"Hooray! it's May!

It's May! Hooray!

And now, it's time to play!"

Hey, look over there! Here's some company headin' over this way right about now. Well I'll be! It's a monk! Why he's just the right fella to come along a-wanderin' with me, 'specially where *I'm* headed this mornin'!

Say what?

Holy moly and I'll be a monkey's uncle! It ain't who I thought it was! God damn! Could it be? Say it ain't so! It's that pain in the ass, Brother Peter Holdup! God damn! No way! It can't be! He looks pale as a sheet! Maybe he ain't had his mornin' pick-me-up yet either!

[*Heading for Brother Peter*]

Okey-dokey, then, I'll do me my wanderin' thataway and try my luck with him: *Bona dies, frater,* and peace be with ya, bro!

BROTHER PETER

Et vobis etiam, frater, likewise, I'm sure! Whaddaya say? Whatcha *gottibus* for *mihi?*

BLOTTO

Holius molius! Ignoramus est. Non speaka da' Latin . . . unless it's when some guy in a robe's orderin' me to do a couple o' Hail Marys or somethin'! *Hailibus Mary-bus!* Although . . . come to think of it, I guess if I say "*Bonjour vobis, mon frère,*" that's better than "*How's tricksibus?*"

BROTHER PETER

You're much too modest! One could hunt high and low and never find anyone around here who masters Latin so good as what you just spoke.

BLOTTO

I done learned it in Paris, I did. You know somethin'? I left all them other schoolboys speechless. It was kinda like I'd speak, and they'd all shut up on a dime.[15] They could hardly believe their ears.

[*Brother Peter might do a double take since Blotto has very big ears.*]

BROTHER PETER

[*Aside or to the Audience with a pleasant anachronism*] Like chalk on a blackboard, I bet!
[*To Blotto*] You know what they say: little pitchers have big ears.[16]

BLOTTO

Say what?

BROTHER PETER

I mean . . . You'd look better with a nice round hat, good sir. Better *coverage,* if you catch my drift.[17]

BLOTTO

I was this close to gettin' into Beaver College[18]—I was almost in, if I woulda just set my mind to it. But I had me a bee in my bonnet in those days, and I said I wasn't havin' none of it.
[*Giving Brother Peter the once-over*] But holy cow! I'd swear you was back in the trenches with me at school! That's what I say!

BROTHER PETER

Oh my God! It *is* you! I saw you take orals, didn't I? The Latin Quarter, eh? Red light district?[19]

[*A brief flashback scene of that exam might enhance the comedy here.*]

BLOTTO

Holy *domine Deus! Par Deum, you speakes truthlily! Comé va vobis?* And how's it *go-go-ere?* How ya doin' anyway, Brother Pete? Doin' well?

BROTHER PETER
Fit as a fiddle.

BLOTTO
Well knock me over with a feather! I ain't seen you in ages! Not since those days. I thought maybe you'd kicked the bucket or somethin'! Where the hell you been anyway?

BROTHER PETER
I've been here, there, and everywhere doing my preaching. You know, up and down, round and round, upstairs, downstairs, in my lady's . . .

BLOTTO
Christ! I can't hardly believe it! Just bumpin' into you like this. Remember that time when we got caught and they came and took you away?

BROTHER PETER
Let's leave that little incident aside, shall we? I did my time! Saints alive![20] You hardly have to remind me.

BLOTTO
I was a good friend to you back then, wasn't I?

BROTHER PETER
You certainly were.

BLOTTO
And I was there for you, buddy, right? I had me some reputation back in those good ol' days, I did. Like no man on the face o' God's green earth!

BROTHER PETER
I'll say! I'd give my eyeteeth to get it all back. Those were the good ol' days! So how's about a little toast to celebrate our reunion?

BLOTTO

Lordy, lordy! Now you're talkin'! Ready when you are, boy! Where should we go?

BROTHER PETER

The gatekeeper over at my place has got good wine . . . well, depending on the time of year, and it only costs a buck or two.²¹ So let's do it!

BLOTTO

Long live the friendly neighborhood barkeep! Long live the grape! Long live the vine!

[*The men repair to the monastery or convent.*]

[Scene 2]

[*At the monastery or convent—the action alternates between the gate and the "tavern" or refectory.*]

BROTHER PETER

Yo! Gatekeeper! Barkeep!

The GATEKEEPER

Who goes there, neighbor?²² What's up? And who's *that* you got there with you?

BLOTTO

I bring you glad tidings: It's me and Bro Peter Holdup! We've come to knock back a few in the name o' the blessed Prince o' Peace! Set 'em up, friend! And, if you please, give us some of the good stuff!

The GATEKEEPER

In the name of our everlasting Father, you'll have a barrelful if you like.

[*The Gatekeeper serves them and may continue to serve other "patrons," possibly alternating—even hurriedly—between his barkeep duties and tending to the gate.*]

BLOTTO

Okey-dokey, so what's new, then, Brother Pete? What's up? What do you say?

BROTHER PETER

I don't know, nothing much, really. Except I heard back in my neck of the woods that you got married.

BLOTTO

It's true. And I married the sweetest, the most joyful, the kindest, the gentlest, the most courteous and gracious lady ever to see the light o' day: Dottie. She's just a blessing on the face o' this earth, and her wish is my command.

BROTHER PETER

Say, pal, is she really that pretty? That beautiful of face and figure?

BLOTTO

Our Father who art in heaven! Everybody thinks so. You've got that gorgeous figure, that adorable little nose, she's always got a smile on those lips o' hers. . . . She's all soft and cuddly, she just melts in your mouth,[23] and she's always game for a little fun. If I'm about to cry, then Dottie cries right along with me. Laughin' one minute, cryin' the next: both at the same time when I have my way with 'er . . .
[*He might make a noise that sounds like an orgasm à la* When Harry Met Sally.]
. . . if you know what I mean. Wink, wink, nudge, nudge, say no more . . .

BROTHER PETER

Hell's bells and God damn, boy! You are blessed! I should be so lucky. I sure wish I could pull that off!

BLOTTO

And then, here's the other thing. So it's like . . . if I'm out and about somewhere and she comes to get me, as God is my witness, she's all over me![24]

[*Possibly acknowledging the Audience*] It don't even matter that folks is watchin'.

BROTHER PETER

God! You lucky dog, boy![25] You sure hit pay dirt! She really just throws herself at you like that?

BLOTTO

You bet your ass! Honest, sometimes she just goes crazy on me, like she's possessed or somethin', hangin' all over me like she does. You should see 'er go at it! I swear on a stack o' Bibles: Our heavenly Father himself doesn't get this much attention in church!

BROTHER PETER

Okay, I give up! I'm begging you: you think you might let me take a crack at her? At least for just the greeting and salutation part? It would do me good. Come on! In honor of our reunion! Just a heavenly kiss or two on those sweet little lips . . .

BLOTTO

In the name of all that's holy! Take a crack, you say?
Sure! Help yourself! Do her as much as you like.[26] But here's how it's gonna go down so you don't get caught.
[*Giving him the once-over*] Those clothes have gotta go. Strip down. Take off your cassock—and, God! that collar!
Then, you're gonna put on *my* clothes. And she'll just rush up and she'll be all over you because she's gonna think it's me.

BROTHER PETER

Say what?

BLOTTO

No kidding. Just do exactly like I told you.

BROTHER PETER

God strike me dead if I don't get mine too! Coming right up! I'll be a new man if I can just kiss that sweet face.
[*He changes clothes offstage or perhaps merely downstage.*]

[*Enter Dottie, looking exasperatedly for her husband*][27]

DOTTIE, *alone*
Holy Mary, Mother of God! Where the hell is that husband o' mine this time? What's he gone and gotten himself into now? God forbid he'd be out working for a living. God damn him! Come on, Lord: send him a plague o' locusts, would ya?
[*From outside the "tavern," Dottie notices her husband—that is, Brother Peter in Blotto's clothing.*]
Look at that jolly-ass drinkin' like a fish over there, on another bender, God damn it! Every penny he earns goes straight to the booze. My mama taught me better! I swear to God, if I can't keep him in line, then our Father might as well just strike me dead! Not that I'd wanna die without getting into a state of grace or anything . . .

BROTHER PETER
[*Still blissfully unaware of Dottie*] How do I look?

BLOTTO
Holy moly! You're a dead ringer! You're all set to go. But just be careful: no matter what happens—come hell or high water—not a single word outta your mouth until she's had a chance to wrap herself around you.

BROTHER PETER
Jumpin' Jehosaphat![28] She can do whatever she wants with me!

BLOTTO
Make sure you don't give it away, you hear? No dirty tricks now. And no droolin' all over her or, I swear, you're really gonna piss me off.

BROTHER PETER
And I'd piss myself off if I were *ever* up to no good, I swear to God!

DOTTIE [*approaching the gate*]
Knock knock!

The GATEKEEPER
Who's there?

DOTTIE
    Dot!

The GATEKEEPER
    Dot who?

DOTTIE
    Dot's for me to know and you to find out!

The GATEKEEPER
    What do you want?

DOTTIE
    Holy smokes!²⁹ My husband Blotto's in there, isn't he? Hasn't he been
    drinking in there for over an hour?

The GATEKEEPER
    Holy smokes yourself, lady! Blotto, you say? As God is my witness, I
    don't think I know him.

DOTTIE
    You don't know your ass from a hole in the ground! You can't fool me!

The GATEKEEPER
    Well . . . we got a real guzzler inside *gettin'* blotto. Old Cobbledy-Gook
    over there! Is that him?

DOTTIE
    You bet it is.

The GATEKEEPER
    Well golly gee! I guess I just didn't see him come in. Barely recognized
    'im.³⁰ But come on in, honey. He's havin' dinner right over there.

DOTTIE
*The WIFE starts beating the MONK, thinking that it is her husband
[because Brother Peter is wearing Blotto's clothes, of course] and says:*
    Mary, Mother o' God, let him choke to death on his dinner!

This is where you come to conduct your business, you rotten louse! This is why you leave your post?

[*Hitting the successfully disguised Brother Peter*]

Take that! And that!

BROTHER PETER

Ow! Mother Mary! Talk about gettin' hammered! What *is* this? A bat outta hell?

DOTTIE

Who the hell are you callin' a bat? It's your wife, for Chrissakes!

BROTHER PETER

I'm all weak and dizzy all over.

BLOTTO [*sotto voce to Brother Pete*]

Ssssshhhhh! Shut the hell up, for God's sake! She'll recognize your voice!

BROTHER PETER

Who cares! She's whuppin' the bejesus outta me! Ow! My stomach!

DOTTIE

Oh shut up![31]

BROTHER PETER

Jesus H. Christ! I'll be hog-tied! She's gonna break every bone in my body!

DOTTIE, *hitting him*

Had enough yet? You goddamn lousy drunk! Vile, stinkin' pig! Dishonoring our good name!

[*Indicating, with more courteous language, the "Monk," i.e., her husband, Blotto, who is equally effectively disguised as Brother Pete*]

Lucky for you that kindly gentleman o' the cloth is standin' right over there, otherwise I'd've really given you what for! You woulda been the sorriest-ass character in your whole family!

BROTHER PETER

My good woman, I now tender a humble prayer to God that . . . He take your ass down pronto!

[*Exit Dottie, and the men change back into their own clothes.*]

You've gotta be kidding me! Holy smokes! This is the adorable wife you were telling me all about? If this is what you had in mind all along, Blotto, then you can hang by the neck till you're dead!

BLOTTO

Hell no! I swear to God! Don't get sore! I don't know what got into her . . . unless it's . . . well . . . maybe she's havin' one of them spells o' hers again. Come to think of it, she does get those things two or three times a week. They hit 'er just like that, and she just loses it! She goes totally nuts. You just caught her on an off day is all.

BROTHER PETER

Yeah, well fuck that shit! I hope she gets hers but good![32] Look at me! I'm standing here minding my own business and she beats the crap outta me!

[*The two men pause for a little number, perhaps in rap.*]

BLOTTO[33]

Pity the poor soul:
Dug himself a hole,
Then he can't get out!

BROTHER PETER

Mad enough to shout!
What a turnabout!
Hurts too bad to laugh.

BLOTTO

Mad enough to pout!
What a martyred lout!
Always feel her staff!

BROTHER PETER

    Didn't you advise
    That she was a prize?
    That you had your leave?

BLOTTO

    Comes as no surprise,
    Seen it with your eyes.
    Now, you must believe.[34]

BROTHER PETER

    The Devil take her—and the horse she rode in on! I think she gave me
    a black eye. Look at this bump on my head! God damn her!

BLOTTO [aside]

    Was that a kick-ass gag, or what? I saw that one comin' from a mile
    away, I did. I knew it! I'd've staked my life on it that, the minute he was
    wearin' my clothes, he was really gonna get . . . what was comin' *to me!*

BROTHER PETER [*to Blotto*]

    So, I got my ass kicked good, got smashed, thank you very much. Bully
    for me! But, I swear to God, if you'll go in on it with me, I think I
    know how to settle the score and get back at her.

BLOTTO

    How?

BROTHER PETER

    Here's what we're gonna do:
    You're gonna send her my way so she can make her full confession. And
    you can bet your ass that I'm gonna give her one hell of a penance![35]
    She'll be beggin' for mercy!

BLOTTO

    In the name of the Blessed Virgin, I promise you she won't do it. I'm
    ready to place my hand on the Bible and swear to it right now.

BROTHER PETER

And I'm telling you that this is the Gospel truth. She'll do it—and that's a promise.

BLOTTO

Jeez Louise, there's never been a confessor who could get two words out of her.

BROTHER PETER

And I'm telling you, my friend, she'll do it because I know how to make her do it. I'm gonna make her understand that just turning to God is not enough: she's gonna have to go and see the Pope himself for a special dispensation! You know, to seek forgiveness for the shame and the outrage that she perpetrated upon me. Get it?

BLOTTO

Jesus H. Christ! That just might work. Only the wisest and, if I may say, the classiest o' fellas coulda thought things through like that. It's a deal: I'll have her come over your way.

BROTHER PETER

Well, go to it then!

BLOTTO [*aside*]

Honest to God, when I think of the ass kickin' of that poor sod, it just cracks me up! I got him but good!

BROTHER PETER [*aside*]

Holy smokes! Old Blotto the Clodhopper over there might've fooled me once, but I'll figure out some way to get him back like he's never been gotten before! [Fool me once, shame on you. Fool me twice . . . um . . . um . . . you're not gonna get fooled again!]
He'll get his, all right. And he'll never even see it coming!
And, Holy Christ, I'll take his wife for a spin too while I'm at it, as soon as I get 'er all *holed up* . . . if I can pull it off, that is.
You've always got to keep your eye on a guy like that! But I'll cut him down to size, I will! Tricksters have got to get tricked.

Okay. Enough standing around here. Away I go! Better head off and wait for her. Because if I don't stop for her, I doubt she'll kindly stop for me.[36]

[*Blotto now catches up with Dottie outside the monastery or convent while Brother Peter occupies himself elsewhere but not too far away. He might even eavesdrop on their conversation.*]

DOTTIE

Where the hell have you been anyway? You lousy stinkin' drunk! Of all the goddamn gall! I hope God gives you a pain in your joint . . . I mean joints![37]
And now tell me, my good man: You've been out all day. Where's all the money that you made, huh?

BLOTTO

Guess what? That's none of your concern. And, by the way, you better hurry off now and make your confession. You're overdue, you know. Hop to it, woman!

DOTTIE

My confession?

BLOTTO

That's right. Your confession.

DOTTIE

Quit playin' around, you damn lush. I swear, if I have to put up with one more o' your stupid jokes, you won't soon forget it![38]

BLOTTO

Why heavens to Betsy! You did beat up a priest after all.

DOTTIE

A priest?

BLOTTO

That's right. I swear, it's the God's honest truth. The whole truth and nothing but the truth.

DOTTIE

A priest? [*Making the sign of the cross*] *Benedicite,* bless my soul, and Lord have mercy! What priest?

BLOTTO

Oh for God's sake! The guy's a monk who used to be a drinking buddy o' mine.

DOTTIE

Jesus H. Christ! If I sucker punched anybody, it wasn't *him!* It was *you!* I know that for a fact.

BLOTTO

And in this case, you happen to be wrong.

DOTTIE

So I guess he was wearing a disguise, then. You two switched clothes, I suppose.

BLOTTO

By God, I think she's got it!

DOTTIE

How the hell did you two geniuses cook that one up?

BLOTTO

How the hell do you think? For Chrissakes! He wouldn't get off my case, askin' me if I was married and stuff. So I told him "yes" and he was all happy for me, it's true, but Jesus H. Christ! It was all on accounta [*puckering up and maybe making smooching noises*] he was all hot to kiss that sweet little face o' yours.

DOTTIE

That's a hell of a show you're runnin' there.[39] And now I'm gonna get excommunicated!

BLOTTO

So far, nobody knows about it except us. [*With a wink at the Audience*] It's not exactly common knowledge, you know.
But you better get over there and get down on your knees right in front of him and confess. Tell him that you're there with contrition in your heart and you're wantin' absolution. Come to think of it: whatever you do, better watch out for his tricks. If he tries to hit on you, you've gotta tell me about it right away!

DOTTIE

Good God, you're such a jackass! He's a monk for God's sake. You're telling me that monks are like that?

BLOTTO

What the hell do you think? Eight days a week,[40] come what may! I don't trust him.

DOTTIE

All right then. If it seems like he's sayin' anything that's not for my own good—if he goes off script just one little bit—then I'll tell you all about it.[41]

BLOTTO

Okay, good.
[*She starts to leave.*]
Wait! Come back here for a second!
I know for sure that one of the things he's gonna tell you is somethin' like . . . that you've gotta beg me for mercy. Don't you forget it!

DOTTIE

Lord have mercy! It'll be a cold day in hell before I ever beg mercy from the likes o' you! I'd rather see you dead and buried than ask *you* for mercy. I don't care what he says or what kinda story he tells me.

BLOTTO
    Don't you think I deserve it?

DOTTIE
    Don't hold your breath.

BLOTTO
    Jesus H. Christ! You sure got a bug up your ass! You're a real she-wolf,
    you are! [*With some diabolical chortling*] Better watch your step! Bo-
    geyman's gonna get you! You look like a sweet young thing, but it's my
    judgment that you're pretty darn proud and uppity.

[*Blotto begins to exit as Brother Peter enters.*]

DOTTIE
    [*To the exiting Blotto*] Your judgment, that's a good one, Daddy.[42]
    [*Brother Peter probably think that* he *is "Daddy."*] God give you good
    day, Father.

BROTHER PETER
    God give you good day, pretty lady, and may He grant you all that your
    heart desires.

DOTTIE
    You got that right, Father. I'm truly pained deep in my heart, for sure.

BROTHER PETER
    And why is that?

DOTTIE
    On accounta what my husband . . . you know . . . when you were drink-
    ing with him and you put on his clothes and all. But I swear to you on a
    stack o' Bibles that I was—that I *am*—truly sorry . . . and that I'm more
    than happy to do any kind of penance that you like.

BROTHER PETER
    Why certainly, my dear. And I must admit that anyone gazing into
    those baby blues o' yours would be most ungracious were he to hold

anything against you. So you shall have my counsel on this matter, my little chickadee . . . but all in due time.

DOTTIE

What do you mean?

BROTHER PETER

Dear sister, anyone desirous of getting to the bottom of this affair must seek the wisdom of Rome. I don't see how we can avoid it . . . unless . . . I could probably come up with some way of getting around it in no time if you're interested. It's entirely up to you.

DOTTIE

Count me in. Whatever it takes. Just say the word, and I'll do it. [*Perhaps kneeling*] So, bless me, Father, for I have sinned. How's about a little absolution for the trespass that I committed against you and all?

BROTHER PETER

Why certainly. But, the better to provide the full absolution treatment, I'll first need to study up on the matter at greater length in my book.

DOTTIE

I beg your pardon?

BROTHER PETER

Yeah, that's the ticket. I need to study up. Do some research.

DOTTIE

Well, if you could be quick about it; I've got other things to do today.

BROTHER PETER

I don't think that's a very good idea. You could get into a whole lot of trouble.

DOTTIE

What do you mean?

BROTHER PETER
My book. I don't have it on me: the one that I need to consult.

DOTTIE
So where is it?

BROTHER PETER
Where else? It's where I do my studying. [*Throwing up his arms in feigned, reluctant resignation, followed by real hope*]
Then again, if you're really in a hurry, you could come back tonight—over to my cell. I could grant you absolution there.

DOTTIE
Alas, Father! I don't think I can do that! My husband would have a fit!

BROTHER PETER
Well, then, you won't be absolved if you don't come. I never heard of such a thing! You better do what I say for the eternal salvation of your soul! I've saved the souls of many a woman—and of some pretty high-class ladies too.

DOTTIE
Lord have mercy! All right. But, if I have to go over there, then you better tell me which one is your room.[43]

BROTHER PETER
Of course, I'll tell you. It's straight ahead. Just follow the path to salvation. I'll give you a road map.[44]

DOTTIE
What's your name anyway, sport?

BROTHER PETER
I'm Brother Peter. And, I swear to God, I'm not playing around here. I'll fix you right up once we're all *holed up.*
[*Exit Dottie and Brother Peter in opposite directions, both heading to their respective homes*]

[*As Brother Peter heads back to the monastery or convent toward the Gatekeeper, he makes the upcoming remarks aside.*]

    I'll fix you up good, all right, honey, when you fall into my little trap.[45]
    Ooooohhh baby! As soon as I hold her in my arms, I'll be a new man!
    There's the gatekeeper! All I've gotta do now is let him in on it!
    Yo, gatekeeper!

The GATEKEEPER

    What's up, Brother Pete? What can I do you for? Whatcha need?

BROTHER PETER

    Actually, I need a favor, son. But you've got to keep it to yourself.
    Tonight, a real classy lady is going to be paying me a private little visit
    in my room. She's coming to make her confession, get it? So, if you'd be
    good enough to show her in. And not a word about it to anyone.

The GATEKEEPER

    Whoa! I get it! On the QT. You got it, by God. Mum's the word.

BROTHER PETER

    But be careful nobody sees her when you let her ass in. Just imagine the
    hurly-burly if the abbot were to recognize her.[46] Get it?

[Scene 3]

[*At Blotto's house*]

[*Blotto is relaxing at home, engaged in his favorite pastime: getting blotto. Given that he's about to get dressed up as a woman, that fortification will doubtless come in handy.*]

[*Enter Dottie*]

DOTTIE

    A blessing upon our house and peace be with you, brother! Was I gone
    too long?

BLOTTO

Praise the Lord! You seem much more reasonable to me now. But first things first. Tell me, dear sister, have you been absolved of all your sins?

DOTTIE

Heaven forbid! He told me that my sins are so horrible and hideous that there wouldn't be any forgiveness for me at all until he did some research in his book. Anyway, to make a long story short, I won't be absolved unless I go over to his room tonight between seven and eight o'clock. That's the appointed hour when he's supposed to absolve me.[47]

BLOTTO

Good God, Woman! May the Lord strike him dead! I'll knock his block off! He won't be planning his little confession session if I get my hands on him. And you can make book on it![48]

DOTTIE

Don't get excited. I figured out a helluva way for him to get what's coming to him.

BLOTTO

I'm still in shock here! What is it?

DOTTIE

Well hang on for a second, and I'll tell you!
So . . . I'm gonna help you get into my dress. And, then, when you're all dolled up, you're gonna go to his room. And then, what's gonna happen is that he'll see you all dressed up like that and he's gonna think it's me: no doubt about it. And—good God Almighty!—just be sure you turn the tables on him but good! In his face! Choke 'im till he turns blue! As that prick has sown, so shall he reap!

BLOTTO

God's Blood! I'll cook his goose all right! *A la royale!*[49]

DOTTIE

Just do exactly like I told you and do a good job pretending to be a woman.[50]

[*Dottie dresses up her husband. He will bring along a stick for protection.*]

BLOTTO, *as a woman*
[*He should also answer in a woman's voice.*][51]
>Mother Mary, you bet I will. I know all there is to know about playing women.[52] So where does he live? What room is he in? I don't have a clue how to get there.

DOTTIE
>You're supposed to find the gatekeeper. He'll show you in and take you there.

BLOTTO
>Jesus H. Christ on the Cross! He's got plenty o' tricks up his priestly sleeve but he's sure gonna get his! I'll punch his tonsured lights out if he thinks he's gonna get outta this one! Nobody gets the best o' me!

[Scene 4][53]

[*At the monastery or convent*]

BLOTTO
>[*Aside*] There's the gatekeeper. I see him. He's the one who's supposed to take me in. I think he wants to talk to me.

The GATEKEEPER
>Where you headed there, babe?

BLOTTO, *as a woman*
>I'm supposed to make my confession to Brother Peter. What room is he in?

The GATEKEEPER
>Oh yeah! Now I remember!
>I'll take you right to him. Just wait here for a moment. He went off to say vespers.

But come on over here a little closer, sugar. How's about a little kiss to get things started?

BLOTTO
Good God! I've got other things on my mind. Don't you think your timing's a little off?

The GATEKEEPER
Seems like the least I can do is take you for a spin since we got some free time here. And that's just what I'm gonna do.

[*He grabs "her."*]

BLOTTO
Oh, for pity's sake, back off, would ya? Get away from me! Go over there!

The GATEKEEPER
Hey, what's your beef, lady? What the heck's your problem anyhow? Holy moly! It's not like you'll be gettin' in and out without me! [*Making an obscene gesture*] I'll catch you on one end or the other, you know. Comin' or goin'!

BROTHER PETER
[*Entering; aside*] Time to repair to my chamber and hit the hay because I bet my little sweetie pie's arrived by now.
There she is over there! [*Gesturing*] I'd know her anywhere with that physi-*oh-my-God!*[54] You can't miss her!
[*Making a move on "her"*] Welcome, welcome, my little muffin, come right on in. Come on over here and give me a little kiss, honey-lamb.

BLOTTO, *as a woman* [*throughout*]
Hey! Quit it!

BROTHER PETER
Just one or two. No extra charge. They're on me.

BLOTTO
Aren't you ashamed of yourself? You better watch your step!⁵⁵

BROTHER PETER
Saints alive! My step! You're the one steppin' out! And, in the name of the shoes of the fisherman, [*pointing to his bed*] you're spending the whole night here! And then, come morning, I'll just knock that full absolution right off for you.

BLOTTO
What kind of a way is that to treat a lady? I come here in a spirit of contrition to ask for absolution, and you just hold me hostage like that?

BROTHER PETER
Uh huh, that's right. That's the way I do it.

BLOTTO, *hits him*
I don't think so, sir! You're a very bad boy! A couple of whacks of this stick oughta teach you! What are you trying to do? Sow the seeds of discord in my marriage?

BROTHER PETER
And I'm telling you: this is how it's done!

BLOTTO [*in a pugilistic posture*]
Jesus Christ Almighty! Then put up your dukes, Brother Prick!⁵⁶

BROTHER PETER
What the hell kinda broad is this anyway? God damn it to hell!

BLOTTO
See how you like the feel o' this rod on your sorry ass! There! How does *that* feel?

[*The noise of the ensuing fight sounds like the "couple" is having sex.*]

BROTHER PETER
It's a she-devil if I ever saw one! I've never been so sore in my life!

BLOTTO

This is how you take women's confessions, is it? And then, *you* wanna give *them* absolution?

BROTHER PETER

Help! I pray you, madam! Oh the hell with you, you goddamn hothead!
And here I thought it was party time! Boy, oh boy, I hurt all over.

[*"She" heads for the gate.*]⁵⁷

The GATEKEEPER
[*Aside, overhearing the commotion*]

Holy Christ! Master Peter's gettin' his rocks off right now with that little tart! That's some rockin' robin in there!
But, honest to Christ, if that little bird thinks she's sneakin' outta here without talkin' to me first . . . A bird in the hand is worth two in the bush!⁵⁸
[*To Blotto as "she" tries to leave*]

Whoa! Hey! Hold up! Where do you think you're goin'? We still have some business to attend to, if you know what I mean. Time to pay the toll!

BLOTTO

Oh for God's sake! Nobody's talking to you. Get out of my way!

The GATEKEEPER

I'd be one heck of a nincompoop if I let you get away this time.

BLOTTO, *hitting him*

And I said you better not try and hold me up! No more beating around the bush! Gotta make like a Catholic and pull out!⁵⁹

The GATEKEEPER

And I say I want *my* share, by God! Same as Brother Peter! It's only fair.

BLOTTO, *hitting him*

I'll give you fair in a minute! You want your share? How's about in the name of *Saint* Peter, I let the both o' you stew in your own juices!

The GATEKEEPER

You don't gotta overextend yourself, you know.

BLOTTO

That's what you do when women come around confessing? You just stop 'em in their tracks?

The GATEKEEPER

All right, all right, *ma'am*! I give up!
[*Aside or to the Audience*] Christ Almighty, that's some feisty broad! What she needs is the back o' my hand![60]

BLOTTO

What's that you're saying?

The GATEKEEPER

Uh . . . what a *hand*some woman you are—honest to God—a real sweetheart.
[*The Gatekeeper flees the scene, perhaps running back to the tavern.*]
[*Aside or to the Audience*] That's all I could think of to say so I could get the hell outta there. God only knows what she was gonna do next!

BLOTTO [*back in character?*]

There! That oughta do it! They're both all black and blue; and they got just what they deserved.
[*To the Audience, perhaps joined by the Company*][61]
Adieu until the next time, folks. We hope and pray that you've enjoyed the show because, now, we've gotta go!

The END

10.

Getting Off on the Wrong Foot, or, Who's Minding the Whore? for Three Actors, to Wit, the Lover Minding the Store, the Cobbler, and His Wife

Farce de Celuy qui garde les Patins

CAST OF CHARACTERS

BOOTIE, the Shoemaker [Jack's Wife's Lover]
JACK, the Cobbler
DESIRÉE, Jack's Wife
[Bootie's unnamed Wife]

PRODUCTION NOTES

The *Farce nouvelle de Celuy qui garde les Patins, à trois personnages* appears as #21 in Cohen, *Recueil,* 165–70. The play is 310 octosyllabic verses; to my knowledge, it survives in the *Recueil Cohen* only, but in two versions.[1] I know of no modern French translation. Alternative titles: *Playing Footsie; The Slippery Slope; By the Bootstraps; Loose Lips Sink Slippers.*

Plot

In a new domestic comedy about two—count 'em, two!—unfaithful spouses, the dimwitted cobbler Jack falls prey to the ruse of his wife's lover, who lives next door. To round out the cast in which Jack is the only named character— and even *that* might be a pejorative nickname along the lines of "Jacko" or Jack-Off"—I have scripted the Lover as Bootie and Jack's Wife as Desirée.

For one thing, it gets very confusing to talk about the plot if the Lover in this triangle doesn't have a name; for another thing, Bootie refers to Jack's Wife as "my object of desire"—*ma desirée* (v. 7)—which is exactly what he would say if he were calling her by name.[2] The now familiar battle of the sexes is coupled here with a commercial conflict between two specialists of the shoe, Jack versus good neighbor, Bootie. In the hierarchy of cobbling, Bootie is an illustrious shoemaker or *patinier* who creatively fabricates footwear himself—and he's an expert fabricator, all right—whereas Jack is a lowly cobbler or *savetier* who merely repairs and sells old shoes.[3] Jack's more pressing dilemma? The poor cobbler suspects that his wife is stepping out on him. In order to catch her in the act, he enlists the assistance of his good neighbor, Bootie, who is only too happy to get in on the act. Needless to say, it won't be an act.

Bootie gets things off on the right foot by tricking Jack into a test of Desirée's fidelity: a test that has the added advantage of getting the two amorous adulterers together (again). Bootie is the better salesman—the whole minidrama was *his* idea—so he oh-so-kindly volunteers to stand in as Jack's bait. Bootie sends Jack over to mind his store, which frees up Bootie to mind *Jack's* store, a professional courtesy that includes servicing Desirée. With the two male characters each installed in one another's shops, Bootie and Desirée proceed with their overtures. Any subsequent "repairs" have nothing to do with shoes at all but, rather, with Desirée's "repairing" to the bedroom with the handier of the two men. Naturally, Bootie has promised to give Jack a sign: Bootie will cough or whistle to cue Jack's reentry on the scene so that the outraged husband can catch the two lovers in flagrante delicto. But, regardless of when, if *ever*, Bootie gives the sign, Jack waits much too long for it . . . and then some. He *does* get it in the end. So too do Bootie and Desirée "get it" when he tans their hides. What else was a cobbler to do?

Reminiscent of the open-endedness with which the curtain comes down on the beloved *Pathelin* (above, Introduction, § "Question of Genre"), the final lines of *Getting Off on the Wrong Foot* also promise more trickery to come—perhaps in the form of another play? One could almost stage this play as a prequel to #2, *Edict of Noée* (with which it shares many features) or, conveniently, to our next play, #11, *Cooch E. Whippet*.

Characters and Character Development

Jack is not the sharpest tool on the belt; in fact, he's just an old shoe, stupidly unaware that his neighbor Bootie is coveting his wife. (Compare him with

Dummy Downer in #6, *Playing Doctor*, or Molière's Orgon in *Tartuffe*.) He has a bit of a split personality to boot, making frequent asides, some to the audience. As noted above, I've called him Jack because, in Scene 1, she seems to call him, with all due irony, *Sire Jehan* (my lord John).

Bootie is quite the artist, Lothario, and metteur en scène and, when we first meet him, he is singing a happy tune about his illicit love for his neighbor's wife. In hatching the whole scene of entrapment, he does a good job of concealing from Desirée that she is but a pawn in the drama that he has designed to play out at her expense (but for which he too shall pay). He lies as easily as he breathes, such that one is reminded of the wisdom of Judge Judy: How can you tell he's lying? His mouth his moving. Let us not forget, moreover, that, although there is no sign anywhere of Bootie's wife, he's a married man. Physically, we also know that he has curly hair.

The lead female character is scripted as the Cobbler's Wife (*La Savetière*), her identity deriving solely from that of her husband. But this highly sexual character takes a back seat to no man, even if, at first—like Dottie in #9, *Monk-ey Business*—she is the only character who is not in on the ruse. Desirée is assuredly a trickster on her own terms, expert in the role-playing that aids and abets cuckolding one's husband. Furthermore, she is a jealous adulteress who suspects Bootie of cheating on *her* with yet *another* mistress; and she is a bit of a practical joker who enjoys a laugh at Bootie's expense.

Given their theatrical propensities, coupled with grammar and syntax that are so excellent that they border on the highfalutin (below, § "Language"), all three characters do a fair amount of overacting.

Language

Wordplay on foot-related issues predominates, starting with my title. I could never have guessed, by the way, that there would be so many puns in the English language about shoes, feet, and other footwear. The adulterous duo is also amusingly devoted to keeping score, counting, and chronologies ("in the past three years or so," "maybe a year and a half," Desirée should choke "for three years runnin," and the like [Scene 1]). In English, it also seemed perfect to have them play some footsie as well as a little game of "This little piggy went to market."

All three characters speak remarkably good French, although when it comes to deciding definitively about using *vous* versus *tu*, they trip up. Sometimes, they even go so far as to offer both polite and impolite versions of the same sentence. It all makes for a nice contrast with their frequent cursing, which is particularly blasphemous in a couple of instances. In addition to deploying the wealth of euphemisms that have peppered this collection, they truly *do* take the name of the Lord in vain.

Key in production is the fact that Desirée's performance calls for her to do a musical number that might include some erotic dancing and the Middle French lyrics of which are integrated into the script. Companies might supply original compositions for these moments or weave in the lyrics to a popular ditty that seems appropriate, provided that all requisite permissions have been cleared. I have indicated these instances via formatting.

Sets and Staging

The entire play takes place inside and outside the two homes of our three protagonists, mostly inside the home of Jack and Desirée (with Jack situated for a time inside Bootie's home). One of the things that we know for sure is that Jack's house (like the set in #2, *Edict of Noée,* and #11, *Cooch E. Whippet*) must have a front door *and* a back door. But, as we wondered of #6, *Playing Doctor:* Where exactly *are* the characters and when? Jack and the lusty Bootie are neighbors; so their homes might be close enough together to see easily inside each other's homes. Today, the French call that *vis-à-vis,* and it is quite the disadvantage on the real estate market. Onstage, however, it offers the comic advantage of multiple voyeuristic efforts on Jack's part as he "minds Bootie's store," such as peering through Bootie's window into *his (Jack's) own home,* or using a sort of rudimentary spyglass (and so on). Indeed, there are some exceptionally erotic moments for him to witness between Bootie and Desirée.

The set for Bootie's home can be fairly elaborate, as he is the better artisan. The most glorious of shoes should bedeck his dwelling (or storefront); recall the closet at *Runway* magazine in the film *The Devil Wears Prada.* If additional physical comedy is desired, it would be possible to cast a nonspeaking character as Bootie's wife.

Given Bootie's propensity for song, this play might also be staged as a musical with any number of interludes (for which all requisite permissions have been cleared). Such musicality is common in the farce repertoire, and it so happens that there is another play in the *Recueil Cohen* (#37) in which yet another cobbler gives his wife a literal song and dance to each one of her requests: the *Farce of the Cobbler Who Answers Only in Song (Farce nouvelle à quatre personnaiges du Savetier qui ne respont que Chansons* [287–94]). In the notes, I offer a variety of tips about modern numbers that might be close to the original sense of the Middle French musical clichés. (See also below, Appendix: Scholarly References to Copyrighted Materials.)

Finally, there are two beating scenes, the first of which bears a resemblance to that of #2, *Edict of Noée* (Scene 1), in which it is the wife who beats the husband but with the husband endeavoring to "save face" by claiming that it is the other way around. The second beating scene of the play's denouement is supposed to be a pretend beating (part of Jack and Bootie's plan), but, to Bootie's dismay, it is a real one instead at the hands of the clobbering cobbler Jack. Since the script is fairly detailed on the subject, it will be necessary to produce some good fight choreography or ballets such as those that we saw in #5, *Blind Man's Buff,* or #6, *Playing Doctor.*

Costumes and Props List

Jack needs a tool belt with various cobbler's implements, among them an awl; and he needs a stick or a staff for the final scene. Jack's house should contain all his merchandise as well: old shoes, socks, stockings, and so on, the rattier the better. (He will throw some of these at Bootie in the final scene.) Bootie's "shop" should contain more elegant merchandise: lots and lots of shoes. Think Imelda Marcos.

Scholarly References to Copyrighted Materials (in order of appearance)

"I Only Want to Be with You." By Michael Edwin Hawker and Ivor Raymonde. (ASCAP)

"Wouldn't It Be Nice?" By Tony Asher, Michael Edward Love, and Brian Wilson. (BMI)

"Sunshine Superman." By Donovan Philips Leitch. (BMI)

"When Will I See You Again?" ["Precious Moments"]. By Kenneth Gamble and Leon Huff. (BMI)

"Happy Together." By Gary Bonner and Alan Lee Gordon. (BMI)

"Build Me Up, Buttercup." By Michael D'Abo and Instone Anthony Gordon. (ASCAP)

"Gimme Some Loving." By Spencer Davis, Muff Winwood, and Stephen Lawrence Winwood. (BMI)

"Wishin' and Hopin'." By Burt F. Bacharach and Hal David.

"Footloose." By Kenneth Clark Loggins and Dean Pitchford. (ASCAP)

"It's in His Kiss." By Rudy Clark. (BMI)
"I'm So Excited." By Trevor Lawrence, Anita Pointer, June Pointer, and Ruth
    Pointer. (BMI)

═══════════

[*The entire play takes place inside and outside the home of Jack and
Desirée. Jack might be occupied elsewhere on stage selling his merchandise
in the open air.*]

BOOTIE, *singing* [*to any original melody*][4]

[*Bootie might begin his song* chez lui *and continue singing as he heads
toward Desirée's door or window. As the scene and his overtures progress,
he insinuates himself closer and closer until he is inside the house.*]
    "My own true love, my darling dear
    May God see fit to bring you near
    For that's the one thing I require:
    That you release me from this fire
    That burns me as I fight for you.
    My joyful heart is ever true.
    My heart's desire, you draw nigh.
    And I'm transported to the sky
    And, thus, a joyful song I sing
    I love her more than anything."
[*Bootie now delivers the same message in prose.*]
    Whenever I think about my little Desirée, I get all warm and fuzzy all
    over! She sure is built! No wonder I've gotta break into song! She's the
    only one for me. I've just got to be with her!
    [*To Desirée*] How's it goin' anyway?

DESIRÉE
    What's it to ya? You know goddamn good and well how I am. Besides,
    you don't even care!

BOOTIE
    Sure I do! I swear by all that's holy!

DESIRÉE

Oh for Chrissakes! No need to swear. I believe you already.

BOOTIE

So calm down a little bit, would ya? What are you tryin' to do? Pick a fight? Let's get things off on the right foot, shall we?

DESIRÉE

[*Punctuating her practical joke*] Gotcha![5]
Don't worry. I was just playin' around! Just a little joke, I promise, honey.

BOOTIE

Saints alive! Thank God for that! What a relief! I feel much better now.

DESIRÉE

[*Emphasizing her various physical attributes*] Actually, I'm fit as a fiddle![6]
[*Giving him the once-over*] How's about you? How're you doin' anyway? Good?

BOOTIE [*lasciviously*]

Okay, I guess. Not much doin', if you know what I mean. . . .
[*Looking around*] Isn't that husband o' yours around here somewhere?

DESIRÉE

Not right now. I hope he drops dead of the pox and never comes home again.

BOOTIE

From your lips to God's ears!
Oh, baby! So . . . remember what you told me the last time? I'm in the mood for a little bit o' lovin'.

[*Possible musical interlude*][7]

DESIRÉE

My little devil!

BOOTIE

My one and only!

DESIRÉE

My honey, my sweetie, my darling, my everything.

BOOTIE

I swear by our Lord who was crucified on the Cross: I ain't never loved another woman on earth the way I do you. [*Aside*] At least, not in the past three years or so.

DESIRÉE

Yeah, yeah, I get it. You think I just fell off the turnip truck? That's what you say to all the girls! You're just lookin' to get your paws on me. Besides, I know darn good 'n' well that it was barely a year ago—well, maybe a year and a half—that you had some other "one and only."

BOOTIE

What do you mean? Who?

DESIRÉE

A cousin of mine.

BOOTIE

Don't you believe it for it a minute, neighbor dear! I could *never* have done such a thing to my wife . . . as you very well know!
But, come to think of it [*perhaps modeling his own footwear*], maybe you're just pullin' my leg again. I wanna be with you forever and ever, you know. If only I might be worthy!

DESIRÉE [*swooning*]

Aaaahhh! I can't fool you! I love you too!

BOOTIE

    Yeah, I know, bless your little heart! When I see you, I feel sooooo good. And now . . . just one little kiss. I can't resist . . . I don't care who sees us.

[*Jack enters, still desperately hawking his wares even as he gets to his own door.*]

JACK

    Shoes for sale! Secondhand shoes right here! Secondhand shoes and stockings! Step right up, my friends, step right up!

DESIRÉE

[*Overacting to fit the different lexicon that follows*]

    Alas! Begone with you! It's my husband![8] You must withdraw forthwith!

    Quick! Back off! Get outta here! Go on! Make like stockings and run!

BOOTIE

    I'll go sneak out the back. He's already at the front door!

[*Bootie, however, shall linger out of eyeshot and observe the couple.*]

JACK [*entering his home, also overacting*]

    Yo! Housewife! Are you here within?

    Oh, for God's sake! Hello! It's like talkin' to a wall! Christ, I think she's hard o' hearin' or somethin'!

    How can she not deign to tender a reply?

DESIRÉE

    [*Perhaps curtseying*] My lord. What do you require?[9]

    May our Lord Jesus Christ confound your body and soul!

JACK

    Good God Almighty! If you would be so kind as to shut up, milady!

    As it happens, I should infinitely prefer silence around here to that kind of racket in my general direction.

Am I not a good husband to you, my dear? I haven't been excommunicated or anything, and people look me right in the eye when they're talking to me. Deep down, I know you're a good girl at heart.
So just shut up, then, and I'll shut up too![10]

DESIRÉE

You goddamn louse. You and your goddamn ideas can go straight to hell!

JACK

Here we go. It's that time o' the month again! Watch out boys!

DESIRÉE

Whaddaya need anyway?[11]

JACK

I didn't say a word. Just let me do my work.

DESIRÉE

Jesus H. Christ! If I hear one more peep outta your ugly mug, I'm gonna give you what for!

JACK, *aside*

Good God in heaven! Come on, now, Jacky-boy: do you really have to put up with this kinda pain and suffering?
Christ in a bucket! I guess big boys don't cry. Otherwise, if it weren't for the shame of it, I surely would. But I'm scared stiff of her is all!
So there you have it. I'm wracked with shame.
I call upon our Father, who art in heaven:
May He strike you dead . . . or send some kinda plague or somethin' your way!
God's death! I don't even know what I'm sayin', but, in the name of Jesus Christ who died for our sins, you're gonna get yours! You'll see. What goes around comes around. I'm sure gonna give it *my all*!

DESIRÉE

What's that you're saying?

JACK

Uh ... [*indicating his cobbler's tools*] My *awl!* I'm askin' that you give me my *awl!*[12]

[*Aside*] God damn you to hell, woman! I hope He makes you choke on your own bile! Month in, month out, while He's at it! You can choke on it for three years runnin'! Hell! Make it ten! I don't give a rat's ass! As God is my witness, that is my prayer!

DESIRÉE

And *now* what are you saying?

JACK

I was just wishin' and hopin' and thinkin' and *prayin'* that,[13] if I had a nickel for every shoe I made in the good old days when I was a cobbler's apprentice, I'd be a wealthy man.

DESIRÉE

What are you talking about?

JACK

I'm wishing for gold and wealth, the better to get you a beautiful winter coat, my dear.[14]

[*Aside or to the Audience*]

She's got me by the bootstraps, all right! I'd rather the lousy bitch had married any other schmuck but me and they could both drop dead o' the plague before she'd ever get what I was just sayin' to you! She's *insane*, folks!

DESIRÉE

What's that now?

JACK

I was just *sayin'* ... that, for this pair over here, it would be ... *insane* not to charge folks a good bit more. Whoever buys these won't find a bargain like that anywhere.

DESIRÉE

Are you ever gonna learn to shut your trap, Jacko? You better watch your step or you're really gonna get what's comin' to you! If I weren't such a lady, you'd get the back o' my hand to boot!

[*She prepares to start landing blows.*]

JACK

Whoa! Hold up! For God's sake, dear, what will the neighbors say?

DESIRÉE

You're headed down a slippery slope, you are. And you're really gonna get it this time!

JACK

I swear, just try it and I'll scream bloody murder! And then what'll people say when they hear me? You better just drop it.

DESIRÉE [*hits him*]

Holy Christ! I will not!

JACK

Good God Almighty! I'm not playin' around!¹⁵
[*He makes good on his promises and screams to the Audience for help.*]
Help! My wife's beating me up!

[*To Desirée*] That's enough! Let's give it a rest now, shall we?

DESIRÉE

No way, for God's sake! Not till I teach you a lesson!

JACK

God Almighty! Don't think I'm scared o' hittin' a girl!

DESIRÉE

[*Tossing in a few more whacks for good measure*] Is that so? Now get the hell out of my house!

JACK [*aside*]

She beat the crap outta me! I swear, I'm all weak and dizzy all over!

[*Jack exits through the front door; Bootie, through the back. They meet out front.*]

BOOTIE

What's up neighbor? What's with the hubbub? I heard quite a racket!

JACK

No, no, it's nothing. Just my fine lady of a wife gettin' a little hot under the collar again is all. God only knows I gave her what was comin' to her and, believe you me, she's sure hurtin' now! What a hothead! I can barely put up with her another minute.

BOOTIE

If it were me, I'd just git rid of her, send her packing! Send her back where she came from! Give 'er the *boot*, eh? [Wink, wink, nudge, nudge, say no more!]

JACK

I'll *never* be rid of her. I'd have to show just cause and all.

BOOTIE

I'm sure I could think up some kind of a pretext: something in the fine print, you know? We'll catch her in the act and she won't be able to get out of it.

JACK

If only we could, good neighbor shoemaker! If you could just give me a bit of advice about what to do. I'd sure like to get back at her.

BOOTIE

Damn! You got it! I know exactly what to do. Here's the plan: You'll be at my house, see? And you'll be the one selling my merchandise. But I'll be at your place with your wife.[16] And, as soon as I give you the sign, you'll come right back over here. I'll whistle for you—I know

how to whistle, don't I?—because that'll mean that I've got her right
where we want her:

[*Pointing inside, thus indicating that he knows exactly where the bed is!*]
Right there on the bed. I'm not planning to stray too far from that
particular location.

And then, you'll stroll along home, mindin' your own business. And
then you'll catch us in the act! You'll be able to prove that she's a slut.
And then, you're gonna get physical: you'll pitch one helluva fit. And
you can really let me have it.

JACK

Wow, that's some plan, buddy. I owe you one.

BOOTIE

Something will be afoot, all right. And, once you catch us in the act, I
don't know how I'm going to keep from bursting out laughing when
you let loose on me!

JACK

Laughing? Good Lord, not a chance! You've got to pretend to be
moaning and groaning, for God's sake!

BOOTIE

Oh shut up! I know exactly what to do. No more dawdling. I better
head on in there.

JACK

And I'll go mind your store. You can count on me, I assure you.

[*Exit Jack, staff in hand. He need only go as far as Bootie's neighboring
house. Bootie goes inside Jack's house and rejoins Desirée.*]

BOOTIE

And how are things going with you now, my darling little neighbor
lady? How's tricks? Hope all's well.
So . . . where is he?

DESIRÉE

He goes from place to place with his slipshod stuff. God only knows I
really socked it to him!

BOOTIE [*setting up his mark*]

He's drinkin' it off, I bet. Hobbling off to guzzle up his earnings. That
was some racket I heard just now.

DESIRÉE

Nah, we were just playin' around! [*Metacommentary alert!*] You can't
take anything we say seriously.
Did you say you saw him heading out to get drunk?

BOOTIE

[*Fabricating narratives as easily as he does footwear*]

That's right, I caught a glimpse of him just now. There's a whole group
of 'em—seven or eight guys—all headed off to drink. And you know
that they're gonna be there all night.

DESIRÉE

So, while the cat's away the mice will play, baby. Step right up!

BOOTIE

Oh, sweetie, I thought you'd never ask! How's about a little kiss?

DESIRÉE

How's about a big one? How's about playin' a little footsie?
They sing
[*I recommend that, whatever song is cleared for production, they perform
it as an erotic ballet. Bootie shall bow to her when the "dance" is over.*][17]
Why thank you, kind sir.

BOOTIE

And now . . . let's make hay while the sun shines. Seize the day! Seize
the play!

[*More footsie: perhaps a game of "This little piggy went to market"*]

JACK [*aside while at Bootie's place*]

Jesus H. Christ! That guy's sure takin' his sweet time! Good God! He hasn't even given me the sign yet! No whistling, no coughing. Nothin'!

BOOTIE

Sing me a little song now, honey. I love it when you sing.

[*Possible musical interlude, likely full of erotic gestures and/or a bona fide striptease*][18]

JACK [*aside*]

Maybe I better go over there and listen in on what they're up to all alone over there.

DESIRÉE

I think I'd like to do "Gimme Somethin' Good!"[19]

JACK [*aside*]

You're gonna *get somethin' good* in a minute![20] You're singing, are you, madam?[21]

[BOOTIE]

[I got *somethin' good* for you right here. What do you say, baby?]

DESIRÉE

I'm some cantor, eh?

BOOTIE

Christ Almighty, you bet your sweet ass! I'd join you in the chorus if I could . . . but my voice is all shaky now. Your voice rises and falls so strong and clear. . . . And then, there's other things risin' around here . . .

JACK [*aside*]

Over my dead body![22] I'm gonna beat some nice rhythms out with this here stick on the both o' you in a minute, and you'll soon be singin' a different tune!

BOOTIE

Come on. Don't stop! Keep on singing. One more chorus! Encore! Encore!

DESIRÉE

[*She can begin singing one more chorus of "Gimme Somethin' Good" with any suitable bumping and grinding*]²³

"Gimme somethin' good.
Sock it to me, baby, with all you got."

JACK [*aside*]

Come on yourself! You can start sayin' your prayers right now, you lousy little . . .

DESIRÉE [*still singing demonstratively*]

"Sock it to me,
Sock it to me!
Gimme somethin' good."

JACK [*aside*]

What in the name of . . . ? You've gotta be kidding me!

BOOTIE

Come on over here, now, baby. Come on over and get a little kiss now, sugar, for that beautiful song you just did.
[*Groping her*] Ooooh, God! You weren't kiddin' about bein' fit as a fiddle. How great thou art!

DESIRÉE

And away we go!

BOOTIE

Ooooh, baby, baby . . . I can't keep my hands off you. I swear!

JACK [*aside*]

Jesus H. Christ Almighty! I don't think so! Talk about mindin' the store! You give 'em an inch, and they take a foot! Well, I never! This is the last straw! Where's the sign anyway?

DESIRÉE

[*She might start—or continue—to remove some of the clothes that "constrain" her. This is a good moment for both lovers to "dance" their erotic ballet.*]

I can barely keep it together when you talk to me like that. My heart's gonna give out . . .

JACK [*aside*]

Oh for God's sake! What the devil? Is this for real?

BOOTIE [*reading her palm*]²⁴

Let's see . . . what do we have here? Hmmmm . . . a rebellious spirit! But I also see a good strong lifeline right there. That's a very good sign.

JACK [*aside*]

Sign? What sign? Where's the sign? I'm startin' to losing my patience here. Why, I'm fit to be tied, all right! Jesus Christ Almighty! I bet he forgot to whistle!

DESIRÉE

Alas and alack! So . . . whatever shall I do about that husband of mine? One of these days, maybe I can just get rid of him.

JACK [*aside*]

And how much longer am I supposed to keep mindin' his store? I tell you, good neighbor, good buddy pal o' mine:
That's a helluva chum you turned out to be! For Chrissakes! Are you gonna whistle already or what?

BOOTIE

And now, my little cream puff, what do you say we turn that husband o' yours into a cuckold?

JACK [*aside*]

Oh yeah? I get it! You want her to ride the baloney pony on my dime! That's baloney, all right! You wanna hit the sack with her? We'll see who gets hit!²⁵ You'll get what's comin' to you, you will!

No . . . wait. . . . I can't do that! What the hell have I gotten myself into?[26] This was the whole plan: to test her. And that's just what he's doin'! He's testing her! I'm sure that's why he said that.

DESIRÉE

What pretty little curls you have . . .

BOOTIE

[*He cuts off a lock of his hair. leaving room for Jack to misunderstand—if Jack has looked away momentarily or even he has not—just what exactly Bootie is "giving" his wife.*]

You know what? I'm gonna give you this one to keep. But, sure as I'm standin' here, you're gonna give *me* somethin' too. I'm gonna have my fill o' you before this day is through, I swear to God!

JACK [*aside*]

Oh yeah? Mary, Mother of God! And *you* know what? I've had my fill o' you too! We'll see who's gonna be through in a minute! Good God Almighty! I'm not kidding around! And that's no joke!

[*Here Bootie and Desirée should be experimenting with different positions, reprising their erotic ballet.*]

DESIRÉE

If only my husband could get a good look at us now! It would sure serve him right!

[*Enter Jack*]

JACK

Aha! And just what do you think you're doing there, my fine lady? Serve me right, eh? That's some position you're in now![27]

DESIRÉE

Oh my God! It's my husband! Mother Mary!

JACK

I swear to God, you're gonna get yours now, you little whore![28]

DESIRÉE

    Whore! Alas!

JACK

    That's sure how it seems! Here! [*Hitting her*] Take that! And that!

DESIRÉE

    Lord have mercy!

BOOTIE [*sotto voce*]

    Hey, neighbor! Don't forget to hit me too! It's part of the act!

JACK

[*He should hit Bootie about the face.*]

    Christ Almighty, you got it! Take that! You screwed me over, all right!

BOOTIE

    Whoa, help! [*sotto voce*] Didn't you hear me? It's an act! Knock it off!
    Or take it down a notch, would ya?
    [*Jack continues to hit him.*] Take it down, would ya?
    [*Jack hits him below the belt, prompting the usual pained response.*] Not
    that far down! You don't gotta sock it to me quite so good!

[*Desirée runs out of the room.*]

JACK

    [*Still hitting him*] *Sock* it to you? [*Perhaps throwing some of his mer-
    chandise at Bootie*] You want *socks*? Here you go! Take it *down*, you say?
    [*Hitting lower and lower*] Will do!²⁹

BOOTIE

    Ow! You're hurting me! Whoa! Cut it out! You don't have to keep hit-
    ting me like that, you know. Your wife's already split!

JACK

    That's some good turn you did me there! And now that the shoe's on
    the other foot . . .

[*He continues to beat Bootie.*]

BOOTIE

Knock it off! Quit it!³⁰ Owwww! Jesus Christ! No kidney punches! No fair! Owww! My ribs!

You know, my good man, I'm not wild about this little farce you're playing.

Fool me once, shame on you. Fool me twice . . . er . . . Wham, bam, thank you, man! Enough is enough!

JACK

At least you're managing to keep from burstin' out laughing! God damn you! A pox on your house!

BOOTIE

Whatever you say, for God's sake! *Pox, shmox* . . . socks. Whatever!

JACK

And don't you forget it! Good God! This is just what you deserve!

Boy oh boy, I was sure in good hands, I was, goin' in feet first like that! Trustin' a smooth-talkin' salesman like you!

[*He might address the Audience as he pins Bootie, holding him in place.*]

How did he pull it off? I've got to admit that the way he set me up so he could go after my wife, he plain outsmarted me.

BOOTIE

[*Thus restrained, Bootie might address the Audience as he tries to get a peek at his nearby store, currently unattended.*] At least he kept an eye on my shop while I was mindin' his store!

JACK [*releasing Bootie*]

Go on, get lost! Get the hell outta here! Right now! Get out of my sight! Get out of my house! Shove off! On your way!

BOOTIE

I'm going, I'm going. But I'm gonna get you back. You can count on it. Just you wait and see. . . .

[*To the Audience*]

Christ Almighty! He woulda killed me! I hardly know what else I
could've said . . . and I still got the raw end of the deal.

[*He might be joined by the rest of the Company.*]

They always say it, it's no trick:
That all those tricksters, they get tricked!
That's why, my Lords, I must repeat
Please take in stride our little jokes.
Be careful as you leave your seat!
Don't trip and fall now. That's all, folks![31]

The END

11.

Cooch E. Whippet, or,
The Farce of Martin of Cambray

Farce de Martin de Cambray

CAST OF CHARACTERS

> Martin Eric Whippet, the Cobbler, better known as COOCH
> (Martin de Cambray)
> WILHELMINA, his Wife (Guillemette)
> Their parish Priest, FATHER JOHN (Le Curé)

PRODUCTION NOTES

The *Farce nouvelle à troys personnages* appears as #41 in Cohen, *Recueil,* 317–26; and as #64, *Martin de Cambrai,* in Tissier, *RF,* 12: 143–204. To my knowledge, this farce of 489 octosyllabic verses survives in the *Recueil Cohen* only; but, as Tissier has shown, it is an expanded copy and reworking of another play: *Le Savetier Audin.*[1] Tissier also translated our play into modern French as *Martin de Cambrai* (#64 in *FFMA,* 4: 251–66). Alternate title: *Below the Belt.*

Plot

Cooch E. Whippet is another play—one of Cohen's personal favorites (*Recueil,* xvi)—about who wears the pants in the family or, in this case, the *belt.* Is it the husband or the wife? It also stages a beloved yet fearsome medieval folktale about the theater in general: Beware, lest a thoughtless imprecation of the Devil prompt an appearance by the pointy-eared menace in person! (The Devil was even known to have made multiple such appearances in plays devoted to his story, *Dr. Faustus* being the prime example.)[2] Most of all, our farce recalls a bit of popular wisdom often attributed to Michel de Montaigne: "You can't tell your friend you've been cuckolded; even if he doesn't laugh at you, he may put the information to personal use." And do watch out for your friendly neighborhood priest!

Cuckold now and evermore, the doltish Cooch the Cobbler likes to lock up his wife, Wilhelmina, when he leaves the house to hawk his slipshod wares. Annoyed by those impediments, Wilhelmina devises a ruse with her lover (their priest, of course), for an escape and an escapade. The next time Cooch curses her out with "The Devil take you!" Father John—in a brilliant piece of typecasting—will come forward costumed as the Devil and do just that: *take her. Could it be . . . Satan?* Cooch *does* curse her out; their priest *does* make his diabolical entrance; and Father John and Wilhelmina do what they do. But do notice that Wilhelmina really has to lay it on thick to provoke Cooch into that particular curse (which, by the way, he uses not a single time as the two spar in Scene 1). The better to extract it, she even gets physical with him—and not in the "good way" that Cooch may or may not have in mind at the beginning of the play (below, § "Language"). During the course of their diabolical little drama, Father John will be dressing and undressing quite a bit; so, as that Devil suit comes on and off, don't forget that *faire le dyable* (make like the Devil) is a synonym in Middle French for the sex act. In any event, when ministering to his parishioners, Father John displays a distinct preference for his *birthday suit.*

One of the farce's funniest moments occurs when a distraught Cooch seeks the counsel of the priestly culprit himself, the latter essentially telling Cooch *exactly* what has happened. Father John states flat out that someone is playing a joke on the hapless cobbler; the man of the cloth simply doesn't happen to mention that he himself is the one who's doing it! After the two lovers have completed their business—and it's not as much you're thinking—the devilish priest (that priestly devil?) transports Wilhelmina back to her home. There, Cooch can but accept his lot as a henpecked husband, all of it related to the special belt with which he shall be girded ceremonially in the final scene. With that belt, Wilhelmina newly baptizes her mate as "Cooch E. Whippet." That's right. Sorry, but this is a farce: he is "coochie-whipped." (More on that belt very shortly.)

Characters and Character Development

Our title character is a lowly cobbler with delusions of grandeur about his future in the hierarchy of shoe specialists (Pinet, "Role of the Cobbler"). He is also a pathologically jealous husband—and with cause: he has already caught his wife in the act on at least one prior occasion. For now, let's just say that his wife has got him by the . . . *belt*. Literally. Indeed, the whole play is based on his French name, Martin de Cambray. According to a famous proverb, Martin was a cuckold, roundly mocked for being "belted at the ass."[3] In the French original we don't actually hear his moniker in full until the end, when Wilhelmina *belts* her husband with these words: *Vous estes Martin de Cambray, / Vous en estes saint sus le cul* (vv. 475–76), which means "You are Martin of Cambray. [I dub you Cooch E. Whippet.] / You're belted at the ass." In this feudal dubbing (drubbing?), she also hits him *below the belt* with a hell of a pun on "saintly" (*saint*) and "belted" (*ceint*). Surely not a chastity belt, right?[4] To make the most of his all-important name, I've taken some liberties with my translation. For example, no one calls the French characters "Mr." or "Mrs." Cambray; but the pun comes through better in English if audiences hear "Cooch's" first and last names periodically. (I have Wilhelmina set up his full name in Scene 1, but reserve the big payoff for the belting scene.)

Wife Wilhelmina is another scheming, sexually voracious shrew whose marriage is an impediment to her happiness and, in this case, a physical prison. Like the Lady of #7, *At Cross Purposes, she* is the director of the play's devilish mise-en-scène. All that will change once she toys with Cooch's superstitions about the Devil's omnipresence (which the medieval audience likely shared). With some not-so-divine but eminently dramatic intervention, she outsmarts her husband and gains mastery over her household and her "freedom" to run wild.

Father John, the Priest, is interested in many things, but preaching the word of God does not appear to be one of them. Even so, he understands quite well his duties to his flock. He is more than happy to offer a helping hand when needed. Perhaps it's best, though, not to think about where he puts it.

Language

The play's first ten lines or so are so challenging to translate that even the term Clintonesque scarcely does them justice. Cooch opens with a spiel devoted to Wilhelmina's various attributes; but everything he says may be understood as extremely amorous, extremely insulting, or, more plausibly, *both*. The trick—and that's just what it is, I think, a *trick*—is to tweak the ambiguities for all they're worth. Does Cooch want to have sex with his wife or belt her one? Unfortunately, those two activities are not mutually exclusive.

At first glance, Cooch seems to be in the midst of one of those usual rants against marriage.[5] I certainly thought so, and so did Faivre (*Répertoire*, 282–

83). So imagine my surprise when I turned to Tissier only to hear that Cooch is "orgging out" (*s'extasier*) about his wife's body. Which is it? Is Cooch insulting her? Or is he demanding that she "put out"? If we accept Tissier's reading, then Wilhelmina's rejections become the medieval equivalent of "Not tonight, dear: I have a headache." Could Tissier be right?

Tissier doesn't mention it, but there is, in fact, another commonplace from medieval theatrical lore in which the husband presses his uninterested wife for sex. More precisely, it is a commonplace about the *Devil's* role in such activities, as when, in the beloved *Miracle of the Child Given Over to the Devil*, the wife wishes "to the Devil" any fruit of the coerced union that she endured with her sexually aggressive husband (which today we call "marital rape").[6] Here's the problem—correction, here are the numerous philological problems (for the full Middle French text, see below, note 14):

For one thing, even if we agree that the play opens with Cooch rattling off a series of flattering epithets about Wilhelmina—and, really, the only term that's *not* ambiguous or in dispute is *poitrine* (her bosom)—there's no reason that he can't be talking about somebody else! After all, #3, *Confession Lessons*, opens with another cobbler singing a happy tune about his mistress. The key terms in Cooch's speech are *courcier, carrelet, musequin, corcelet, mirouer, cuninet, faire lait, torchay, cheminer, fourbiray, chief gros*, and *besogner;* and Tissier finds an appropriate *positive* meaning for each one (*RF*, 12: 159–62n). I am not so sure and, instead, I find an appropriate *negative* one. I suppose that the French would accuse me of having *l'esprit mal tourné:* that's a twisted mind focused on the dark side of everything. The glass half empty. Potato, po-*tah*-to; tomato, to-*mah*-to. Instead of calling the whole thing off, let's take them one by one, shall we?

A *courcier* is a fast warhorse, and that doesn't sound especially complimentary; but the word looks an awful lot like the verb "to get angry" (*correcier*). Plus, adjectivally, it means (of *women*) "wanton," "easy," or "licentious"—exactly what Cooch fears about his wife. The term also designates the cannon on a warship, along with one of the pieces that keeps the wheel of a windmill going. (Remember the mouth, be it male or female, as the "big wheel [that] keep on turnin'" from #2, *Edict of Noée*, and #8, *Shit for Brains?*) And then, from among many other meanings, there's the *porte corsière*, a secret door used for spying on women of questionable repute (nothing less than Cooch's primary concern). Talk about a "trap" door! In sum, Tissier hears a good place to mount; I hear an old warhorse, a battle-ax, and a loose woman who runs her mouth. Ideally, we need to hear all those things at the same time.

A *quarelet* (or *carrelet*) is a small arrow, as well as a more specialized cob-bler's tool that is basically a large needle. Tissier finds a verbal meaning of "to resole shoes"; but surely one of the other verbal meanings, "to pierce" is more relevant: "give it your *awl* and stick it in?" Furthermore, in light of the subsequent *corcelet* (which sounds like *porcelet,* a little piggy), mightn't the whole combo conjure something like "to pork?" Also, sorry to mix meta-phors and critters, but a *carrel* is a kind of fish, and Wilhelmina is a classic "fishwife." And, regarding that *corcelet,* it is either a bodice or a diminutive term for body (little bod?). However, it also looks like one of the many vari-ants deriving from *courser/corrocer/correcier* (again, "to get angry"). *Corcelet* appears, moreover, with *musequin,* for which we find one definition of "fine linen fabric" and another indicating an (affectionate) diminutive of *museau* (an animal's mug).[7] Feisty little bod . . . or broad?

Mirouer or "mirror" normally refers to the eyes: mirrors into the soul and what have you. So, at least that one seems relatively straightforward . . . except that it can also mean "masterpiece," "model," or, as a verb, to attend to one's person, to reflect, and even to go tit for tat.

Cuninet, with its darling diminutive suffix of *-inet,* can be a "little rabbit" (*conin* or *coninet*), evocative of the adorably fluffy coneys of various medieval comic tales.[8] Sure, why not? A term of endearment, a caress, a cuddle, *my little rabbit.* But it also looks like, sounds like, and *is* the word for "little cunt" (*con* or *coninet*), another popular topic from the fabliaux.[9] Come to think of it, that's how Wilhelmina seems to understand it, and she's not happy about it. In his modern French translation, even Tissier grants that she responds with something like: "Leave *my pussy* [her *coochie*] out of it!" (*FFMA,* 4: 251).

Fourbir, which sounds like "to trick," also means to wipe clean, pol-ish, steal, or groom a horse . . . who may be related to that other warhorse (*courcier*) of the first verse of the play.

Faire lait sounds like "to make," "prepare," or "heat up the milk"—which is what Dolly is doing in when we meet her in #12, *Birdbrain,* Scene 2—but it also connotes "to do somebody wrong" or, as a homonym, "to make ugly."

Torcher normally signifies to "clean out"; but the word is situated much too close for comfort to *cheminer* ("to make one's way"). *Cheminer* is a homonym of *cheminee* (which means "chimney"), yielding what seems to be an allusion to snaking out the chimney, one of the most popular, farci-cal metaphors ever for the sex act. Indeed, there are any number of farces devoted to vile puns on "sweeping chimneys," which are all about stickin' it in and snakin' things out.[10] Plus, sleazy chimney sweep is the very profession of Wilhelmina's dad, as Cooch insultingly reminds her as they go tit for tat (see?) in Scene 1. Call me a hopeless romantic, but that doesn't sound so amorous.

Although *chief gros* (or *chégros*) refers to a cobbler's heavy thread for sewing leather—we just saw one of those in #10, *Getting Off on the Wrong Foot*,[11]— let's investigate its parts. A *chief* is a head and *gros* is fat: a fathead! This is reminiscent of Harpee's head-obsessed imprecations in #8, *Shit for Brains*.

Finally, *besogner*—the term that Cooch employs when he heads off to cobble—is "to work" as well as to be "in (*sexual?*) need." But it also means "to get down to business," especially if he's been giving his wife the business.

So I hope that you can see, dear Reader, that, at a very minimum, it's all open to interpretation. If Cooch's opening lines are about having sex with his wife, then what he has in mind may not be so very nice. I've split the difference by doubling his meaning and even quadrupling it. That is to say, I have attempted to preserve *all* possible readings of violence, eroticism, erotic violence, and violent eroticism.

Otherwise, of linguistic note in *Cooch E. Whippet* are the many shifts between formal and informal modes of address, some ill-fitting, as when husband and wife use *vous* in the midst of hurling multiple insults. One of the dramatic high points (and marital low points) of Scene 1 is when, amid every foul and vulgar name in the book, Cooch finds that Wilhelmina's greatest impropriety is her having addressed him with the informal *tu*!

Cooch uses *vous* when addressing his parish priest as "sir," "sire," or "lord," which I have rendered (more consistently with American usage) as "Father." As for Wilhelmina, her grammar and stylistic grandeur improve when she is speaking with her paramour, Father John.

Sets and Staging

Although the text gives few specifics, at least two sets are needed: one for the home of Cooch and Wilhelmina, the other either a marketplace or a more rudimentary spot "in town" where Cooch sells his stuff; a possible third might be the home of Father John (a manse? a cell in a monastery? behind the altar at church?). Like other houses that we have seen (in #2, *Edict of Noée,* and #10, *Getting Off on the Wrong Foot*), Cooch and Wilhelmina's place must have a front door and a back door.

On one perplexing question, the text is silent. Where do Wilhelmina and Father John actually *go* after the Devil comes to take her away? Back to her paramour's place? To church? Into the fields? It could be quite entertaining if they go nowhere at all and perform their verbal foreplay (and afterplay?) right under Cooch's nose.[12] There is also some question as to where and when the Priest should disrobe (and rerobe) as he switches back and forth multiple times between the Devil and himself. In literal costumer's terms, he might overdress and underdress.

Costumes and Props List

Father John needs his ecclesiastical look as well as his Devil costume, for which actors have several choices. Check out William's Devil gear in #7, *At Cross Purposes* (§ "Costumes and Props List"); or see below (note 49) for the troublesome possibility that the Devil is played in blackface (although the play's rapid costume changes would likely rule out the latter.) Depending on the costuming choices of Devil suit versus birthday suit, Father John might place the Devil costume over his priestly vestments. In fact, popular medieval wisdom had it that the Devil could be played in a flesh-colored body suit, which would work especially well here, given the goings on. Cooch, the "tool," wears the most important prop of the play: his telltale tool belt, which contains an awl and a highly visible house key. The better to conjure his blue-collar status, that belt might hang low enough for the audience to see his butt crack! The company might also wish to provide a drum to preface, with a drumroll, Father John's momentous appearances as the Devil. Finally, if the company wishes to perform the final dubbing by analogy to contemporary knighting ceremonies, Wilhelmina might use a sword.

Scholarly References to Copyrighted Materials (in order of appearance)

"Every Breath You Take." By Sting. (BMI)
"Eight Days a Week." By John Winston Lennon and Paul James McCartney. (ASCAP)
"Bat Out of Hell." By James Richard Steinman. (BMI)
"Little Less Talk, and a Lot More Action." By Keith W. Hinton and Jimmy Alan Stewart. (BMI)
"Signed, Sealed, Delivered, I'm Yours." By Lee Garrett, Lula Mae Hardaway, Stevie Wonder, and Syreeta Wright. (ASCAP)
"Embraceable You." By George Gershwin and Ira Gershwin. (ASCAP)

[Scene 1]¹³

[At the home of Cooch and Wilhelmina]

COOCH, *begins*
Talk about a fast-movin' filly!
Talk about a squeaky wheel!
Talk about a little snout and a piece of [*he stops short of saying "ass"*] . . .
Holy bazongas! Talk about a piece o' work . . . that's a work of art.
[*Trying to grope her*] Hang me by the neck if I don't soon get off . . .¹⁴

WILHELMINA
Screw you!¹⁵ I have a headache already.

COOCH
Tell me you're not getting angry again, my little pussycat. Because I'll
have me a thing or two to . . .

WILHELMINA
Pussy yourself, mister! What the devil's got *you* all churned up, anyway?¹⁶ For Chrissakes, knock it off, would ya? And keep your paws to
yourself.

COOCH
Jesus H. Christ, Mrs. Whippet, I'm not kiddin' around. I'm all rarin'
to go and I'll clean your clock. Takes a lickin' and keeps on tickin'. You
think *you* can stick it to *me*? And, besides . . .

WILHELMINA
I'll give you a lickin' in a minute. Just keep it up. I'll show *you* where to
stick it! Stick to your own business.

COOCH
We'll see who's gonna stick to what. I'll be stickin' it in! And I'll fix
your wagon, all right, when I wipe the floor with you.

WILHELMINA

Over my dead body! [*Perhaps making the sign of the cross and, with a hasty afterthought*] May God bless the souls of the dearly departed.

COOCH

Just keep this up and I'm gonna belt you one. Gonna give it my all.

WILHELMINA

Oh yeah? [*Grabbing the awl off his tool belt*] You'll get your *awl* in a minute! Right off this belt! I'll stick it up your ass. Like I'd service a lousy drunk like you.[17]

COOCH [*with ironic foreshadowing*]

Jesus H. Christ! We'll soon see who gets belted.

WILHELMINA

Jumpin' Jehosaphat! We will not.

COOCH

What are you anyway? A she-devil? Quit playin' around. Get over here!

WILHELMINA

I *am* here.

COOCH

Are you gonna do what I tell you?

WILHELMINA

No fuckin' way![18] I'm a lady. What kind o' bill o' goods are you tryin' to sell me anyhow?

COOCH

Jesus H. Christ! I *will* be master of this house!

WILHELMINA

And God Almighty, *I'll* be the mistress!

COOCH

Get over here!

WILHELMINA

And I'll be goddamned if I will!

COOCH

If only there were some blasted way to get around her.[19] You've really gotta be shittin' me with this goddamn act o' yours.

WILHELMINA

Go on, then. Shit a brick, why don'tcha.

COOCH

Shut up, you piece o' shit!

WILHELMINA

Eat shit yourself!

COOCH

No, you.

WILHELMINA

No, you.

COOCH

What a racket!

WILHELMINA

Go on. Do your worst.

COOCH

My fine lady?

WILHELMINA

Good sir?

COOCH

Please, after you.

WILHELMINA

No, after you.

COOCH

I just don't get it. Look at this. Get a load o' her.

WILHELMINA

Likewise, I'm sure.

COOCH

What the hell's wrong with you anyway? Shut up!

WILHELMINA

Shut your own gob!

COOCH

You're the one with the big fat trap, you shit-head!

WILHELMINA

And you're the shitty cobbler!

COOCH

Your father cleaned chimneys.

WILHELMINA

And yours cleaned up shit! Talk about a charming profession.

COOCH

[*With some obscene mime*] And, I'm telling you, yours *really* swept them chimneys: stickin' it in everywhere.[20]

WILHELMINA

And yours was always so full o' shit that they called him Brownie Brown. My, my, my, why aren't you from a fine family!

COOCH

> Your grandfather was a hangman.

WILHELMINA

> And yours killed dogs and skinned 'em during hunting season.

COOCH

> Jesus H. Christ! What does *that* have to do with it? When I married you, what did *you* have?

WILHELMINA

> And what about *you*? You were practically naked. You barely had two cents.[21]

COOCH

> And you been puttin' in *your* two cents' worth ever since. 'Cept when I first met you, you were wearin' some *schmatta*—except you had it on backwards.[22]

WILHELMINA

> And you! You had lice crawlin' all over your head and suckin' your brains out.

COOCH

> And there's one more lie outta your vile, stinkin', filthy, trap!

WILHELMINA [*menacingly*]

> You're lyin' again, you lousy, rotten, hothead! Prepare to meet your maker.

COOCH

> And there's another lie. You're a real diva, aren'tcha? Diva!
> [*Aside*] More like a *deviant*!
> You're a fiery little devil![23] Gone all hog wild! By the faith that I owe our Father, the Pope, I'll haul your ass before a judge.

WILHELMINA

> And by the faith I owe ... whoever ... you're not even a man!

COOCH

    Shut up!

WILHELMINA

        No, you.

COOCH

                What the hell is this anyway?

    God damn you! Damn! Damn! Damn!

WILHELMINA

    Damn, damn yourself, dum-dum! Goddamn hick and your crummy
    clodhoppers!

COOCH

    Just wait'll I get my hands on you . . . I'll teach you who's in charge
    around here.

WILHELMINA

    Well I'll be! Big man! I'm sooooooo scared o' you, jackass.

COOCH

    And just who do you think you're talking to? I'll thank you to employ a
    more respectful tone when addressing your husband! How dare you dis
    me! A distinguished practitioner of the shoe like myself.[24] You should
    be ashamed of yourself.

WILHELMINA

    Shit! Good thing you let me know about it, bub.

COOCH

    In the name of the Kingdom of Heaven, this is some flippin' state of
    affairs. You know what? I'm gonna tell you: I can barely get a word in
    edgewise[25] around here when I'm the one in charge.

WILHELMINA

    Oh for Chrissakes,[26] sure you can, you big pussy! All you gotta do is try.

COOCH

    Will you put a lid on it, woman! There you go again.

WILHELMINA

    [*With her best sneer*] And it is you, *sir,* who won't let it go. How's that
for a respectful tone, *sir*? I wish, *sir,* that you were dead, *sir*! And—what
do they say?—I solemnly affirm that you are in grave error . . . or somethin' like that.

[*Father John, the Priest, possibly spotlighted as the set of Cooch's place
goes dark, makes his entrance elsewhere on stage, talking to himself but,
perhaps, to the Audience too. During his monologues, the quarreling
couple freezes.*]

FATHER JOHN

    Sweet Mother Mary, I'm in love with a lady! And what does it mean to
be in love?
    For God's sake! There are worse things I could say. I'm not actually
doing anything about it. I'm just a poor clergyman vowed to poverty.
We men of the cloth have a hard time of it, we do: day in, day out, eight
days a week, from place to place, coming and going, going and coming.[27] Real hard.
    Good Lord! I can't even get my act together to talk to her. Can't figure
out the right moment. Her husband, Cooch, over there is so jealous
that she's afraid to even take that first step and come out of the house.
But, I swear to God, he'll be a cuckold or they can rip my eyes out!
I can see clearly now: I'm going to have to put an end to this or I'll go
stark raving mad.

[*Father John remains still, perhaps straining to hear the couple fighting
from a distance. He shall draw ever nearer during their ongoing dispute.*]

COOCH

    I'm telling you, now, Wilhelmina, I have to go into town. Even if it kills
me, I've gotta get outta here and go hawk my wares, do you hear? You
watch out for the house while I'm gone or, mark my words, I'll tan your
hide!

WILHELMINA

Watch out yourself! I have other affairs to attend to, for God's sake.
And attend to them I will.

COOCH

You'll take care of the house because that is what I want you to do.

WILHELMINA

If that's what you want, you can do it yourself.

COOCH

Good God! What a drama queen! This is some lot in life I've got
here.[28] Lord have mercy!

WILHELMINA

God damn you, Martin Eric Whippet, and your goddamn wild and
crazy jealousy!

COOCH

Oh yeah? I know what I know and I know what I saw that time. When
the cat's away, the mice will play. This is a very serious matter.

WILHELMINA

Holy shit! It would be easier if you were dead already, or if God would
just hang you by the neck!
[*More elegantly*] In the name of the God, in whom I believe with all my
heart, are you really suggesting that I ever did such a thing? No, no, not
I! I'd never be with more than one man!
[*Possibly to the Audience*] At least, not with more than one man *at a
time*.
I'm not that kind of girl.[29]

COOCH

Jeezy Creezy, Wilhelmina! Why most certainly, yes indeedy, I take you
to be a noble woman in that regard . . . but, I swear by Mary, the mother
of our Lord: I'm really not so sure. You know what they say: trust but
verify.

WILHELMINA

That's some cockamamie oath. I'd rather be dead and buried.

COOCH

Jesus Christ! Whatever you say, my dear. But, better safe than sorry. I'll be locking you up just the same. For peace of mind.

WILHELMINA

Screw you! You think you can just hold me against my will like that?

COOCH

Go out of your mind, for all I care! But you're not going out of this house![30]

WILHELMINA

One of these days, buster, you'll be sorry.

COOCH

There's no escape. No use even tryin'.

WILHELMINA

May God strike you dead, you putz!

COOCH

And you're still keeping this up? What did I just tell you about how to address me?[31]
Go out of your mind, for all I care! But you're not going out of this house!

WILHELMINA

Before it's time for evening Mass tomorrow, I swear, you'll be sorry.

COOCH

Go on. Do your worst! Give it your best shot!

WILHELMINA

I will.

COOCH
[*Modeling the key with which he will lock Wilhelmina inside*]
   And, by the way, what do you think *this* is, right here, hangin' on my
   belt? Looks pretty nice, don't it?

WILHELMINA
   I have to go keep an eye on the house.

COOCH
   God give you good day, Wilhelmina.

WILHELMINA
   Heavenly Father, hear my prayer!
[*Father John, who is by now very close, might overhear this and hope to be
the "heavenly father" in question.*]
   Can't you just go and break his neck or somethin'?

COOCH
   Gone with the wind!
   Women! I swear by all that's holy: you can't live with 'em, can't live
   without 'em! And you gotta be nuts to listen to anything they have to
   say. Always bitchin' and complainin' and raisin' hell . . . And, frankly,
   my dear, I don't give a damn.[32]

[*Exit Cooch to market*]

FATHER JOHN [*aside or to the Audience*]
   Isn't that Cooch I see leaving his house?
   If it's him this time,[33] then I'm all ready to make hay while the sun
   shines. Boy, oh boy, I sure am hot to trot for that wife of his. Can't wait
   to get my hands on her.
   Like it or not, I'm going to go see her, I am. I don't care what people say.

COOCH
[*Setting up shop elsewhere onstage*]
   Hmmm . . . This looks like a good spot to set up. Let's see if I can't make
   a few bucks on these old shoes.
   Step right up, folks! Get your used shoes and stockings right here!

FATHER JOHN
[*Aside, still seeking the right moment and swearing prophetically*]
Should I go over there? If he's really going to be out for awhile, then the coast is clear. I pray you, Saint Julian . . . and Saint Lizzie . . . and Lizzie Borden[34] . . . let him never come back again unless I go and get him myself! In the name of Saint John, he's going to get what's coming to him, all right!

[Scene 2]

[*At the home of Cooch and Wilhelmina*]

FATHER JOHN
Hello! Anybody home?

WILHELMINA
Who's there?

FATHER JOHN
Open up and find out.

WILHELMINA
Who's there? Who is it? I don't have the keys, for heaven's sake! Cooch has got me all locked up in here.

FATHER JOHN
Good Lord! What the heck are you saying?

WILHELMINA
Who is it?

FATHER JOHN
It's me. Your parish priest, Father John.

WILHELMINA
I remember *you*! You've got a thing for me.[35] Now I really can't let you in.

FATHER JOHN
    Come on, baby, help me out here.

WILHELMINA
    You can see very well that I can't.

FATHER JOHN
    Jesus Christ! I'll break the door down!

WILHELMINA
    Oh no you won't! You'll do no such thing!
    But I *will* tell you something else I've thought of so that we can get
    outta this one.

FATHER JOHN
    Do tell.

WILHELMINA
    You're gonna hang around outside the door, and you'll have to wait till
    Cooch gets home. And you're gonna need a Devil costume—no two
    ways about it. And then, when he gets here, I'll start in on him again,
    yellin' my head off and cursin' him out at the top of my lungs. You
    know, stuff like: "God damn it to hell!" and "God strike you dead right
    this instant!" That sorta thing. Get it?

FATHER JOHN
    I get it. Go on, keep going.

WILHELMINA
    And then, after he gets home and I keep it up for awhile with all the
    cursin' and screamin', God only knows it shouldn't take too long before
    he shouts right back and says: "The Devil take you!"
    And then, when you hear that, you're gonna be the Devil, see?—
    straight outta hell. And you're gonna come right up to me and put me
    on your back and take me away.

FATHER JOHN

I swear, you thought the whole thing out, all right! Your wish is my command. That's exactly what I'll do.

WILHELMINA

Don't be long now.

FATHER JOHN

Not another word. I get it. You can take that to the bank. I'm off right now to get my costume. I'm pretty sure I can find one backstage.[36] Farewell!

WILHELMINA

Farewell!

[*Possible musical interlude, during which Father John will position himself near Cooch's house to wait for his cue*][37]

COOCH

[*At the marketplace, still hawking his wares, and not having much luck*]

Mary, Mother of God, maybe if I keep at it a bit longer . . .

Step right up, folks! Right over here! Stockings! Used stockings right here! Old ones! Used ones! Old ones good as new! All in reasonable condition, I swear to God![38]

[*Possibly performing a mime*]

One, two, buckle my shoe.

Three, four, shut the door.

Five, six, pick up chicks.

Seven, eight, lay them straight.

Nine, ten, a big fat hen.

Eleven, twelve, dig and delve.

Thirteen, fourteen, maids a-courtin'.

Fifteen, sixteen, maids in the kitchen!

Seventeen, eighteen, maids a-waitin'.

Nineteen, twenty, my platter's empty. . . .

As far as I can tell, my whole profession's a thing of the past. Everybody's doin' it.[39] God, I might as well just go on home. There's no place like home.

[Cooch returns home.]

[Scene 3]

[At the home of Cooch and Wilhelmina]

COOCH
What's up with you, Wilhelmina?

WILHELMINA
I pray to God our Father:
He who saves all souls from that nasty rash of Saint Anthony's fire,
He who saves 'em from swelling and edema, from epilepsy, and from
all kinds o' welts ... or tumors ... or infectious diseases ... or purple
blotches all over your skin ... or all them other serious illnesses ... like
that awful one that kills horses ... May you drop dead from each and
every one of 'em, you big jerk![40]

COOCH
That's a fine how-do-you-do, for Chrissakes! How lovely.

WILHELMINA
You think I'm the kinda woman you can just lock up? I pray God that
He let loose ...

COOCH
You better shut up if you know what's good for you.

WILHELMINA
I wish I'd never been born.

FATHER JOHN
[Aside, attempting to eavesdrop from his vantage point]
Let's see if I can hear what's going on.
Cooch is back now, I see. It's high time I get into this costume.
[Father John makes his first costume change.]

WILHELMINA

You can make me keep house, but I can sure make it pretty damned uncomfortable for you around here, bub!

COOCH

Go on, go on, give it your best shot! A little less talk, a lot more action.[41]

WILHELMINA

Action, is it? Wait'll I get my hands on ... You got me chained up in here like a dog![42]

COOCH

Go on and try me if you think I'm kidding around! I'd rather be hanged at the gallows!

WILHELMINA
[She should make some kind of move against him: striking, poking, shoving, etc.]
Here! Take that, you rotten lout! Take that! And that!

COOCH

Mary, Mother of God!

WILHELMINA

Serves you right! You had it coming.

COOCH

Help! She's trying to kill me!

WILHELMINA

Get your sorry ass out of my sight!

COOCH

May God grant a pox on your house!

WILHELMINA

Get outta here, you filthy peasant!

COOCH [*drum-roll please . . .*]
> My Lord, I call upon you:
> The Devil take you! Come here from hell today! Come here! Take 'er
> away![43]

FATHER JOHN
> [*Aside*] That's my cue!
> [*Father John enters their home, dressed as the Devil.*]
> Yoo-hoo!

COOCH
> Jesus H. Christ! What in the name of God is *this*?
> Blessed Virgin Mary, Mother of God. Help! I'm a dead man! Mother
> Mary, beatific virgin! People will say that I killed her!
> It's true. People always say to be careful what you wish for: it might
> come true.
> Help! Mother Mary, this is crazy!

[*Father John carries Wilhelmina off; but they needn't go far. He does not
necessarily set her down. Cooch might hesitate stupidly, or run around the
house before setting off in not-so-hot pursuit.*][44]

[Scene 4]

[*Wilhelmina and Father John alone, at first in a more public place*]

FATHER JOHN
> So, how am I doing? How was my Devil?

WILHELMINA
> The performance of a lifetime.

FATHER JOHN
> And now that it's just the two of us . . . I can have my way with you.[45]

WILHELMINA

You can do anything you want, God willing. Here I am: signed, sealed, delivered. I'm all yours! [46]

FATHER JOHN

My darling!

WILHELMINA

My love!

FATHER JOHN

My little chickadee. I gotcha now.
Oooooh, you feel so good.

WILHELMINA

My dear.

FATHER JOHN

My little angel.
May God grant you . . . good health.

WILHELMINA

And for God's sake, don't I wish!
But I've got an idea for better cover. I've got a reputation to watch out for, you know.

FATHER JOHN

Huh? What do you mean?

WILHELMINA

You better hotfoot it over there and find out what my husband is up to. And you're gonna need to pretend that you haven't got a clue about what's goin' on.

FATHER JOHN

Oh! I get it. Jeezy Creezy! You certainly make one helluva point there. Off I go!

[He might make the sign of the cross and install her somewhere, potentially close enough to watch the performance to come.]

WILHELMINA
Careful! Don't let on, now. Fake it till you make it. And, whatever you do, don't get all religious on me!⁴⁷

FATHER JOHN
Not to worry. I'll do it up right. Just sit tight. I'll be right back. I think I see him over there and he looks like he's in quite a state.

[Scene 5]

[Father John changes clothes again, exchanging his Devil costume for his priestly one. He rejoins Cooch in town, where a hysterical Cooch is searching for his missing wife.]

FATHER JOHN
God keep you, Cooch!

COOCH
Oh my God! Father, I'm so glad to see you.

FATHER JOHN
How's it goin'?

COOCH
I'm goin' straight to hell!

FATHER JOHN
You seem troubled, my son. What's the matter?

COOCH
I lost it.

FATHER JOHN
I'm not sure I understand what you're saying.

COOCH

I swear to God, I've lost my mind!

FATHER JOHN

Lost your mind? Jeezy Creezy! Surely not.

COOCH

Nope, it's true. I'm a dead man.

FATHER JOHN

Come now, why is that? Is it your wife? Is she sick?

COOCH

No, it's much worse than that, for Pete's sake!

FATHER JOHN

So what is it? Has she passed away, then?

COOCH

The Devil in hell has taken her away!

FATHER JOHN

Sweet Jesus! And *gesundheit*! What are you saying?

COOCH

It's the God's honest truth. He came right in and he took her! Right over there!

FATHER JOHN

What? I can't believe it! You'll have to tell me the whole story.

COOCH

Ahhh, Father, it's true. It's all true. She was a real pain in the ass, and a troublemaker, a real hell-raiser, and a bit of a schemer. And I've always had my doubts about her . . . for which I repent most sincerely . . . And, to tell you the truth, the whole truth, and nothing but the truth, I must confess that I used to lock her up when I left the house, and that's the God's honest truth.

So, when I got home just now and she was all harpin' on me again . . . all that yellin' and screamin' and cursin' and callin' me every name in the book. . . . So I finally said: "The Devil take you! Come here from hell today! Come here! Take 'er away!"

FATHER JOHN
Not your best choice of words, I'll grant you.

COOCH
And then he just showed up! Right then and there, as soon as I said it, and he hauled her off.

FATHER JOHN
Good God, man, you're an idiot if you think that was really the Devil. You can't possibly believe that.

COOCH
Saints alive! You bet I do.

FATHER JOHN
Oh for God's sake. Somebody's pulling your leg. I'm sure you're mistaken.

COOCH
Am not! For God's sake, I saw it with my own eyes!

FATHER JOHN
Don't you believe it for a minute; it's nonsense. It's a farce! Some joker's playing a trick on you; and he's come to get her so he can have his way with her. A little afternoon delight. So don't you believe any of it.

COOCH
Really? No kidding? You really think that's how it went down?

FATHER JOHN
Why certainly. That's just how she went down. [*Catching himself*] I mean *it: it* went down that way. My scenario is totally plausible.

[*Pausing to appreciate Wilhelmina*] She's totally doable. [*Catching himself again*] I mean *it*: the *scenario! It's* totally doable.[48] Don't you believe for a minute that the Devil came here. It's a joke.

COOCH

Alas and alack, Father! [*Genuflecting*] I'm begging you. Look: I'm on my knees here. Could you just go and ask around for her? All over the parish? Here, there, and everywhere. If the man who's got her doesn't bring her back right this minute, maybe you could excommunicate him?

FATHER JOHN

Not sure that's much of a disincentive, but sure thing. I'm happy to give 'er a try.

COOCH

Mary, Mother of God, I'll buy you a round, I promise.

FATHER JOHN
[*To the Audience*]

Okay, listen up, now, everybody!
I hereby excommunicate the person or persons out there who, this very morning, took the wife of my good neighbor, Cooch! Your eternal soul's at risk if you don't 'fess up right now and say: "I've got her!"
[*To Cooch*] How am I doing? How was that?

COOCH

That was great, Father. But, if you wouldn't mind, could you also say something like ... well ... that I'd like her brought back in good working order. . . . Or, at the very least—in the same condition that he found her in. . . ? Or I'll sic the law on 'im.

FATHER JOHN
Good idea.
[*To the Audience*]

Hey, listen up again, guys! If you've got her, you better come forward right now, right this minute, step right up and bring 'er back or we're gonna tan your hide just like we would the *real* Devil.[49]

[*Here, both men pause to wait for a response.*]

COOCH
  No one's breathin' a word. I've lost her for sure.

FATHER JOHN
  Don't worry, we'll find her; but, Jesus Christ, I'm sore afraid!
  Get down on your knees right here and now and tender an earnest
  prayer to God.
[*Indicating the general direction where the Audience sees Wilhelmina
waiting*]
  And I'll be right over there, downstage,[50] I promise you, on my knees
  offerin' up something just as tender. Adieu!

COOCH
  Adieu to you too, Father, and for God's sake, [*to Father John, the Audience, or both*], get her back here![51]

[*Cooch gets down on his knees to pray, within eyeshot of his wife.*]

FATHER JOHN
  Before you know it, she'll be back knockin' on your door. You won't
  lose a thing except the shame of it all.

COOCH
  Alas, from your lips to God's ear, Father!

FATHER JOHN
  [*Aside*] My lips, all right. *Ear*, there, everywhere.
  [*To Cooch*] Enough now. Just rest assured that I'll be giving it my all
  because I too love her above all things.
[*As he heads back toward Wilhelmina, Father John might provide some
obscene mime about his own "awl," not Cooch's.*]
  [*Aside*] Christ! That's the God's honest truth! Oh baby! We got that
  poor schmuck but good! Wait'll his wife hears *that* one!

[Scene 6]

[*Father John rejoins Wilhelmina at the spot where he has left her. He might start removing his vestments, and he may or may not need his Devil costume at this moment.*]

FATHER JOHN
>   I'm back! How's tricks?

WILHELMINA
>   What does the poor schlub have to say for himself now? He oughta be drowned in the river like a cat!

FATHER JOHN
>   Believe it or not, he's beside himself. Lordy, lordy, he's crying and flailing like a babe in the woods! He can hardly believe that the Devil came and took you away. And, to top it all off, he's over there—get this!—praying on bended knee, begging God most humbly to send you back his way right soon, or he's a goner.

WILHELMINA
>   Oh yeah? Well I'm beggin' God just as humbly to let loose all the hell fire and brimstone He's got on that bum!

FATHER JOHN
>   Oh, for Pete's sake, it's all perfectly clear: he really loves you.

WILHELMINA
>   Screw him!

FATHER JOHN
>   I'll tell you what I'm gonna do:
>   In just a little bit, I'm gonna carry you back to the spot where I took you before. And, in the same getup, just like before, I'm gonna put you back where I found you. A place for everything and everything in its place. Back in the right spot.
>   And speaking of the right spot . . . First, I've gotta do this . . .

WILHELMINA

God Almighty, you sure do a lotta talkin'.

FATHER JOHN

Ooooooooh. You melt in my mouth. Ooooh . . . you feel so good.
Come on, gimme some sugar.[52]

[*Possible musical interlude. Since the couple is dawdling, the company
might consider having them perform some kind of romantic duet, so long
as all requisite permissions have been cleared prior to performance.*]

WILHELMINA

Shut up and do it, already![53]

FATHER JOHN

You sure are built. When nature made you, she really broke the mold.

COOCH [*outside, still in prayer*]

Saint Dennis, hear my prayer! In the name of all that's holy, in the
name of Saint John, and Saint Matthew, and my patron saint, Saint
Martin—the maker of miracles[54]—and Saint Hubert, and Saint Ma-
turinus the Exorcist, and Saint Peter, and Saint Paul, and our blessed
Mother Mary:
Please get my wife back to me. I'll light a candle for each and every one
of you with my own two hands. I swear to God, I won't fail you!

[*Father John enters in his Devil costume carrying Wilhelmina on his back.
The company may decide when he should put her down. There will be a
number of positional ups and downs in the upcoming denouement.*][55]

FATHER JOHN

Yoo-hoo!

COOCH [*springing to an upright position*]

Mary, Mother of God!
How the hell are you, Wilhelmina?

WILHELMINA

Alas! Mother of God, I hardly know myself. Oh the pain! Oh the suffering!

COOCH

The Devil's brought you back! I knew it! I knew he had you! Where have you been?

WILHELMINA

Where do you think? Here I am. Like a bat outta hell!

[*This is a good moment for Father John to set her down.*]

COOCH

You were in hell? *Gesundheit!* In hell?

WILHELMINA

For sure.

COOCH

Welcome back, my dear Mrs. Whippet. But tell me: what kind of people are down there?

WILHELMINA

All kinds, really. There are butchers and bakers and candlestick makers . . . and tailors and tanners . . . But mostly, cobblers.

COOCH

Cobblers?

WILHELMINA

You betcha!
And, I swear, I can pretty much vouch for the fact that the whole lot of 'em's gonna wind up down there. Plus, they got so many of them jealous types down there that they barely know where to stick 'em.

COOCH

So which ones get the full torture treatment?

WILHELMINA
Which ones?

COOCH
Yeah.

WILHELMINA
The jealous ones.

COOCH
What the devil are you saying?

WILHELMINA
The truth. It's just like I say.

COOCH [*falling to his knees again*]
My darling, I beg your forgiveness most humbly! I'll never, ever do it again. From here on in, I'll give *you* the keys and you can come and go as you please.
[*Handing over the keys, still on his knees*]
Here, darling, here you go. Go wherever you need to go. See to your affairs as you see fit. And here: here are the keys to the back door too. I'll never defy you again.

WILHELMINA
So let's all of us live together in peace from here on in. Let's the both of us agree to do that.

COOCH [*standing up again*]
I'm on board, I swear, whatever it takes, for richer or for poorer.

WILHELMINA
Here: I'll belt you one. Take this belt. I'm giving it to you now as a token of our peace treaty. And [*preparing to belt Cooch*] we'll see who wears the pants in *this* family.
[*To maximize the upcoming double entendres on* high vs. low, *Cooch might try out the belt in a higher vs. lower spot, he might speak in a*

higher feminine vs. lower masculine voice, or at a higher vs. lower pitch or volume.]

Holy moly! Look how good it looks on you. This is exactly what we need.

COOCH
Like this?

WILHELMINA
No. That's too high.

COOCH
Lower then.[56] [*Cooch repositions the belt and drops again to his knees.*]

WILHELMINA
There you go. Just right! Lordy, lordy! Now you're all done. All dressed up and ready to go. [*Cooch hears "up" and stands up again.*]

COOCH
Holy moly! I *do* look good.
[*The actor might solicit praise from both Wilhelmina and the Audience.*]
And now . . . what do they have to say about me?

[*After a disapproving look from Wilhelmina, Cooch kneels again, upon which Wilhelmina dubs him, possibly with the flat point of a sword.*]

WILHELMINA
Rise, Martin Eric Whippet. [*Cooch stands up for the last time.*] You're *Cooch E. Whippet!*
We know who wears the pants in *this* family. And you bet your sweet ass I've got the keys to *your* kingdom.

COOCH
I don't think I've ever looked so good or so fetching.

WILHELMINA
You're *Cooch E. Whippet.* You're *coochie-whipped!*

[*Wilhelmina might invite the Audience to say this line with her a few times. For his closing speech, Cooch might continue to be confused as to whether he should be standing or kneeling.*]

COOCH

I swear to God, my darling, for as long as I live, I'll be a good husband to you; and you'll be the keeper of my heart. And, I promise, I'll never forget that saying. How does it go again?

"'Tis better to have loved and lost than never to have loved at all!" Or how's about: "Be careful what you wish for; it might come true."

But, for now, how's about: "What goes around comes around."[57]

[*To the Audience*]

And thus, ladies and gentlemen, high and low,[58] I humbly pray you that you remember this lesson well:

For sure, for sure, I'll never go off script,

Now and forever, I am Cooch E. Whippet.

The END

12.

Birdbrain: A Musical Comedy? or, School Is for the Birds

Farce joyeuse de Maistre Mimin

CAST OF CHARACTERS

The Illustrious PROFESSOR (Le Maistre d'escolle)
MASTER MIMIN, a Student (Estudiant)
ROLLO, Mimin's father (Raulet)
TRIXIE, Mimin's mother (Lubine)
WOLFY CHEWY, Mimin's future father-in-law (Raoul Machue)
[And featuring] DOLLY, the Fiancée of Master Mimin (Et La Bru
   Maistre Mimin)
[Mister Gobble, Mimin's first tutor]

Original production: *Birdbrain* was first produced as *Monkey See, Monkey Do* at the University of California, Santa Barbara, on 2 May 2009, directed by Andrew Henkes, choreographed by Tarah Pollock. Chickens were generously donated by Gerry Hansen, and their coop designed by Rose Elfman and Courtney Ryan.

CAST

Jason Bornstein as Wolfy Chewy
Melani Carroll as Trixie
Beth Faitro as Dolly, the Fiancée
Andrew Fromer as the Professor
Jordan Holmes as Mimin
Sigmond Varga as Rollo

PRODUCTION NOTES

From the *Recueil du British Museum,* the *Farce joyeuse de Maistre Mimin, à six personnages* appears in Fournier, *TFR,* 314–21; and as #17 in Tissier, *RF,* 3: 213–72.[1] Tissier also translated the play into modern French as *Maître Mimin, Étudiant* (#17 of *FFMA,* 1: 301–17), as did Bernard Faivre (*Farces,* 2: 331–407). It is 418 octosyllabic verses in the Tissier edition (Fournier does not provide verse numbers). This farce was first published, it seems, between 1547 and 1557, although Tissier estimates that it was written between 1480 and 1490 (*RF,* 3: 218; and *FFMA,* 1: 303). Other possible titles or subtitles: *Starting from Scratch; Parrot, Carrot, or Stick?* (My first title—ultimately, insufficiently ornithological—was *Monkey See, Monkey Do.* I came very close to choosing, as a subtitle, *Polly Wanna Slacker* because of the play's unabashedly sexist take on the role of women in learning and unlearning.)

Plot

How do you keep 'em down on the farm? This play is about learning, unlearning, and the mixed feelings that surround the upward social mobility that allegedly accompanies an education. Even the elusive Monsieur Delepierre—remember Tridace-Nafé-Théobrome?—considered it "a real find" (*Description et analyse,* 91n) and, unlike the "disgusting" *Farce of the Fart* (#1 herein), he transcribed our play almost in its entirety (above, About This Translation, § "Editions and Printed Sources"). If anything, *Birdbrain* is a play about intellectual "rehab." Make that *anti*-intellectual rehab: it is a medieval *intervention* into that addiction known as book learnin', a veritable "peasants' revolt" against snooty professors. What happens, it asks—doubtless to the sheer delight of university students everywhere—when schooling turns a young man into such a jargon-spouting, Latin-speaking fool that he forgets his mother tongue, ordinarily useful in communicating with one's fiancée. The answer? Get him down off that perch and back on the farm.

In the opening scene, we learn that Master Mimin has been sent off by his parents to a new tutor so that he can make something out of himself. Under the intimate tutelage of an illustrious Professor, young Mimin has become so besotted with academia that he forsakes his native French. It's Latin only for the lad: all in the obscurantist tones that enrapture his teacher but sound like gibberish to everybody else. (Does *that* sound like anybody we know?) Correction: what Mimin speaks is a highly inept and idiosyncratic version of what he *thinks* is Latin, and which is probably just what his highly imperfect prof *taught him*. Those who can't do, teach. Those who can't teach, teach Latin? Rollo and Trixie (Mimin's Ma and Pa) are so concerned that, with Mimin's fiancée Dolly and future father-in-law Wolfy in tow, they set off to collect the idiot savant. How on earth, they worry, will Mimin talk with "the girl"? Nothing to do but get that trained parrot the hell out of there for a little bit of good old-fashioned homeschooling. So much for the best laid plans of mice, men, and hens.

Once Mimin is back on the farm, the families begin his reeducation. Since, by nature and by name (below, § "Characters and Character Development"), the boy is happy to parrot whatever he's taught, they place him inside a cage—a dirty chicken coop, to be exact. Correction again: technically, they put only *his head* in the cage. Talk about starting from scratch! From that new perch he repeats, after the women, a series of French phrases and musical refrains until he recovers his native tongue, the better to redeploy it for French . . . and, we assume, for French kissing. For all the medieval musical refrains (for which all requisite permissions for any substituted modern equivalents must be cleared), recall that music was a traditional pedagogical aid to the memory:[2] it's easier to memorize a poem if it's set to music, isn't it? Or to retrieve some forgotten lyrics once you have the melody? And who better to take charge of his vocal indoctrination than the loquacious women, those "magpies" from countless misogynistic pieces? As the play draws to a close, even the Professor is forced to admit that it is women who *rule the roost*. LOL. Except that . . .

I suspect that many modern readers will not be cracking up about the farce's strong implication that the women's success is Mimin's failure. It is true that, like John-Boy of #4, *Student Who Failed,* Mimin fails because he has insufficient knowledge and class to be able to penetrate what passed back then for the ivory tower. But the play also insinuates that wives and mothers impede the progress and cultural evolution of men. In that respect, *Birdbrain* joins a long-standing conversation about who should be entrusted with the education of young people and, more particularly, of young men. Such early Roman writers as Tacitus once decried the practice of assigning early child rearing to "some silly little Greek serving-maid" who spoke Latin badly; whereas, on the subject of his medieval schooldays, Guibert de Nogent had to convince his reluctant mom, on a daily basis, that the beatings he was administered were good and good for him.[3] By the way, it is in this "nursemaid" context that the play's curious allusions to women's breasts (Scenes 1 and 4) finally start to make a strange kind of sense, especially considering that Dolly is boiling *milk* when we first meet her.

Despite Tissier's valiant effort to interpret the asides about the "tits" of Trixie and Dolly as a pun on *sain* (healthy) and *sein* (breast), there's no getting around the fact that this is just plain weird. At first, it almost sounds like Trixie is a wet nurse. All in all, I believe that such features speak to a medieval brand of intellectual nurturing that calls for men to wrest from women, as Caroline Walker Bynum argues, even the physiological capacities of lactating and nursing.[4]

There is also something passing strange about Mimin's ornithologically inspired prison from which "his ass can hang out the back." Again, dear Reader, my own head might well have been in my farcical cage for too long but, in light of the tortures of medieval educational training (above, Introduction, § "Performance and Performance Records"), this *sounds* to me like a gender-reversed usage of the implement of torture known as the "brank." Resembling a muzzle—except that it was a full head cage—the brank was a metal mask designed to discipline, punish, and humiliate gossipy, *talkative* women by literally *pinning the tongue* of the unfortunate female wearer.[5] Alas, the brank is perfectly consistent with the play's theme of speech reeducation.

Characters and Character Development

With six characters, this play boasts the largest cast of our collection. Virtually everyone's French name, except that of the unnamed future daughter-in-law, is a play on words.

Mimin derives etymologically from mime, mimicry, aping, imitation, or impersonation. Since those meanings come through to the English eye and ear, it seemed unnecessary to translate his name (although it might be enhanced with a nickname like Master Parrot).[6] The playtext also offers some clues as to his physical appearance, which is described succinctly by Wolfy Chewy in Scene 4. Suffice it to say that Mimin is a hunk (and the Professor clearly thinks so too); the actor playing Mimin should look buff, as if he has been working out—with the exception of one area still in need of work: his gut or pot belly. Additionally, there are a number of references throughout to the size of a man's nose as a means of measuring brainpower. For Tissier, this is not so surprising, given that clever, long-nosed fellow Cyrano de Bergerac (*RF*, 3: 233n); thus one might either cast an actor with a pronounced proboscis or create such a beak for him.

Regarding Mimin's schooling, Tissier clarifies a point that might otherwise have caused some confusion (*RF*, 3: 233n), namely, that Mimin has actually been under the tutelage of *two* different pedagogues. His first teacher was the local schoolmaster, *Mangin,* a name that is etymologically suggestive of eating, gnawing, and biting, but also of a famous remark by Robert of Sorbon (whose own name gives us that of the acclaimed *Sorbonne*): medieval scholastic training demanded that scholars chomp on everything with the "teeth of disputation."[7] (Although Mr. Mangin is not a bona fide role, it would be possible to create a flashback scene of his pedagogy.) I thought of calling him "Mr. Eatem" (from *manger*); but, given the play's overarching (high-flying?) bird metaphors, I've opted for Mr. Gobble. He was probably a turkey anyway.

As for the schoolmaster (Le Maistre d'Escolle), he goes by his honorific title throughout the script: *Magister.*[8] (Channeling a 1995 episode of *Seinfeld,* and given the importance of music, one might also refer to him to as The Maestro.) He is a prof with the grandest of academic pretensions and he should sound as grandiloquent as possible as he plays his integral part in a medieval educational system that anointed Latin language learning.[9] In production, one might go so far as to expand his title to "My Lord, Professor." (I bet American academics would just eat that up. This isn't Germany, after all, where faculty holding the Ph.D. are addressed with the overkill title of *Herr* or *Frau Doktor Professor.*) Our unnamed *Magister* is no *Mangin* but he does gobble, all right; in fact, he seems to find young Mimin good enough to gobble up (a proclivity not lost on mom Trixie, who finds his pedagogical relationship with her son "perverted" [Scene 3]).[10] The actors will have multiple opportunities to stress that unsavory side, as when the Professor practically swoons when Mimin is speaking. (Imagine the over-the-top response of Molière's Bélise, Armande, and Philaminte upon hearing the mediocre sonnet delivered by Tissotin in *The Learned Ladies,* act 3, sc. 2.) Another possible inspiration for this character might be the Wizard of Oz (invoked earlier for #4, *Student Who Failed,* § "Characters and Character Development"), who is much more plain-spoken once the fanciful trappings of Emerald City are removed and he reverts to being a regular man in front of the curtain.

Mimin's father is *Raulet,* a homonym for *rollet,* which evokes the "scrolls" upon which contracts might be written. (In addition to one such contract that we've already seen in #2, *Edict of Noée,* famous scrolls on the medieval French stage include the domestic charter of the *Farce du Cuvier* [*The Washtub*], detailing the husband's household duties; and, more seriously, the contract between the Devil and the fallen priest, Theophilus, in Rutebeuf's *Miracle of Théophile.*)[11] It also denotes "roll," as in "roster," "roll call," or "taking roll": whence, *Rollo.* Dad Rollo has all that he can handle and displays little initiative, yielding virtually throughout to the superior wisdom of his wife.

The name *Lubine* sounds like a clever or quick fix—a Mrs. Fix-it with her bag of tricks—so I've called her Trixie. Trixie has a taste for both overacting and ironic understatement. She is smarter than she looks or than she lets on. That will be apparent in her speech patterns as the play moves forward and as Mimin progresses . . . or is that *regresses*? (Below, § "Language").

Master Mimin's future father-in-law is the widower *Raoul Machue.* Although Tissier notes (*RF,* 3: 218) that this is a Norman version of *massue* (which means "club," à la caveman), I prefer a different pun. Chew on this: his last name—*pace* Robert of Sorbon—recalls *mâcher* (to chew); whereas his first name, Raoul, is said to derive from "wolf." I have called him Wolfy Chewy; but he might also be called "Mashey," "Cuddy," or even "Gumby." Whether the cause be scribal error or authorial choice, Wolfy Chewy tends to repeat himself a lot; so, in the production of May 2009, Andrew Henkes cleverly staged Wolfy as an alcoholic (with wine bottle in hand at all times) who simply had trouble keeping track of what had already been said . . . by himself or by anybody else.[12]

Mimin's unnamed Fiancée drags her little doll around with her everywhere (a gift from Mimin); so she can be called Dolly. Truth be told, she is a bit of a "living doll" whom Trixie finds rather coquettish and who seems to have someone's mitts on her person all the time. In Scene 2 she must be taken by the hand, in Scene 3 by the arm, and in Scene 4 by the whole body when Mimin carries her piggyback. This particular cast list also gives her final billing in a sequence that is neither alphabetical nor chronological in order of appearance: *et la Bru Maistre Mimin.* Thus, one could almost make Dolly a featured role.

Finally, my translation involves some rereadings and reassignments of who says what, especially during Scene 3 at the Professor's. In the associated notes, I indicate when I have taken the lines away from men and placed them into the mouths of women. It makes for an exceptionally long note or two. Sorry about that; but, from the Bible to the *Play of Adam,* there is a fascinating history in textual editing of wresting language from female speakers. As the feminist theologian Phyllis Trible has demonstrated so compellingly for the voices of Moses and Miriam, we do well to put it back where it belongs.[13]

Language

Although this translation was first produced as *Monkey See, Monkey Do,* my original title was not insistent enough on that all-important ornithological register. The play is full of birdies and bird metaphors that translate well into English: "for the birds," "a chicken with its head cut off," "cook your goose," "take a gander," "be chickenshit," "rule the roost," and many others besides. You name it: if it walks like a duck and talks like a duck—rather, a *chicken*— it's in here. So too is the vocabulary of the contemporary "intervention": the boy is an addict, drunk on the books. He needs one.

Otherwise, this farce, particularly thick with wordplay and double entendres, was far and away the most difficult to translate but, in many ways, the most fun. Its greatest linguistic challenge was how to convey—to postmedieval, English-speaking audiences who are largely unproficient in Latin— Mimin's hysterically funny inability to speak Latin correctly. Short of singing *Adeste fidelis* in choir or hearing *Gaudeamus igitur* at their high-school graduations, most American students have little or no exposure to the late, great *lingua latina*. Moreover, the reality is that, if only from church, the average medieval spectator would have understood far more of Mimin's so-called Latin than we would today. Each time Mimin opens his mouth to pontificate in the mangled mess that the French now call "kitchen Latin" (*latin de cuisine*), medieval students doubtless enjoyed a good laugh at the expense of the poor country boy trying to gain access into their secret society. In fact, Faivre brilliantly summarizes the play's content with a pun of his own, even though he finds the farce somewhat deficient from a literary standpoint (is he *kidding?*). He writes that Master Mimin has "lost his Latin" (*perdre son latin*), an expression meaning, basically, to get so confused that you don't know which end is up (*Répertoire*, 241)—or, in Mimin's case, which end is hanging loose out of the back of a non-Latinate chicken coop.

What to do? My solutions include recommendations for mime as well as a quirky anglophone Latin which, by analogy to franglais, I suppose one could call *flatin*. I draw on the few key Latin phrases that have crept into the English language along with a variety of Latinate suffixes (*-ibus, -issima*) that will be recognizable enough to at least *sound like* Latin. Additionally, where any given Latin term was likely to be more recognizable than another (without compromising meaning), I have replaced, for instance, "chapter three" with "chapter two" (*capitro tertialy*, e.g., becomes *capitro duo*). Still, there is really no way to do justice to the biggest in-joke of all except to flag it in an endnote when it happens: the very first Latin phrase uttered by the illustrious Professor is grammatically *wrong*. I won't bore you with a Latin lesson—especially since Tissier offers one (*RF*, 3: 244n); but, if you can imagine what an extremely pretentious Mrs. Malaprop might sound like, that is the right feel for the Professor's language.

As to the speech patterns of the other characters, I have exaggerated their grammar and original Norman dialect (*RF,* 3: 217–18), peppering their lines with mostly Southern regionalisms (see above, Introduction, § "Language and Style"). Their French is actually a good bit better than the English I've provided; and the women's grammar and lexicon start out rough-hewn but gain in correctness and elegance toward the end. Elsewhere, I have conveyed the Professor's preciosity by having him throw in a few *French* expressions, such as *entre nous,* or some archaic English phrases, such as "he doth." All "foreign-language" terms should be exaggerated, mispronounced, and/or overacted.

In addition to Wolfy's repetitiveness cited above—which constitutes a good instance of the refrain-like structures of the poetic *rondeau triolet* that signaled characters' entrances, exits, and changes in emotional state—this play boasts some interesting usage of masculine pronouns.[14] By offering a variant line or two, I have attempted to navigate the perilous path between the default linguistic conventions of gender (which call for masculine pronouns when speaking of gender-mixed subjects) and the repressive misogyny that, at least for Luce Irigaray and a host of feminist critics, lurks behind such conventions. (For an example of such a linguistic convention, see below, note 18.) I readily admit that my suggestions (at notes 54 and 57) go against the grammatical grain; but, to paraphrase Irigaray's *This Sex Which Is Not One:* when it comes to a protofeminist triumph *that is not one* (*qui n'en est pas un*), the men's last bastion for dominance, it would seem, is grammar.

Sets and Staging

There are three sets: the farm of Mimin's parents; the neighboring farm of Wolfy Chewy; and the school, which is "in town" (also Tissier, *RF,* 3: 226–27). The two farms might even be close enough together to be within earshot, encouraging some shouting between the two rustic habitats. Based on his interpretation of the scenography, Tissier thinks that the "reprogramming" scene takes place at the chicken coop at Wolfy Chewy's farm (*RF,* 3: 269n). Maybe that's the case; but the only evidence that it is *Wolfy's* chicken coop (as opposed to Rollo and Trixie's) is that Wolfy's daughter Dolly uses the possessive "our": *dedans* nostre *cage à poussins*.[15] Since both families live on farms, since the closing celebration takes place back at Rollo and Trixie's, and since the whole plot is initiated by mom Trixie so that her son can relearn his *mother* tongue, Tissier's reading seems to place an awful lot of weight on one word that might easily have been an error in the possessive adjective that goes with the chicken coop: *nostre* versus *vostre.* Thus, I prefer to stage the all-important final scene at the home of Mimin's parents. When, in Scene 4, Rollo proposes that they "party at their place," he might just as easily be indicating that everyone should head back to the house—his own house—as opposed to raising a few at his own chicken coop. Likewise, Mimin might just as easily ask his *parents* as his *neighbors* whether they can eat their own chicken for dinner: specifically, the caged bird that has been pecking at his nose during his brief residency inside the cage. (Sorry, folks, but the image that keeps pecking at my brain was much in the news as I was preparing this collection: Sarah Palin being interviewed against the backdrop of a turkey being slaughtered. Updated staging, anyone?)

At other moments, the text alludes to how Mimin speaks "Latin." Whenever he does so, it is *haultement* or *hault,* presenting actors with several choices: he should speak very *loudly,* or with a *high* voice, or in an *elevated* or *high*falutin manner, or perhaps using some combination of all of those.[16] And never forget that professors spend a lot of time giving their students a song and dance—so get ready for the grand finale! It would be perfectly in keeping with the medieval spirit to produce this play as a musical, chock-full of choreography and production numbers, so long as all requisite permissions have been cleared. From time to time, I have shared my various impressions as to how one might capture the spirit of the play's music, as always, in keeping with the specifications of the Appendix: Scholarly References to Copyrighted Materials.

Costumes and Props List

For Trixie: an apron and, to support one of the puns, a hat and a relatively long dress ("cap and gown"). For Dolly: a doll, of course, which—given the play's obsession with gendered learning—might be a *talking doll* that says "mama." The Professor's classroom should have a desk of sorts and preferably, a throne-like chair: this is the professorial *chaire* whence we get expressions like today's "endowed chair." (Remember Woody Allen's line from *Annie Hall*? "Two more chairs they got a dining room set.") The classroom should contain other "learning aids": a dunce cap as well as rulers, whips, and so on for corporal punishment. The coop is full of chickens, one of which is especially large.

Scholarly References to Copyrighted Materials (in order of appearance)

"Teacher, I Need You." By Elton John and Bernie J. P. Taupin. (BMI)

"Bloody Well Right." By Richard Davies and Charles Roger Pomfret Hodgson. (ASCAP)

"Wonderful World" ["What a Wonderful World"]. By Lou Adler, Herb Alpert, and Sam Cooke. (BMI)

"Merrily We Roll Along." By Eddie Cantor, Murray Mencher, and Charles Tobias. (ASCAP)

"We're Off to See the Wizard." By Harold Arlen and E. Y. Harburg. From *The Wizard of Oz,* © Metro Goldwyn Mayer, 1939. (ASCAP)

"The Madison Time." By Ray Bryant and Edwin L. Morrison. (BMI)

"When I First Came to This Land." Traditional folk song. Writer unknown. (BMI)

"I Can't Help Myself, Sugar Pie" ["Sugar Pie Honey Bunch"]. By Lamont Herbert Dozier, Brian Holland, and Eddie Holland Jr. (BMI)

"Do Re Mi." By Oscar Hammerstein II and Richard Rodgers. From *The Sound of Music,* © 1959. (ASCAP)

"My Boyfriend's Back." By Bob Feldman, Gerald Goldstein, Richard Gottehrer, Miriam Nervo, Olivia Nervo, and Paul Lancaster Wiltshire. (ASCAP)

"Together, Wherever We Go." By Stephen Sondheim and Jule Styne. From *Gypsy.* (ASCAP)

"We Go Together" ["Grease"]. By Warren Casey and Jim Jacobs. From *Grease,* © 1972. (ASCAP)

"You Never Can Tell" ["Teenage Wedding"]. By Chuck Berry. (BMI)

[Scene 1][17]

[At the home of Rollo and Trixie]

[Trixie arrives home, perhaps a bit out of breath.]

ROLLO *begins:*

>There you are, Trixie! It's about time! One of these days . . . POW! Right in the kisser! Where you been anyway?

TRIXIE

If you must know, I've come from the oven to see if we can use it tomorrow. I can't be runnin' around all the time like a chicken with its head cut off, you know!

ROLLO

Now *that's* a good one. What's wrong with you anyway? Are your tits botherin' you or somethin'? They still sore?

TRIXIE

I've just had some terrible news about our son.

ROLLO

Okay, if you insist: What is it?[18]

TRIXIE

What it *is* is that he won't speak French no more. His Professor's got 'im so under his thumb and he's so taken with 'im[19] that you can barely understand what he's sayin'. He might as well be speakin' English!

ROLLO

Well bless my soul and God help us! What in God's name are we supposed to do?

TRIXIE

What are we supposed to do? Lord have mercy! Whatever it takes, come hell or high water. He needs an intervention! You know good 'n' well that he's engaged to Wolfy Chewy's girl. She's the prettiest one on her street; and no one's more dolled up on the holidays. You know: what they call *une coquette.*[20]

ROLLO

I put him in that there school so's he could make somethin' of hisself. Maybe even go on to law school.

TRIXIE

You put 'im in there to put the fear o' God into 'im!
Didn't he already know all them books inside out? They cost us a

fortune! I even heard his old teacher, Mr. Gobble, sayin' that he had the best mind o' any boy he ever did see. You can tell just by lookin' at the size of his . . . nose. The nose knows.[21]

ROLLO

[*Making the sign of the cross*] Jesus H. Christ! You got a point there. We can't have him not speakin' French no more. God forbid! The girl won't be able to understand him when they're havin' a conversation.

TRIXIE

Alas and alack! No, she won't. And thus methinketh that we gots to get to that there school so's we can see the kinda state he's in.[22] Just think about it: if he stays there one more day, he's gonna speak such highfalutin Latin that even the dogs won't understand a thing!

ROLLO

Well said, Trixie. But we better stop by and pick up Wolfy Chewy on the way, and his kid too, our son's fiancée. Because I'm thinkin' that, with Dolly, he ain't got no problem with French. [*He might make a few kissing sounds.*] He'll talk French to her!

TRIXIE

What do I know about nothin'? But I swear by the hem o' this here cap and gown:[23] all's I can say is that you done made me real happy, hearin' you say that 'n' all.
So let's be on our merry way!

ROLLO

We'll be there in a jiffy; it's just down the road apiece.[24]

TRIXIE

Up and at 'em! Merrily we roll along! We'll be there in a jiffy!

[*Rollo and Trixie head off to Wolfy's place, singing as they go. They sing loudly enough for Wolfy and Dolly to hear the commotion from some ways away.*][25]

[Scene 2]

[At the home of Wolfy Chewy and his daughter, Dolly]

WOLFY CHEWY
What's this I hear?

DOLLY *[en déshabillé]*
Hey, it must be Trixie. Yoo-hoo!

WOLFY CHEWY
Let's go take a gander, then, honey.
[Counting out the beats as a prelude to more choreography to come and yelling to the approaching group]
And a-one, and a-two, and a-one-two-three . . . Come on in, folks!

ROLLO *[yelling back]*
We'll be there in a jiffy; it's just down the road apiece.
[Singing again in step as they approach Wolfy's farm, they arrive and find Wolfy.]
[To Wolfy] And howdy-do to you!

WOLFY CHEWY
God give you good day, Rollo, my brother, and you too, my sister, Trixie.

ROLLO *[seeking a private word with Wolfy that Dolly won't overhear]*
C'mere for a sec, why don'tcha. Come on over here.

TRIXIE
And howdy-do to you too.

WOLFY CHEWY
God give you good day, Rollo.

ROLLO
What's the girl up to?

WOLFY CHEWY

She's boilin' some milk.

DOLLY

It's done! It's done!

TRIXIE

That's a good girl, honey.

ROLLO

And howdy-do to you too.

WOLFY CHEWY

God give you good day, Rollo, my brother, and you too, my sister, Trixie. But good God! What brings you our way? We don't usually see you 'round these here parts.

TRIXIE

Alas and alack! May God watch over us!

WOLFY CHEWY

What's the matter?

ROLLO

It's no big deal, really . . . But let's talk in private for a moment. I can't really talk about it in front o' your girl.

WOLFY CHEWY

What's goin' on? Is the village on fire? Did Master Mimin die or somethin'?

ROLLO

Okay, here's the deal:
We pulled him outta the school 'round here so's we could really make somethin' out of 'im. [*The actor might pause here to accommodate the absurdity of the coming anachronism.*] A real rocket scientist.[26] Maybe even a famous lawyer! And all that so's he'd be able to hang onto any little somethin' we'd be able to pass on to 'im.

But we ain't exactly happy about how it all turned out. All that lookin'
and bookin' and cookin' the booken he undertooken that, with all that
Latin textbookin', all that insanin' declaimin'. . . .[27] Why he done gone
and forsooken all his French, and he can't barely speak a word of it no
more!
So, seems to me like we better hotfoot it over there, fast as we can, and
git 'im so's we can fix this mess.

WOLFY CHEWY

Are you tellin' me that he's really doin' all that studyin'?
Better watch out! Next thing you know, he'll be spoutin' mumbo
jumbo and callin' up the Devil!

TRIXIE

Let's head on over there, partner, and get a good look at 'im. We'll see
for ourselves.

WOLFY CHEWY

So we better hop to it! Off we go! Step lively! Swing your partner! [*To
Dolly*] And you there, lazybones: lickety-split, girl! Get dressed!

[*Dolly excuses herself to dress to see her fiancé.*]

ROLLO

So we better hop to it! And away we go!

[*Dolly takes forever to get ready. While the others wait, they might
perform a musical number as a prelude to their not-so-speedy departure.*][28]

TRIXIE

Do you think he'll be happy to see her?

ROLLO

What do you think? Enough talk now. So we better hop to it! Off we
go! Step lively! It's time to hit the road . . . and fast! That's what we
gotta do.

WOLFY CHEWY
[*To Dolly, who has just emerged*] Come on, girl! Where you been any-way? What are you dawdlin' about?
Trixie, take her by the hand, would ya?

DOLLY
I was just gettin' my little dolly that Master Mimin, my boyfriend, done give me.

TRIXIE
She ain't no dunce! Is that a pair o' lovebirds or what?

[Scene 3]

[*At the Professor's*]

The PROFESSOR
And may you, therefore, not blame me, my son, inasmuch as I too might seek to be in a position whence to derive honor from your repu-tation once you become a great nobleman.
Master Mimin, read and learn:
Respondez-vous! Quod librum legis?[29]
Please to answer in French.

MIMIN
[*Whenever Mimin speaks "Latin," he does so loudly, pretentiously, and/or in a high voice; he may even "elevate" himself atop a desk.*]
Ego non will say: *non speakere* in Frenchly because *ego allibus forgettibus.*

The PROFESSOR
Never have I seen such an apt pupil nor one so burning to learn! Unceasingly, he gazeth upon proverbs and epistles; he studieth the commentaries and, if I so direct, he doth check all the references and the footnotes! Such is the deep and profound knowledge of the truly intellectually adventurous, of those who take everything they can from the world around them!

Thus, if you must know, I shall make such a great man of you that all the clerics in Pavia, Rome, and Paris[30] will envy your little self insofar as you, my boy, shall know more than they.

MIMIN

> *Mundo variabilis*
> *Adventuribus goodlibus*
> methinketh is meaning:
> [*In pig latin*:] *Ake-tay ut-whay at-they an-cay gettibus;*
> *Non lastus longus forevribus;*
> *non take-us* with-us.
> *Dicatus in capitulo* eight-us:
> Live it up-us along the way.
> *Carpe diem,* man!

The PROFESSOR

> So well said, my boy! Honest to God, people that declaim thusly are no fools! I've never seen anything like it. With every word, he speaks the truth—and all in his own voice—without lifting a thing from anywhere else. No plagiarist, he![31] Why, he shall be a pillar of society, he shall, in this great kingdom of ours!
> Now go on, my son, and find me the psalm about why the honor of the world is hanging by a thread.

MIMIN, *reading aloud* [*with lots of miming*]

> *Adeste fidelis et gaudeamus igitur!*[32]
> *In capitulo* dynamic duo,
> *Nobis* read-imus *quod*
> *noster universibus et* globe-us *honorabile*
> is hang-ere *via threadibus littlissima.*
> *Nobis* liveth *et vivabit* subject to *fortuna!*
> *Ergo: cloakibus et daggeribus*
> *Meekes inheritaberunt* globe-us *et terra!*

The PROFESSOR

> Will you look at that! He's a Renaissance man![33] See how the Latin comes trippingly off his tongue. See how he makes the Latin tremble, even though it looks like butter wouldn't melt in his mouth.

[Enter the rest of the Company]

ROLLO

    Well what do you know! Here we are!

TRIXIE

    You men folk go on in first. We'll follow along behind you, me and her.
    [*To Dolly*] You be good now, sweetie, you hear?

DOLLY

[Perhaps miming what "being good" looks like]
    Here, look! Watch this! Aren't I doin' good?

ROLLO

    [*To Wolfy*] You go first. I insist. After you.

WOLFY CHEWY

    Not on your life!
    The father o' the boy goes first.
    After you.

ROLLO

    You go ahead.

WOLFY CHEWY

    Why, certainly, sir. After you.

DOLLY

    Quit it, would ya? And you say it's us girls who's always puttin' on airs!
    What are we a-s'pposed to do anyhow if all you're gonna do is bicker
    like that? You're stubborn as mules, the both o' you!

[Dolly goes in first and promptly sits down to play with her doll.]

ROLLO

    God give you good day, Doctor Professor, and my boy too.
    How are y'all doin'?

MIMIN
>*Bene.*

The PROFESSOR
>Greet your parents, *domine,* in French.

MIMIN
>[*He can, for example, shrug his shoulders to indicate that he does not how to.*]
>*Ego non comprehendo!*
>*Mommibus et Daddibus, et Wolfibus Chewibus,*
>Girly-girliba, baby-dolliba,
>*donare* to giveth in holy *matrimonia,*
>Howdy-doodibus!
>Greet-imus *et salutationis compania!*

ROLLO
>I don't get it.

The PROFESSOR
>He's greeting you, my friends.

MIMIN
>*Pater, pater; Mater, mater; Wolfibus Chewibus,*
>Girly-girliba, baby-dolliba.

TRIXIE
>Speak French! Speak *ipso facto.*

MIMIN
>*Ipso schmipso!*
>*Lingua latina speakere! Latina parlaria!*

DOLLY
>He sure does talk funny, Daddy! He's gonna make me laugh!

ROLLO
>Holy moly! He really knows a lot!

MIMIN

Pater, pater; Mater, mater; Wolfibus Chewibus,
Girly-girliba, baby-dolliba.
donare to giveth in holy *matrimonia,*
Howdy-doodibus!
Greet-imus *et salutationis compania!*

TRIXIE

Well I never! And in front of his mother!
[*She urges Dolly to intervene "Frenchly" as soon as possible, but Dolly continues to remain seated.*] Go on, get up! Get over there! I didn't mean for you to be *that* good.[34]

ROLLO

Have you forgotten the language that you learned on your mama's knee and that you used to talk so good?

The PROFESSOR
[*The Professor too might speak loudly, pretentiously, in a high voice, and/ or atop the desk.*]

You mark my words: it may indeed seem that his intellect has taken a turn for the worse; but the truth of the matter is that he's on fire, burning with the passion for learning, hot to trot, if you will.
Sometimes, he attains such heights when he talks that it's enough to make the both of us crazy. Why, I'm all hot and bothered just thinking about it.

TRIXIE

Yeah, yeah. And we know exactly where he's gettin' all o' this from. It's all them professors! They're just a bunch o' perverts: beatin' their students just for gettin' a line o' poetry wrong! You had your way with 'im for long enough! No more of this "Spare the rod and spoil the child"! We're gettin' 'im outta here!

The PROFESSOR [*more colloquially*]
See if I care! It's no skin off my nose.[35] And I'm made of strong stock. What the hell kinda show are you runnin' around here anyway?[36]

ROLLO

[*To Mimin*] The Professor can't do nothin' more to you now. And he did what he could.[37]

MIMIN

Burn-ibus learn-ibus!
[*Here, he might gesture toward the dunce caps. Dolly rises to see what's troubling him.*]
Non desirare non dunce-us cap-us!

WOLFY CHEWY

The Professor can't do nothin' more to you now.

TRIXIE

Ain'tcha never gonna speak French no more, honey? Come on now, sweetie pie, just a little word or two for mama.

DOLLY

The Professor can't do nothin' more to you now. And he did what he could.

TRIXIE

At least give her a little kiss, honey! You hear me? Did I bring you up like that?

MIMIN, *kisses her*
[*First a peck, then perhaps a French kiss*]
Kissimee minima . . . et maxima!
Post hoc marriagibus et receptionis,
Weddeth to beddeth:
Master Miminus virilibus lickety-split *cum novima bridella*
Et makimus petite baby-kins.

ROLLO

What kinda gibberish. . . ? To hell with all this Latin-speak! What does he mean, Professor?

The PROFESSOR
    Not to worry. He's just making a little joke! But *entre nous,* it's a bit on the *risqué* side.

WOLFY CHEWY
    What's he sayin'?

The PROFESSOR
    Er . . . That he's looking forward to getting his wife into bed, as a man does on his wedding night, and . . . *comment dit-on? . . .* to *being* with his wife . . . for procreation purposes, as the Lord commands.

ROLLO
    That's some smooth talker!

TRIXIE
    His mouth's waterin'! That's a fine way to talk about a little bun in the oven![38]

ROLLO[39]
    You can't tell me you're surprised now, Trixie! Why, as God is my witness, when I was his age and I was . . . gettin' lucky . . . it was wham, bam, thank you ma'am! I got what I wanted on the double![40] But I kept my nose clean!

TRIXIE
    Keep your voice down, will you, in front of the girl![41] I don't care if he trots out all the fancy lingo he wants. They're so lovey-dovey 'n' all that she'd still understand every word.
    Okay, then. Enough o' that now. Listen up:
    [*Her grammar takes a sharp turn for the better.*]
    Mister Doctor Professor, you just admitted—with no evidence to the contrary—that our son knows more than you do. That's what you just told us. So it is *your* turn now to study under *him* because we shall take him home with us immediately, this very instant!

The PROFESSOR

Don't let me stop you. I'd be happy to accompany you to assist in his . . . reindoctrination, the better to see if we might find some way of tempting him—seducing him, if you will—into speaking French again.

ROLLO

He still knows how to sing, don't he? It would be a great way to pass the time along the way.

WOLFY CHEWY

The girl sings really good.

DOLLY

He still knows how to sing, don't he?

The PROFESSOR

Yes, indeed, of course he does.

TRIXIE

So . . . merrily we roll along. Come on, lover boy, escort the young lady! Take the girl by the arm. Swing your partner!

[*The farm folk rehearse their traveling music, possibly the same music as earlier, so long as all permissions have been cleared.*]

WOLFY CHEWY

He still knows how to sing, don't he? It would be a great way to pass the time along the way.

The PROFESSOR

He's all the rage around here.

ROLLO

Let's all hum a few bars, then.

[*As they head to the home of Rollo and Trixie, the farm folk entertain the Audience and themselves with one or two songs of their choice for traveling*] *music, so long as all requisite permissions have been cleared. It is unlikely that, at this stage, the Professor would join in any such song and dance.*]

[Scene 4]

[*Back at the home of Rollo and Trixie*]

ROLLO
Enough of that now! We got work to do!
You over there, Prof, what are we a-s'pposed to do to get 'im back to normal? We gotta make it so it feels more . . . natural-like . . . for 'im to speak French.

The PROFESSOR
It's all that reading that has put him in the state that he's in; so, in my opinion, he would be in grave danger if, at this juncture, we were to leave him all alone with his books. Therefore, here is how we might proceed with his rehabilitation:
He cannot be let out of our sight. Night and day, we have to keep an eye on him. And, should he fall asleep, then he must be reawakened instantly.[42] Above all, he is not to have any books or reading matter whatsoever.[43] That's what got him into all this trouble to begin with. He's drunk with learning, so we can't have him falling off the wagon. He's an addict.

TRIXIE
Got it: no books.
We'll find another way to instruct him in his mother tongue again. I know! We'll put him in a cage! You teach birds how to talk, right?

ROLLO
Now you're talkin'!

WOLFY CHEWY
That's a right good idea you got there, Trixie!

DOLLY

Oh my God! You are soooooo smart! You're smarter than all our neighbors put together.

What about the chicken coop?[44] Wouldn't that be a great place to cook him up right?

WOLFY CHEWY

And I say don't count your chickens before they hatch. I don't think he'll fit. He's so tall, so broad-shouldered, so brawny, so well-built . . . well, except for that gut . . . that I don't think he's gonna squeeze in there.

DOLLY

Hang on! I'm gonna show you how to do it. Haste makes baste!
[As she speaks, Dolly might try to demonstrate slowly by pushing Mimin's head into the cage. Mimin will not fully "enter" the cage until his mother tells him to do so.]

All we really need to do is get his head inside. Like so. See? His mouth and all his teeth: just like that. His ass can hang out the back.[45] That oughta do it. [Perhaps gently swatting Mimin on the bottom] A bird in the hand is worth two in the tush!

ROLLO

Don't be chickenshit, boy! I, your own father, Rollo, and Wolfy Chewy, and the Professor: we're gonna teach you how to talk.
[Gasp] Look! He's breakin' out into a sweat. His goose is cooked, all right. This is pathetic.

MIMIN

Imprisonabus est cum chickibus! Cage-y-atus imprisonare!
Non libris, non codexes, non textis-bookis non studiare
Et lingua latina necessarius est forgettere!
Lingua latina tabula rasa!
Professoris meum non pedagoguit; ego non educare!
Non explicando non gettin' outta here-ibus!
Rustica lingua franca ressurexit!
Miserere, miserere!
Nix et ix-nay lingua latina! Nix et ix-nay lingua latina!

[*To the Professor*]
    Et tu, Magister?

ROLLO
    What's he sayin'?

The PROFESSOR
    That he feels such passion for those books that he shall die
    straightaway!

TRIXIE [*pushing him into the cage*]
    He doesn't know which end is up, and we've got to start somewhere.
    Okey-dokey, now, Master Mimin, one step at a time. Right side up. In
    you go!

WOLFY CHEWY
    Be a gentleman, boy. Go on and do like you're told.

TRIXIE
    What a good boy he is. It's a miracle! See how nicely he's going in? No
    muss, no fuss.

MIMIN
[*Perhaps banging his head or bumping into something*]
    Owwww![46] *Oops-us daisy-bus!*

TRIXIE
    He hurt his ear.

ROLLO
    What a good boy he is. It's a miracle!

The PROFESSOR
    I've never seen anything like it! He's obeying your every word.

TRIXIE
    What a good boy he is. It's a miracle! See how nice he's goin' in? No
    muss, no fuss.

ROLLO

First of all, Doc Professor, since we's all gathered together here today, let's talk to him man to man; seems to me that's what we gotta do. Go on, then: say somethin' to 'im.

The PROFESSOR

I'm willing to do that.

However, without levying, in no wise, blame upon one side or the other, I would say *irregardless* that, while our own manly words go together with those of women like two peas in a pod, it is the case nonetheless that, as men, we have greater knowledge and are more influential. Women! Now, that's a horse of a different color!

[*To Mimin*] May God grace you with perfect eloquence in French. Go on then, Master Mimin, in beautiful French:

Speak!

DOLLY

[*Rejecting the horse metaphor in favor of the dominant birds of the play*]

Oh no you don't! And who are you calling a horse? When it comes to talking, it's us girls who rule the roost!

The PROFESSOR

I'll say: too much so.

DOLLY

We have much sweeter voices than menfolk. Men are too rough. You don't know the first thing about how to handle kids when school's out.

TRIXIE

You tell 'em!

[*To Mimin*] Now: Repeat after me: "My darling."⁴⁷

MIMIN

Answers like a woman [*i.e., imitating his mother*]

"My darling."

TRIXIE

"Mother dear, forgive me."

MIMIN, *crying*
    "Mother dear, forgive me."

TRIXIE
    "And my father, Rollo, too."

MIMIN
    "And my father, Rollo, too."

TRIXIE
    "And Monsieur Wolfy Chewy."

MIMIN
    "And Monsieur Wolfy Chewy."
    [*At last, Mimin utters his first words in the target language of "French";
    but it's English here, of course. To capture the spirit, I've given him a few
    words in French.*]
        Merde alors! Get me outta here, Mom, I'm sweatin' like a pig! You don't
    smell what I smell in here.[48]

TRIXIE
    Did you hear that? See how he's making sense again? Now the chickens
    have come home to roost! *We're* the teachers now.

DOLLY
    That's right! Back off, boys!
    [*With a marked change in register*] How's that lesson of yours proceed-
    ing anyway? Go on: go ahead! Make him speak. I'm not holding my
    breath. But you're just going to make him sound like more of an idiot.
    [*To Mimin*] Okay, repeat after me: "My darling, my honey lamb."[49]

MIMIN, *responding like a student*[50]
    "Okay, repeat after me: 'My darling, my honey lamb.'"

[*The subsequent lines are delightfully ambiguous. It is unclear whether
Dolly is continuing to have Mimin repeat after her, whether she is trying
to express her love for him in earnest "French" communication—with
Mimin merely continuing, idiotically and unromantically, to parrot*

her—or whether, in fact, the young couple now start to exchange their first words of love in "French." Their lines are scripted as the first possibility, as an echo of the preceding exchange between Mimin and Trixie but any of the three options would work well.]

DOLLY

"Sugar pie, my honey bunch."[51]

MIMIN

"Sugar pie, my honey bunch."

DOLLY

"I love you baby, now and forever."

MIMIN

"I love you baby, now and forever."

DOLLY

And now, once more with feeling, to the Professor.

MIMIN

Oh no you don't! I wouldn't dare! Only Latin with the Professor! I'll speak French again if you want, but only for my mama! *Je ne veux pas! Maman! Maman!*

DOLLY

Just listen to that beautiful voice! Doesn't he sound great? He's making sense again.

ROLLO

It's a miracle!

WOLFY CHEWY

You can say that again.

The PROFESSOR

And thus, one is obliged to acknowledge that women are indeed in possession of certain talents: more than I might hitherto have warranted.

Why, they're more wily than ... the *Dev*—[*catching himself just in time*] ... No, let me not misspeak!—than the *day* is long.[52]

DOLLY

And I think that's worth saying twice. With all their sweet talk, it's women who make them sing in their cages! And I'm not just talking about magpies and parrots and parakeets and cockatoos.
[*To Mimin, but also pausing to appreciate the anachronism*]
"Here came the airplane, he opened up the hangar!" And that's how we do it, isn't it, sugar?

TRIXIE

So let's get out of here. It's time to wrap things up and have a couple of rounds. You're buying![53]

MIMIN, *humming*

Listen, mom, I'm a little tweetie bird! I'm a-whistlin' like a yellow-bellied warbler! Doodlee-doo, doodlee-doo, doodlee-doo, doodlee-doo. Lemme give it all I got: after all, I know why the caged bird sings.

ROLLO *lets him out* [*of the cage, possibly with disapproving looks from the women who ought to be exercising that power*] *and says:*
Come on out now, my son, come on. We'll sing all the way there!

MIMIN, *now out* [*of the cage*]
I talk goodly, goodly now!

The PROFESSOR
This is women's work.

MIMIN

Good God and, oh, Daddy! I talk goodly, goodly now! So let's get outta here and raise us a toast to all this!
[*To Dolly*] Hey, what about you, honey? Whaddaya think? I talk goodly, goodly now, right?

The PROFESSOR
This is women's work. Not that there's anything wrong with that ...

Very well, I must admit that, all the world's a cage, the men and women merely players. Without wishing to impute blame to anyone in particular ... [*gesturing toward the women*] they've really got it down pat![54] When it comes to talking, women rule the roost. Chicks rule!

ROLLO

So, off we go, then. C'mon! Let's go! We can party at our place![55]

MIMIN

Are we gonna eat that big bird that was peckin' at my nose?

ROLLO

You betcha!

DOLLY

Come on, come on along, let me take you by the hand. But, for Pete's sake, let's take it easy! I'm exhausted!

MIMIN, *lifts her piggyback*

How's about if I carry you? I think you deserve a ride: hop on!

ROLLO

This is what you call takin' it easy? Are you kiddin' me?
[*To Mimin*] Careful for her titties now!

MIMIN [*warming up for the final number*]

Everybody sing along with me: do-re-mi![56]

TRIXIE

This is what you call takin' it easy? Are you kiddin' me?

MIMIN

Dad, her ass is really soft!

WOLFY CHEWY

I absolutely affirm that she's a virgin.

The PROFESSOR
    This is what you call takin' it easy? Are you kiddin' me?
    Careful for her titties now!

ROLLO
    So let's sing along the way. And you, my pretty, I promise we'll do it up
    right.

The PROFESSOR
    At least we all done seen now that, when it comes to talkin', women
    rule the roost. Chicks rule!

ROLLO
    You got that right. I'll swear to it! At least we all done seen now that,
    when it comes to talkin', they rule the roost![57]

The PROFESSOR
    And, truth be told, sometimes, without hardly tryin'!

WOLFY CHEWY
    At least we all done seen now that, when it comes to talkin', women
    rule the roost. Chicks rule!

MIMIN
    Enough of that now! We gotta make like a chicken and get the flock
    outta here!
    A little closing music, please! We'll do it up right, come what may!

They sing.[58]

The END

Appendix: Scholarly References
to Copyrighted Materials

It is a frequent occurrence throughout this repertoire that a character intones a few poetic verses, parodies a famous or infamous medieval character, breaks into song, or refers to a popular medieval ditty without necessarily singing it. When that happens, I share some ideas about possible modern analogues that any theater company might consider in production. For the most part, this takes the form of underscoring the importance of music and musicality to medieval life as well as its relevance to the contemporary musical theater (see above, About This Translation, § "Prose, Verse, and Music"). However, my brief allusions to a variety of song titles are neither citations per se nor official parts of the script. They represent my dramaturgic thoughts only, and I present them as such, usually in the notes, in accordance with scholarly conventions of fair use. Prompting a number of difficulties is the fact that the Middle Ages had no such notion of fair use: all was fair in literature.

All over medieval Europe, music was performed in streets and public squares. Like poetry, epic, romance, and drama itself, it was part and parcel of a long lost pop culture, accessible and readily identifiable—without attribution—to numerous and diverse audiences (even though the actual melodies have typically been lost to history).[1] In fact, much of what we now call "medieval lyric poetry" ought actually to be designated "medieval music." What is more, music was so integral to daily life that many of its phrases entered the Middle French language, prompting my scholarly interest in what I have called—with no disrespect intended to lyricists and composers everywhere—the "musical clichés" of our dozen farces. I use that term to denote the recurring moments in which song lyrics took hold in the phrases, idioms, and expressions of everyday medieval linguistic usage. Please note that in no way am I implying that there is anything trite or vacuous about the music that

I reference. Far from it. Rather, I am offering evidence that medieval music was so stunningly influential that key phrases entered the Middle French language as idioms, commonplaces, and—yes—clichés. That language includes the language of farce. Thus, this bears repeating: to modern aficionados of all things literary, it is true that clichés feel dead in much the same way as many character "types" feel stereotypical. But music and drama are—and always have been—marvelous ways to bring all such standard usages back to life.

Although a musical cliché is harder to capture than clichés or idioms from other sources—precisely because the melodies that complete the cultural picture have disappeared—there are multiple modern-day examples from many venues that help us to decipher the all-important medieval musical practice. Allow me to explain:

Regarding the contemporary American language alone, if the sniffling individual seated next to you asks you for a "kleenex," a trademark sign does not appear in a bubble over his or her head to proclaim the primacy of the rightly trademarked brand of Kleenex™. Nor would you tend to respond: "Sorry, I have the generic brand. May I offer you a paper tissue instead?" Likewise, the word "thermos" is an official noun in the English language by which we denote a vacuum flask, even though the term started out as a trademarked brand name that most consumers encountered for the first time in stores or advertisements (just as they did those other products that help them with their runny noses). Similarly, in Old French, the word for *fox* was *goupil,* but it was no match for one of the most popular literary protagonists of all time, *Renard* the Fox, such that *renard* became—and still is—the French word for *fox.* What happened with music, language, and the medieval theater is roughly equivalent. In current French linguistic use, we still find the expression that means "let's get back to the point": *Revenons à nos moutons!* Its literal meaning is "let us return to our sheep!" but its connotations were institutionalized because the phrase appeared in the denouement of a beloved farce: the famous trial scene of none other than the fifteenth-century *Pathelin,* in which a tricky lawyer babbles incoherently about stolen cloth when he is supposed to be litigating about stolen *sheep.*

It's *language.* It *evolves.* That's why *Webster's* puts out a yearly list of lexical items whose widespread usage has made them unworthy of the designation "neologism." (The 2010 list included the term *unfriend,* born of social networking sites like Facebook and MySpace.) Twentieth- and twenty-first-century American audiences are well acquainted with the phenomenon. We too encounter it each time a phrase from a piece of pop music—or, for that matter, from television, cinema, or such Web sites as YouTube—makes its way into contemporary usage. Consider *Grey's Anatomy. Seriously!* That does not mean that, each time we say the word "seriously," we need to pay royalties to Ellen Pompeo or to find out who wrote the first script of *Grey's Anatomy* in which the term was used. The same holds true for Alicia Silverstone's "as if!" in the film *Clueless* or of Dana Carvey's "could it be Satan?" when he is playing the Church Lady. (I use these expressions all the time myself, especially in the classroom.) Another prime example is the phrase with which witty individuals pepper their double entendres: "Wink, wink, nudge, nudge, say no more!" (At least, that's how *my* British friends say it.) Perhaps unbeknownst to them, they are referring to a delightful bit from *Monty Python's Flying Circus*, specifically to "How to Recognise Different Types of Trees from Quite a Long Way Away." If you look up the phrase "Nudge Nudge" in Wikipedia (as I did on 26 October 2010), you encounter this statement: "The quote, 'nudge nudge, wink wink' has entered the English language as an idiomatic phrase implying sexual innuendo." So it has. Today, it is a relatively simple matter to trace the origins of that particular expression to the brilliant comedy that spawned it. In the Middle Ages, such a quest for origins relied mostly on the memory, be it reliable or unreliable.

Therefore, as far as the musicality of our farces is concerned, it is important to understand that the evolution of language depends not just on linguistic attention to phonology and morphology but to an entire network of sociocultural influences that I have endeavored to translate to the best of my ability, especially in the case of the rampant medieval theatrical use of song lyrics. The music that makes an appearance in the medieval French farce was as ingrained in the minds of medieval playwrights and spectators as is such a song as today's "Happy Birthday." You scarcely seek the rights—do you?—each time you sing that song, nor do those who sing it to *you*, presumably once a year. Perhaps you heard it for the first time while watching *Romper Room*. Perhaps a medieval townsperson first heard *Bon temps, reviendras-tu?* (which appears in #5, *Blind Man's Buff*) while walking through the marketplace. Today, we can search a number of musical registries and learn, much to the surprise of many, that "Happy Birthday" is protected by copyright, registered to Mildred J. Hill and Patty Smith Hill. In the Middle Ages, that was not only impossible: it was unnecessary. In the myriad cases in which one of our plays seems to be alluding to another artistic source—sometimes to another farce—I have indicated my awareness of that allusion and have made every effort to document the extratextual source. The problem for the farcical echoes of medieval music, however, is related to all those lost melodies.

Whereas numerous medieval epics, romances, and poems are extant to assist us in putting the dramatic puzzle back together again—we have a good example of this in #4, *Student Who Failed*, in which familiarity with an epic story is the only way to get the French joke—that is by no means the case for songs. It is as if one were being handed the score for a Broadway musical with nary a musical note on the page. In all likelihood, our twelve plays channel plenty more in-vogue but unidentifiable medieval songs for which one can only venture a best guess. Sometimes, the only guide is a suspicion (often deriving from a change of poetic meter) that a metrical string of words would have been sung. Thus, my challenge throughout has been to provide an evocative, comparative musical tool (in the form of song titles only) that will convey to readers, at least in part, what has been lost musically in translation. That does not mean that I've even come close to identifying each and every musical cliché; so I hasten to sound a cautionary note.

Musical clichés are so ubiquitous nowadays in American popular culture that it is entirely possible that I happen to use here the occasional idiom or set phrase that originates in a modern song or a television show, but that the expression in question is so institutionalized by regular English usage that I am simply unaware of its origin. Alas, it is just as possible that I'm not hip enough to know it. Otherwise, if one of our farces contains—or seems to contain—a song, if there is reason to believe that, consistent with medieval performance practice, a bona fide musical interlude might have been inserted into a given farce, I do the following:[2]

For purposes of scholarly understanding (and usually in the associated endnote), I have taken to gesturing toward the *titles only* of a song or two that strike me as rough, translational analogues for what is happening in the medieval text. At the same time, however, it was key not to be too specific. Like language, music too evolves; so, what seems musically contemporary to me will cease to be contemporary as these translations age. My readings of medieval music are temporary and unscripted, if you will, and of the moment. With the exception of those few phrases that are bona fide parts of contemporary English language, I do not cite any actual lyrics from any of the songs that I mention, nor any specific performances by recording artists. Instead, when I give the name of a song, I acknowledge the author(s) of that song: i.e., the individuals (if known) responsible for the music and lyrics.

Since I am concerned in this translation with medieval musical *language*—as opposed to those largely irrecoverable medieval melodies—I name the writers only of the songs in question (which may have been recorded by more than one artist). Again, my intent is to illustrate for readers the full extent to which musical allusions or subtexts run through the farces. Doing so was crucial to any postmedieval understanding of what passed in the medieval day for a veritable multimedia event: the theater.

Should any theater company wish to follow up on my thoughts about the medieval spirit of the farces by inserting musical materials or interludes into any given performance—even to perform one of these farces *as a musical*—the detailed list below is designed to assist them in taking their first steps toward obtaining permission for use. And please do note that rights may be held by lyricists, composers, performers, corporations, and other entities as well, such that, for any given musical selection it may be necessary to seek separate permission from separate entities for the rights to perform lyrics, melodies, specific performed versions, etc. As a lifelong fan of many of the songs that I mention in translational support of the spirit of these twelve farces, I am happy to publicize the work of the gifted lyricists and composers who created them, even though I do not cite directly from their work nor do I have the casts of characters perform their songs. However, it must be emphasized in no uncertain terms that *before contemplating production, theater practitioners are required to investigate and resolve any and all issues of copyright, fair use, or royalty arrangements related to the following copyrighted materials to which I make scholarly references in the plays.*

Finally, in the event that my own idiomatic mention of these songs inspires theater companies to seek, as they must, performance rights, I also provide the relatively simple guide below. In each and every instance where I give the title of a specific and knowable song, I indicate the professional registry—here, ASCAP or BMI—to which interested users may turn, the better to facilitate the identification of the legal title of the song. Since no actual musical performances are scripted in these twelve farces, and, since I mention any song subject to all the linguistic, translational specifications above, I have opted for a simplified way of naming the "authors" only of all of these songs, whom I designate by the term "by." If a company wishes to use any such song in performance, however, that style of reference will necessarily change to reflect distinctions, for example, between composers, lyricists, recording artists, and the like. Consistent with those guidelines and reflective of my commitment to identifying a song's legal authors, I also list those authors alphabetically, as per the song's legal title (even though, under other circumstances, those authors might be listed in order of priority).

Next to each title listed below, you will find your likely first stop for further details about how to obtain the rights to use any given song: ASCAP (ascap.com) and BMI (bmi.com) be it inside or outside the United States.

"Adelaide's Lament." By Frank Loesser. From *Guys and Dolls*, © 1950. (ASCAP)

"All That You Dream." By Paul Barrere and William H. Payne. (ASCAP)

"Anything You Can Do." By Irving Berlin. From *Annie Get Your Gun*, © 1946. (ASCAP)

"Baby Got Back." By Anthony L. Ray. (BMI)

"Back in the Saddle Again." By Gene Autry and Ray Whitley. (ASCAP)

"Bad Case of Lovin' You" ["Doctor, Doctor"]. By John Moon Martin. (BMI)

"Bat Out of Hell." By James Richard Steinman. (BMI)

"Behind Closed Doors." By Kenny O'Dell. (BMI)

"Bloody Well Right." By Richard Davies and Charles Roger Pomfret Hodgson. (ASCAP)

"Build Me Up, Buttercup." By Michael D'Abo and Instone Anthony Gordon. (ASCAP)

"Bye Bye Baby" ["Bye, Bye, Baby (Baby Goodbye)"]. By Bob Crewe and Robert Gaudio. (BMI)

"By the Light of the Silvery Moon." By Hawley W. Ades, Gus Edwards, and Edward Madden. (ASCAP)

"Can't Buy Me Love." By John Winston Lennon and Paul James McCartney. (ASCAP)

"Come and Get It." By Paul James McCartney. (ASCAP)

"Come Away Death." [Words by William Shakespeare.] By Danny Apolinar and Hal Hester. (ASCAP)

"Creep." By Colin Charles Greenwood, Jonathan Richard Guy Greenwood, Albert Louis Hammond, Michael Edward Hazlewood, Edward John O'Brien, Philip James Selway, Thomas Edward Yorke. (ASCAP)

"Do Re Mi." By Oscar Hammerstein II and Richard Rodgers. From *The Sound of Music*, © 1959. (ASCAP)

"Eight Days a Week." By John Winston Lennon and Paul James McCartney. (ASCAP)

"Embraceable You." By George Gershwin and Ira Gershwin. (ASCAP)

"Every Breath You Take." By Sting. (BMI)

"Footloose." By Kenneth Clark Loggins and Dean Pitchford. (ASCAP)

"Get Down Tonight." By Harry Wayne Casey and Rick Finch. (BMI)

"Get Ready." By William [Smokey] Robinson. (ASCAP)

"Gett Off." By Prince. (ASCAP)

"Gimme Some Loving." By Spencer Davis, Muff Winwood, and Stephen Lawrence Winwood. (BMI)

"Goin' Co'tin'" ["Going Courting"]. By Gene de Paul and John H. Mercer. From *Seven Brides for Seven Brothers,* © Metro Goldwyn Mayer, 1954. (ASCAP)

"Going Up the Country." By Alan C. Wilson. (BMI)

"Goin' Out of My Head." By Teddy Randazzo and Bobby Weinstein. (BMI)

"Handy Man." By Otis Blackwell, Jimmy Jones, Charles Merenstein, and Unart Music Corporation. (BMI)

"Happy Birthday to You." By Mildred J. Hill and Patty Smith Hill. (ASCAP)

"Happy Together." By Gary Bonner and Alan Lee Gordon. (BMI)

"The Happy Wanderer." By Friedrich Wilhelm Moeller, Antonia Florence Ridge, and Florenz Siegesmund. (ASCAP)

"Hard to Handle." By Alvertis Isbell, Allen Alvoid Jones Jr., and Otis Redding. (BMI)

"Hey, Marty!" By Paddy Chayefsky and Harry Warren. Theme song from *Marty,* © 1955. (ASCAP)

"Hot Blooded." By Louis A. (Andrew) Grammatico and Michael Leslie Jones. (ASCAP)

"Hound Dog." By Jerry Leiber and Mike Stoller. (BMI)

"I Can't Help Myself, Sugar Pie" ["Sugar Pie Honey Bunch"]. By Lamont Herbert Dozier, Brian Holland, and Eddie Holland Jr. (BMI)

"If Ever I Would Leave You." By Alan Jay Lerner and Frederick Loewe. From *Camelot,* © 1960. (ASCAP)

"I Have a Song to Sing-O!" By William Schwenck Gilbert and Sir Arthur Seymour Sullivan. From *The Yeoman of the Guard* (1888). Revised version of Gilbert and Sullivan classic also attributed to Milton T. Okun, Noel Paul Stookey, Mary Allin Travers, and Peter Yarrow. (ASCAP)

"I'll Take You There." By Alvertis Isbell. (BMI)

"I'm Called Little Buttercup." By William Schwenck Gilbert, Cameron Nicholas Patrick, and Sir Arthur Seymour Sullivan. From *H.M.S. Pinafore* (1878). (BMI)

"I'm Every Woman." By Nickolas Ashford and Valerie Simpson. (ASCAP)

"I'm So Excited." By Trevor Lawrence, Anita Pointer, June Pointer, and Ruth Pointer. (BMI)

"I'm So Lonesome, I Could Cry." By Hank Williams. (BMI)

"I'm Telling You Now." By Frederick Garrity and Mitch Murray. (ASCAP)

"In the Midnight Hour." By Stephen Lee Cropper and Wilson Pickett Jr. (BMI)

"I Only Want to Be with You." By Michael Edwin Hawker and Ivor Raymonde. (ASCAP)

"I Think We're Alone Now." By Ritchie Cordell. (BMI)

"It's in His Kiss." By Rudy Clark. (BMI)

"It's My Party." By John R. Gluck, Wally Gold, Seymour Gottlieb, and Herbert Wiener. (ASCAP)

"I Will Follow Him" ["Chariot"]. By Paul Julien André Mauriat, Jacques Plante, and Franck Marius Louis Pourcel. (ASCAP)

"Jealousy." By Freddie Mercury [Frederick Mercury, Freddie Bulsara, Farrokh Bulsara]. (BMI)

"Judy Blue Eyes." *See* "Suite: Judy Blue Eyes"

"Let Me Entertain You." By Stephen Sondheim and Jule Styne. From *Gypsy*, © 1959. (ASCAP)

"Let the Good Times Roll." By Shirley M. Goodman and Leonard Lee. (ASCAP)

"Little Less Talk and a Lot More Action." By Keith W. Hinton and Jimmy Alan Stewart. (BMI)

"Lover's Cross." By James J. Croce. (ASCAP)

"The Lusty Month of May." By Alan Jay Lerner and Frederick Loewe. From *Camelot*, © 1960. (ASCAP)

"Madeleine." By Eric Blau, Jacques Romain G. Brel, Jean F. Corti, and Gérard Emile Jouannest. (BMI)

"The Madison Time." By Ray Bryant and Edwin L. Morrison. (BMI)

"Merrily We Roll Along." By Eddie Cantor, Murray Mencher, and Charles Tobias. (ASCAP)

"Mon Homme" ["My Man"]. By Jacques Mardochée Charles, Albert Lucien Willemetz, and Maurice Yvain. (ASCAP)

"My Boyfriend's Back." By Bob Feldman, Gerald Goldstein, Richard Gottehrer, Miriam Nervo, Olivia Nervo, and Paul Lancaster Wiltshire. (ASCAP)

"My Man." *See* "Mon Homme"

"Night and Day." By Cole Porter. (ASCAP)

"Nowhere to Run." By Lamont Herbert Dozier, Brian Holland, and Eddie Holland Jr. (BMI)

"Over My Head." By Christine McVie. (BMI)

"Poor, Poor, Pitiful Me." By Warren William Zevon. (BMI)

"Proud Mary." By John Cameron Fogerty. (BMI)

"Quando, Quando, Quando." By Charles E. Boone, Elio Cesari, and Alberto Testa. (ASCAP)

"Rescue Me." By Raynard Miner and Carl William Smith. (BMI)

"Respect." By Otis Redding. (BMI)

"Rocky Raccoon." By John Winston Lennon and Paul James McCartney. (ASCAP)

"Saving All My Love." By Gerald Goffin and Michael Masser. (ASCAP)

"She's Not There." By Rod Argent. (BMI)

"Signed, Sealed, Delivered, I'm Yours." By Lee Garrett, Lula Mae Hardaway, Stevie Wonder, and Syreeta Wright. (ASCAP)

"Silver Threads and Golden Needles." By Dick Reynolds and Jack Rhodes. (BMI)

"Silvery Moon." *See* "By the Light of the Silvery Moon"

"Smoke Gets in Your Eyes." By Otto A. Harbach and Jerome Kern. (ASCAP)

"Smooth Operator." By Helen Folasade Adu, Paul Anthony Cook, Andrew Ralph Potterton, and Raymond William St. John. (ASCAP)

"Suite: Judy Blue Eyes." By Stephen A. Stills. (BMI)

"Sunshine Superman." By Donovan Philips Leitch. (BMI)

"Teacher, I Need You." By Elton John and Bernie J. P. Taupin. (BMI)

"Teenage Wedding." *See* "You Never Can Tell"

"Think." By Aretha Franklin and Ted White. (BMI)

"Tired of Waiting for You." By Raymond Douglas Davies. (BMI)

"Together, Wherever We Go." By Stephen Sondheim and Jule Styne. From *Gypsy*. (ASCAP)

"Upside Down" ["Round 'n' Round"]. By Sandra Jacqueline Denton, Bernard Edwards, Cheryl James, and Nile Gregory Rodgers. (ASCAP)

"The Vatican Rag." By Tom Lehrer. (ASCAP)

"Volare." By Francesco Migliacci and Domenico Modugno. (ASCAP)

"Walking the Floor over You." By Ernest Tubb. (BMI)

"We Go Together" ["Grease"]. By Warren Casey and Jim Jacobs. From *Grease,* © 1972. (ASCAP)

"We're Off to See the Wizard." By Harold Arlen and E. Y. Harburg. From *The Wizard of Oz,* © Metro Goldwyn Mayer, 1939. (ASCAP)

"When I First Came to This Land." Traditional folk song. Writer unknown. (BMI)

"When Will I See You Again?" ["Precious Moments"]. By Kenneth Gamble and Leon Huff. (BMI)

"Wishin' and Hopin'." By Burt F. Bacharach and Hal David. (ASCAP)

"(What a) Wonderful World." By Lou Adler, Herb Alpert, and Sam Cooke. (BMI)

"Wouldn't It Be Nice?" By Tony Asher, Michael Edward Love, and Brian Wilson. (BMI)

"You Can Leave Your Hat On." By Randall S. Newman. (ASCAP)

"You Never Can Tell" ["Teenage Wedding"]. By Chuck Berry. (BMI)

"You Really Got Me." By Raymond Douglas Davies. (BMI)

Notes

Preface

1. Unless otherwise indicated (in the Bibliography), all translations from the French are my own, as for the citation from *RF*, 1: 55.

Introduction

1. Shaw is cited by Davis, *Farce*, 22. (I'm assuming that there was no pun intended with the phrase "at bottom.") Among the best introductions to this philosophical bent: Bergson's enduring treatise on "Laughter," 62–64—though Le Goff found it disappointing ("Laughter in the Middle Ages," 40); and Marshall, *Surprising Effects of Sympathy*. For a discerning general history, see Barish, *Antitheatrical Prejudice;* plus Clopper, *Drama, Play, and Game*, chap. 1.

2. When citing the primary-source documents from this volume, I give their text number as well: E84 in this case.

3. The question of *when* these pieces were written, compiled, and published is addressed below, About This Translation, § "Editions and Printed Sources."

4. On the *Recueil Cohen*, see below, About This Translation, § "Editions and Printed Sources." Thanks to such critics as Tissier, Harvey, Knight, and Bowen, we know, e.g., that the anonymous author of the celebrated *Farce of Master Pierre Pathelin* was a Basochien; and, thanks to Koopmans's new introduction to the *Recueil de Florence* (the original name of the *Recueil Cohen*), we also know (or suspect) that most of the authors of the twelve farces assembled here were Basochiens as well.

5. Even though the commentator might well have exaggerated, on the performance situation of Bourges and the *Adam*, see *DBD*, 98–102, 148–49.

6. See, e.g., Young's pronouncement in *Drama of the Medieval Church*, 1: 1; and my analysis of it in *ROMD*, 66–68.

7. For some extant tropes, see Bevington, ed., *Medieval Drama*, 25–29.

8. "*Vecy, veez dan chie-en-escole. . . . / Je vueil son cul breneus torchier*," vv. 992–94; cited in *MTOC*, 149, where I include many examples of pedagogical violence (129–52).

9. I have never seen Davis's insight adequately treated elsewhere. John Stevens, e.g., explores the practice of "farsing," but, oddly enough, he privileges the narrative concerns of reading over the performance concerns of drama (*Words and Music*, 241–42).

10. Still invaluable is Chambers on medieval folk drama, as performed by mimes, min-strels, and bards (*Mediaeval Stage,* 1: chaps. 2–4; also its invaluable appendices). For more on gesture as drama, see esp. Davidson, ed., *Gesture in Medieval Drama;* and my "Of Miming."

11. I cite this passage in "Of Miming," 1; as does Adam Kendon in *Gesture: Visible Action as Utterance,* 17–19. See esp. the excellent essays in Bremmer and Roodenburg, eds., *Cultural History of Gesture;* in Davidson, ed., *Gesture in Medieval Drama;* plus Bur-row, *Gestures and Looks.* Nichols also studies the visual language of "corporeal gesture" in "Aux frontières du rire."

12. On the impeccable scholarship of both Koopmans (who rediscovered the *Recueil Cohen*) and Tissier (to whom we owe some of the finest editions of medieval French farce), see below, About This Translation, § "Editions and Printed Sources." For Koop-mans's remarks, I quote, in my own translation, from the typescript introduction to his in-press edition of the *Recueil de Florence* (i.e., the original name of the *Recueil Cohen*).

13. Although Davis reedited *Farce* in 2003 (with a new introduction and corrections), the newer edition is unusually difficult to find; thus, I cite from the original 1978 edition.

14. See, e.g., on court culture Walker, "Learning to Play," 1–14; and, on the *Rederijkers,* Kramer, "Rederijkers on Stage"; plus the interesting essays in Happé and Streitman, ed., *Urban Theatre in the Low Countries.*

15. This phrase appears in the 1875 ed. of Fabre's *Clercs du Palais,* viii; also cited in *ROMD,* 130. In *ROMD,* chap. 3, I give a full overview of the secondary literatures on the Basoche, including Fabre; Harvey, *TB;* Delachenal, *Histoire des avocats;* and Genty, *Basoche notariale.* On the law as dramatic structure, see *ROMD,* chaps. 1, 2, also as re-flected by today's law and literature movement: exemplary work includes Brooks and Gewirtz, eds., *Law's Stories*; and Sarat and Kearns, eds., *Law in Everyday Life.*

16. I'll be citing throughout from a very interesting article by Pinet, "Role of the Cobbler."

17. Scholars have yet to reconcile the author-actor theory with Pinet's fascinating if undocumented claim about the ubiquitous cobbler of farce: namely, that it is "clear that before the advent of semi-professional companies of actors in the mid-sixteenth century, the tradesman-actor played himself in farce" ("Role of the Cobbler," 309).

18. Petit de Julleville, *Les Mystères,* 2: 190; and Fabre, *CP* (1875), 132–33, my emphasis; also cited in *ROMD,* 140. As actors, the Basochiens took full philological advantage of the meanings of *actor* (prosecutor), *auctor* (author, authority), and *actio* (rhetorical deliv-ery) (*ROMD,* 8–9).

19. Tissier describes the *sots'* costumes (*RF,* 9: 137–38). Still known to us today is the legendary *sot* Pierre Gringore, whose identity is wrapped up in his role as the *sottie's* Mother fool or Mère Sotte (*MES,* 334).

20. See Huizinga, *Homo ludens,* 76–77; 191–94; Burns, *Courtly Love Undressed,* esp. introd. and chap. 1; and Crane, *Performance of Self,* introd. and chap. 1.

21. On the Feast of Fools, see, e.g., Chambers, *Mediaeval Stage*, 1: chaps. 13, 14; and Bakhtin, *Rabelais and His World*, 4–58.

22. As noted below in About This Translation, § "Critical Apparatus," I indicate the most self-conscious of these moments by the phrase *Metacommentary alert!* Among our savviest metteurs en scène: the Lady in #7, *At Cross Purposes;* Colette in #3, *Confession Lessons;* Goguelu and Thomasina in #5, *Blind Man's Buff;* Frigid Bridget and Doc Double-Talk in #6, *Playing Doctor;* pretty much everybody except the Gatekeeper in #9, *Monk-ey Business;* Bootie and Desirée in #10, *Getting Off on the Wrong Foot;* and Wilhelmina and Father John in #11, *Cooch E. Whippet.*

23. On the theater of everyday life, see, e.g., de Certeau, *Practice of Everyday Life;* or Read, *Theatre and Everyday Life.* Superb introductions to the wide range of medieval theatrics include Symes, *Common Stage;* Clopper, *Drama, Play, and Game,* 3–19; Axton, *European Drama,* pt. 1; Olson, "Medieval Fortunes of 'Theatrica'" and *Literature as Recreation,* 64–77; Dox, *Idea of the Theater,* chap. 1; and Henri Rey-Flaud on *mystère/ministerium* in *Pour une dramaturgie,* 75–76.

24. For more on the disputational spectacle of the medieval university exam, see the § "Production Notes" for #4, *Student Who Failed.*

25. See *Etymologies,* bk. 18, analyzed at length in *ROMD,* 77–89. For a terrific initiation to performance studies, see Bial, ed., *Performance Studies Reader.* I also summarize that interdiscipline's relevance to medieval theater in *MBA,* esp. chap. 2.

26. Among the most remarkable documents: the detailed contracts for the Passion plays at Mons in 1501 and Valenciennes in 1547 (see *MES,* 540–52). Cohen edited the Mons contract as *Le Livre de conduite du Régisseur.* I analyze the Valenciennes contract at length in "Performing Miracles."

27. See my review in *Theatre Journal* 54.4 (2002).

28. If you read French, Bernadette Rey-Flaud provides a helpful review of some of the etymological difficulties of the term, ultimately refuting the "alimentary" hypothesis in favor of the "trick" (*Farce,* 155–70). We return to that "tricky" meaning below, § "Question of Genre."

29. For additional sources on medieval rehearsals, see, e.g., *MES,* 299–307, 542, 549–50; and *MBA,* chap. 2.

30. Here, I draw on *CE,* 4; *RF,* 1: 37, 46–48. We return to the *sottie* below in § "Question of Genre."

31. To put it all into a contemporary American perspective, see, e.g., Savran on "highbrow vs. lowbrow" in *Queer Sort of Materialism,* esp. chap. 1.

32. In "Spectacle of the Scaffolding," I retell the sordid story first related by Thomas in "Le Théâtre à Paris et aux environs."

33. These are case studies in my *MBA,* chaps. 1–3. Petit de Julleville, e.g., found only a handful of earlier fragmentary records from 1290, 1333, 1351, and 1376 (cataloged chronologically in *Les Mystères*).

34. Excellent introductions to the Grand Guignol include Gordon, *Grand Guignol*; Hand and Wilson, *Grand-Guignol* and *London's Grand Guignol*.

35. I discuss these ideas in *MTOC*, 120–52, 170–202, including Gatton, "There Must Be Blood"; Woolf on singsong musicality (*English Mystery Plays*, 255); Holsinger's brilliant *Music, Body, and Desire*, esp. chap. 5; and States on pain and pleasure, *Pleasure of the Play*, chap. 12.

36. Interestingly enough, Austin believes that theater is *not* performative, a notion that I refute in *MBA*, 7–13.

37. On such incidents, see *DBD*, esp. chaps. 3–7, 13, and 14; and *MBA*, chaps. 1 and 2.

38. Again, I quote, in my own translation, from Koopmans's typescript introduction to his edition of the *Recueil de Florence* which was in production at the time of this writing. See below, About This Translation, § "Editions and Printed Sources."

39. Preface to *A Duke and No Duke* (1693), cited by Davis, *Farce*, 1.

40. Bentley is also cited by Davis, *Farce*, 1.

41. "Farce," Wikipedia, http://en.wikipedia.org/wiki/Farce (accessed 9 October 2009). Interestingly enough, when I reaccessed this source on 21 July 2010, the excellent bracketed phrase had already been deleted in favor of a purely theatrical definition limited to "in theatre."

42. Vol. 1 of Faivre's anthology of farces in modern French translation is called *The Battle of the Sexes* and vol. 2 is *Dupes and Tricksters*. Tissier notes that most fools are men (*RF*, 1: 42).

43. See Guynn on ethics in the *Pathelin* in "Justice to Come."

44. Unfortunately, Beam fails to provide a bona fide bibliography and also neglects reams of scholarship in theater and performance studies: to wit, the groundbreaking work of Knight and Bowen, whom she relegates to minimalist footnotes (26n, 12n).

45. Excellent general introductions to rhetoric include Kennedy, *Classical Rhetoric*; and Murphy, *Synoptic History*. See also my revised take on the medieval rhetorical tradition as cultural studies, "Rhetoric in the Middle Ages," in the forthcoming *Norton Anthology of Rhetoric and Writing*.

46. Guilhamet's chaps. 2–4 are devoted to demonstrative (epideictic), deliberative, and forensic rhetoric respectively. I elaborate further in my review of that book for *Continuum*. Although Beam does not cite his work, she too hesitates between calling farce a comic *mode* or a comic *genre* (*LM*, 27–29).

47. The passage appears in the *Mystère de la Résurrection*, ed. Servet, vol. 1, Day 1, 218–25; also discussed in *MBA*, 39–40.

About This Translation

1. Online at http://english.cua.edu/faculty/drama/index.cfm (accessed 26 September 2010).

2. Tissier gives full details about each manuscript or printed source (*RF*, 1: 15–19) and also enumerates all modern French translations thereof (*RF*, 1: 19–22). See also Faivre,

Répertoire, 9–28; Koopmans, introd., *Recueil de Florence;* Boucquey, *SMFF*, 1–4; and Maxwell, *French Farce*, 164–67.

3. Koopmans has written a lengthy and learned introduction to his *Farces du Recueil de Florence*. However, since that work had not yet been published at the time of this writing, I cite him in two ways: (1) I refer, as above, to several e-mail "conversations" that we had in English, this one, from 30 August 2009 (the only such conversation cited here); and (2) since he was kind enough to share his typescript with me, I indicate the section of his introduction from which a given quote (in my English translation) is taken. Lest there be any confusion, my own citations from the playtexts of the *Recueil Cohen* refer to the printed source of 1949, which I cite as *Recueil*, whereas I refer to the unconsultable primary source by its common proper name: the *Recueil Cohen*.

4. In generalizing thus, I draw from such signature works as Saenger, "Silent Reading"; Treitler, "Oral, Written, and Literate Process"; Huot, *From Song to Book;* and Gellrich, *Idea of the Book*.

5. Cohen wrote of his own experiences in "The 'Théophiliens.'" On his life as a theater practitioner, see Solterer, "Waking of Medieval Theatricality" and *Medieval Roles*.

6. So far, thanks to my ingenious copyeditor, Michael Gnat, who located a French anagram-finder, I see that it is possible to make out the following anagram, which is not bad at all: *Brio, nom de Café-Théâtre*. I've been unable, however, to locate any former or current Café-Théâtre by the name of "Brio."

7. *Lippin* appears in *Medieval Dutch Drama*, trans. Prins, 43–53.

8. See esp. Gatton, "There Must Be Blood," 87.

9. I am eternally grateful to Clareann Despain for suggesting this.

10. Chatelain published an exhaustive catalog of variant forms of the *rondeau*, along with an explanation of their uses and function, in *Recherches sur le vers français*, esp. 213–20. Note, however, that he does not appear to have cataloged their usage in the farce. Such *rondeaux* appear in Passion plays as well, notably in the musical beating scenes; see also Tissier, *RF*, 1: 39–40; and Warning, *Ambivalences of Medieval Religious Drama*, 187–90.

11. The linguistic particularities of this collection are almost exclusively American; but it's a relatively simple matter to change the slang to reflect other sensibilities. Try reading Father John, for instance, of #11, *Cooch E. Whippet*, with an Irish brogue or Scottish burr. It's no problem to replace his "boy oh boy" with "Crikey!" or his "baby" with "lassie."

12. See, e.g., Paxson, "Structure of Anachronism."

13. The better to clarify that convention, I've highlighted it, e.g., in #7, *At Cross Purposes* (note 10) and in #12, *Birdbrain* (notes 18, 54). See also #2, *Edict of Noée*, note 25.

14. For both these moments, see § "Language" in the "Production Notes" for #8, *Shit for Brains,* and #12, *Birdbrain*.

Actors' Prologue

1. Or try this variation in performance: "And last, if you should wish to start to hector, / If you don't like it, just blame the director!"

Play 1. *Farce of the Fart*

1. I follow Viollet le Duc's edition in *ATF,* drawing on Tissier as needed, as well as on Lewicka's facsimile edition of the *Recueil du British Museum.* On the published sources, see also Tissier, *RF,* 10: 23–24.

2. There is also evidence that the *Farce of the Fart* was known in Italy; it was published in Asti in 1521 in a collection of plays based on French farces (*RF,* 10: 31).

3. [Delepierre], *Description et analyse,* 12. He reproduces only a twelve-line excerpt. Faivre gives a much better picture in *Répertoire,* 340–41. On Delepierre's pseudonym, see *Notes and Queries* (25 January 1851): 77; cited above, About This Translation, § "Editions and Printed Sources." Compare his indictment to Bouchet's words, *MES,* E84, 332; cited above, Introduction. I offer a literary analysis of this play in *ROMD,* 216–21.

4. Don't get me wrong: Mark Jordan has treated the subject with the utmost seriousness and erudition in *Invention of Sodomy.*

5. See, e.g., Mandel's translation of the *Pathelin,* which he calls *Peter Quill's Shenanigans,* in *FCMF,* 131. The Judge is impatient to adjourn before the trial even begins!

6. See also Tissier's chart of the distribution of scenes and speeches, *RF,* 10: 27.

7. This is the *esguillette* cited above, § "Costumes and Props List."

8. This stage direction was Tissier's idea (*FFMA,* 4: 17).

9. In French, he swears by an imaginary saint (*FFMA,* 4: 37n).

10. To reinforce the impending trial, one might also add: "Or any accessory after the *fart!*"

11. Here is an example of how I account throughout for a change from *vous* to *tu.*

12. For Tissier, the literal meaning of this line—*c'est qu'il en peult de cela*—is something like: "There are some people who do not deserve to be served; one sees the result" (*RF,* 10: 39n); or, more idiomatically: "That's the thanks I get for waiting on you hand and foot!"

13. Apparently Jehannette has not seen #11, *Cooch E. Whippet,* where uttering this phrase causes the Devil himself—well, a priest in a Devil costume—to put in an appearance. Editors have typically corrected what appears to be a scribal error in which the text reads "the Devil take *him!*" (*RF,* 10: 40n).

14. I have added some extra dialogue to maximize the double entendre.

15. It's not entirely clear whether the Lawyer is speaking to Jehannette, Hubert, or both.

16. Another possible interpretation: "You can't tell each other's side of the story!"

17. Jehannette is smart enough to be ironic here; another reading of her line is: "There's a good man! *That's* the way to do it!"

18. Tissier argues that only Hubert should answer here because Jehannette is too "polite" throughout to utter the actual word *fart* (*RF,* 10: 45n). I beg to differ.

19. Wonderful wordplay results if the actor uses a cheesy French accent to create a homonym for *sheet/shit.*

20. Here I try to capitalize on that potential homonymy between *pet* (fart) and *paix* (peace, silence, or "shut up"); see above, § "Language."

21. Tissier thinks that, both here and in the final address to the public, the term *seigneurs* applies to men and women alike (*RF,* 10: 63n). Again, I beg to differ.

22. "(*Non est*), *il n'en est riens,*" v. 163. Tissier has another reading of this line, namely that Hubert is being "conciliatory," saying that it's no big deal and that all Jehannette need do is simply admit her culpability (*RF,* 10: 26). Yet again, I beg to differ.

23. Since a verse is missing here, Tissier proposes a line such as this one (*RF,* 10: 52n).

24. I suggest that Jehannette might eavesdrop because she seems particularly well prepared for the legal arguments to come. Then again, it's possible that she is simply *that* smart.

25. To which one could also add "Back off!" or "But[t] no!" or "Blow it out your ass!"

26. Literally, the French proverb is "as you brew, so shall you drink" (*ce qu'il brasse, il le vous fault boire*); see also Tissier, *RF,* 10: 57n. But what's bubbling over here is from the asshole. Yuck. In more civilized social intercourse, we would say: "as you sow, so shall you reap."

27. How about a Boston accent: "the guilty *potty*"? Or this could be a good moment to interpolate "an accessory after the fart."

28. In Middle French, Hubert wishes upon Jehannette the *fièvre quartaine,* that all-purpose expression cited above, About This Translation, § "Language and Style" (Cursing and Expletives).

29. Based on this line, and drawing on contemporaneous woodcuts from the legalistic comedy of the poet (and lawyer) Guillaume Coquillart, Tissier believes that the Judge is addressing a nonspeaking character, the Judge's Scribe or Clerk (*FFMA,* 4: 22; 305). If so, there are marvelous opportunities for mime: How might such a Clerk attempt to transcribe (or otherwise capture) a fart?

Play 2. *Edict of Noée*

1. Compare esp. with the similar difficulties in #4, *Student Who Failed*; and #11, *Cooch E. Whippet.* I offer a literary analysis of this play in *ROMD,* 210–16; as does Perfetti, *Women and Laughter,* chap. 5.

2. On the universal language of gesture, see above, Introduction, § "History, Development."

3. See below, note 29, for why I've scripted it this way. Faivre seems to agree (*Répertoire,* 138).

4. In *Répertoire,* 154–56, Faivre writes that the site is localized in Paris: *la place Baudoyer* near the Hôtel de Ville. He also cites a related proverb that means "the winner takes all" (*qui est battu l'amendera,* i.e., the loser pays court costs.)

5. For the lyrics, e.g., see Bryant, *Best English and Scottish Ballads,* 349–51.

6. See Harvey, *TB,* 19n; and *ROMD,* 151–52.

7. Edict of 13 April 1553, Delachenal, *Histoire des avocats*, 109n; cited in *ROMD*, 151-52.

8. Pinet, "Role of the Cobbler," 309; my emphasis.

9. I refer to the hit single "I'm Every Woman," by Nickolas Ashford and Valerie Simpson (ASCAP).

10. If opening music is desired, such a song as "Respect" (provided that all requisite permissions have been cleared) might capture the medieval spirit, as would the more pleasantly ironic classic "Smoke Gets in Your Eyes."

11. Compare, e.g., with the Company begging for cash at the opening of #5, *Blind Man's Buff*. There is plenty of evidence, by the way, that entrance fees were charged for medieval dramas, as in the famous extant accounting for the Valenciennes Passion play of 1547. See my "Performing Miracles," 56–57; and also, above, Introduction, § "Performance."

12. Cleverly, *elle me fait noise* refers to both the Cobbler's noisy belly and the legal dispute (*noise*) to come. The Cobbler refers to the wine "repeating on him" (*s'une fois le vin se reveille*) but, nowadays, I suspect that he'd have a brewski.

13. The smoke (*fumée*) appears in the expression *je m'enfume*: "I'm suffocating," "I can't stand the stench," "I'm smoked out," etc. You can see how one might think of this play as a sequel to the *Farce of the Fart*.

14. This is the signature line of the play: *Allez le fermer!* (above, § "Language"). I've added some extra profanity. Also, Chailley notes in his review of Cohen's *Recueil* that there is a medieval song called "*Il est temps de fermer son huis*" (*Time to shut one's door* or *trap*).

15. Used in spinning, the distaff holds on its cleft end the unspun flax or wool from which thread is drawn.

16. Specifically, he vows the legal *noyse* of a trial. But not before the opposite of noise: the mute, dumb-show contest of the wager to come.

17. She employs—*correctly*, no less—the ponderous imperfect subjunctive; in English, "shan't" seems to cover it. Readers may recall a similar usage from an episode of *Cheers* ("An American Family," 1984).

18. The ambiguity continues: she is urging him to shut the door, his mouth, or both.

19. The more site-specific insult is that he would be better off in Boulogne.

20. We have evidence of such intermingling with the crowd as early as the twelfth-century *Play of Adam* (*DBD*, 98–101). See, e.g., Bevington's edition of that play, published as *The Service for Representing Adam*, in *Medieval Drama*, 85, 89.

21. He yells *haro!*—the juridical cry mentioned above, § "Language." Again, on the reality of medieval domestic violence, see above, Introduction, § "Performance and Performance Records."

22. Compare with the Professor's endorsement of the misogynistic motto that women talk too much in #12, *Birdbrain*, Scene 4.

23. She calls him *Jehennin*—Jonny, John-Boy, John-John—which can't be good . . . and which may or may not be his actual name. I suspect not. In fact, I think we could almost call him "Hubert."

24. If a musical interlude is desired, such a song as "Proud Mary" (provided that all requisite permissions have been cleared) might reflect the medieval spirit.

25. Grammatically speaking, the Cobbler says: the first *male* to get up (*le premier*) shall shut the door and, yes indeed, *he* shall. True, the masculine pronoun is the default position for gender-mixed subjects (as for this man and this woman); but, technically, the Cobbler gets this exactly right. See also above, About This Translation, § "Language and Style" (Masculine and Feminine).

26. It's Saint Lawrence in the text; but any town will do. Try a local one.

27. Does anyone recall the similar bit in the *Seinfeld* episode "The Lip Reader" (1993) featuring Marlee Matlin?

28. The phrase "finger signs" appears in the text (*Fait des signes du doy*).

29. Again, I'm confident that this is the same Judge who asked directions moments earlier: the Cobbler soon alludes to that "earlier meeting."

30. *Se seroit trop fait en bejaune* (v. 264): this is a Basochial idiom referring to the *bec-jaune*, the inexperienced attorney who, by analogy to the young, yellow-billed bird, is still learning to sing.

31. Here the Judge invokes the great medieval interpretational practice of text and gloss (*teste et glose*), namely, the quest for hidden, often allegorical meanings.

32. A rhymed insult this time for *fièvre quartaine*: "*La fievre cartaine / Vous tiengne en male sepmainne!*" See above, About This Translation, § "Language and Style" (Cursing and Expletives).

33. On *malle fame/mala fama*, see above, § "Language."

34. With scholastic logic, she even cites her husband's fallacies of reasoning (*la falace*).

35. *Se non en bien* might also mean: "unless it's good for him," "unless we interpret the law in the spirit intended," etc.

36. Compare this list of duties with the famous contract between Jack and his Wife in *The Washtub*, trans. Mandel, *FCMF*, 144–46. Come to think of it, *The Washtub* could be a sequel to the *Edict of Noée!*

37. As in #1, *Farce of the Fart*, one might consider a nonspeaking clerk in this final courtroom scene (*FFMA*, 4: 22, 305).

38. A few nonspeaking female extras might wander onto the stage to hear the momentous ruling.

39. The versification scheme changes here (see below). Having rendered in prose the Cobbler's speech that immediately precedes the play's closing lines, I also render those lines in verse (as per the original). He might deliver those versified lines in rap, the better to hammer home the moral of the story,

Final Verses in Middle French

LE SAVETIER
> *Chères dames, par ma simplesse,*
> *Il me conviendra fermer l'uys*
> *Et ma femme sera mestresse.*

LA FEMME

Se vous dictes chose qui blesse
e vous jett[e]ré en ung puis.

LE SAVETIER

Chères dames, par ma simplesse,
Il me conviendra fermer l'uys.
Adieu vous dis, tant que je puis,
Vous supliant hault et bas,
Recevés en gré nos esbas!

Literal Translation

THE COBBLER

Dear Ladies, due to my simplicity
I am obliged to close the door
And my wife will be mistress.

The WIFE

If you say anything hurtful,
I shall toss you into a well.

The COBBLER

Dear Ladies, due to my simplicity
I am obliged to close the door.
I bid you adieu, as much as I am capable of doing so,
Praying you, high and low,
That you take our play in the right spirit.

Play 3. *Confession Lessons*

1. For a helpful introduction to this complex theological topic, see Tentler, *Sin and Confession*, 103–30.

2. *Noah's Flood* is available in many editions: see, e.g., *The Chester Mystery Cycle*, ed. Mills, 57–59; and the very accessible edition (ed. Ward) in *Everyman and Other Miracle and Morality Plays*, 6–8.

3. Compare her too, e.g., to the no-longer-so Frigid Bridget in #6, *Playing Doctor*. Also, Faivre's plot summary of our #3 is laugh-out-loud funny (*Répertoire*, 87–89).

4. See, e.g., the opening scenes of *Paphnutius*, in Wilson's translation that she titles *The Conversion of the Harlot Thais* (at 103).

5. See also *MTOC*, 170–85; and Woolf, *English Mystery Plays*, 253–60. Such choreography is also crucial in #5, *Blind Man's Buff*, and #6, *Playing Doctor*.

6. If opening music is desired, such a song as "Hot Blooded" might reflect the medieval spirit, as would such songs as "Jealousy" or "The Vatican Rag" (provided that all requisite permissions have been cleared).

7. These are the more-or-less literal lyrics to a popular medieval song for which a company might craft its own melody. Alternatively, a contemporary lyric might be substituted in production, so long as all requisite permissions have been cleared. Under those conditions, possible modern song choices (of various sensibilities) that might capture the medieval spirit might include: "I Will Follow Him"; "Goin' Co'tin'"; "Get Ready"; or "Suite: Judy Blue-Eyes."

8. As above (§ "Language"), this scene begins with the Wife using *vous* with her husband while he uses *tu* with her.

9. Fittingly, since *dire* means both singing and speaking (above, About This Translation, § "Prose, Verse, and Music"), *contredire* can also mean "to sing against": exactly what the Wife is doing.

10. This is a good example of a musical cliché in daily linguistic use. Please note that, should the Wife sing these lines, the requisite permissions must be cleared for "Anything You Can Do."

11. Again, the production might supply its own melody or substitute an appropriate contemporary ditty. Possibly reflective of the medieval mood might be such song choices as "My Man"; or "Saving All My Love" (provided that all requisite permissions have been cleared).

12. This is the moment where the *tu* and *vous* forms are inverted as the Husband begins to address his Wife with *vous* and she uses *tu* with him.

13. Here is another good example of a musical cliché in everyday linguistic use. Please note that, should the Husband sing these lines, the requisite permissions must be cleared for "Let Me Entertain You."

14. The Wife will deliver this line five times: *Par Dieu, la chanson vous cuyra,* literally, "In God's name, that song will 'cook you' [get you in the end]." She might also sing this refrain to an original melody that a company might craft; or, alternatively, substitute in production an appropriate musical refrain (provided that all requisite permissions have been cleared).

15. *Garde bien l'hostel hault et bas:* literally, watch the house "high and low" or "upstairs/downstairs." It seems unlikely that this is a two-story mansion but, in production, the line could be very funny, especially if their home is a small set.

16. She might actually sing a few bars of whichever song has been selected for the performance (again, provided that all requisite permissions have been cleared).

17. There is a marked change of grammatical register, full of imperfect subjunctives.

18. A wonderful visual pun on the two-syllable *marrye* is lost in translation: it means "grief" or "sadness" but looks like the one-syllable word for "spouse."

19. As noted above (§ "Plot"), how Colette happens to have these clothes is left to the imagination.

20. There is another terrific pun on *ordonnance,* which connotes theatrical casting, performance, last rites, and today's medical prescription.

21. In this scene, the Wife uses *vous* during her entire performance, whereas the Husband uses *tu* when addressing her.

22. For the phrase *le curé ou son vicaire,* the Wife's meaning is likely that she might get the second-in-command to stand in for the parish priest. I've used ecclesiastical offices more familiar to American audiences.

23. *Brunette* is a fine, much sought-after fabric died jet black. Moments earlier, her husband was too pale whereas, now, he is too "black"; but let's split the difference and say that he's colorless or "ashen." Ashes to ashes, dust to dust: he looks like death. It is unclear whether he is wearing black as the attendee or as *the corpse* at the funeral. Or whether it is *she* who is wearing black to *his* funeral.

24. Protesting that he is dying of thirst, the Husband invokes the hero of the *Song of Roland* (who, as folk wisdom had it, died of thirst on the battlefield). A bit over the top, *n'est-ce pas?*

25. I take full advantage, once again, of the phallic connotations of *membre.*

26. The expression *faulce mort tu faiz la vieilles* is difficult to translate. Given a certain confusion among *vielle, viel,* and *vieille* ("viol, the musical instrument," "waiting up," "old"), it might mean any of these: Death is coming too soon, Death is playing tricks, Death is "fiddling" while Rome burns.

27. She might also say: "Nothin' to lose, all right and [*indicating her husband*] not much to gain either!" or "I don't know where to turn."

28. To enhance the comedy, I've rendered two two-verse speeches as four lines of dialogue.

29. Cohen thinks that she delivers this line *to Colette,* in which case it would make sense to translate her first sentence as "You should see how I got him to take the bait!" as she rushes to Colette's place.

30. Compare to how long it takes Dolly to get ready in #12, *Birdbrain,* Scene 2.

31. I've tried to capture the theatricality and sexuality implicit in her use of *charivari,* a kind of crazed community parade (writes Rey-Flaud, *Charivari*), which yields the English term "shivaree" (the noisy, mocking harassment reserved for newly married couples).

32. This synesthesia is in the original, reminding one of the truly unmedieval expression "How can I know what I think until I see what I say?"

33. I've added these lines to give a better flavor for the Latin phrases of the play.

34. This is my farcical solution to another great pun. When Colette says "confess to God," the French reads "*à Dieu*"; and, although Cohen does not appear to have caught the pun, the Husband clearly hears *adieu* (as in "bye-bye").

35. Again, remember that dresses were a form of identity; see above, esp. in connection with the Basochiens, Introduction, § "History, Development."

36. I have rendered the Persian provenance of *une perse* as "exotic."

37. The *grands jours* or the *jours des grandes assises* refer to days when a visiting monarch or his dignitaries arrived in town to adjudicate legal matters.

38. Again, the term for the color is *brunette,* as above, note 23.

39. Compare with Wolfy Chewy's similar affirmation about his daughter in #12, *Birdbrain,* Scene 4.

40. Those with a taste for a more vulgar economy might substitute for these last two lines something like "He shot half his wad on your daughter." Yuck. Should a company wish to bring the preceding musical clichés back to life, all requisite permissions must be cleared for "Night and Day" or "Gimme Some Loving."

41. Such a beating also invokes the tortures of schooling, as with the switch-wielding grammar teacher. See, e.g., *MTOC*, 136–44.

42. *Metacommentary alert!* When the Husband asks, *Où sont les pièces?* he is asking, legalistically, for evidentiary support; but the phrase also means: "Where are the *plays?*"

43. In Cohen's *Recueil* (18), this line is attributed to the Wife, but it makes more sense coming from Colette, disguised as the priest.

44. Like John-John the Blind Man in #5, *Blind Man's Buff*, he actually *knows* that this will not end well but plays along anyway.

45. This stage direction appears after the subsequent line in Cohen; but it seems more logical here. Try having the ladies yell and scream in "hushed tones," a device familiar from the delirium scene of *Pathelin* (see Mandel, *Peter Quill's Shenanigans*, in *FCMF*, 121–23).

46. In the *Recueil*, the stage direction indicates that these lines are spoken to the "Neighbor" (19); but the Husband might direct them just as easily to both women as well as to the audience. These verses were probably sung to the tune of yet another familiar song, with the parts divided among the three characters. Below, I provide a literal translation of these lyrics. A company might also include a song of its choice, provided that all requisite permissions have been cleared.

Original French of Five-Foot Verses

LE MARY [*à la VOYSINE*]
> *Mal suis fortunez,*
> *Vous m'avez du nez*
> *Bien tirez les vers.*

LA VOYSINE
> *Les propos ouvers*
> *Et motz decouvers*
> *Souventesffois nuysent.*

LA FEMME
> *Ceulx qui se devisent*
> *Et les motz n'avisent,*
> *S'en treuvent deceuz.*

LA VOYSINE
> *Puis que née suis*
> *Nouvelles je n'euz*
> *Si très desplaisantes.*

LE MARY

Bien l'ay-je senty
Quant j'en suis batu
De verges poingnantes.

Literal Translation

The HUSBAND [*to the NEIGHBOR*]
What hard luck I had
You really pulled the wool
right over my eyes.

COLETTE
Speaking openly
but with hidden meaning
sometimes gets you into trouble.

The WIFE
People chattering away
who don't watch what they say
often get what's coming to them.

COLETTE
Since the day I was born
I never heard
such bad news.

The HUSBAND
I sure felt it
when I got beaten
with those prickly switches.

47. Over the next seven verses, octosyllables return, but with a different rhyme scheme. The better to convey that shift, I've doubled this bit.

48. Another fabulous example of religious ignorance. No such excommunication has occurred! And you've got to love the way he keeps using the masculine singular pronoun for Colette, even though he has recognized *her*.

49. The play ends with a new, somewhat inconsistent versification pattern, whence my shift to poetry; see below.

Original French of Final Address to the Audience

LE MARY
[*au Public*]
Pour ce, vous tous, gardez-vous bien,
Quant parlerez n'en quel endroit.

Mais qui jamais ne mesprendroit
Aurait de sens trop largement.
Seigneurs, vueillez pour orendroit
Prendre en gré nostre esbatement.

Literal Translation

The HUSBAND
[to the Audience]

> And that's why, all of you, be very careful
> about where and when you speak up.
> The man who never messes up is
> certainly someone with a great deal of good sense.
> My lords, for now and ever more,
> [we hope] that our little play has been to your liking.

Play 4. *Student Who Failed*

1. For a careful review of the versions and the character type, see Tissier, *RF,* 5: 113–14.

2. On the influence of the quodlibet on medieval drama, see *ROMD,* 2–3, 162–204.

3. See Faivre's habitually tongue-in-cheek *Répertoire,* 98–99.

4. I mean, really, what's the difference? Sorry to sneak this in, but this *is* a collection of farces. I have never forgotten the preexam advice of my friend from graduate school, Bruce Thomas Boehrer, now a distinguished scholar of the English Renaissance. To calm my nerves about my impending doctoral orals, he advised that I should state to the department chair: "You can give me an oral if I can give you a rectal!"

5. If opening music is desired, such a song as "(What a) Wonderful World" might capture the medieval spirit (provided that all requisite permissions have been cleared).

6. As noted earlier, John-Boy should mispronounce this term along with any other "foreign" words.

7. Try *Char*-[as in "charming"]-*dough-nay.* The text calls for German wine.

8. *Gringotter* refers to the songs of small birds—relatives of the Basochial *bec-jaunes* (see #2, *Edict of Noée,* note 30)?—or to people who can't carry a tune. The term also looks a lot like *grignoter,* to nibble or nosh.

9. I've added, for color, another food exclamation which means "Crack your yolk!"

10. To this day, there is a traditional *pot*—a small reception (rhymes with *dough*)—immediately after a French doctoral defense.

11. The term is *en court,* as described above, § "Sets and Staging."

12. He says Saint Gervais, which is now a ski resort near Mont-Blanc. I have substituted a Virginia counterpart for winter sport with a funny name.

13. Recall when Houseman as Professor Kingsfield (*Paper Chase*) gives struggling law student (Timothy Bottoms as Mr. Hart) a dime so that Hart, after an unacceptable answer to the prof's question, can call his mother to tell her that he shall never become a lawyer.

14. *Il en est beaucoup d'ainsi fais qui cuident sans elles voller:* literally, "there are many [fools] who think they can fly without wings."

15. Although anyone who had attended a medieval sermon would doubtless know that Hebrew was the language of the Old Testament, the odds that the "scholarly" author(s) knew a single word of Hebrew are pretty slim. In my opinion, since this remark isolates a different linguistic and religious community, the odds are rather better that it had anti-Semitic ramifications. In performance, one could substitute Greek or other so-called difficult languages.

16. If this play is performed at its most likely venue—a college campus—one might substitute, e.g., "You gotta be a college professor. . . ."

17. In the text, his name is more like Colin Smith (*Collard le Fèvre*) or Colin Marshall; but I've taken liberties to capture the pun.

18. In the French text, the boy is probably even more confused: *marichau* is the word for a blacksmith but, potentially, also a field marshal. It also sounds like a *mari chaud* or a hot (to trot) husband (the "profession" that John-Boy turns down).

19. Here is the big joke about the *quatre fils Aymon.* To make sense of it in English, I offer a different site—a tomb—where a family name would be absolutely clear. Literally, the text reads: "And doesn't he [Aymon] have four sons?" (Remember that the medieval epic is called *The* Four *Sons of Aymon.*) "Yup! Two big ones and two little ones. I'd know them anywhere."

20. Here, he says *soit sens ou folie,* meaning, "whether it be reasonable or foolish." But the nose, mentioned in our other academic farce, #12, *Birdbrain,* is supposedly—so says mom Trixie in Scene 1—a sign of intelligence.

21. In French, the Examiner asks how it's possible that the Aymon boys have *two* fathers because John-Boy has just said that the father of the *quatre fils Aymon* is one Collart le Fèvre. More confusion: as Koopmans reminds us in his own plot summary, Collart le Fèvre is an infamous cuckold who is, more than likely, not even the father of his *own* children!

22. What's *that*? An imperfect subjunctive? Is this a liminal moment where the actor has to show that he—the *actor*—is much smarter than the character? Have fun!

23. Here he originally says, "If you want to become priests."

Play 5. *Blind Man's Buff*

1. In *Stumbling Blocks before the Blind,* Wheatley analyzes the whole play from the standpoint of disability studies.

2. Cohen, "La Scène," esp. 368–72.

3. The *Boy and the Blind Man* appears in Axton and Stevens, *MFP,* 193–206.

4. Or so thought Jason Narvy, when he brought John-John to life during a read-through.

5. There is an example of just such a rape by a valet in the *Mistere de la Sainte Hostie;* see my "Theater Makes History," 995–1006.

6. There, the torturers invent new games, as here, by which to torment Christ, including a sort of blind man's bluff. See, e.g., Woolf, *English Mystery Plays*, 253–60; and *MTOC*, 170–85. See also above, Introduction, § "Performance and Performance Records."

7. On violence in and out of context, see *MTOC*, 6–7. In Gréban's *Mystère de la Passion* (22803–13) and the anonymous *Passion d'Auvergne* (3335–40), e.g., the "counting out" of blows upon Christ's body—as many as eleven—is explicit; I cite both in *MTOC*, 146–48. See also Axton, *European Drama*, chaps. 2 and 3; Woolf, *English Mystery Plays*, 255.

8. Chailley identifies *Bon temps reviendras-tu?* as an actual medieval song, the title of which means literally "Good times, will you return?" Apparently the melody was popular enough that even medieval people could make up new lyrics of their choice, perhaps parodic ones at that.

9. One might consider a flashback scene in which John-John is begging (unsuccessfully) with the very cup into which Thomasina pees.

10. Aficionados of Molière may recall a similar moment in *The Miser* when Harpagon accuses the audience of stealing his strongbox with all his money (act iv, sc. 7).

11. The French text actually specifies that she *pretends* to pee in the glass: *Fait semblant de pisser dedans.* I am assuming that the *pretense* in question is that of the *actor*, not the *character*, who really *is* peeing; but there is some ambiguity.

12. There is a play on words between *dégoutter* and *goutte* (dripping/disgusting). One also thinks of the expression *n'y voir goutte*, which amply befits the context: i.e., to be unable to see a thing or to be almost blind.

13. Fans of *Cheers* will recall that Carla always succumbed when ex-husband Nick summoned her to "a private chat." We meet another go-between in #8, *Shit for Brains*.

14. Should a company wish to bring this musical cliché back to life as Lancelot might have done in *Camelot,* all requisite permissions for "If Ever I Would Leave You" would need to be cleared prior to performance.

15. *Mausouppé* is, literally, a bad supper, bad service, etc.; so an exclamation with a foodstuff does the trick. Consider also fiddlesticks! or "Holy *crudité*!" *à la* Robin in TV's 1960s *Batman*. (I know, I know: no Batman in the Middle Ages, but I'll need him again shortly.) Koopmans believes that *Mausouppé* is actually the Blind Man's name, but I am not so sure. (See also my take on Blotto as *Fin Vertjus* in #9, *Monk-ey Business.*)

16. Oddly, there is a medieval tradition of the capital punishment of animals: pigs, e.g., were hanged at the gibbet (if not burned at the stake: too close to cooking?). See Evans, *Criminal Prosecution and Capital Punishment of Animals;* and my "Homicidal Pigs."

17. Literally, she says that he is as "jealous as a cat," perhaps deserving of the cat-o'-nine-tails?

18. To maximize the humor associated with the barrel of the earlier "wine scene," one might add here a line such as: "Either that or—what do the Brits say?—you're taking the piss!"

19. John-John says *on ne gaigne plus rien* ("one earns nothing anymore"), which recalls his opening lines about the theater troupe being unable to make a living.

20. Technically, he asks for *trois gros du roy,* three valuable coins.

21. That's right. The Middle Ages knew neither Batman nor Little Orphan Annie: but they did know worms, a component of the expression *Vermoulu!* Worms, lizards: any creepy crawler will do.

22. Here John-John continues his dual mode of address, speaking as both actor and character: i.e., the trio will indeed perform just such a musical number at the end of the play.

23. The French is ambiguous: Does Goguelu mean that both he and Thomasina will serve John-John, or that he—Goguelu—will serve both John-John and Thomasina?

24. He actually says *demoiselle,* that "girl" or "young lady." And, since he is practically conjuring the Devil, he clearly hasn't seen #11, *Cooch E. Whippet.* Plus, if you buy the possibility that the couple is having sex, that's exactly what *faire le dyable* means (below, #11, § "Plot").

25. The French expression is *bastu comme beau seigle vert:* literally, he will be beaten as if she were pounding the grain to make rye bread.

26. Needless to say, should a company wish to enliven this musical cliché with such a possibility as "You Can Leave Your Hat On," all requisite permissions must be cleared.

27. Literally, it's the *mode lyonnaise:* how women are dressing in the city of Lyon (that contemporary capital of gastronomy).

28. She uses *templete* and *gorgeri,* both technical milliner's terms.

29. *Apointée* is the basis of another play on words: cooked, appointed, or, perhaps just *pointed*—as in poked!

30. Here, the term is the sexual, theatrical *charivari;* see above, #3, *Confession Lessons,* note 31.

31. The verb in question appears to be *batre,* but the spelling is odd: *baptu,* which recalls—at least to the eye—"baptism." Whence my use of the term "hazing," to suggest the baptism by fire that was school learning (as in Ong's groundbreaking work in *Rhetoric, Romance, and Technology,* chap. 4).

32. Literally, *à broche cul* means "ass—or asshole—on a spit." Delicious!

33. If a musical interlude is desired, such a song as "Goin' Up the Country" (with all requisite permissions cleared) might capture the medieval spirit, especially given its allusion to water tasting like wine.

34. *Boulleaux à foison:* technically, these would be cudgels or clubs made of straw, such as those typically used in the scourging scenes of Passion plays.

35. And it turns out that that is *not* how they do it. Thomasina does not wait around to act out the fake beating.

36. There is another wonderful play on words on *ensacher:* to put something into a bag / to pull the wool over someone's eyes.

37. The text identifies marjoram, but doubtless for the rhyme of *marjolaine/villaine.*

38. The wordplay is between *esbatre/batre* and *lier/liesse,* as described above (§ "Language").

39. *Par la foy que je doy à mon Parrain:* literally, "by the faith that I owe my godfather." Note that, contrary to the rules that Thomasina announced earlier, Goguelu doesn't seem to be tying anybody up.

40. Instead of the metaphor from the granary (*gerbe de forment*), I've chosen another register consistent with the spirit of the play. Or one could continue the food metaphors with "sealed tight," "air-sealed," or, if you don't mind the anachronism, "tighter than a pressure cooker."

41. She uses—at least, she *tries to use*—some Latin here: "Est-il bien à propos *ilum*?"

42. *Metacommentary alert!* Goguelu employs the rich theatrical term *contrefaire*.

43. She says *comme loches:* literally, fat as carps; but a *loche* is also a ladle, of the sort that might even be used for scooping up all sorts of "shit" (as in #8, *Shit for Brains*). I've kept the metaphor off *one* pot and in another (in the kitchen).

44. The English is ambiguous because the French is too: "Take this one!" denotes either handing over the implement or hitting him with it. Perhaps both?

45. *Party* is deliberate: I mean to evoke, from the history of torture, the beating en masse that is called a "tea party." Note that this phrase bears no relation (other than coincidental) to the contemporary American "Tea Party," which is, for some, a particular kind of torture.

46. *Tondu* denotes shorn (like a sheep), stripped, plundered, but also tonsured like a monk.

47. If a musical interlude is desired, such a song as "Nowhere to Run" (provided that all requisite permissions have been cleared) might appropriately reflect the medieval sense.

48. Again, this was not part of Thomasina's original plan, which called for her to endure a fake beating.

49. The text contains an unusually detailed stage direction that speaks directly to theatrical pretense: *en faignant sa voix et en lui troussant le cul et en frappant dit ce qui s'ensuit.*

50. This is a very clever set of speeches: Goguelu is pretending to be a passing policeman who believes—the ersatz policeman, that is—that he has caught a highwayman (what John-John might *appear* to be) as that highwayman lies in wait, the better to rob people strolling through the woods. Goguelu also refers specifically to having seen the chambermaid fleeing the scene with none other than . . . himself, Goguelu.

51. As indicated above (§ "Sets and Staging"), I offer a kind of double translation of the musicality of this scene (song, dance, rhythmic beats, and even cheerleading).

52. Should the production wish to enliven this musical cliché with actual singing, all requisite permissions for "Let the Good Times Roll" must be cleared prior to performance.

53. As above (§ "Language"), the term "discipline" also denotes the whip (*disciplina*).

54. To be "back in the saddle" is a Middle French cliché that signified all manner of bodily activities and that predates its country-western American equivalent by several centuries. Here, as elsewhere, I follow the rhyme-scheme of the original verses and, in this instance, the octosyllabic meter as well. Should my doggerel strike you as a parody of

Gene Autry's "Back in the Saddle Again," I assure you that my verse rendering contains nary a quotation from that wonderful classic song. Poetic license notwithstanding, my translation is, in fact, fairly literal. However, it is crucial to emphasize that, should a theater company wish to evoke or perform the actual Autry song, all requisite permissions for words and music must be cleared. For the original French and a literal translation, see below. Also of linguistic note: a gruesome counterpart from religious drama appears in the *Geu Saint Denis*, in which the saint's tormentors force him to "ride the horsey," an implement of torture, and get him "back in the saddle" (*a la selete*), vv. 621–27; cited in *MTOC*, 44–45. In modern French today, going to the "saddle" still denotes moving one's bowels (as we shall see in #6, *Playing Doctor*, and #8, *Shit for Brains*).

Original Lyrics in Middle French

TOUS ENSEMBLE

> *Asoir, ung gentil compaignon*
> *Trouvesmes, je vous certify,*
> *Qui faisoit cela et cecy*
> *O une fille de regnon,*
> *Je ne fus onc plus esbahy,*
> *Tant branloit fort le croppion.*
>
> *La fillette dont nous parlon*
> *A bien près de dix huit ans*
> *Et a le plus gentil teton*
> *Que je vis oncques, je me vens.*
> *Quelle viande pour frians*
> *Qui ayment le dedhuyt du hon,*
> *Aprochez-vous gentilz gallans,*
> *Mes que vous ayez argenton.*
>
> *Mais si d'argent n'estes garnis,*
> *Se ne vous en aprouchez jà,*
> *Si vous en estes bien fournis,*
> *Elle ne vous escondira,*
> *Portez-luy escuz et ducas,*
> *Elle sera à vostre bandon,*
> *D'elle vous ne chevirez pas,*
> *Si vous ne portez argentum.*
>
> *Ainsi qu'entendu nous avon*
> *Elle estoit encore pucelle*
> *Et si a le fourchu menton,*

Je la vy hier en la ruelle,
Elle a une blanche fourcelle
Et ung regard qui est mignon,
Les bien venus serez o(u) elle
Mes que vous ayez argentum.

Literal Translation

ALL TOGETHER

> One evening, we happened upon a nice fella,
> That's the God's honest truth,
> Who was doing this and that
> With a noble young lady.
> I've never been so astonished as when
> I saw them bouncing up and down in the saddle.
>
> The young lady that I'm talking about
> Is almost eighteen years old
> And she has the nicest tits
> I've ever seen, if I do say so myself.
> Any of you boys out there who'd like to
> Sink your teeth into that kind of tasty meat,
> Step right up, good fellas,
> But you better have some silver on you.
>
> But, if you don't have any money you,
> Then you'd better not come any closer,
> If you've got lots on you,
> Then she won't lead you astray.
> Bring her crowns and sovereigns,
> And she'll be yours for the taking,
> But you'll be left high and dry
> If you've got no legal tender.
>
> From what I hear,
> She was still a virgin
> And she has a cleft chin.
> I saw her yesterday in the street
> She has a white cleavage
> And she looks at you in this really cute way
> You're welcome to take her for a spin,
> But you've gotta have the legal tender.

Play 6. *Playing Doctor*

1. See Douin de Lavesne, *Trubert*. Eustache Deschamps also wrote the *Farce de Maître Trubert et d'Antrongnart*, in *Oeuvres complètes*, 7: 155–75. For terrific summaries of both plays, see Faivre, *Répertoire*, 141–43; and 257–59.

2. This, by the way, is a famous old bit from the French version of *Candid Camera*: bystanders intervene to hector an unchivalrous man whose wife struggles to carry all their luggage.

3. Similar issues beset #3, *Confession Lessons*, and #10, *Getting Off on the Wrong Foot*. See Axton, *European Drama*, chaps. 2 and 3; Woolf, *English Mystery Plays*, 253–60; and *MTOC*, 170–85.

4. The stick or staff also assumes importance in #2, *Edict of Noée*.

5. Vignettes are printers' marks, but do try a mimed sketch. If opening music is desired, such a choice as "All That You Dream," which refers to being down, might work well to convey the medieval spirit (so long as all requisite permissions have been cleared).

6. If such music is desired in performance, one could consider—so long as all requisite permissions have been cleared for production—such possibilities as "Bad Case of Loving You" ["Doctor, Doctor"], "Hard to Handle," "Smooth Operator," "Hot Blooded" (also evoked for #3, *Confession Lessons*), "I'm Called Little Buttercup," "Handy Man," or "Come and Get It."

7. His remedies—surprise, surprise!—have a high alcoholic content: brandies plus "verjuice" (also important in #9, *Monk-ey Business*), which refers to the highly acidic, vinegar-like potion that is squeezed from underripe grapes and frequently used in medieval sauce making. Pun intended.

8. See above, § "Sets and Staging," on the ambiguity of place.

9. On *sellette*, see above, § "Language."

10. The implication here—*sa femme est mal assenée*—is that Dummy also beats his wife.

11. Again, should the production wish the good doctor to channel "Adelaide's Lament" from *Guys and Dolls*, all requisite permissions must be cleared.

12. The double entendre continues: Does he want Bridget by his side as company? Or as the medieval equivalent of the newspaper next to the toilet?

13. *Et que fillés vostre quelongne:* see above, § "Language." It sure takes gall to demand her assistance in his "business," while telling her to "mind her own business." I've retained some of his violence with expressions from that site of "women's work," the kitchen.

14. *Harnas* denotes belongings and household items, but also the male genitalia.

15. *Froide joye de ses genoulx:* literally, a cold welcome in his lap. Shrinkage?

16. Alternatively, if the scene plays out at market, Dummy can easily be occupied elsewhere onstage.

17. Literally, she wishes that he were in the river six feet above his armpits!

18. He uses the juridical term *plait*, which denotes pleading a case or a court proceeding.

19. Here, as elsewhere in this collection, should a company wish to enliven this musical cliché with actual music, all requisite permissions must be cleared for "Let the Good Times Roll."

20. Literally, he says "*soit blanc, soit noir comme charbon*" (149): something on the order of "white as snow or black as coal."

21. Again, as above, should a company wish to enliven this musical cliché with actual music, all requisite permissions must be cleared for "Come and Get It."

22. There is at least a visual pun in the original on *jeune* (young) and *jeusne* (fasting).

23. Alternatively, should a company wish to enliven this musical cliché with actual music, all requisite permissions must be cleared for "Night and Day."

24. That's the number in the text: one wonders what she's doing for the other two hours.

25. The verb here is *baiser,* now notorious in French classes across the nation because of its ambiguity. Sometimes, a kiss is just a kiss. Sometimes, it's sexual intercourse. Either way, Doc makes a sportsmanlike allusion to his personal best.

26. In French, it's "cook his goose" (*Nous luy ferons menger de l'oue*). I've expanded this speech to maximize the punning.

27. Have some fun with the fact that she asks for a doctor and he offers a pharmacist!

28. Compare with a similar moment in #3, *Confession Lessons*, sc. 4.

29. The medical remedies are *deadragon* and *diaculun.* I've opted for a contemporary homeopathic remedy that fits the bill and permits extra punning: Gotu Kola (*Centella asiatica*) is a medicinal herb used to "heal wounds, improve mental clarity, and treat skin conditions such as leprosy and psoriasis." http://www.umm.edu/altmed/articles/gotu-kola-000253.htm (accessed 4 October 2010).

30. Fortunately, the nature of this particular enema has been lost to history: *Ung clistoire / Qu'on dit barbarin.* I thought of "necessitarian barbarian," but The Expunger seems "barbaric" enough, thank you.

31. If a musical interlude is desired to reflect the medieval spirit here, companies might possibly consider, so long as all requisite permissions have been cleared, such a choice as "I Think We're Alone Now."

32. Since, as noted above (§ "Plot"), the couple does not proceed to the business at hand but, rather, prepares to do so later, one might consider any time-wasting song (so long as all requisite permissions have been cleared). Compare with Scene 4 of #11, *Cooch E. Whippet.*

33. *Par ma foy, il est bien, Trubert, / De mon plaisir venir seullette:* even in Middle French, her evocation of pleasure sounds as sexually suggestive as it does in modern English. It *sounds* like not only the usual call for discretion (as in the Lady's alleged need to disguise her suitors in #7, *At Cross Purposes*) but a suggestion that she's capable of taking her own sexual gratification "in hand."

34. Technically, *degoisier* is not "disguise" (although it likely evoked it) but, rather, to make a joyful noise by singing (*gosier* = "throat"). I have preserved both possible meanings.

35. Again, as above (note 19), should a company wish to enliven this musical cliché with music, all requisite permissions must be cleared for "Let the Good Times Roll."

36. "*Et certes je suis bien Dando, / Dando, mais plus que Dandinastre, / Dandinastre, mais vray folastre....*" George Dandin is a famous cuckold (after whom Molière named a play); so I've rendered the wordplay of these complex verses with variations on "chump."

37. What he says is *crousler ses pois*, literally, shucking peas. Other possibilities for performance (with some mime to keep the play's numerous food metaphors alive): churning the butter, corking, porking, sowing his wild oats, having a pickle tickle, etc.

38. *Prendre par la moue:* to get the better of someone by means of trickery.

39. *Metacommentary alert!* The line is *ainsi qu'on se joue:* to play someone/to play out/ to be in a play. One might also substitute for the previous line, e.g., "if they're playin' downstage...."

40. *Il ne fauldra soucier / Que l'ung ou l'autre vous y voye.* I suspect that it is *nous y voye,* which would be: "neither one of us will have to worry about being seen there."

41. *Metacommentary alert! Farcy* means to get had or "stuffed," as in one of the standard meanings of *farce* as comic "stuffing" between "serious" dramatic offerings (above, Introduction, § "Performance and Performance Records").

42. Compare my translation with the French original, shown below.

Original French of Final Beating Scene

TRUBERT
    Avez-vous plus mal de cela?

FRIGALLETTE
    Je n'en ay plus, la Dieu mercy.

TRUBERT *en frappant*
    Saint Jehan, vous aurés de cecy,
    C'est remède contre cela.

FRIGALLETTE
    Ha! faulx meurdrier, tu m'as meurdry!

TRUBERT [*la battant*]
    Saint Jehan, vous aurés de cecy.

FRIGALLETTE
    Au meurdre!

TRUBERT
        [*Je criray aussi:*]
    Avez-vous plus mal de cela?

FRIGALLETTE
    Je n'en ay plus, la Dieu merci.

TRUBERT *en frappant*
> Saint Jehan, vous aurés de cecy,
> C'est remède contre cela.

FRIGALLETTE
> Ha! faulx traistre, tu m'as meurdry!

TRUBERT
> Saint Jehan, vous aurés de cecy.

FRIGALLETTE
> Au meurdre.

TRUBERT *en frappant*
> Je criray aussi.

FRIGALLETTE
> Vous me tuez, pour Dieu! holà!

TRUBERT *en frappant*
> Saint Jehan, vous aurés de cecy,
> C'est remède contre cela. . . .

DOUBLET
> Je m'en vois, adieu vous commande!
> Comment il sert à descouvert,
> De m'en aller je suis expert,
> Vous priant trestous hault et bas
> Que prenés en gré nous esbatz,
> Je vous en prie, sans villenye.
> Adieu toute la compaignie!

Literal Translation

DUMMY DOWNER
> Feeling better now, are you?

FRIGID BRIDGET
> I'm feeling much better, praise the Lord.

DUMMY DOWNER *hitting* [*her*]
> In the name of Saint John, take *this!* Here's the cure for what ails you!

FRIGID BRIDGET
> Ow! Criminal! Murderer! You're hurting me!

DUMMY DOWNER *hitting* [*her*]
> In the name of Saint John, take *this!*

FRIGID BRIDGET
> Help! Murder!

DUMMY DOWNER
> I'll scream too! Feeling better now, are you?

FRIGID BRIDGET
> I'm feeling much better, praise the Lord.

DUMMY DOWNER *hitting* [*her*]
> In the name of Saint John, you'll get *this!* That's the cure for what ails you!

FRIGID BRIDGET
> Help! You rotten louse! You're hurting me!

DUMMY DOWNER
> In the name of Saint John, you'll get *this!*

FRIGID BRIDGET
> Help! Murder!

DUMMY DOWNER *hitting* [*her*]
> I'll scream too.

FRIGID BRIDGET
> Stop! You're killing me! Help!

DUMMY DOWNER *hitting* [*her*]
> In the name of Saint John, you'll get *this!* Take your medicine! Here's the cure for what ails you! ...

DOC DOUBLE-TALK
> I'm leaving, so I bid you adieu!
> When it comes to being under cover,
> I know what I'm doing.
> I pray that all you folks, high and low
> Take our ribaldry in stride.
> If you please, no offense!
> Adieu to all!

43. There are at least two possible readings of her repeated couplets, both deeply misogynistic. Between "I'm cured" vs. "I'm all fixed up," I've opted for the *slightly* less offensive "fixed up" because it, at least, retains some of the agency of the violent sexist "fixer" rather than implying exclusively that the bludgeoning of women "cures" their "disease" of sexual desire.

44. Here, as elsewhere in this collection, should a company wish to enliven this musical cliché with actual music, all requisite permissions must be cleared for "Hard to Handle."

Play 7. *At Cross Purposes*

1. On an extant fragment of the play, see Tissier, *RF,* 11: 117–22.

2. See *Grand Parangon,* ed. Mabille, 58–65; also discussed by Tissier, *RF,* 11: 128.

3. Although our playtext does not specify that the cross is at the cemetery, I borrow this useful detail from the *Grand Parangon.*

4. See *RF,* 11: 124; 367–68. Images of these coins may be found on a variety of Internet sites.

5. See also Tissier's chart of the distribution of scenes and speeches (*RF,* 11: 126).

6. I borrow this detail from the *Grand Parangon;* see also *RF,* 11: 129.

7. The fire-breathing tricks also appear in the *Grand Parangon;* see Tissier, *RF,* 11: 130. No kidding, medieval actors have been known to catch fire! See *DBD,* 62–63.

8. If opening music is desired, one might consider such choices as these, so long as all requisite permissions have been cleared. Tissier suggested Jacques Brel's "Madeleine," the tale of the poor schlub who's waiting and waiting for his date, a certain Madeleine, who will be standing him up. Other possibilities that might capture the medieval spirit might possibly include: "Lover's Cross," "She's Not There," "Can't Buy Me Love," or "I Have a Song to Sing-O!"

9. A literal translation of Martin's sad five lines appears below, for which a company might compose an original melody. Otherwise, any sad song of the lovelorn and brokenhearted would work well here, so long as all requisite permissions have been cleared prior to performance: possibilities that might convey his meaning could include "I'm So Lonesome, I Could Cry," or "Come Away Death."

Original Lyric in Middle French

MARTIN, *premier amoureux commence en chantant:*
> *J'ayme mieux mourir, bref que languir;*
> *Ce m'est douleur mendre!*
> *Puis qu'aultrement ne puis guerir,*
> *Me vienne donc la mort querir*
> *Sans plus attendre!*

Literal Translation

MARTIN, *the first lover, begins by singing:*
> I'd rather die than languish like this any longer;
> That would be a lesser pain!
> But, since I can't be cured any other way,
> Then, let Death come for me
> Without delay!

10. *Sont-ilz joliettes?* The male subject pronoun, *ilz,* belongs linguistically with *amours* but refers to the plural of "lady love." See above, About This Translation, § "Language and Style" (Masculine and Feminine).

11. With all requisite permissions cleared, one possible song choice that might capture the medieval spirit would be along the lines of "Poor, Poor, Pitiful Me."

12. The French has him "tied up" and "released" (*lier/deslier*).

13. Should a theater company wish to bring this musical cliché back to life in production, all requisite permissions would need to be cleared for "Silver Threads and Golden Needles."

14. As described above (§§ "Characters and Character Development"; "Sets and Staging"), the precise amount here is ten *ducats*. If Martin is portrayed as cheap, one might substitute "a twenty." Alternatively, if the prop is a purse, try: "Will this little sack tide you over?"

15. *Vela l'enseigne du bergier:* "the sign of the shepherd" is usually the "evening star" (*RF*, 11: 142n); but I propose a different metaphor, with pigs and a she-wolf.

16. *En chassant du nez la roupie:* the phrase denotes ridding one's nose of mucus.

17. Should a musical interlude be desired here, a possible song choice along the lines of "Hound Dog" might capture the medieval spirit (so long as all requisite permissions have been cleared).

18. Tissier emphasizes Martin's guilt at heading to the cross for a romantic assignation (*RF*, 11: 146n). In Scene 7, Martin does indeed appear to feel quite guilty.

19. Apparently, now that the audience is in on the joke, no further explanation is required about that jealous husband of hers and the need for disguise! It's almost as if the Lady is staging the farce for *us*.

20. One might add "Walter Falter" or a string of rhymed—even rapped—insults. Literally, the Lady says Walter of Cambrai (a character from the *Roman d'Alexandre*, a twelfth-century epic about Alexander the Great). She likely means William's literary brother-in-arms, the henpecked *Martin* of Cambray of #11, *Cooch E. Whippet*.

21. Should the Lady launch into song, a possible choice along the lines of "Nowhere to Run" might capture the medieval spirit (so long as all requisite permissions have been cleared).

22. Should a theater company wish to bring this musical cliché back to life in production, all requisite permissions must be cleared for "In the Midnight Hour."

23. Should the Lady launch anew into song, a possible choice along the lines of "Creep" might capture the medieval spirit (so long as all requisite permissions have been cleared).

24. The text does not call for a third costuming scene; but, for symmetry, I interrupt Walter's speech to provide one.

25. In French, he is wishing his compatriot off to Frise (Friesland), a bilingual Dutch province. The best fit in American English would be to "put him on a slow boat to China" or to "wish him into the cornfield" (as in the famous *Twilight Zone* episode "It's a Good Life.").

26. Among those sins: messing around at the cross. See above, note 18.

27. *Requiem eternam cunctis pro fidelibus defunctis!* Martin is reciting a Latin prayer for the dead; but for Anglophones, a few well-known Latin phrases ought to do the trick.

For more on the general difficulties of translating the farces' Latin, see #12, *Birdbrain*, §
"Language."

28. Technically, Walter is wishing him all sorts of loveliness: gout, diarrhea, pink
eye ... you name it, it's a disease to be wished upon one's enemies!

29. A pun here on *membre:* extremities like the arms and legs but also the virile
member.

30. These lines are attributed to Walter in the *Recueil* (vv. 326-27); but I've attributed
them instead to Martin, for whom they make more sense. Martin has continually ex-
pressed his guilt at what he is doing.

31. Fans of *Four Weddings and a Funeral* might substitute "the Holy Spigot."

32. I reproduce these two lines in Latin exactly as they appear in the text; the rest is as
macaronic and idiosyncratic as it will be in #12, *Birdbrain.*

33. If, somehow, the audience isn't laughing, he could heckle *them* with the line about
being dead and buried.

34. Parts of what we recognize as the Lord's Prayer are indeed interspersed in this
speech. Amen. Imagine Sandra Bullock's character in *Miss Congeniality* asking God to
forgive her for taking a bite of her bagel and schmear before she said grace.

35. Since Martin is not exactly a learned fellow, he might pronounce this word so it
rhymes with "vagina" and then giggle. Representative of the irreverent spirit here would
be the tone of something like Tom Lehrer's "Vatican Rag" or the performances in *Sister
Act.* Should a theater company wish to insert any such music into the script, all requisite
permissions must be cleared.

36. Should a theater company wish to bring this musical cliché back to life in production, all requisite permissions must be cleared for "Quando, Quando, Quando."

37. What a coincidence! Consistent with medieval misogyny, the "misbehaving" is
attributed to both Woman and the Devil, practically one and the same ever since the
Fall.

38. Again, he uses *membre,* so some kind of obscene mime could be appropriate here.

39. Should a theater company wish to bring this musical cliché back to life in production, all requisite permissions must be cleared for "Upside Down."

40. When Walter-as-Dead-Man says that Death chased him there, it sounds almost as
if he's been chasing his own tail ... or is that tale? Very confusing! Perhaps the scribe made
a mistake and he meant that the *Devil* chased him there, which would mean William!

41. Yes: it may well be a scribal error but Martin really does repeat himself.

42. So long as all requisite permissions have been cleared, one might possibly have him
break into a few verses of "Volare."

43. Alternatively, depending on which prop William's devil has been assigned, Walter
could say: "and chains me up."

44. Here is another excellent example of a musical cliché. Should a company wish to
bring either or both back to life with "By the Light of the Silvery Moon" or "Rocky Raccoon," all requisite permissions must be cleared prior to performance.

45. This is the bit discussed above (§ "Characters and Character Development"). Martin says that, if he (Martin) breaks his word, then his interlocutor—*Walter* (Gaultier in French), whom Martin does not recognize—can call him (i.e., Martin) Gaultier, "a Walter," which means a "welsher": *nommés moy hardiment Gaultier* (v. 491). One more time: Martin says to Walter (whom I've called the Welshman, the better to enable the pun) that Walter can call Martin (who is *not* the Welshman) "Walter-the-Welsher/Welshman." Martin tells Walter that he wishes to be called by Walter's name. Whence Walter's considerable confusion.

46. *Cornardie* implies fools and almost cuckolded fools.

47. The text indicates only that "they sing" (*Ilz chantent*). Although the melody is not extant, the Middle French lyrics appear below. The twelve verses are divided equally between the three suitors. Alternatively, a company might interpolate a bona fide musical number before their final rap performance. Any number of modern song choices might convey the medieval mood, so long as all requisite permissions have been cleared. Possibilities might include "You Really Got Me," "She's Not There," or "Hard to Handle" (this last also evoked in #6, *Playing Doctor*).

Original Lyric in Middle French

GAULTIER
> *Tous trois avons gardé la lune,*
> *On n'avoit garde de la perdre.*

MARTIN
> *Des plus fines fames c'est l'une.*

GAULTIER
> *Tous trois avons gardé la lune.*

GUILLAUME
> *Dea! elle a eu de ma pecune*
> *Dix royaulx. Qu'on la puisse ardre!*

MARTIN
> *Tous trois avons gardé la lune,*
> *On n'avoit garde de la perdre.*

GAULTIER
> *Mais comme se ose femme herdre*
> *De farcer ainsi les galans?*

MARTIN
> *Compaignons, se en somme blans,*
> *Aussy sont plusieurs compaignons.*

GUILLAUME

> *Je conseille que nous prenons*
> *Congié à nostre seigneurie;*
> *Puis que on joue de tromperie,*
> *Je n'en vueil plus estre assoté.*

GAULTIER

> *Vous qu'estes en amours bouté,*
> *Gardés-vous de telles finesses.*

MARTIN

> *Nos ebas s'il vous plaist notez,*
> *Vous qu'estes en amours boutez.*

GUILLAUME

> *Les tromperies redoubtés*
> *De telles qui en sont maistresses.*

GAULTIER

> *Vous qui estes en amours boutés,*
> *Gardez-vous de telles finesses.*
> *Ne vous fiés pas en promesses*
> *Ainsi qu'avons fait simplement.*
> *En joyes, festes et liesses,*
> *Prenés en gré l'esbatement.*

Literal Translation

WALTER

> The three of us wasted our time howling at the moon,
> And we scarcely risked losing it.

MARTIN

> She's certainly the cleverest lady of them all.

WALTER

> The three of us wasted our time howling at the moon.

WILLIAM

> Good Lord! She got some of my money!
> Ten *royaulx*! May she be burned at the stake!

MARTIN

> The three of us wasted our time howling at the moon,
> And we scarcely risked losing it.

WALTER

> But how does a woman dare to devote herself like that
> To playing a trick on her suitors?

MARTIN

> We haven't got a penny left to our name, fellows,
> And it's the same thing for other fellows out there.

WILLIAM

> I suggest that we now
> Take our leave of the fellows out there.
> Since this whole thing is a farce,
> I'd prefer not to look any more foolish.

WALTER

> All of you [men] who are set in the ways of love,
> Be careful of tricks like these.

MARTIN

> And learn your lesson from this play,
> All of you who are set in the ways of love.

WILLIAM

> Be careful of all those tricks that ladies play
> Because they master them the best of all.

WALTER

> All of you who are set in the ways of love,
> Do be careful of tricks likes these.
> Don't believe her promises
> as we did like fools.
> And, as you take your leave happy, joyful, and rejoicing,
> We hope that you liked the show and took it all well.

48. The expression used here is *garder la lune,* probably in the sense of *garder la lune des chiens ou des loups,* literally "to protect the moon from dogs or wolves," which connotes: "to go to a whole lot of trouble for nothing" (i.e., the moon needs no such protection). Exactly what the three gents have done here.

49. Here, as elsewhere, should a company wish to enliven this musical cliché with actual music, all requisite permissions must be cleared for "Hard to Handle."

50. Here, and in the next speech, I've switched Walter and William for a better fit.

51. If closing music is desired, one might consider such a choice as "Bye Bye Baby," so long as all requisite permissions have been cleared.

Play 8. *Shit for Brains*

1. Tissier (*RF,* 10: 74) cites Lewicka, *Études sur l'ancienne farce française,* 123–24.

2. In *RF,* 10: 69–74, Tissier discusses the derivation and meaning(s) of these names, which also appear in Rabelais. The expression *tarabin-tarabas* also comes into the English language as "tut, tut," "folderol," or the all-purpose American "Whatever!"

3. Compare him with the geezer in #5, *Blind Man's Buff.*

4. After all, that is how John-Boy addresses Master Peter in #4, *Student Who Failed.*

5. I am indebted to my colleague, Ron Tobin, for lending his expertise to my exploration of this possible reading. If my reading is deemed ridiculous, that's my fault, not his.

6. For a marvelous essay that is as funny as it is erudite, see Persels, "Sorbonnic Trots."

7. See above, About This Translation, § "Language and Style" (Masculine and Feminine).

8. *Fables,* bk. 7, fable 9, trans. Shapiro, 170, my emphasis.

9. See Harvey, *TB,* esp. 19–23; and Tissier (*RF,* 10: 24–25), who draws on Bowen, *CE.*

10. Tissier also briefly discusses staging in *RF,* 10: 77–78.

11. Compare with a similar moment at the close of #11, *Cooch E. Whippet* (Scene 6).

12. My translations of these two monologues are far from exact. But it almost doesn't matter what they say, so long as they say "head" and "ass." Harpee's "heady" speech is sixteen verses long; Harpo's "asinine" speech, seventeen verses.

13. Both characters express that they are "in pain" by using the expression *triboullé(e),* as if to predict the arrival of that other "pain," Payne N. Butts (*Triboulle Mesnage*).

14. Should a company wish to bring this musical cliché back to life with "Goin' Out of My Head," all requisite permissions must be cleared prior to performance.

15. Should a company wish to bring this musical cliché back to life with "Over My Head," all requisite permissions must be cleared prior to performance.

16. Again, should a company wish to bring this musical cliché back to life with "Baby Got Back," all requisite permissions must be cleared prior to performance.

17. The French is even more vile: *cul qui porte la semence / Où se prent le puant enfant* (vv. 38–39). This means: the "asshole" or, with great anatomical confusion, perhaps *another hole* that "carries the seed where stinking children take hold?" Recalling the sodomy of #1, *Farce of the Fart,* as well as Rabelais's tale of Gargantua's "shitty" birth (which coincides with mom Gargamelle's diarrhea from eating too much tripe), one can only wonder about the biological impossibility of a pregnant rectum (or is that a rectal pregnancy?). If there can be a farce devoted to a pregnant husband (*Le Galant qui a fait le coup*), and if Kathleen Biddick can write about "The Devil's Anal Eye," then, alas! I fear that the impossible is possible. For Harpo, a hole is a hole.

18. *Grivellé* suggests "variegated" (Tissier, *FFMA,* 4: 32); but this ain't no carnation.

19. I know: Harpee usually sticks to the head, but let's not break her ass about it. This is an adaptation, after all.

20. *Metacommentary alert! Si vous jouez tousjours si hault* implies overdoing it but also playacting too loudly.

21. He calls her a *marastre de paix:* someone who *engenders* trouble (see *RF,* 10: 87n); but consider too the play on words of *paix/pet* ("shut up"/"fart") that we also saw in #1, *Farce of the Fart* (all continuing that most curious notion of the engendering rectum, above, note 17).

22. This is one of the spots, e.g., where he says *mon maistre* (v. 105).

23. Harpee says *teste dyablesse,* which is grammatically correct for something like "devilish head." It is also conceivable that Payne thinks Harpee has just insulted *him.* As noted above (§ "Language"), I've emphasized the possibility of gender-bending.

24. Tissier thinks that this line is addressed to Harpo because Payne never uses *tu* when addressing his "mistress" (*RF,* 10: 94n). I beg to differ; I've written Harpee as the one who keeps interrupting, which is consistent with the medieval stereotype of the loquacious female, even if this farce focuses on her talking out of her ass.

25. *De toutes testes princesse:* his head is the "princess" of them all! As for henpecked Harpo, first he's a "fairy" and now he's a "queen."

26. As always, should a company wish to bring this musical cliché back to life with "Proud Mary," all requisite permissions must be cleared prior to performance. Compare with a similar insult in #2, *Edict of Noée,* Scene 1, where it applies to women.

27. Literally, his (princess-)head is the size of a king who is sticking his nose—an appropriate body part here, one must say—into everyone's business; and her ass is as fat as the pope's, and maybe farts like it too.

28. Again, credit where credit is due: this is Tissier's idea (*RF,* 10: 98n).

29. *Se je casse un pot / Mon fait sera hydeulx.* Call me crazy, but this is where I hear that proverb about the pitcher breaking (cited above, § "Language"): *Tant va la cruche à l'eau qu'enfin elle se casse.*

30. These names sound as if they came right out of Rabelais: Pop *Bouteffu* sounds like "fire starter" (*bouter le feu*); and *Tiremelle*—a cousin of Gargantua's tripe-loving mom Gargamelle?—sounds like "pull the tits" (*tirer mamelles*).

31. Another possible interpretation: "What? You think this is *my* job?"

32. The playtext refers to ashes (*cendres*), which were used—believe it or not—in laundering. We can capture some of that with Cinderella (*Cendrillon,* from *cendre* in French).

33. *C'est affin que amont ou aval ne soit dit:* more wordplay on up vs. down (*amont/aval*), which will take on new importance when the couple tries to load Payne up.

34. Anachronistic, yes, but not by much. He does indeed wish to weigh the "crap" that will soon weigh *him* down.

35. The all-purpose *fièvre quartaine* appears once again; as I suggested in #1, *Farce of the Fart,* late in Scene 2, a more vile interpretation is possible along the lines of "on the rag."

36. This is the legalistic *Item* from contracts, more familiar today as "Article 1, 2, etc." Remember too that Rabelais was famous for his lists, such as the one devoted to young Gargantua's asswipes (*Gargantua,* chap. 13, in *Complete Works,* trans. Frame, 34–37).

37. What else could I do? *Le coissin de Tarabin* simply *had* to be Harpee's "whoopee cushion."

38. If you believe me that Payne could be a lawyer, then substitute "shyster."

39. In other words . . . any woman wearing the pants in the family is full of shit!

40. To fans of *Saturday Night Live:* perhaps someone has been eating Colon Blow cereal.

41. Normally, the apron would belong to *Harpee,* not Harpo (as it does later at v. 268). This *could* be a scribal error; then again, she *does* taunt him by comparing him to queens and princesses.

42. *Tenés-vous estau.* Keep cool—but *estau* also means urination (of animals).

43. Although the French *selle persée* might sound here like a Persian saddle, it is, rather, a rudimentary toilet. On this kind of "saddle," see Tissier, *RF,* 10: 107n; and, above, #6, *Playing Doctor* (§ "Language"). However, I do *not* think that this is the saddle in question in the closing song of #5, *Blind Man's Buff.*

44. This is the *pot aux choux gras* (above, § "Language"): nice lard-laden cabbage stew—yum!—that might well have led to the very digestive excesses in question. I've teased out the other senses with other "crocks," alimentary or what have you.

45. As Tissier points out (*RF,* 10: 107n), *la chausse d'Ypocras* refers to a sweet wine known to have aphrodisiac properties. But *chausse* also refers to a particular kind of hose or britches—the very site of some of the filth problems.

46. For *ceillier,* I propose "bucket" (*seel*), evoking again that rudimentary toilet. Tissier thinks that it is a variation of "spoon" (*RF,* 10: 108n); but a spoon's a scooper, eh?

47. That's right: he does indeed invoke Saint Francis of Assisi! (*RF,* 10: 108n). Bless the pigs and the children?

48. This is a pun on *fourbis:* a *fourbe* is also a trickster.

49. This is the proverbial *pot au lait;* see above, § "Language."

50. That's right: earlier, the apron was Harpo's; see above, note 41.

51. *Ung sanglant estront de chien* is a dog turd and a bloody one at that. Charming.

52. I know: Harpo usually gets the shit puns, but the timing seemed right.

53. Again, we encounter the legal term *haro!* See Basin, *Apologie,* 258–61; cited above #2, *Edict of Noée,* § "Language."

54. You have to *hear* the French, which sounds like singing (la-la-la): *En! voy*la là, *plus par en bas* (v. 302).

55. For Tissier, this line indicates that Payne is a *badin*—the stereotypical drunken jester figure of *sotties* (*FFMA,* 4: 30). But the "big fat wino" could also be her husband, Harpo.

56. Again, substitute "shyster" if you like my lawyerly reading.

57. Another possibility might be: "If you lay down with dogs, you get . . . to take it all to the flea market yourself!"

58. For Tissier (*RF,* 10: 76) this is where Payne resigns as their valet: *Plus ne seray vostre servant!* (v. 321).

59. *Pardonnez-nous si nostre farce / A esté ung bien petit grace / Et prenés en gré je vous prie. / Adieu toute la compaignie!*

Play 9. *Monk-ey Business*

1. See Tissier, *RF,* 9: 134; and Faivre, *Répertoire,* 395. The traditional reading is that the Cobbler goes by the name of *Fin Vertjus*—whence the nickname "Blotto"—so I'm happy to continue to use that nickname, which fits the character well. Indeed, it is often practical to use both "Blotto" and "The Cobbler," given that both Cohen and Tissier script him as the latter. I do think it's possible, however, that *fin vertjus* is simply an exclamation (which we have seen before), related to "verjuice," i.e., the potion extracted from underripe grapes (above, #6, *Playing Doctor,* note 7). See also below, note 29.

2. On these hats, see, e.g., Tissier, *RF,* 9: 150n; and Arden, *Fools' Plays,* 28; above, Introduction, § "Performance and Performance Records." See also #8, *Shit for Brains,* in which Payne might be wearing such a bonnet.

3. Recall also the importance of the door/threshold of #2, *Edict of Noée.*

4. The episode, "I, Mudd," aired in November 1967.

5. Compare with #7, *At Cross Purposes,* Scene 7; and #12, *Birdbrain,* § "Language"; and Scene 3.

6. See Tissier's excellent analysis and chart of speeches/scenography in *RF,* 9: 139–41. It's true: a monastery or convent would normally be situated behind walls; but this particular devotional site needs a bar where the townspeople may congregate as well. Do note that, to this day, if you want to buy the very best *Époisses* a truly fantastic *fromage*—you must leave your *supermarché* behind and go pick one up from the monks instead.

7. For me, the image that comes to mind is an old commercial for Dunkin' Donuts: the "man who makes the doughnuts" checks out a competing doughnut shop by "disguising himself" as a female customer. He covers up his moustache with his finger and is addressed, hesitatingly and repeatedly, by the clerk as "ma'am." Or recall the mustachioed Lou Jacobi in Woody Allen's *Everything You Ever Wanted to Know about Sex.*

8. On this double drag, see Tissier, *RF,* 9: 138–39; and, for Francophones, see Roy, "Déguisement dans la farce." Faivre's hunch is that Dottie was played by a woman (*Répertoire,* 397).

9. See Bloch, *Scandal of the Fabliaux,* 35–36.

10. If opening music is desired, such a choice as "Behind Closed Doors" might work to convey the spirit here, so long as all requisite permissions have been cleared.

11. *L'autre jour jouer m'aloye / L'orée d'ung pré herbu, / Je ne sçay que je queroye / Ne que j'avoye perdu* (vv. 1–4). Literally: "The other day, I went off to play in the fields. I don't know what I was seeking or what I'd lost." If he sings in the production, an appropriate choice might be such a tune as "The Happy Wanderer," so long as all requisite permissions have been cleared.

12. If you prefer a different sensibility, try "y'all," "everybody," "fellas," "you guys," "guys," etc.

13. Tissier interprets this speech as a hawking cry (above, § "Staging"). If he's right, it's one of the shortest sales pitches in history.

14. *En ce moys de may, hauvay! / Doit-on faire amye* (vv. 13–14): "In this month of May, tra-la, a man must find a sweetheart." If he sings again in the production, an appropriate choice might be Lerner and Loewe's joyous mating tune from *Camelot*, "The Lusty Month of May," so long as all requisite permissions have been cleared.

15. Tissier reads this as "they could barely get a word in edgewise" (*RF*, 9: 148–49). My "dime" might sound anachronistic, but it's from Anglo-French *disme*, the tenth part, which yields the English "tithe."

16. It is almost impossible to capture the sense of *il emporte bien les oreilles d'estre des dames d'Aigremont*. According to Cohen (*Recueil*, 268n) and Tissier (*RF*, 9: 149–50n), this expression seems to have something to do with Latin study in the convent. Tissier's best guess is that it also refers to one of the "fools' companies" (*RF*, 9: 149n). I've preserved the academic subtext; plus chalk on a blackboard is high-pitched, conveniently anticipating the effeminate performance to come.

17. If desired, Blotto should have his fool's hat and scepter in the final scene; the company may decide when we see them for the first time.

18. As Cohen notes (*Recueil*, 268n), the Cobbler's imaginary school, *Logeotruie*, means both "stay somewhere else" (*loge autrui*) and "pigsty" (*loge aux truies*). By the way, the pigs in question are not even *male* pigs but *female sows*. I've opted for any college with a funny name: Slippery Rock, Ball State, Beaver, or even an educational institution local to the performance.

19. Remember that oral exams were public affairs (above, #4, *Student Who Failed*, § "Plot"). However, as Tissier notes, the *Petit Pont* cited here—an actual Parisian site near Notre Dame cathedral—hosted not university exams but fishwives! (*RF*, 9: 151n; *FFMA*, 3: 236; also Cohen, *Recueil*, 268n.) I've substituted another recognizable initiation space for the testing of male mettle.

20. Since Rémy, by whom he swears, is the patron saint of debtors (*RF*, 9: 152–53n), he could also say, "I paid my debt to society!"

21. "Two bits" or any appropriate currency would work.

22. The Gatekeeper presumably recognizes at least Brother Peter but perhaps Blotto as well, since it is the latter who answers.

23. *Faicte comme de cire* is a memory image of the reusable wax tablets upon which students inscribed their lessons; see *MTOC*, 96–99. The phrase also has religious connotations, as in Psalm 68:2: "As wax melteth before the fire, so let the wicked perish at the presence of God."

24. Here's *baiser* again: Does Dottie kiss him, "embrace" him, or "fuck him over?"

25. Brother Peter now switches to the *tu* form for a while.

26. The most vulgar interpretation of *volentiers vous la baiserez* might be: "Sure thing, you can fuck her."

27. Tissier suggests that she might walk by the spot where he should normally be hawking his wares (*FFMA*, 3: 161).

28. Maybe I'm hearing things again but, when Brother Peter swears by the imaginary *Sainct Nichaise*, I hear *Saint n'y . . . touche*, an idiom that means "butter wouldn't melt in her mouth" ("a saint wouldn't touch her"). A saint *wouldn't*; but *this* monk is no saint.

29. Dottie exclaims *fin vertjus!* (above, § "Characters and Character Development"). Is it her husband's nickname? Does she mean "Holy cannoli"? I suspect the expression is based on another popular imprecation that survives in Rabelais: *Vertus Dieu!* which Donald Frame translates as "Power of God!" in *Quart Livre,* bk. 10 of *Complete Works,* 459. Bloody hell!

30. The Gatekeeper might be telling the truth, since Blotto and Brother Peter have by now switched clothes.

31. For Tissier, this is the Cobbler's line (*RF,* 9: 163), in keeping with Blotto's previous line that Brother Peter shouldn't speak. But I'm with Cohen that it's the exasperated Dottie's. Or *both* could say it.

32. Literally, he wishes upon her the "bloody gout."

33. Tissier thinks that the following verses might have been sung (*RF,* 9: 165n); I agree, and suggest a choreographed, perhaps rap, version. Of course, a company might add original music or, alternatively, substitute an appropriate song of their choice for which all permissions have been cleared.

LE SAVETIER
> *Ha! qui mal s'en sent*
> *Brief sus luy descent*
> *Ung cas qui l'empire.*

LE MOYNE
> *A verité dire,*
> *Je ne m'en puis rire,*
> *La chose m'est dure.*

LE SAVETIER
> *Par mon âme, sire,*
> *Voiez le martire*
> *Que d'elle j'endure!*

LE MOYNE
> *Comment! tu disois*
> *Que d'elle faisois*
> *Tout à ton vouloir!*

LE SAVETIER
> *Si veu ne l'eussiez,*
> *Pas ne creussiez*
> *Pour nes ung avoir.*

Literal Translation

The COBBLER
> Ouch! The man who is feeling poorly
> Often finds that there descends upon him
> something even worse.

The MONK
> Truth be told,
> I can't even laugh about it.
> It hurts too bad to laugh.

The COBBLER
> Upon my soul, my lord,
> Look at the martyrdom that
> I'm forced to endure on her account!

The MONK
> What? You were just saying
> that you had your way with her,
> whatever you wanted.

The COBBLER
> If you hadn't just seen it
> You would never have believed it
> for anything in the world.

34. Blotto almost implies that he has provided the whole performance only so his old drinking buddy would believe him!

35. Compare with Colette and friend's use of penance in #3, *Confession Lessons*, Scene 5.

36. The farces are teeming with literary allusions so, that's right: I am channeling Emily Dickinson's "Because I could not stop for Death."

37. Technically, more gout; but that ailment *does* present with *joint* pain.

38. *Metacommentary alert!* She uses the verb *farcer,* i.e., joking around *and* playing a farce.

39. Again, *farce* in the French.

40. Should a theater company wish to bring this musical cliché back to life in production, all requisite permissions must be cleared for "Eight Days a Week."

41. *Sachez se il fait significance de me dire:* Dottie's brilliant language contains a legal loophole. If Brother Peter only *seems to be* doing something, rather than actually *doing it,* then she'll absolutely tell her husband all about the *semblance . . .* but perhaps not about the *reality.*

42. Dottie's line is *Dieu vous gard, sire!*—potentially ironic to her husband but polite to a monk. I have her repeat it to capture both meanings.

43. The anachronistic "Just give me your room number" could be very funny here, almost as if the monastery were Brother Pete's "motel."

44. Literally, he says that there is a stone step outside his door. Personally, I think it would be funnier to tie a necktie on his cloister cell (à la fraternity house)!

45. *Je vous auray par beaux baratz:* literally, "I will have you"; "You will fall into my little trap!" (*baratz* = ruse). I've doubled the line to retain both possibilities.

46. Technically, it's the *prieur;* but I've rendered it as an ecclesiastic who "outranks" a monk. Perhaps the abbot would be wanting his share of penitent booty too.

47. Several lines must be missing from the earlier scene between Dottie and Brother Peter: he does not give the "hour" for her absolution. Either that, or the play needed a better script supervisor.

48. There is a terrific pun on *relier:* "knocking his block off" and bookbinding. Alternatively, "gotta book," e.g., as in "gotta run."

49. *Par le sang que beuf respendit:* this is a version of "God's Blood!" in which *Dieu* is *beuf,* an "ox." Sorry, but I hear a *recipe* here like rabbit—actually, *hare—à la royale:* i.e., cooked in its own blood (if not *God's* blood). It's delicious, I assure you.

50. Again, the verb is the theatrically resonant *contrefaire.*

51. The stage directions remind us repeatedly that the Cobbler is dressed as a woman, answers like a woman, etc. As if we could forget.

52. One wonders how indeed he knows all about being a woman, unless he plays her role all the time at home or—*metacommentary alert!*—he's a professional actor.

53. If a musical interlude is desired for the scene change, a mercy-obsessed tune such as "I'll Take You There" might work well, so long as all requisite permissions have been cleared.

54. *Philosomye* is some sort of punning neologism on *philosophy* + *mye* (a term of endearment, as in *ma mie*). I have him starting instead to say the word "physiognomy."

55. If a musical interlude is desired here, such a tune as "Think" might capture the medieval spirit well, so long as all requisite permissions have been cleared. Remember that, technically, his room is the one with the "stone step" outside the door (above, note 44).

56. He calls him *Frère Frappart,* literally, "Brother Hitter." "Prick" seems to capture it, esp. since switches are often described as prickly (as in #3, *Confession Lessons,* Scene 5).

57. If exit music is desired, the company might possibly consider, so long as all requisite permissions have been cleared, such a choice as "It's My Party."

58. Anybody hear a pun? The rhyme of *rouge/gouge* sounds like *rouge gorge* (robin redbreast), esp. since the next line mentions *batant:* beating, but also flapping one's wings.

59. *Il m'en fault aller tout batant,* above, as in "flapping one's wings," note 58. Also, on the frequent pairing of *batre* (to beat, pummel) and *ébatre* (to enjoy oneself, to have a good [sexual] time), see *MTOC,* 146–49. The actor may also be announcing that the company will soon go its merry way.

60. He says *rebelle* (feisty, rebellious, disobedient) and pretends to have said *belle* (beautiful). Jack the Cobbler has a similar technique in #10, *Getting Off on the Wrong Foot.*

61. Tissier wonders when or *if* Blotto gets back into his own clothes (*RF,* 9: 193n). Regardless, during a contemporary "curtain call," he will become yet another self (see States, *Great Reckonings,* 197–206).

Play 10. *Getting Off on the Wrong Foot*

1. The other version, similar in many respects but not as snappy as this one, appears as #35 in Cohen, *Recueil,* 273–82. Faivre discusses both (*Répertoire,* 326–27).

2. Alternatively, one might call her Buttercup (necessitating line changes indicated in the notes).

3. On these distinctions, see Pinet, "Role of the Cobbler," discussed above, Introduction.

4. Although the music to his song has been lost to history, Chailley has identified its lyrics (below) as quite well known. If a company prefers to update this musical number, the medieval spirit might be captured by such choices as these (so long as all requisite permissions have been cleared): "I Only Want to Be with You"; "Wouldn't It Be Nice"; "Sunshine Superman"; "When Will I See You Again?" ["Precious Moments"]; "Happy Together." If the Cobbler's Wife is called "Buttercup," the opening number might be "Build Me Up, Buttercup." In the event that a company does indeed prefer to substitute a modern song for Bootie's opening verses, I have also scripted him speaking a prose version of his medieval lyrics so that their precise meaning is not lost.

Original Lyrics in Middle French

LE PATINIER *en chantant*
> *M'amour et ma parfaicte joye,*
> *Dieu (vous) doint que brefvement vous revoye,*
> *Autre chose ne vous requier*
> *Pour moy oster hors de dangier*
> *Que pour vous souvent me guerroye.*
> *J'ay le cueur droictement en joye*
> *Quant je pense à ma desirée,*
> *Elle est tresbonne cariée.*
> *Voulentiers certes me degoise,*
> *Avecques luy fault que je voise.*

Literal Translation

The SHOEMAKER, *singing*

> My love and my perfect joy,
>
> May God grant that I see you again, if only briefly
>
> That is all that I ask of you in order to
>
> Release myself from [the] danger
>
> of waging war for so long on your behalf.
>
> My heart is truly joyful
>
> when I think about the object of my desire
>
> She is marvelously built.
>
> With pleasure, I rejoice in song,
>
> I must go with her.

5. In other words, he's been *Punk'd*?

6. Her line, conceivably directed at Bootie, is *vrayment en bonne santé* or "truly in good health." Maybe he's looking pretty good too; so I've doubled the line accordingly.

7. If Bootie's "song and dance" is emphasized in production, he might break anew into song. Should a company wish to include such a choice as "Gimme Some Lovin'," which bears a resemblance to his lines in the Middle French, then all requisite permissions must be cleared.

8. Yikes! It's the canonical French wife's cry when her cuckolded hubby arrives on the scene: *Ciel! Mon mari!* ("Oh my God! It's my husband!"). For a good laugh, see Chiflet's masterpiece of franglais, *Sky My Husband! Ciel mon mari!*

9. Here, she uses the very polite *Que vous fault-il, sire?*

10. This moment is also reminiscent of #2, *Edict of Noée* (Scene 1): but, here no wager is necessary. It is out of the question that this particular couple shut up, even for a moment.

11. Here, she asks, more informally, the same question as above (note 9): *Qu'esse qui te fault?*

12. The play on words is on *gros: tu auras ton gros* (roughly, "you'll get yours!") and *je demande du chief gros* (Jack's request for one of the tools of the cobbler's trade, i.e., a type of thread for sewing leather [see Tissier, *FFMA*, 3: 154]). I've preserved the pun with an *awl*, one of the few shoemaking implements still instantly identifiable today.

13. Should this musical cliché be brought back to life with "Wishin' and Hopin'," then all requisite permissions would need to be cleared.

14. Jack doesn't have a snappy comeback this time, but he will again soon.

15. *Metacommentary alert! Ce n'est pas jeu!* means "this is not a game," i.e., not a *play*.

16. I have added this line (which is only implicit in the original).

17. For obvious reasons, a song that might work well to convey the medieval spirit, so long as all requisite permissions have been cleared, would be "Footloose."

18. The couple might possibly break into song again here to whatever number seems appropriate in production. So long as all requisite permissions have been cleared, such a choice as "It's in His Kiss" might capture the spirit.

19. If the couple has already done a musical number, precede this line with "And now." Desirée may well be proposing "Dueil angoisseux," a lovely poem penned by none other than the great fifteenth-century author Christine de Pizan and set to polyphonic music by Gilles Binchois. See also Chailley's review of Cohen's *Recueil* (67). The point is that Desirée picks a song whose lyrics are integrated into the dialogue and for which I've proposed an imaginary, apropos title. I have indicated via formatting all such melodic moments (for which other synonymous phrases about love, lust, pain, or some combination thereof, may be substituted). Should a company wish to integrate and perform musical phrases from a copyrighted song of their choosing—"I'm So Excited" could be considered—all requisite permissions must have been cleared.

20. If all requisite permissions have been cleared for use of a different lyric, then a phrase from the song in question needs to be substituted in this line.

21. Cohen attributes the line "*Chantez-vous?*" to Bootie, but it makes more sense for Jack to say it. I've made room for both possibilities by means of Bootie's subsequent line.

22. Cohen attributes this line to Desirée, which would suggest this translation: "Calm down, already, don't get so excited" (*Recueil*, 168n).

23. In the original, she adds another verse to her song; so she will continue to perform whichever song has been selected and cleared for production.

24. In the place of medieval physiognomical interpretation, I've substituted modern palmistry. The point is that Bootie is talking about "signs," prompting Jack to wonder where *his* sign is.

25. The pun is on *giber/regiber,* a more violent allusion akin to whipping a horse, a beast who survives in my other metaphor.

26. The exclamation is the legalistic call for help, *haro!* See Basin, *Apologie,* 258–61; cited above, #2, *Edict of Noée.*

27. A great pun on *estat,* which denotes the state that she's in, her social position, and whatever *sexual* position she and Bootie have gotten themselves into.

28. Depending on the production values, one could add, "'Tis pity she's a whore?"

29. Another play on words on *plus bas,* along the lines of higher–lower, up–down, which also appears in #8, *Shit for Brains;* #11, *Cooch E. Whippet;* and #12, *Birdbrain.* But *bas* also means "stockings," and Jack sells used shoes and stockings. Thus, when Bootie says *plus bas!* (v. 275), Jack understands *stockings* and asks, "What stockings?" (*Quel bas?*).

30. I could be dreaming but, when spoken, Bootie's cry of *Ostez ce!* sounds like *hôtesse* (i.e., the mistress of the house). Is he calling the *woman* for help?

31. The use of *de degré en degré* is likely a variant on the typical adieu to spectators "regardless of their social standing." But "high and low" might also refer to the spatial level of the "bleachers" on which spectators are seated. *Degré* means step, so this may represent advice that the spectators "watch their step" as they "walk down the steps" at the end of

the show. Cohen too suspected that this was an architectural term important to theater history (*Recueil,* 170n).

Play 11. *Cooch E. Whippet*

1. Tissier's edition of *Audin* is #53 of *RF,* 12: 107–42; Faivre also discusses both plays in *Répertoire,* 282–84, 391–92.

2. See *DBD,* 94–97; and Cox, *Devil and the Sacred,* 125.

3. Surprisingly, Cohen missed the reference, inserting only a question mark next to Martin's name (*Recueil,* xvi n). But Le Roux de Lincy explains the name in *Livre de proverbes,* 2: 55; see also Tissier, *RF,* 12: 148–52. Martin also appears in the fifteenth-century *Fifteen Joys of Marriage,* the 11th Joy (or chapter), as translated by Pitts (96); but Pitts doesn't get it either (146n).

4. Faivre thinks that the belt is a souvenir from hell (*Répertoire,* 283).

5. Compare, e.g., with the opening of #8, *Shit for Brains,* or of the *Second Shepherds' Play* (e.g., in the Dover Thrift edition).

6. The *Miracle of the Child Given Over to the Devil* was performed, e.g., in the city of Metz on 10 October 1512. On this and other diabolical rapes, see *DBD,* 91–95.

7. The term is also a synonym for *molequin,* a fancy woman's dress made of linen. Tissier notes (*RF,* 12: 159n) that *corcelet* and *musequin* appear in close proximity—in a positive sense—in *Le Pauvre Jouhan,* vv. 135 and 148 (see #52 in *RF,* 10: 225–96). But, in between those two uses, we find *ne vous coursez point* (v. 140), i.e., "Don't get *angry!*"

8. For a great (shaggy) rabbit story, see Coldewey, "Thrice-Told Tales."

9. The title of one fabliau ought to do it here: "The Knight Who Made Cunts Speak." See Bloch, *Scandal of the Fabliaux,* 107–10.

10. The *Farce of the Chimney Sweep* (*Farce du ramonneur*), #30 in Cohen, *Recueil,* is disgustingly clear in that respect, revolving around double entendres on chimney sweeping and sex. My translation of that one is projected for volume 2! In the meantime, see Boucquey's translation in *SMFF.*

11. See #10, *Getting Off on the Wrong Foot,* note 12; and also Tissier on *Le Savetier Calbain* (*FFMA,* 1: 353, n. 131).

12. See also Tissier's charts of the distribution of scenes and speeches, *RF,* 12: 152–53.

13. If opening music is desired, "Every Breath You Take" might capture the medieval spirit perfectly, so long as all requisite permissions have been cleared.

14. This is it: here begin the challenges enumerated above, § "Language"; see below. You'll see that—gasp!—I've even conveyed the possibility of erotic asphyxiation (unless he's only "getting off" to work.)

Opening Lines in Middle French

MARTIN *commence*
> *Quel courcier et quel quarelet,*
> *Quel musequin, quel corcelet,*

> *Quel mirouer, quelle poitrine,*
> *On me puist pendre au gibet*
> *Si je ne . . .*

GUILLEMETTE

> *Vostre fièvre cartaine!*

MARTIN

> *Vous courroucez-vous, mon doulx cuninet[?]*
> *Ce je vous dy . . .*

GUILLEMETTE

> *Qui luy fait lait?*
> *Laissez-moy en paix de par le dyable.*

MARTIN

> *Par le sang bieu! ce n'est pas fable!*
> *Doncques ne fustes mieulx torché*
> *S(e) il fault que je . . .*

GUILLEMETTE

> *Très bien cheminer.*

MARTIN

> *Ha! je vous fourbiray pensser.*

GUILLEMETTE

> *Dieu ait l'âme des trespassez!*

MARTIN

> *Ça du chief gros que je besongne . . .*

15. Again, for *fièvre quartaine*; see above, About This Translation, § "Language and Style" (Cursing and Expletives).

16. For *faire lait* (above, § "Language"), I milk the dairy metaphor in another way.

17. Tissier thinks that she is ordering her unseen servant to fetch Cooch's dinner (*FFMA*, 4: 251). And, yes: we have seen this pun before in #10, *Getting Off on the Wrong Foot.*

18. Her language is not quite that vulgar, but, seeing as she says mentions shit a few lines later, this captures the tone. "Hell, no!" is probably more literal.

19. Again: opportunities for physical comedy, given the double entendre of "doing without her" but also "getting around her." Perhaps a commotion at the threshold, as in #2, *Edict of Noée?*

20. Again, the key text is that *Farce du ramonneur* (above, note 10).

21. Her term, *nicquet,* also denotes a prank or a nasty trick.

22. A *roquet* is a peasant's blouse; the Yiddish term seemed fitting.

23. *Dyable aspic* sounds almost like a recipe. How about a devil's food cake in their kitchen?

24. This is the moment (above, § "Language") when Cooch complains about Wilhelmina addressing him with the informal *tu*. I've found other ways to render her "disrespect."

25. Tissier thinks that this means "I don't know what to say" (*FFMA*, 4: 254).

26. The cursing here is more "Easter-like" (*Pasque*) with references to precious blood.

27. He says, "every day of the week"; one might also substitute the expression "24/7." Again, should a theater company wish to bring this musical cliché back to life in production, all requisite permissions must be cleared for "Eight Days a Week." Compare with Brother Peter's description of his activities in #9, *Monk-ey Business*, Scene 1.

28. With rich theatrical resonance, *mistere* also denotes a "mystery play"; its etymon, *ministerium*, connotes daily activities, things that one does every day.

29. Especially rich and varied, this speech boasts the word *chier,* used as "dear" (cf. the modern *cher*), but the term reads like "to shit": whence my "holy shit."

30. *Se vous deviez du sens issir, / Si serés-vous (cy) enfermée* (starting at v. 143). This verse is repeated: a musical refrain of some kind would work well, provided that all requisite permissions have been cleared.

31. Again, Cooch is not pleased that Wilhelmina has lapsed back into using *tu*.

32. Cooch uses the French expression for empty promises: *autant en emporte le vent,* which is how *Gone with the Wind* is translated into French.

33. Alternatively: "That's him all right."

34. I use this phrase to reflect his unusual choice of saints: Julian killed his parents.

35. Wilhelmina's phrasing is a bit more ambiguous, possibly referring to past consummation (and all very politely): she says *aymé m'avez!* (you have loved me). Father John implied earlier that he's not doing anything about his love; but maybe he means only that he's not doing anything about it *today*. Perhaps he is simply concerned about "what the meaning of *is* is."

36. *Dessus ung paintre* probably means "I've got one hanging by the door." But *paintre* denotes "painters," who were heavily involved in set design. See also Cohen, *Recueil,* 326n.

37. If a musical interlude is desired, "Bat Out of Hell" might convey the medieval spirit perfectly, so long as all requisite permissions have been cleared.

38. "Old ones, bad ones" can refer to people as well as to hose. Since Cooch's words are likely from a popular ditty, I've provided an eerily appropriate nursery rhyme.

39. For Tissier, this means "anyone can do it," i.e., fix his own shoes (*RF,* 12: 182n). Compare to the Cobbler's lament that opens #2, *Edict of Noée*, Scene 1.

40. Wilhelmina uses the affectionate *tu* as she invokes the *mal Saint Quentin* (hydropsy); the *mal Saint Leu* (erysipelas or Saint Anthony's fire, a skin infection that often follows a bout with strep); and the *mal Saint Jehan* or *Saint Valentin* (epilepsy).

41. Again, should a company wish to enhance this musical cliché with an actual melody, they must clear all requisite permissions for "Little Less Talk, a Lot More Action."

42. The literal meaning of *oncques ne fus en tel bicestre* is closer to "I've never been in such a prison." I've not completed the sentence because there is a nice double meaning of her use of the expression *mettre les mains*: putting her hands on her husband and putting her hands on the house (to clean it).

43. I've used rhyme to reinforce the fact that this is supposed to sound like conjuring. Also, given all the metacommentary about theater, I've given Father John an extra line.

44. There is no such stage direction in the play; but the dialogue reveals that Wilhelmina and Father John should be alone, at least momentarily.

45. Tissier thinks that Father John removes his Devil costume here. My own opinion is that it's funnier if he leaves it on to make the most of the term *faire le dyable,* that synonym for the sex act (above, § "Plot"). Obviously, he must remove it before returning as himself to torment Martin.

46. If a musical interlude is desired to reanimate the musical cliché, "Signed, Sealed, Delivered, I'm Yours" might work well, so long as all requisite permissions have been cleared.

47. The phrase *gardez d'en faire signe* is a brilliant pun on both "letting on" (or "giving oneself away") *and* making the sign of the cross.

48. Another double entendre on *elle est fesable:* the thing is possible; the *wife* is *doable.*

49. In both addresses to the public, Father John uses the second person plural—indicating politeness toward one culprit or normal usage toward many. More interesting: he says that such persons will be "black as the Devil." Sorry to report again that "blackface" is one medieval way to be in Devil costume (see *RF,* 12: 194n).

50. Or "stage left," "stage right," whatever the director has decided.

51. Alternatively, the company might ask the audience to applaud—as in the musical *The Mystery of Edwin Drood*—if they want the Wilhelmina character to come back to the stage.

52. Literally: it feels so good to hold you. Embrace me (à la Gershwin)? Should a company wish to perform any part of Gershwin's "Embrace Me," all requisite permissions must be cleared.

53. Is this kiss just a kiss? That's right: *baiser* again. I've left the English ambiguous.

54. Saint Martin, our title character's namesake, was renowned for performing miracles. On the cult of Saint Martin and on the pilgrimages in his honor, see esp. Farmer, *Communities of Saint Martin.*

55. Tissier suggests that Father John must depart quickly to avoid being recognized (*RF,* 12: 198n).

56. Again, high vs. low (*hault* vs. *bas*) can refer to both volume of speech (loud vs. soft) and to how high (or low) Cooch is wearing his belt.

57. *Qui pert y retreuve pour tout vray ne soit que deuil certainement:* literally, the expression means: "He who has lost something shall truly find it again, even if he regrets it."

Depending on the performance values, one might also try: "Sometimes in a democracy, you get what you deserve." Or remember the proverb scene in the film *Amélie*? Or, from any edition of Spenser's *Faerie Queene* (as recited in *Sense and Sensibility*), Book V, Canto II, stanza 39: "For there is nothing lost, that may be found if sought."

58. Here, we find the same double entendre as above (note 56) for *hault et bas*.

Play 12. *Birdbrain*

1. For other published editions and adaptations, see Viollet le Duc, *ATF*, 2: 338–59; Philipot, *Trois Farces*, 141–63, with its learned commentary and analysis (61–95); and [Delepierre], *Description et analyse*, #44, 91–109. Gustave Cohen's theater troupe, the Théophiliens, also performed the play; see Tissier, *RF*, 3: 216–17; and, on the Théophiliens, see Solterer, "The Waking of Medieval Theatricality" and *Medieval Roles for Modern Times*, chaps. 2 and 3.

2. See Isidore of Seville (d. 636), e.g., on the commonplace that the Muses (whence *music* got its name) were the daughters of Memory (*Etymologies*, 1: bk. 3, chap. 15.)

3. See *Dialogus de oratoribus*, bk. 1, chap. 29; and Guibert, *Self and Society*, esp. 46–50.

4. Here, I refer to Bynum's paradigm-shifting work, e.g., on Sermon 23 of Bernard of Clairvaux, in *Jesus as Mother*, 118.

5. I explore the gendered nature of the punitive brank and provide three images of these devices in "Violence, Silence, and the Memory of Witches," 220–23.

6. By the sixteenth century, the Mimin character was known and beloved (*RF*, 3: 219–20).

7. See Durkheim, *Evolution of Educational Thought*, trans. Collins, 142.

8. Christ himself is mockingly called *magister* in the scourging scenes of the *Mystère de la Passion de Troyes* (2: Day 2, 7233–34); see above, Introduction, § "Performance and Performance Records."

9. On the agonistic ritual of Latin learning in the Middle Ages and Renaissance, see Ong, *Rhetoric, Romance, and Technology*, chap. 5.

10. Some of this is manifest, e.g., when the Professor shifts from *vous* to *tu* while addressing his charge.

11. See, e.g., the translation by Axton and Stevens in *MFP*, esp. 191–92.

12. Another possible reading—this one suggested by the clever Michael Gnat: take literally Wolfy's use, with Rollo and Trixie, of the terms "my brother" or "my sister." Perhaps Wolfy is so out of it because there has been rather too much intermarriage between cousins in this family tree!

13. See esp. Trible's exemplary restoration of the female voice to biblical narratives in "Bringing Miriam out of the Shadows" and, more generally, *God and the Rhetoric of Sexuality;* and, for *Adam,* see Lerer, "Making Mimesis." See also Tissier's charts of the distribution of scenes and speeches, *RF*, 3: 225–27.

14. See above, About This Translation, § "Language and Style" (Repetition and Repetitiveness; Masculine and Feminine).

15. See Fournier, *TFR*, 319, col. 2; or verse 218 in Tissier, *RF*, 3: 259. In the *Recueil du British Museum,* however, there is no ambiguity. It's definitely written as "nostre." While "v's" and "n's" often looked identical in Gothic script, that is not the case here.

16. Similar wordplay appears in #8, *Shit for Brains;* #9, *Monk-ey Business;* and #11, *Cooch E. Whippet.*

17. If opening music is desired in performance, one could consider—so long as all requisite permissions have been cleared—such possibilities as "Teacher, I Need You," "Bloody Well Right," or "(What a) Wonderful World."

18. Rollo uses the masculine *ilz* when referring back to *les nouvelles* (feminine plural). See above, § "Language"; and above, About This Translation, § "Language and Style" (Masculine and Feminine).

19. He is *fourré,* which could also be an allusion to the furry hats typically worn by the legalistically inclined Basochiens (see *ROMD,* 136–41; and above, Introduction, § "History, Development").

20. Trixie should exaggerate her French pronunciation or mispronounce this term (which is not used here in the French original).

21. In addition to the importance of the nose (above, § "Language'), the French wordplay targets "signs" (*seignes*) and "teaching" (*enseigner*).

22. A play on words is lost in translation: *cette cole/cette école,* which suggests both "too far gone" and "that school." It *almost* works in English with *kinda state/kind estate.*

23. Actually, she swears by the hem of her apron, but this fits the themes better!

24. Other possibilities, depending on production values, include "within spitting distance," "within shouting distance," "just a stone's throw away," etc.

25. If a bona fide musical interlude is desired in production, any happy folk song will do, so long as all requisite permissions have been cleared. Alternatively, one might consider such possible selections as "Merrily We Roll Along" or a parodic version of "We're Off to See the Wizard," substituting "teacher" for "Wizard."

26. The anachronism is deliberate; plus, medievalists know all too well that anachronism was rampant in the medieval theater, most notably when Old Testament characters extol the virtues of a Christ who has not yet been born (see, e.g., Paxson, "Structure of Anachronism").

27. The rhyme scheme in French involves wordplay on the following infinitives: *comprendre, prendre, apprendre, reprendre, entreprendre* (i.e., understand, take, learn, start up, undertake).

28. If a bona fide song-and-dance number is desired, one might consider something like "The Madison Time," subject, of course, to clearing all requisite permissions.

29. I have reproduced this particular Latin phrase exactly how it appears, i.e., with a *mistake.* And why the Professor, in his next breath, expects an answer *in French* to a question in so-called *Latin* is anybody's guess! I take liberties with the rest of the Latin (above, § "Language").

30. Do add the city of the place of performance, as Henkes did with "Santa Barbara."

31. Actually, there's really no medieval equivalent for "plagiarism." Don't get any ideas, you undergrads, but in the Middle Ages the "authorship" (of an *auctor*) often involved mere rote citation (and even unattributed citation) of "authorities" (of *auctoritas*).

32. He might hum *gaudeamus igitur*. Remember that one from high-school graduation?

33. It takes Tissier almost two pages to explain a reference to a know-it-all (*maistre Aliborum*) who is really a charlatan (*RF,* 3: 246–47n). I've gone with a more user-friendly allusion.

34. Tissier disputes Philipot, contending that Trixie is speaking not to Mimin but to the Professor (*RF,* 3: 251–52n). I maintain that she is speaking to neither! I believe that she is speaking to *Dolly,* clarifying her earlier imperative that the girl "be good." She has just said, "*Faictes bien la sage, ma belle*" (p. 317, col. 2) and, now, she says, "*Levez-vous; vous estes trop sage*" (p. 318, col. 2). Plus, while it's true that Dolly's dad, Wolfy, uses *tu* when speaking to his daughter, there is no evidence that the other characters do.

35. My reading is consistent with Tissier's (*FFMA,* 1: 311); but it's incongruous nonetheless: i.e., how can the Professor be simultaneously hot to trot *and* indifferent? Methinks the pervert doth protest too much! Yes he doth.

36. It is difficult to translate *me baillez-vous cest entremetz? Entremetz* is one of many synonyms for a *farce* (which accounts for my theatrical metaphor); but it's also a food-stuff—more like the sorbet between the meat and the fish than the generic farcical "stuffing" itself. In my humble opinion, given the various markings of Norman dialect (above, § "Language"), it can scarcely be coincidental that we call that sorbet the *trou Normand* (literally, "the Norman hole").

37. So long as all requisite permissions have been cleared, this recurring verse might be sung to the tune of such a traditional folk song as "When I First Came to This Land" or another appropriate tuneful selection.

38. *Cuer à la cuisine* is literally "heart in the kitchen"; so I've kept the metaphor in that location. Tissier explains (*RF,* 3: 256n) that this popular expression refers to the olfactory pleasures of cooking scents (the nose again?); but he misses the pun between *bonne chère* (good food/good times) and *bonne chair* (good flesh/good sex)! Remember that we saw an oven in the opening lines of the play.

39. Fournier attributes this line to Rollo; but Tissier believes that it should be spoken by Wolfy Chewy (*RF,* 3: 256n), as indicated in the *Recueil du British Museum.* It seems more likely to me that Rollo would be off-color in front of *his wife* than would Wolfy in front of *his daughter.* See also below, note 41.

40. *Sur pied, sur bille* comes from woodcutting or tree felling, and means "immediately" (*RF,* 3: 256n). Tissier suggests that Rollo make an obscene gesture (*FFMA,* 1: 312). Great idea!

41. Tissier attributes this line to Rollo, as per the *Recueil du British Museum,* but also because Rollo was "sensitive" enough to advise discretion in front of Dolly in Scene 2. However, I agree with Fournier that Trixie is the one speaking for the following reasons:

(1) Trixie is invoked by name in the preceding speech; it makes sense that *she* would answer. (2) Given her initiative throughout, *she* would be likely to initiate bringing her son home. (3) One woman might well seek to protect another woman from hearing the gory details of sexual conquest. (4) If Trixie were to *yell* at the men to keep their voices down, she would be in the good company of the likes of Guillemette in *Pathelin* (see Mandel, *Peter Quill's Shenanigans*, in *FCMF*, 121–23; cited above, #3, *Confession Lessons*, note 45). There are other possibilities, which would necessitate other changes, such as reinforcing the stereotype of the talkative female by having Rollo deliver the first line while Trixie continues to talk. Actors may redistribute some of these lines as they see fit.

42. Sleep deprivation fits with the other "tortures" of medieval education invoked by the likes of Saint Augustine (*Confessions,* bk. 1, 1.9) and Guibert de Nogent (*Self and Society,* 47; 49–50). See also *MTOC,* 129–52.

43. For comic anachronism, one might add: "And you can forget about the Cliffs-Notes, books on tape, Kindle, and his iPod!"

44. This is the spot where Dolly uses *nostre* (above, § "Sets and Staging"). I've deleted the possessive as I think that this coop needn't be "theirs."

45. See above on the brank (§ "Plot").

46. What is the meaning of the mysterious *Anno!* (*RF,* 3: 261–62n)? Allow a medievalist geek to point out that this is phenomenally interesting in that I think it's possible that Mimin *is actually speaking English,* as in *Ah, no!* So to maximize the foreignness, one could have him say "no" in any other language: Chinese, or perhaps the Russian "yes–no!" (*da nyet!*) Sorry, general Reader, but this one's for the medievalists. I feel the way Samuel Stern did upon discovering that the poetic *kharjas* of the medieval Hispano-Arabic *muwashshahas* were not in Arabic at all but in Old Provençal. Eureka! For the stalwart seeking to learn what in the world I'm talking about, see Menocal on Stern's "Les vers finaux" in *Arabic Role,* 83–85.

47. One might also try a game of Simon Says. Compare with the confessional of #3, *Confession Lessons,* Scene 5.

48. *Sentir* means "to feel"; but, since Mimin is (at least partially) inside a chicken coop—and so too is that all-important and most dispositive nose—the olfactory meaning of "to stink" works perfectly.

49. To make the most of Dolly's courtly commonplaces and refrains, one might expand this section with selected snippets from any number of love songs that could be sung rather than spoken, so long as all requisite permissions have been cleared for performance.

50. *Respont si cler* is another play on words: he responds "happily," "clearly," but also "like a cleric."

51. I consider "sugar pie, honey bunch" to be a prime example of a musical cliché; but if it is sung in performance, the production will need to clear all requisite permissions for "I Can't Help Myself, Sugar Pie."

52. See Tissier on the work of Philipot (*RF,* 3: 267n).

53. Tissier thinks that Trixie is talking to her husband (*RF*, 3: 267n); but she might just as easily be talking to the Professor.

54. This is the moment when the Professor refers to the women (as will Rollo shortly) with *ilz*, the male subject pronoun: *Mais pour parler ilz ont le bruyt* (p. 321, col. 1). See above, "Language"; and About This Translation, § "Language and Style" (Masculine and Feminine). In any production that challenges the notion that gender is mere convention, one might substitute a variant such as "those *guys* have really got it down pat!"

55. This is the spot where Tissier thinks that the whole Company travels back to Rollo and Trixie's farm. But, again, Rollo might merely be suggesting that they go back inside to raise their toasts. See above, § "Sets and Staging."

56. The text specifies the musical scale: *ré, fa, sol*. Recall the lyre-tuning moments from #5, *Blind Man's Buff*. If a longer musical number is desired, one might consider having the Company sing "Do Re Mi" or another number, so long as all requisite permissions have been cleared.

57. See above, note 54. Possible variant in that same spirit: "when it comes to talkin', those *guys* rule the roost!"

58. The Company's parting number is likely a popular refrain: *Et à Dieu, vogue la gallée,* which sounds like a medieval version of "Row, Row, Row Your Boat," a song that does not really fit the sensibilities of my translation (and which song, by the way, gets sixty different hits on ascap.com). In modern French, the expression *vogue la galère* basically means "Hang in there, come what may!" If a company wishes to substitute a postmedieval closing number that captures the modern spirit, one might consider—so long as all requisite permissions have been cleared—such possibilities as "My Boyfriend's Back," "Together, Wherever We Go," "We Go Together," or "You Never Can Tell" ["Teenage Wedding"].

Appendix

1. Important exceptions include the signature musical reconstructions by van der Werf and Bond in *Extant Troubadour Melodies* and Margaret Switten's multimedia teaching applications (with CD-ROMs) of *The Medieval Lyric* (see http://www.mtholyoke.edu/acad/medst/medieval_lyric/ [accessed 6 October 2010]). I shall also have occasion to refer to Chailley's important recuperative work in his book review of Cohen's *Recueil,* in which he identifies some of the precise songs that appear in farces. See above, About This Translation, § "Prose, Verse, and Music."

2. See Introduction, § "Performance and Question of Genre" for more information on musical interludes.

Bibliography

Editions of French Farces

Cohen, Gustave, ed. *Recueil de Farces françaises inédites du XVe siècle*. Cambridge, Mass.: Mediaeval Academy of America, 1949. [*Recueil*]

Droz, Eugénie, and Halina Lewicka, eds. *Le Recueil Trepperel*. 2 vols. 1935. Rpt. Geneva: Droz, 1961–74.

Faivre, Bernard, ed. and trans. *Les Farces: Moyen Âge et Renaissance*. 2 vols. Vol. 1: *La Guerre des sexes;* vol. 2: *Dupés et trompeurs*. Paris: Imprimerie Nationale, 1997; 1999.

Fournier, Édouard, ed. *Le Théâtre français avant la Renaissance*. 1872. Rpt. New York: Burt Franklin, 1965. [*TFR*]

Koopmans, Jelle, ed. *Les Farces du Recueil de Florence*. Orléans: Paradigme, in press.

Philipot, Emmanuel. *Trois Farces du Recueil de Londres*: *"Le Cousturier et Esopet," "Le Cuvier," et "Maistre Mimin, estudiant."* 1931. Rpt. Geneva: Slatkine Reprints, 1975.

Recueil du British Museum. Fac-similé des 64 pièces de l'original. Ed. Halina Lewicka. Geneva: Slatkine Reprints, 1970.

Tissier, André, ed. *Recueil de Farces (1450–1550)*. 13 vols. Geneva: Droz, 1986–2000. [*RF*]

———, trans. *Farces françaises de la fin du Moyen Âge*. 4 vols. Geneva: Droz, 1999. [*FFMA*]

Viollet le Duc, M. *Ancien Théâtre françois*. 10 vols. Paris: P. Jannet, 1854–57. [*ATF*]

Collections of Medieval French Drama in English Translation

Axton, Richard, and John Stevens, trans. *Medieval French Plays*. Oxford: Basil Blackwell, 1971. [*MFP*]

Boucquey, Thierry, trans. *Six Medieval French Farces*. Lewiston, N.Y.: Edwin Mellen, 1999. [*SMFF*]

Denny, Neville, trans. *Medieval Interludes*. London: Ginn, 1972.

Mandel, Oscar, trans. *Five Comedies of Medieval France*. 1970. Rpt. Boston and London: University Press of America, 1982. [*FCMF*]

Individual French Farces Available in English Translation

The Boy and the Blind Man. In Axton and Stevens, *MFP*, 193–206.

The Chicken Pie and the Chocolate Cake [*Le Pâté et la Tarte*]. In Mandel, *FCMF*, 151–58.

The Farce of Calbain. In Boucquey, *SMFF,* 69–103.

The Farce of Master Pierre Pathelin. Trans. Alan E. Knight. In Donald Maddox, *Semiotics of Deceit: The Pathelin Era; with a new English prose translation of "Maistre Pierre Pathelin" by Alan E. Knight,* 173–99. Lewisburg, Pa.: Bucknell University Press, 1984.

The Farce of the Bonnet. In Boucquey, *SMFF,* 105–42.

The Farce of the Chimney Sweep. In Boucquey, *SMFF,* 165–96.

The Farce of the Gentleman and Naudet. In Boucquey, *SMFF,* 197–233.

The Farce of the Kettle Maker. In Boucquey, *SMFF,* 143–64.

The Farce of the Miller. In Boucquey, *SMFF,* 13–67.

In the Suds [*The Farce of the Washtub* or *La Farce du Cuvier*]. Trans. Barnard and Rose Hewitt. Boston: Baker's Plays, 1938.

Peter Quill's Shenanigans [*La Farce de Maître Pierre Pathelin*]. In Mandel, *FCMF,* 105–38.

The Pie and the Tart [*Le Pâté et la Tarte*]. In Denny, *Medieval Interludes,* 9–24.

The Play of the Bower [*Le Jeu de la Feuillée*] by Adam de la Halle. In Axton and Stevens, *MFP,* 207–55.

The Washtub. In Mandel, *FCMF,* 139–59.

Other Primary Sources

Aristotle. *The "Art" of Rhetoric.* Ed. and trans. John Henry Freese. Loeb Classical Library. 1926. Rpt. Cambridge, Mass.: Harvard University Press, 1975.

———. *Poetics.* Ed. and trans. W. Hamilton Fyfe. In *Aristotle, Longinus, Demetrius.* Loeb Classical Library. 1927. Rpt. Cambridge, Mass.: Harvard University Press, 1946.

Augustine of Hippo. *Confessions.* Ed. and trans. William Watts. 2 vols. Loeb Classical Library. Cambridge, Mass.: Harvard University Press, 1950.

Basin, Thomas. *Apologie ou plaidoyer pour moi-même.* Ed. Charles Samaran and Georgette de Groër. Paris: Belle Lettres, 1974.

———. *Histoire des règnes de Charles VII et de Louis XI.* Ed. J. Quicherat. 4 vols. Paris: Renouard, 1859.

Bevington, David, ed. *Medieval Drama.* Boston: Houghton Mifflin, 1975.

Bryant, Edward Andem. *The Best English and Scottish Ballads.* New York: Thomas Y. Crowell, [1911].

Champfleury. *L'Avocat Trouble-Ménage.* Paris: E. Dentu, 1870.

Chéruel, Adolphe. *Dictionnaire historique des institutions, mœurs et coutumes de la France.* 2 vols. Paris: Hachette, 1855.

The Chester Mystery Cycle. Ed. David Mills. Medieval Texts and Studies, 9. East Lansing, Mich.: Colleagues Press, 1992.

Chiflet, Jean-Loup. *Sky My Husband! Ciel mon mari! Guide de l'anglais courant. Guide of the Running English.* Paris: Hermé, 1985.

Chrétien de Troyes. *Erec and Enide.* In *The Complete Romances of Chrétien de Troyes,* trans. David Staines, 1–86. Bloomington: Indiana University Press, 1990.

Cohen, Gustave, ed. *Le Livre de conduite du Régisseur et Le Compte des dépenses pour le Mystère de la Passion joué à Mons en 1501.* Paris: Champion, 1925.

Coleridge, Samuel Taylor. *Coleridge's Literary Criticism.* Introd. J. W. Mackail. London: H. Milford, 1921.

Cotgrave, Randle. *A Dictionarie of the French and English Tongues.* 1611.

[Delepierre, Octave Joseph.] *Description et analyse d'un livre unique qui se trouve au Musée britannique.* [London]: Au Meschacébé, 1849.

Deschamps, Eustache. *Oeuvres complètes d'Eustache Deschamps, publiées d'àprès le manuscrit de la Bibliothèque nationale par le Marquis de Queux de Saint-Hilaire.* 11 vols. Ed. Auguste de Queux de Saint-Hilaire (vols. 1–6); Gaston Raynaud (vols. 7–11). Paris, 1878–1903. Rpt. New York: Johnson Reprints, 1966.

Douin de Lavesne. *Trubert: Fabliau du XIIIᵉ siècle.* Ed. G. Raynaud de Lage. Geneva: Droz, 1974.

Enders, Jody, ed. "Rhetoric in the Middle Ages." In *The Norton Anthology of Rhetoric and Writing,* ed. Andrea Lunsford and Susan Jarratt, with Enders, Robert Hariman, LuMing Mao, Thomas Miller, and Jacqueline Jones Royster. New York: Norton, forthcoming.

Farce du Ramonneur de Cheminées. #30 in Cohen, *Recueil,* 235–41.

The Fifteen Joys of Marriage [*Les .XV. Joies de mariage*]. Trans. Brent A. Pitts. New York: Peter Lang, 1985.

Le Galant qui a fait le coup. In Tissier, *RF,* 6: 309–29.

Le Geu Saint Denis du Manuscrit 1131 de la Bibliothèque Sainte-Geneviève. Ed. Bernard James Seubert. Geneva: Droz, 1974.

Godefroy, Frédéric. *Dictionnaire de l'ancienne langue française et de tous ses dialectes du IXᵉ au XVᵉ siècle.* 10 vols. 1881–1902. Rpt. Vaduz, Liechtenstein: Kraus Reprints, 1965.

Gréban, Arnoul. *Le Mystère de la Passion.* Ed. Omer Jodogne. Brussels: Académie Royale, 1965.

Guibert of Nogent. *Self and Society in Medieval France.* Trans. John F. Benton. Medieval Academy Reprints for Teaching, 15. Toronto: University of Toronto Press, 1989.

Hindley, Alan, Frederick W. Langley, and Brian J. Levy. *Old French-English Dictionary.* Cambridge: Cambridge University Press, 2000.

Hrotsvitha of Gandersheim. [*Paphnutius*]. *The Conversion of the Harlot Thais.* In *The Plays of Hrotsvit of Gandersheim,* trans. Katharina Wright Wilson, 93–122. Garland Library of Medieval Literatures, vol. 62, Series B. New York and London: Garland, 1989.

Isidore of Seville. *Isidore of Seville's Etymologies: The Complete English Translation of Isidori Hispalensis Episcopi: Etymologiarum sive Originum, Libri XX.* 2 vols. Trans. Priscilla Throop. Charlotte, Vt.: MedievalMS, 2005.

Izzard, Eddie. *Dress to Kill.* DVD. Ella Communications Ltd., 1999.

La Fontaine, Jean. *The Complete Fables of Jean de La Fontaine.* Trans. Norman R. Shapiro. Urbana and Chicago: University of Illinois Press, 2007.

Le Roux de Lincy. *Le Livre des proverbes précédé de recherches historiques sur les proverbes français et leur emploi dans la littérature du Moyen Âge et de la Renaissance.* 2d ed. 2 vols. Paris: Adolphe Delahays, 1859.

Lucian of Samosata. "The Dance." Ed. and trans. A. M. Harmon. In vol. 5 of *Works.* Loeb Classical Library. 1936. Rpt. Cambridge, Mass.: Harvard University Press, 1972.

Medieval Dutch Drama: Four Secular Plays and Four Farces from the Van Hulthem Manuscript. Trans. Johanna Prins. Asheville, N.C.: Pegasus, 1999.

Meredith, Peter, and John E. Tailby, eds. *The Staging of Religious Drama in Europe in the Later Middle Ages: Texts and Documents in English Translation.* Early Drama, Art and Music, 4. Kalamazoo, Mich.: Medieval Institute Publications, 1983. [*SRD*]

Molière, Jean-Baptiste Poquelin de. *The Flying Doctor* [*Le Médecin volant*]. In *One-Act Comedies of Molière,* trans. Albert Bermel, 29–44. 2d ed. New York: Ungar, 1975.

———. *Georges Dandin.* In *The Miser and George Dandin,* trans. Albert Bermel, 2–43. Vol. 1 of *The Actor's Molière.* New York: Applause Theatre Books, 1987.

———. *The Learned Ladies* [*Les Femmes savantes*]. In *The School for Wives and The Learned Ladies,* trans. Richard Wilbur, 153–316. San Diego, New York, and London: Harcourt Brace, 1978.

———. *The Miser* [*L'Avare*]. In *The Miser and George Dandin,* trans. Albert Bermel, 45–109. Vol. 1 of *The Actor's Molière.* New York: Applause Theatre Books, 1987.

Le Mystère de la Passion de Troyes. Ed. Jean-Claude Bibolet. 2 vols. Geneva: Droz, 1987.

Le Mystère de la Résurrection Angers (1456). Ed. Pierre Servet. 2 vols. Geneva: Droz, 1993.

Les Mystères de la procession de Lille. Vols. 1–4. Ed. Alan E. Knight. Geneva: Droz, 2001–7.

Nagler, A. M. *A Source Book in Theatrical History.* 1952. Rpt. New York: Dover, 1959.

Nicolas de Troyes. *Le Grand Parangon des nouvelles nouvelles.* Ed. Émile Mabille. Paris: A. Franck, 1869.

Noah's Flood. In *Everyman and Other Miracle and Morality Plays,* ed. Candace Ward, 1–11. New York: Dover Thrift Editions, 1995.

Noomen, Willem, and Nico van den Boogaard, eds. *Nouveau Recueil complet des fabliaux.* Vols. 1–2 of 5. Assen: Van Gorcum, 1983–84.

La Passion d'Auvergne. Ed. Graham A. Runnalls. Geneva: Droz, 1982.

Picot, Émile, and Christophe [Kristoffer] Nyrop. *Nouveau Recueil de farces françaises des XVe et XVe siècles.* 1880. Rpt. Geneva: Slatkine, 1968.

Plato. *The Republic.* 2 vols. Ed. and trans. Paul Shorey. Loeb Classical Library. Cambridge, Mass.: Harvard University Press, 1935.

Les Quinze [*.XV.*] *Joies de mariage.* See *The Fifteen Joys of Marriage.*

Rabelais, François. *The Complete Works of François Rabelais.* Trans. Donald Frame. Berkeley: University of California Press, 1991.

———. *Oeuvres complètes.* Ed. Guy Demerson. Paris: Seuil, 1973.

Rutebeuf. *Le Miracle de Théophile*. In *Jeux et sapience du Moyen Age*, ed. Albert Pauphilet, 135–58. Pléaide. Paris: Gallimard, 1951. Published in translation in Axton and Stevens, MFP, 165–92.

The Second Shepherds' Play. In *Everyman and Other Miracle and Morality Plays*, ed. Candace Ward, 12–35. New York: Dover Thrift Editions, 1995.

Tacitus. *Dialogus de oratoribus*. Ed. and trans. W. Peterson, revised by M. Winterbottom. Loeb Classical Library, 1914. Rpt. Cambridge, Mass.: Harvard University Press, 1980.

Tate, Nahum. *A Duke and No Duke: A Farce*. London: Henry Bonwicke, 1693.

Tridace-Nafé-Théobrome. [See Delepierre, Octave Joseph.]

Tydeman, William, ed. *The Medieval European Stage, 500–1550*. Series: Theatre in Europe: A Documentary History. Cambridge: Cambridge University Press, 2001. [*MES*]

Unsworth, Barry. *Morality Play*. New York: Nan A. Talese/Doubleday, 1995.

van der Werf, Hendrik, and Gerald A. Bond. *The Extant Troubadour Melodies: Transcriptions and Essays for Performers and Scholars*. New York: H. van der Werf, 1984.

Walker, Greg, ed. *Medieval Drama: An Anthology*. Oxford: Blackwell, 2000.

Secondary Sources

Allen, Valerie. *On Farting: Language and Laughter in the Middle Ages*. 2007. Rpt. New York and Basingstoke: Palgrave Macmillan, 2010.

Arden, Heather. *Fools' Plays: A Study of Satire in the Sottie*. Cambridge: Cambridge University Press, 1980.

Auerbach, Erich. *Mimesis: The Representation of Reality in Western Literature*. Trans. Willard R. Trask. 1953. Rpt. Princeton, N.J.: Princeton University Press, 1974.

Austin, J. L. *How to Do Things with Words*. Ed. J. O. Urmson and Marina Sbisà. 2d ed. Cambridge, Mass.: Harvard University Press, 1978.

———. *Philosophical Papers*. Ed. J. O. Urmson and G. J. Warnock. 2d ed. Oxford: Clarendon, 1970.

Axton, Richard. *European Drama of the Early Middle Ages*. London: Hutchinson, 1974.

Bakhtin, Mikhail. *Rabelais and His World*. Trans. Hélène Iswolsky. 1965. Rpt. Bloomington: Indiana University Press, 1984.

Barish, Jonas. *The Antitheatrical Prejudice*. Berkeley: University of California Press, 1981.

Bayless, Martha. *Parody in the Middle Ages: The Latin Tradition*. Ann Arbor: University of Michigan Press, 1996.

Beam, Sara. *Laughing Matters: Farce and the Making of Absolutism in France*. Ithaca, N.Y.: Cornell University Press, 2007. [*LM*]

Bentley, Eric. *The Life of the Drama*. 1964. Rpt. New York: Applause Books, 2000. [*LD*]

Bergson, Henri. "Laughter." In *Comedy: "An Essay on Comedy" by George Meredith; "Laughter" by Henri Bergson*, ed. Wylie Sypher, 59–190. Garden City, N.Y.: Doubleday, 1956.

Bermel, Albert. *Farce: The Comprehensive and Definitive Account of One of the World's Funniest Art Forms*. New York: Simon & Schuster, 1982. Reprinted as *Farce: A History from Aristophanes to Woody Allen*. Carbondale: Southern Illinois University Press, 1990. [*FAH*]

Bial, Henry, ed. *The Performance Studies Reader*. 2d ed. London and New York: Routledge, 2007.

Biddick, Kathleen. "The Devil's Anal Eye: Inquisitorial Optics and Ethnographic Authority." In *The Shock of Medievalism*, 105–34. Durham, N.C., and London: Duke University Press, 1998.

Bloch, R. Howard. *Etymologies and Genealogies: A Literary Anthropology of the French Middle Ages*. 1983. Rpt. Chicago: University of Chicago Press, 1986.

———. *The Scandal of the Fabliaux*. Chicago and London: University of Chicago Press, 1986.

Bowen, Barbara C. *Les Caractéristiques essentielles de la farce française et leur survivance dans les années 1550–1620*. Illinois Studies in Language and Literature, 53. Urbana: University of Illinois Press, 1964. [*CE*]

——— [Barbara Cannings]. "Towards a Definition of Farce as Literary 'Genre.'" *Modern Language Review* 56.4 (1961): 558–60. [TDF]

Bremmer, Jan, and Herman Roodenburg, eds. *A Cultural History of Gesture: From Antiquity to the Present Day*. Cambridge: Polity Press, 1991.

———. *A Cultural History of Humour: From Antiquity to the Present Day*. Cambridge: Polity Press, 1997.

Brooks, Peter, and Paul Gewirtz, eds. *Law's Stories: Narrative and Rhetoric in the Law*. New Haven, Conn.: Yale University Press, 1996.

Brown, Howard Mayer. *Music in the French Secular Theater, 1400–1550*. Cambridge, Mass.: Harvard University Press, 1963.

Burns, E. Jane. *Courtly Love Undressed: Reading through Clothes in Medieval French Culture*. Philadelphia: University of Pennsylvania Press, 2002.

Burrow, J. A. *Gestures and Looks in Medieval Narrative*. Cambridge Studies in Medieval Literature, 48. Cambridge: Cambridge University Press, 2002.

Bynum, Caroline Walker. *Jesus as Mother: Studies in the Spirituality of the High Middle Ages*. Berkeley: University of California Press, 1982.

Cannings, Barbara. See Bowen, Barbara C.

Cavell, Stanley. *Must We Mean What We Say?: A Book of Essays*. New York: Scribner's, 1969.

Certeau, Michel de. *The Practice of Everyday Life*. Trans. Steven Rendall. Berkeley: University of California Press, 1988.

Chailley, Jacques. Review of *Recueil de farces françaises inédites du XVe siècle*, ed. Gustave Cohen. *Revue de Musicologie* 32 (1950): 65–68.

Chambers, E. K. *The Mediaeval Stage*. 2 vols. Oxford: Oxford University Press, 1903.

Chatelain, Henri Louis. *Recherches sur le vers français au XVe siècle: Rimes, mètres et strophes.* 1908. Rpt. New York: Burt Franklin, 1971.

Clopper, Lawrence M. *Drama, Play, and Game: English Festive Culture in the Medieval and Early Modern Period.* Chicago: University of Chicago Press, 2001.

Cohen, Gustave. "La Scène de l'aveugle et son valet." *Romania* 41 (1912): 346–72.

———. "The 'Théophiliens': The Resurrection of the Medieval Theater." *Books Abroad* 25.1 (1951): 7–10.

Coldewey, John C. "Thrice-Told Tales: Renegotiating Early English Drama." In *European Medieval Drama 1996: Papers from the First International Conference on Aspects of European Medieval Drama, Camerino, 28–30 June 1996.* ed. Sydney Higgins, 1: 17–34. Camerino: Università degli Studi di Camerino, Centro Linguistico di Ateneo, 1996.

———, ed. *Medieval Drama.* 4 vols. New York and London: Routledge, 2007.

Cox, John. *The Devil and the Sacred in English Drama, 1350–1642.* Cambridge: Cambridge University Press, 2001.

Crane, Susan. *The Performance of Self: Ritual, Clothing, and Identity during the Hundred Years War.* Philadelphia: University of Pennsylvania Press, 2002.

Davidson, Clifford, ed. *Gesture in Medieval Drama and Art.* Early Drama, Art, and Music, 28. Kalamazoo, Mich.: Medieval Institute Publications, 2001.

Davis, Jessica Milner. *Farce.* London: Methuen, 1978. Rpt. New Brunswick, N.J., and London: Transaction, 2003.

Davis, Natalie Zemon. *Fiction in the Archives: Pardon Tales and Their Tellers in Sixteenth-Century France.* Stanford, Calif.: Stanford University Press, 1987.

———. "Women on Top." In *Society and Culture in Early Modern France: Eight Essays by Natalie Zemon Davis,* 124–51. Stanford, Calif.: Stanford University Press, 1975.

Dean, Joan F. "Joe Orton and the Redefinition of Farce." *Theatre Journal* 34.4 (1982): 481–92.

Delachenal, Roland. *Histoire des avocats au Parlement de Paris (1300–1600).* Paris: Plon, 1885.

Dox, Donnalee. *The Idea of the Theater in Latin Christian Thought: Augustine to the Fourteenth Century.* Ann Arbor: University of Michigan Press, 2007.

Durkheim, Emile. *The Evolution of Educational Thought.* Trans. Peter Collins. London: Routledge & Kegan Paul, 1977.

Enders, Jody. *Death by Drama and Other Medieval Urban Legends.* Chicago: University of Chicago Press, 2002. [*DBD*]

———. "Homicidal Pigs and the Antisemitic Imagination." *Exemplaria* 4.1 (2002): 201–38.

———. "Medieval Stages." *Theatre Survey* 50.2 (2009): 317–25.

———. *The Medieval Theater of Cruelty: Rhetoric, Memory, Violence.* Ithaca, N.Y.: Cornell University Press, 1998. [*MTOC*]

———. *Murder by Accident: Medieval Theater, Modern Media, Critical Intentions.* Chicago: University of Chicago Press, 2009. [*MBA*]

Enders, Jody. "Of Miming and Signing: The Dramatic Rhetoric of Gesture." In *Gesture in Medieval Drama and Art*, ed. Clifford Davidson, 1–25. Early Drama, Art, and Music, 28. Kalamazoo: Medieval Institute Publications, 2001.

———. "Performing Miracles: The Mysterious Mimesis of Valenciennes (1547)." In *Theatricality,* ed. Tracy C. Davis and Thomas Postlewait, 40–64. Cambridge: Cambridge University Press, 2003.

———. Review of Leon Guilhamet, *Satire and the Transformation of Genre. Continuum* 3 (1991): 197–201.

———. Review of William Tydeman, ed. *The Medieval European Stage, 500–1500. Theatre Journal* 54.4 (2002): 658–59.

———. *Rhetoric and the Origins of Medieval Drama.* Rhetoric and Society, 1. Ithaca, N.Y.: Cornell University Press, 1992. [*ROMD*]

———. "The Spectacle of the Scaffolding: Rape and the Violent Foundations of Medieval Theatre Studies." *Theatre Journal* 56 (2004): 163–81.

———. "Theater Makes History: Ritual Murder by Proxy in the *Mistere de la Sainte Hostie.*" *Speculum* 79 (2004): 991–1016.

———. "Violence, Silence, and the Memory of Witches." In *Violence against Women in Medieval Texts,* ed. Anna Roberts, 210–32. University of Florida Press, 1998.

Evans, E. P. *The Criminal Prosecution and Capital Punishment of Animals: The Lost History of Europe's Animal Trials.* 1906. Rpt. London: Faber & Faber, 1988.

Fabre, Adolphe. *Les Clercs du Palais.* 1856. 2d ed., Lyon: N. Scheuring, 1875. [*CP*]

Faivre, Bernard. *Répertoire des farces françaises: Des origines à Tabarin.* Paris: Imprimerie Nationale, 1993. [*Répertoire*]

———, ed. *La Farce: Un genre médiéval pour aujourd'hui?* Special issue of *Études théâtrales* 14 (1998).

Farmer, Sharon. *Communities of Saint Martin: Legend and Ritual in Medieval Tours.* Ithaca, N.Y.: Cornell University Press, 1991.

Foucault, Michel. *Discipline and Punish: The Birth of the Prison.* Trans. Alan Sheridan. New York: Pantheon, 1977.

Frank, Grace. *The Medieval French Drama.* Oxford: Clarendon, 1954.

Gatton, John Spalding. "'There Must Be Blood': Mutilation and Martyrdom on the Medieval Stage." In *Violence in Drama*, ed. James Redmond, 79–92. Themes in Drama, 13. Cambridge: Cambridge University Press, 1991.

Gellrich, Jesse M. *The Idea of the Book in the Middle Ages: Language Theory, Mythology, and Fiction.* Ithaca, N.Y.: Cornell University Press, 1988.

Genty, Lucien. *La Basoche notariale: Origines et histoire du XIVe siècle à nos jours de la cléricature notariale.* Paris: Delamotte, 1888.

Girard, René. *Violence and the Sacred.* Trans. Patrick Gregory. Baltimore: Johns Hopkins University Press, 1977.

Gordon, Mel. *The Grand Guignol: Theatre of Fear and Terror*. Rev. ed. New York: Da Capo, 1997.

Guilhamet, Leon. *Satire and the Transformation of Genre*. Philadelphia: University of Pennsylvania Press, 1987.

Guynn, Noah D. "A Justice to Come: The Role of Ethics in *La Farce de Maistre Pierre Pathelin*." *Theatre Survey* 47.1 (2006): 13–31.

Hand, Richard J., and Michael Wilson. *Grand-Guignol: The French Theatre of Horror*. Exeter: University of Exeter Press, 2002.

———. *London's Grand Guignol and the Theatre of Horror*. Exeter: University of Exeter Press, 2007.

Happé, Peter, and Elsa Streitman, eds. *Urban Theatre in the Low Countries, 1400–1625*. Turnhout: Brepols, 2006.

Hardison, O. B., Jr. *Christian Rite and Christian Drama in the Middle Ages: Essays in the Origin and Early History of Modern Drama*. Baltimore: Johns Hopkins University Press, 1965.

Harvey, Howard Graham. *The Theatre of the Basoche*. Cambridge, Mass.: Harvard University Press, 1941. [*TB*]

Holsinger, Bruce Wood. *Music, Body, and Desire in Medieval Culture: Hildegard of Bingen to Chaucer*. Stanford, Calif.: Stanford University Press, 2001.

Huizinga, Johan. *Homo ludens: A Study of the Play Element in Culture*. [Trans. R. F. C. Hull.] Boston: Beacon, 1955.

Huot, Sylvia. *From Song to Book: The Poetics of Writing in Old French Lyric and Lyrical Narrative Poetry*. Ithaca, N.Y.: Cornell University Press, 1987.

Irigaray, Luce. *Ce sexe qui n'en est pas un*. Paris: Éditions de Minuit, 1977. Published in translation as *This Sex Which Is Not One*. Trans. Catherine Porter with Carolyn Burke. Ithaca, N.Y.: Cornell University Press, 1985.

Jonsson, Ritva, and Leo Treitler. "Medieval Music and Language: A Reconsideration of the Relationship." In *Music and Language*, 1–23. Studies in the History of Music, 1. New York: Broude Bros., 1983.

Jordan, Mark. *The Invention of Sodomy in Christian Theology*. Chicago: University of Chicago Press, 1997.

Kendon, Adam. *Gesture: Visible Action as Utterance*. Cambridge and New York: Cambridge University Press, 2004.

Kennedy, George A. *Classical Rhetoric and Its Christian and Secular Tradition from Ancient to Modern Times*. Chapel Hill: University of North Carolina Press, 1980.

Kerr, Walter. *Tragedy and Comedy*. New York: Simon & Schuster, 1967.

Kibler, William W. *An Introduction to Old French*. New York: MLA, 1984.

Knight, Alan E. *Aspects of Genre in Late Medieval French Drama*. Manchester: Manchester University Press, 1983. [*AG*]

Kooper, Erik, ed. *Medieval Dutch Literature in its European Context*. Cambridge: Cambridge University Press, 1994.

Kramer, Femke. "Rederijkers on Stage: A Closer Look at 'Meta-theatrical' Sources." *Research Opportunities in Renaissance Drama* 35 (1996): 97–109.

Le Goff, Jacques. *La Civilisation de l'Occident médiéval*. Paris: Arthaud, 1964. Published in English as *Medieval Civilization, 400–1500*. Trans. Julia Barrow. Oxford: Blackwell, 1988.

———. "Laughter in the Middle Ages." In *Cultural History of Humour*, ed. Bremmer and Roodenburg, 40–53.

Lerer, Seth. "Making Mimesis: Eric Auerbach and the Institutions of Medieval Studies." In *Medievalism and the Modernist Temper*, ed. R. Howard Bloch and Stephen G. Nichols, 308–33. Baltimore: Johns Hopkins University Press, 1996.

Le Roy Ladurie, Emmanuel. *Carnival in Romans*. Trans. Mary Feeney. New York: George Braziller, 1979.

Lewicka, Halina. *Études sur l'ancienne farce française*. Paris: Klincksieck, 1974.

———. "Histoire d'un Thème Dramatique: 'L'Enfant mis aux Écoles.'" In *Études*, chap. 2, 32–46.

Marchello-Nizia, Christiane. *La langue française aux XIVᵉ et XVᵉ siècles*. Paris: Nathan, 1997.

Marshall, David. *The Surprising Effects of Sympathy: Marivaux, Diderot, Rousseau, and Mary Shelley*. Chicago: University of Chicago Press, 1988.

Maxwell, Ian. *French Farce & John Heywood*. Melbourne: Melbourne University Press; Oxford: Oxford University Press, 1946.

McLuhan, Marshall. *The Gutenberg Galaxy: The Making of Typographic Man*. Toronto: University of Toronto Press, 1965.

McLuhan, Marshall, and Quentin Fiore. *The Medium Is the Message*. New York: Random House, 1967.

Menocal, María Rosa. *The Arabic Role in Medieval Literary History*. Philadelphia: University of Pennsylvania Press, 1987.

"Miscellaneous." *Notes and Queries* (25 January 1851): 77.

Morrison, Susan Signe. *Excrement in the Middle Ages: Sacred Filth and Chaucer's Fecopoetics*. New York and Basingstoke: Palgrave Macmillan, 2007.

Murphy, James J. *A Synoptic History of Classical Rhetoric*. New York: Random House, 1972.

Nichols, Stephen G. "Aux Frontières du rire médiéval." In *L'Hostellerie de pensée : Études sur l'art littéraire au Moyen Âge offertes à Daniel Poirion par ses anciens élèves*, ed. Michel Zink and Danielle Böhler, 315–44. Paris: Presses de l'Université de Paris–Sorbonne, 1995.

Nicoll, Allardyce. *World Drama from Aeschylus to Anouilh*. 1949. 2d ed. New York: Harper & Row, 1976.

Olson, Glending. *Literature as Recreation in the Later Middle Ages*. Ithaca, N.Y.: Cornell University Press, 1982.

———. "The Medieval Fortunes of 'Theatrica.'" *Traditio* 4 (1986): 265–86.

Ong, Walter J. *Rhetoric, Romance, and Technology: Studies in the Interaction of Expression and Culture*. Ithaca, N.Y.: Cornell University Press, 1971.

Paxson, James J. "The Structure of Anachronism and the Middle English Mystery Plays." *Mediaevalia* 18 (1995): 321–40.

Perfetti, Lisa. *Women and Laughter in Medieval Comic Literature*. Ann Arbor: University of Michigan Press, 2003.

Persels, Jeff. "The Sorbonnic Trots: Staging the Intestinal Distress of the Roman Catholic Church in French Reform Theater." *Renaissance Society Quarterly* 56.4 (2003): 1089–111.

Petit de Julleville, L. *Les Comédiens en France au Moyen Âge*. Paris: Léopold Cerf, 1885.

———. *Les Mystères*. Vols. 1 and 2 of *Histoire du théâtre en France*. 1880. Rpt. Geneva: Slatkine, 1968.

Pinet, Christopher P. "The Role of the Cobbler in French Farce of the Renaissance." *French Review* 48.2 (1974): 308–20.

Price, Glanville. *The French Language: Present and Past*. London: Edward Arnold, 1971.

Radoff, M. L. "Influence of the French Farce in *Henry V* and the *Merry Wives*." *Modern Language Notes* 48.7 (1933): 427–35.

Read, Alan. *Theatre and Everyday Life: An Ethics of Performance*. London and New York: Routledge, 1993.

Rey-Flaud, Bernadette. *La Farce, ou la machine à rire: Théorie d'un genre dramatique*. Geneva: Droz, 1984.

Rey-Flaud, Henri. *Le Charivari: Les rituels fondamentaux de la sexualité*. Paris: Payot, 1985.

———. *Pour une dramaturgie du Moyen-Âge*. Paris: Presses Universitaires de France, 1980.

Robertson, D. W. *A Preface to Chaucer: Studies in Medieval Perspectives*. Princeton, N.J.: Princeton University Press, 1962.

Roy, Bruno. "Le Déguisement dans la farce: Problèmes d'identité." In *La Farce, Études théâtrales* 14 (1998): 13–20.

Runnalls, Graham. *Études sur les mystères*. Paris: Champion, 1998.

———. *Les Mystères français imprimés*. Paris: Champion, 1999.

Rus, Martijn. *De la conception de l'au delà dans ce siècle qui n'en est pas un*. Amsterdam: Rodopi, 1995.

Saenger, Paul. "Silent Reading: Its Impact on Late Medieval Script and Society." *Viator* 13 (1982): 367–414.

Sarat, Austin, and Thomas R. Kearns, eds. *Law in Everyday Life*. Ann Arbor: University of Michigan Press, 1993.

Savran, David. *A Queer Sort of Materialism: Recontextualizing American Theater*. Ann Arbor: University of Michigan Press, 2003.

Shaw, George Bernard. *Our Theatres in the Nineties*. 3 vols. London: Constable & Co., 1932.

Sheindlin, Judy. *Don't Pee on My Leg and Tell Me It's Raining: America's Toughest Family Court Judge Speaks Out.* New York: Harper, 1997.

Solterer, Helen. *Medieval Roles for Modern Times: Theater and the Battle for the French Republic.* University Park: Penn State University Press, 2010.

———. "The Waking of Medieval Theatricality: Paris—1995." *NLH* 27 (1996): 357–90.

States, Bert O. *Great Reckonings in Little Rooms: On the Phenomenology of Theatre.* Berkeley: University of California Press, 1985.

———. *The Pleasure of the Play.* Ithaca, N.Y.: Cornell University Press, 1994.

Stern, Samuel Miklos. "Les Vers finaux en espagnol dans les muwaššahs hispano-hébraïques." *Al-Andalus* 13 (1948): 299–346.

Stevens, John E. *Words and Music in the Middle Ages: Song, Narrative, Dance, and Drama, 1050–1350.* Cambridge: Cambridge University Press, 1986.

Symes, Carol. *A Common Stage: Theater and Public Life in Medieval Arras.* Ithaca, N.Y.: Cornell University Press, 2007.

Tentler, Thomas N. *Sin and Confession on the Eve of the Reformation.* Princeton, N.J.: Princeton University Press, 1977.

Thomas, Antoine. "Le Théâtre à Paris et aux environs." *Romania* 21 (1892): 606–11.

Tissier, André. "Le Public des farces en France à la fin du XVᵉ et au début du XVIᵉ siècle." In *Das Theater und sein Publikum* [Proceedings of the International Conference on Theater History of 1975 and 1976], 148–59. Vienna: Austrian Academy of Sciences, 1997.

Treitler, Leo. "Oral, Written, and Literate Process in the Transmission of Medieval Music." *Speculum* 56 (1981): 471–91.

Trible, Phyllis. "Bringing Miriam out of the Shadows." In *A Feminist Companion to Exodus to Deuteronomy,* ed. Athalya Brenner, 166–86. Sheffield: Sheffield Academic, 1994.

———. *God and the Rhetoric of Sexuality.* Philadelphia: Fortress Press, 1978.

Walker, Jonathan. "Learning to Play." In *Early Modern Academic Drama*, ed. Walker and Streufert, 1–18.

Walker, Jonathan, and Paul D. Streufert, eds. *Early Modern Academic Drama.* Farnham, U.K., and Burlington, Vt.: Ashgate, 2008.

Warning, Rainer. *The Ambivalences of Medieval Religious Drama.* [1974.] Trans. Steven Rendall. Stanford, Calif.: Stanford University Press, 2001.

Wheatley, Edward. *Stumbling Blocks before the Blind: Medieval Constructions of a Disability.* Ann Arbor: University of Michigan Press, 2010.

Woolf, Rosemary. *The English Mystery Plays.* 1972. Rpt. Berkeley: University of California Press, 1980.

Wright, Stephen (Steve), webmaster. "Medieval Drama in English Translation." http://english.cua.edu/faculty/drama/index.cfm (accessed 26 September 2010).

Young, Karl. *The Drama of the Medieval Church.* 2 vols. Oxford: Clarendon, 1933.

Acknowledgments

O f the many individuals whom I must thank, two graduate-student collaborators merit special gratitude because, in their unique ways, both had a great deal to teach me about the practice of theater: Clareann Despain and Brian Granger.

I have also profited over the past several years from the insights and expertise of many colleagues and just as many students, whom I wish to thank for their generosity, creativity, artistry, intellectual daring, and acting skills, all of which contributed immeasurably to the preparation of these farces. Any and all shortcomings are my own.

It is a distinct pleasure to acknowledge a particularly talented undergraduate class in comparative medieval drama at the University of California, Santa Barbara (fall 2007), for their assistance in vetting the earliest version of my translation of *The Farce of the Fart*. Katie Pajao had superb ideas about some of my puns; and Joey Axiaq, Jeremy Cowan, Jessica Fleitman, and Travis Wong did a terrific job staging that play as their final class project. In a later class, Sebastian Ruan proved an assiduous and thoughtful proofreader, as did S. C. Kaplan in a graduate seminar. In June of 2009, I invited a wonderful group of artists/scholars for a read-through that brought these plays to life with gusto, such that I was able to hear how my translations would fare in performance: for their uncommon gifts—and spotlighting their tour-de-force performances—I thank Kane Anderson (a glorious Goguelu), Leo Cabranes-Grant (scariest Examiner ever), Clareann Despain (fishwife Harpee extraordinaire), Brian Granger (fabulously feckless Cobbler), Andrew Henkes (prickly Master Peter), Dan Jaffe (put-upon Payne N. Butts), Jason Narvy (crotchety, cantankerous John-John Horny), Courtney Ryan (what a Lady!), Christy Simonian (mellifluous as a cross-cast Doc Double-Talk), Annika Speer (wily Wilhelmina), and Beth Wynstra (I still *hear* her as Colette).

Also, I don't know what took me so long but, in 2001, I discovered the American Society for Theatre Research, a marvelous group of historians, theorists, and practitioners of the theater who frequently opened my eyes to aspects of performance that I had earlier taken for granted. My association with that organization has proved to be one of the most stimulating intellectual experiences of my life.

I must also give credit to André Tissier's masterful, scholarly editions of six of the plays presented here (my #1, #7, #8, #9, #11, #12); in his *Recueil de Farces,* Tissier occasionally had the explanation when a Middle French turn of phrase seemed obscure enough to have been lost to history. And no praise is sufficient for the magnanimity of Jelle Koopmans. In the final stages of preparing this manuscript, I learned that Koopmans had discovered the whereabouts of the elusive *Recueil de Florence,* better known as the *Recueil Cohen* (on which ten of my twelve translations are based). He shared with me his edition of the *Recueil* (then in press) so that I could compare his readings with my own and learn of any earlier misreadings by Cohen or by others. For that act of intellectual grace, I am eternally in his debt. Like Koopmans, moreover, I too applaud the anonymous owner of the *Recueil Cohen* for making the collection available (to Koopmans alone) so that future generations might learn and work from it.

At the University of Pennsylvania Press, the ever wise and gracious Jerome Singerman obtained two learned and perceptive readings of my manuscript, both of which offered a painstaking attention to detail and an intellectual generosity rarely seen in the profession. Alan Knight was simultaneously exacting and open-minded, taking me through the paces of any aspect of Middle French that had escaped my notice while keeping the possibilities for performance before his eyes at all times; Claire Sponsler offered invaluable advice about the delicate negotiation of a tone that befits not only college students, general readers, actors, and directors but also medievalists eager to conduct research on these plays. In addition, even though I did not work with him on this project, Randy Petilos at the University of Chicago Press has been a marvelous friend for some two decades who remained willing to counsel me about some of the finer points of publishing artistic work.

I am thankful to the Interlibrary Loan Office at Davidson Library of my home institution, whose staff assiduously assisted me in securing even the most obscure documents, and to several other deeply knowledgeable friends who discussed this project with me at various stages and who never let me forget about the importance of performance: Bradford Lee Eden, Bruce

Holsinger, David Marshall, Jeff Persels, Ron Tobin, David Wallace, and especially Mark Rose. Meanwhile, my colleague William Ashby never once lost his astonishing ability to answer any philological question I had.

And then, there is the copyeditor, the brilliant Michael Gnat. Thanks to Caroline Winschel and Erica Ginsburg at the Press, he was contracted for this project at my request. I first worked with Michael Gnat while serving as the editor of *Theatre Survey*, during which time I came to know him as the most meticulous and inspired copyeditor with whom I've ever worked. Moreover, I knew him to be a working actor and a generous collaborator whose unusually trenchant insights into stagecraft would make him the ideal reader. He surpassed my wildest expectations, occasionally offering an idea of his own about a turn of phrase, a scenic clarification, or a dramaturgical suggestion so compelling that extra footnotes were required in his honor. It is a privilege to thank Michael Gnat for offering, albeit through readerly eyes, what I can only think to call a "a virtual workshop" of these plays.

Above all, and as always, I couldn't possibly do without the love and support of my husband, Eric D'Hoker, who, after almost twenty years of hearing about violence and torture on the medieval French stage, finally got to have a good laugh.

www.ingramcontent.com/pod-product-compliance
Lightning Source LLC
Chambersburg PA
CBHW020647110726
47901CB00001B/77